Blessed Experiences

Blessed Experiences

Genuinely Southern,
Proudly Black

James E. Clyburn

Foreword by Alfre Woodard

THE UNIVERSITY OF SOUTH CAROLINA PRESS

© 2014 James E. Clyburn

Published by the University of South Carolina Press
Columbia, South Carolina 29208

www.sc.edu/uscpress

Manufactured in the United States of America

23 22 21 20 19 18 17 16 15 14   11 10 9 8 7 6 5 4 3 2

Library of Congress Cataloging-in-Publication Data

Clyburn, James.
  Blessed experiences : genuinely Southern, proudly Black / James E. Clyburn ;
foreword by Alfre Woodard.
    pages cm
  Includes index.
  ISBN 978-1-61117-337-6 (hardback) — ISBN 978-1-61117-338-3 (ebook) 1. Clyburn, James.
2. Legislators—United States—Biography. 3. United States. Congress. House—Biography. [1. African
Americans—South Carolina—Biography.] I. Title.
  E840.8.C59A3 2014
  328.73'092—dc23
  [B]
                                2013027984

Dedicated

to
E. L. and Almeta Dizzley Clyburn,
P. J. and Mattie McCants England,
for their lives and legacies;

to my wife
Emily England Clyburn,
for her love and support;

to my siblings,
John B. and Vivian Hilton Clyburn,
Charles E. and Gwendolyn Jones Clyburn,
Mattie England and Robert Wadley,
for their assistance and support;

to my daughters and sons-in-law,
Mignon L. Clyburn,
Jennifer L. Clyburn and Walter Reed,
Angela D. Clyburn and Cecil Hannibal,
for their admiration and support;

to my grandchildren,
Walter A Clyburn Reed,
Sydney Alexis Reed,
Layla Joann Clyburn Hannibal,
for their devotion and support;

to my loyal colleagues and staffs at the
Office of Governor John Carl West,
South Carolina Human Affairs Commission,
The United States Congress,
The James E. Clyburn Research and Scholarship Foundation,
for their nurturing, competence and support;

To constituents and citizens of South Carolina for their confidence and support;

And to all other proud and genuine Americans similarly situated and challenged.

CONTENTS

ILLUSTRATIONS

FOREWORD

I was born in Oklahoma, which, though not strictly speaking a southern state, has a great deal in common with Congressman Jim Clyburn's home state of South Carolina. Both are places where, regardless of class or color, folks will put themselves in harm's way to help a stranger and where a conversation about football or barbecue is not really about a sport or a method of preparing meat; it's about who you are. Yet beneath the cordial surface, social, political, and racial tensions rooted in events that happened a century and a half ago are ever present.

Two of my grandparents were sharecroppers, and my parents both grew up in families of thirteen children. But M. H. and Connie Woodard raised my brother, sister, and me in a pink house with a two-car garage in a grassy middle-class neighborhood on the north side of Tulsa. My daddy drove a midnight-blue Lincoln with a white landau roof, and my mother had a charge account at Neimans. The north side was a thriving, upwardly mobile black community when I was a girl. I walked my first precinct with my mom when I was ten years old. Segregation may still have been a fact of life in Tulsa, but M. H. and Connie made sure it set no limits on their children.

They sent me to Bishop Kelly High, a private integrated Catholic school, and I went on to college at BU in Boston in the early 1970s. I did not have to fight to become what Mrs. Fannie Lou Hamer called a "first-class citizen," and like most headstrong kids growing up in the era of rock and roll, I couldn't fully appreciate how much the world I inherited had been changed by people like my parents, who lived and worked and made a comfortable, happy life for their children despite being surrounded by a hostile society that would have preferred to make us invisible. I felt like a first-class citizen my whole life because my parents would not have had it any other way.

Reading Jim Clyburn's lucid, detailed, and fascinating autobiography, I was struck over and over again by how strangely familiar the stories of his formative years were to me. Strange because as a student leader, schoolteacher, and then staff member for South Carolina governor John C. West, Jim confronted overt political and personal racism far more directly than I did at a young age. His day-to-day life of professional trial and error and political awakening was also very different from mine. But throughout the book there is a sense of balance, pragmatism, and buttoned-down toughness that reminded me vividly of the men and women among whom I was raised on the north side of Tulsa.

In following Jim's career as a congressman, especially once he became House majority whip, I have been deeply moved by how truly "Representative" Jim Clyburn is of modern African Americans and of their parents, whom white people "politely" referred to as "Negroes"; and of their parents and grandparents, who endured being called "Colored"; and of their ancestors, who bore the terrors of slavery. Jim truly represents their collective aspirations, and he has the record, scars, and fighting spirit, to prove it. One has only to attend the annual Jim Clyburn Fish Fry in Columbia, South Carolina, to get a sense of the great respect he has earned from South Carolinians of every color and political persuasion.

As described in these pages, Jim's parents, Reverend Enos Lloyd Clyburn and Almeta Dizzley Clyburn, demonstrated first-class citizenship decades before it was actually granted to them. They were people of dignity, pragmatism, and staunch determination, who were doing foundational civil rights work before most Americans were aware of something called the civil rights movement. For me the early chapters brought back almost tactile memories of teachers, ministers, deacons, and small-business owners who set examples that I absorbed unconsciously, through my skin. When Jim and I first met, I recognized the formative combination of balance and strength, which he so eloquently details here.

I came of age believing I should join with those who storm the ramparts of injustice. Jim has taught me that it's just as important to know what, and especially who, is behind those walls and how one might start a conversation once inside.

Beginning with a truly insider account of the political firefight over the 2008 South Carolina Democratic primary, wherein Jim and President Bill Clinton exchanged famously opposing views, this book reveals a straightforward, unpretentious, deeply patriotic, and principled American who continues to represent his constituents with great skill and integrity.

Alfre Woodard

My life doesn't lend itself to classification or categorization. As a longtime congress-man from one of America's most impoverished districts, I fashioned a career out of being prepared and staying focused. I used my political talents to develop relation-ships and was always willing to steer a course away from predictable channels.

The eldest son of a fundamentalist minister, I joined forces with a white Catholic priest to defend the rights of underpaid black workers during a strike against the City of Charleston and the Medical College of South Carolina (now MUSC) in Charles-ton. As a community organizer, I found ways for hundreds of children from inner-city and seasonal farm workers' families to gain scholarships to colleges and universities throughout the country.

I played the clarinet in my high school marching band and orchestra and the alto saxophone in the dance band. I made only one fielding error in my three years as second baseman on my high school baseball team, but I was too weak with the bat and too slow running the bases to get beyond one year of college baseball. I was a lightweight, second-string linebacker on my high school football team, but my basket-ball skills never advanced beyond junior varsity.

I played a leading role in my high school senior class play and when I entered college, I joined the dance troupe, the debating society, and the theater group, where I played leading roles in *Our Town, An Inspector Calls,* and *The Rainmaker.*

I became a risk taker, organizing sit-ins and protest marches in my college town of Orangeburg, South Carolina, and the state capital of Columbia. I acquired enough jail time to qualify as a veteran of the civil rights movement in the 1960s, and recently celebrated fifty-year reunions in Orangeburg and Columbia with my fellow jailbirds.

I worked with—and was greatly influenced by—Dr. Martin Luther King Jr., Vice President Hubert Humphrey, and Congresswoman Shirley Chisholm. I devel-oped close working relationships with NAACP branches, Urban League affiliates, various voting rights groups, and civil rights activists in the black and brown com-munities.

I incurred the wrath of the leadership of the NAACP's state conference of branches over my role in fashioning a compromise to remove the Confederate battle flag from the dome of the South Carolina capitol building. But at one time or another, I have keynoted Freedom Dinners for most of the NAACP local branches in South Carolina and several branches across the country.

In 1971 I broke the color barrier and became the first black executive staffer to a South Carolina governor and convinced that governor, John Carl West, to create the State Housing Finance and Development Authority, which continues in existence to-day. I helped pass a state-level civil rights bill and later became the enforcing agency's commissioner, serving four governors, two Democrats and two Republicans. I successfully lobbied the state legislature to pass a Bill of Rights for Handicapped Citizens and the South Carolina Fair Housing Law, both considered groundbreaking legislation for a southern state.

I have defied stereotypes throughout my life and have made destroying broadly held myths about black people my highest priority. Growing up under the discipline of a proud black minister and a genuinely southern businesswoman, I developed enough poise and popularity to be elected president of my NAACP Youth Council before my thirteenth birthday—and the first black congressman from South Carolina in nearly a century.

I decided against following my father into the ministry and am still second guessing my decision. I lost three elections—one at the local level and two statewide—before getting elected to Congress in 1992, at an age when many were ending rather than beginning their political careers.

I have held leadership positions in the House of Representatives: president of my freshman class for the second session of the One Hundred Third Congress (1994), chairman of the Congressional Black Caucus (1999–2001), vice chairman of the House Democratic Caucus for three years, and chairman of the House Democratic Caucus for one year. I served four years as majority whip, (2007–10) and have been assistant Democratic leader since 2011.

I used my political clout in Congress to pump millions of dollars into South Carolina and my district, and I used my friendships with congressional moderates and conservatives to retain Affirmative Action in federal grant programs, to lessen sentencing disparities, and to gain passage of legislation to designate a black heritage corridor along the southeastern coast of the United States from Florida through Georgia and South Carolina to North Carolina.

I worked closely with Presidents Bill Clinton and Barack Obama, and occasionally fought with Senator Strom Thurmond of my home state, but I often worked with him and with Senator Ernest "Fritz" Hollings to improve the quality of life for South Carolinians. One of the highlights of my career occurred when the Medical University of South Carolina (MUSC) named the research facilities adjacent to the Hollings Cancer Center and the Strom Thurmond Biomedical Research Center, the James E. Clyburn Research Center.

I have been an outspoken supporter of the Obama administration, but my advocacy of some not-so-popular aspects of health-care reform, educational opportunities for low-income families, and the economic needs of persistently poor communities sometimes make me a vocal critic of some of his administration's actions and policies.

I have been awarded thirty-three honorary degrees by thirty-two colleges and universities. Marc Morial, the president and CEO of the National Urban League, presented me his 2010 Annual President's Award, and I have received scores of awards and citations from various groups and organizations—many of them named in honor of Martin Luther King Jr., Whitney Young, Rosa Parks, Eleanor Roosevelt, Septima Clark, and other notable Americans.

My story is one of national leadership and local advocacy. It is the story of a black youngster who grew up in the Jim Crow South, fought most of his adult life to lower barriers of discrimination, and emerged at the national level as a political pragmatist and consensus builder.

When I decided to write this memoir, I sought the help of my longtime friend and confidant Philip G. Grose Jr. Phil was speechwriter for Governors Robert E. McNair and John C. West and wrote books on both of them. Phil's untimely death, about two-thirds of the way through my project, gave me great pause in more ways than one. We spent many hours discussing our mutual backgrounds, common heritage, and different cultures. He was a tremendous help with style and perspective, but from the very beginning, I reserved unto myself all substance and content. I miss him dearly.

I have always been frustrated by those who explain their questionable expressions and actions toward me and those who look like me, by proclaiming themselves to be southerners, moderates or conservatives. Phil and I shared a low tolerance for such behavior, and for years I told him that if I ever wrote the memoir he always promised to help me with, it would be titled, "I, Too, Am a Southerner."

But long before I became a son of the South, I was an offspring of two dyed-in-the-wool, proudly conservative southerners, Almeta Dizzley and Enos Lloyd Clyburn, who treated me and my brothers, and people who looked like us, with great love and affection.

My mother spent many long hours in her beauty shop, and was a generous contributor to and supporter of the NAACP, as well as many other community causes and political activities. My dad always ate his last meal of the week around 6:00 P.M. on Fridays, to begin preparation for his Sunday sermons and services. He always spent most of his Saturdays fasting, reading, and humming his favorite hymn, "Blessed Assurance."

One day while President Obama and I were enjoying a round of golf, he asked about my parents as we discussed this project. When I told him the working title and why I had chosen it, he broke into his Al Green imitation and started singing one of the hymn's verses.

I did not share with the president a little factoid that I feel certain my dad never knew. My dad's mother and the composer of the music to that hymn shared the same, not-so-common given name, Phoebe. In that hymn's refrain are the words, "this is my story, this is my song."

CHRONOLOGY

1940

July 21   Born James Enos Clyburn in Sumter, South Carolina, to Almeta Dizzley Clyburn and the Reverend Enos Lloyd Clyburn, a Church of God minister

1957

May   Graduates from Mather Academy, an all-black private high school in Camden, South Carolina

September   Enrolls at South Carolina State College (now University), in Orangeburg, South Carolina

1960

February 25   Helps to plan and participates in a march protesting the segregated lunch counter at the Kress store in Orangeburg

March 15   As one of the Orangeburg Seven organizers and leaders of a major demonstration against segregated lunch counters at three Orangeburg businesses, one of the largest such protests in the South, is arrested, jailed, and eventually found guilty of "breach of the peace," a conviction later overturned by the U.S. Supreme Court

1961

March 15   Is arrested and jailed for participating in a civil rights demonstration at the State House in Columbia, South Carolina, which leads to the landmark breach of the peace case *Edwards v. South Carolina*

June 24   Marries Emily England

December   Completes course work for a B.A. at S.C. State

1962

January   Begins teaching eighth-grade English and social studies at Simonton School in Charleston, South Carolina

March 22   Birth of Mignon L. Clyburn

May   Receives degree from S.C. State

1978

June   Loses second political election in a Democratic primary runoff (after finishing first in a three-way race) in a statewide campaign to serve as South Carolina secretary of state

1986

June   Loses third political election in a Democratic primary, again for South Carolina secretary of state

1992

February   Resigns as commissioner of the South Carolina Human Affairs Commission to run for Congress

August   Wins a five-man Democratic primary race for Congress without a runoff

November   Wins general election to Congress, becoming the first African-American to serve in the U.S. House of Representatives from South Carolina since the nineteenth century

1993

January   Begins first term as representative for the Sixth District of South Carolina in the United States Congress

1993–1994 Serves as copresident, with Democrat Eva Clayton of North Carolina, of his 110-member congressional freshman class

1999–2001 Serves as chair of the Congressional Black Caucus

2003–2005 Serves as vice chair of the House Democratic Caucus

2005–2006 Serves as chair of the House Democratic Caucus

2007–2010 Serves as House majority whip

2011–present Serves as assistant House Democratic leader

PART ONE

Blessed by Experiences

"Clyburn," she asked, "how did you vote in this primary?"
It was quite a question. But, given the weightiness of the
previous half-hour's conversation, I was prepared. I looked at
Emily, took a deep breath and said, "How could I ever look in
the faces of our children and grandchildren had I not voted
for Barack Obama?"

1 Conversations with a Former President

My Blackberry vibrated, and I looked at my watch. It was 2:15 A.M. on the morning of January 27, 2008. I answered, and after several intermediate conversations, this powerful voice came on the other end: "If you bastards want a fight, you damn well will get one."

I needed no help identifying that voice. It was Bill Clinton, the former president of the United States, my longtime political friend who some were calling the country's "first black president." Black America, and particularly black South Carolina, had found political refuge in the presidency of this remarkable man.

Tonight, however, that friendship was being tested. His wife, Hillary, had just suffered a major defeat in South Carolina's Democratic primary, which was supposed to be a test of black political strength between Senator Clinton and a charismatic newcomer, Barack Obama. Obama had whipped her, and Bill Clinton wanted me to explain why.

Aboard Air Force One (second from left) with President Bill Clinton, Reverend Jesse Jackson and Senator Ernest Hollings on the way to Greeleyville, South Carolina, to dedicate the first church rebuilt after a rash of black-church burnings in South Carolina in 1996. William J. Clinton Presidential Library.

I told him I had pledged neutrality to the rules committee of the Democratic National Committee as a condition of their authorizing a primary in South Carolina, and I had kept that promise. I asked him to tell me why he felt otherwise. He exploded, using the word "bastard" again, and accused me of causing her defeat and injecting race into the contest.

That charge went back to an earlier disagreement we had about Senator Hillary Clinton's suggesting that, while Dr. Martin Luther King Jr. had done an excellent job promoting the issues of civil and voting rights for black people, it took a sensitive president such as Lyndon Baines Johnson to have the resolution of those issues enacted into law. In a *New York Times* article referencing an interview Mrs. Clinton had with Fox News on Monday, January 5, 2008, she was quoted as saying "Dr. King's dream began to be realized when President Lyndon Johnson passed the Civil Rights Act of 1964."

The article went on to say that Mrs. Clinton thought her experience should mean more to voters than uplifting words by Mr. Obama. "It took a president to get it done," Mrs. Clinton said. It was an argument I had heard before while growing up in the South, even from white leaders who supported civil rights reform. It took black leaders to identify problems, but it took white leaders to solve them, they said. I had accepted that argument for a long time; but in 2008 it seemed long outdated, and it was frankly disappointing to hear it from a presidential candidate. When the reporter called to ask my reaction, I did not hold back.

Whose Role is More Important?

As I read news reports of this little dustup, I thought about the many debates that took place during the civil rights era. Not all of the discussion was black and white. Very often it was a debate within the black community. Was the NAACP more critical to our efforts than SCLC? Was Whitney Young more important than A. Philip Randolph? I hated these debates, having had an early experience that taught me how misplaced they were.

It occurred during my last incarceration during our nonviolent war in the 1960s against racial inequality. We were challenging several "breach of the peace" ordinances that were put in place to stymie our efforts to integrate public facilities in South Carolina. On March 15, 1961, student leaders from several colleges and high schools met at Zion Baptist Church on Washington Street in Columbia to march on the capitol.

My roommate, "Duke" Missouri, and I attended the rally to help them organize, but we were not planning to march. We had had enough of jail for a while. So we dressed as if we were headed to church and went to Columbia. I wore a relatively new three-piece olive green suit, a new gold shirt, and a paisley-printed tie. Zion Baptist Church was packed.

When the NAACP field secretary, the Reverend I. DeQuincey Newman, saw us, he figured from the way we were dressed that we were not planning to do much that day. He also knew that we were graduates of Mather Academy, a highly regarded secondary school in Camden, South Carolina, sponsored by the United Methodist Church.

Dr. Newman was a master politician. He came over to where Duke and I were seated and told us that a group of Mather Academy students was on the other side of the church who wanted to meet us. We went over to meet them, and it was clear that they wanted to participate in the march and wanted us to lead their group. Duke and I agreed that we would march with them to the State House, with the understanding that they needed to get back to their campus in Camden and we needed to get back to our campus in Orangeburg. They all agreed that, when we were ordered to turn around, we were going to obey that order. So we marched to the State House.

When we got there, we were met by Chief J. P. Strom of the State Law Enforcement Division (SLED). I was a bit surprised when the chief called me by name, and ordered us to turn around. Just as I turned toward the students, the Reverend David Carter from Newberry came over and started his standard tirade about nobody turning us around.

Those students got caught up in his rhetoric and decided that they were not going to turn around. Duke and I looked at each other and before we knew it, all of us were under arrest and headed to jail. This stint in jail provided me with one of the most important life lessons that I have ever experienced.

There were 187 protestors arrested on that day, and a group of us were taken to the Columbia City Jail. To accommodate us, city authorities had sent out to Fort Jackson for canvas cots, which were lined up in rows on the firing range in the basement of the building. Late that night one of the Mather students came to me and asked when we were going to get out of jail. I told him I thought we would get out by morning, just as soon as Reverend Newman rounded up the bail money.

The young man left, but he returned a little while later and asked, "Clyburn, who did you say was out raising the bail money?" I repeated, "Reverend Newman." The student asked, "Is he that little man with the goatee?" I said, "Yes." He said, "Well, he's over in that corner over there." Surely enough, Reverend Newman was in jail with us. As a result, it was three days before we got out because Reverend Newman was there with us rather than out raising bail money.

The biggest lesson I learned from that experience was that we all have roles to play, and no one of them is more important than the other. For some of us the role was to march, sit-in, and, if need be, go to jail. But others should stay out of jail and raise the bail money.

I told the *New York Times* reporter Carl Hulse that we should be careful how we speak about that era and its personalities in American politics. While it may be historically factual that Dr. King and President Johnson shared roles and responsibility for important legislation of the 1960s, it was disingenuous to suggest which was more important or that those same roles applied a half-century later. It's one thing, I said, to run a campaign and be respectful of everyone's motives and actions, and it's something else to denigrate the efforts of others. That episode bothered me a great deal. One of the regular arguments by defenders of the status quo, I said, is to recognize input from black people but give substantive credit to white people.

The middle-of-the-night Clinton-Clyburn debate drifted into another area of contention. Less than a week earlier—on the occasion of the debate in Myrtle Beach

With Senator Hillary Clinton (left) and Mayor Joe Riley (right) at the International Longshoreman's Hall in Charleston during her 2007 presidential campaign. Unless otherwise stated, all photographs are from the author's collection.

five days before the South Carolina primary—I touched another nerve with the former president. I told CNN's John Roberts that I fully understood Bill Clinton's standing up for his wife. It's the thing spouses do. We had gotten word, however, that Hillary had questioned whether she should even contest the South Carolina primary. She worried for good reason. Obama's strength was growing in the state, and it would be a risky undertaking for her. We were also hearing that it was on the advice and assurances of her husband that she entered the South Carolina primary race. President Clinton had apparently counted on his own political clout in the black strongholds of the state to carry the day for his wife. He had used his considerable influence to recruit the lion's share of political officeholders to his spouse's team. But racial pride was trumping political chips and gender equity.

Some Political Hazards

For all his disappointment at her loss—and whatever feelings he may have had toward me and other Democratic leaders in the state—there were other issues in play. I told him that being a former president put him in a rather unique and peculiar position. I suggested that he should be careful not to say or do things so divisive that the nomination would be worthless.

All this was taking place in a delicate political atmosphere in which South Carolina's most influential black political leaders—many of whom had stuck by the Democratic Party since before the days of Lyndon Johnson—found themselves torn between a sense of loyalty to Senator Clinton and a sense of history in the making with Senator Obama. Friendships were being strained, and at times like that we could have used a little restraint from the candidates and their campaigns. That's the signal I intended to send when Roberts asked if I had any advice to offer President Clinton.

Just before going on the air, John and I had been talking about the unseasonably cold weather in Myrtle Beach that January, and—meaning no disrespect—I said in response to John's question that I would advise the president to "just chill out." The comment was carried widely, and it probably sounded a little provocative. I guess that's how Bill Clinton took it.

By this time the Clinton-Clyburn debate was getting steamy on both sides. Inevitably the question arose about who played the "race card" first. I suggested that it had happened a few months earlier with reports that Andrew Young, former United Nations ambassador, had made off-color remarks about rumors of President Clinton having had interracial affairs. The reports of Mr. Young's comments were unfortunate, the president said, but that Andy had called and apologized for having made them. This time the former president and I agreed, but for only a moment. I exploded. Maybe a private apology made it OK for President Clinton, but it did not erase the racial aspect that was already in the public arena.

By then we were both rhetorically worn out and concluded our conversation with abrupt good-byes. It was clear that the former president was holding me personally responsible for his wife's poor showing among South Carolina black voters, and it was also clear that our heated conversation had not changed his mind.

As we hung up, my wife, Emily, was stirring fitfully and eventually asked me about the spirited conversation that had awakened her. When I told her it was Bill Clinton and that he was accusing me of sabotaging his wife's campaign in South Carolina, she asked a question she had never asked before in more than forty-seven years of marriage.

"Clyburn," she asked, "how did you vote in this primary?"

It was quite a question. But, given the weightiness of the previous half-hour's conversation, I was prepared. I looked at Emily, took a deep breath and said, "How could I ever look in the faces of our children and grandchildren had I not voted for Barack Obama?"

In my entire adult life in one of the nation's most racially conscious and sensitive states, I had rarely felt such certainty in a decision I had made. For once my heart, my soul, and my mind converged at a moment that was both spontaneous and exhilarating. For all the claims politicians may make about being absolute in their feelings, the fact is that even the best of them leave the field of combat with partial victories and mixed feelings.

Not so that evening. It was life changing. There was even something curiously energizing about being called out in the middle of the night by an angry former president of the United States. Bill Clinton and I were friends, and always would be.

Presidential candidate Barack Obama at my 2007 "World Famous Fish Fry"

I understood how he felt. I had known my share of political defeats and disappointments. We would have time to reconcile, which we did; but not on this night.

Emily was less forgiving. She was not only upset about the nature of the call and its tone, but she disagreed strongly about the claims that I had been pro-Obama. She didn't think so. By then she was wide awake, and went to her computer to check e-mails. I was exhausted, and fell off to sleep.

Venting and Then Some

It took a while for me to realize that my middle-of-the-night telephone conversation with Bill Clinton was not just an exercise in venting for the former president. He meant what he said about a fight. The next morning when I turned on the television news, the magnitude of it all began to hit me. There was President Clinton, making his comparison of Obama's South Carolina primary victory with that of Jesse Jackson's caucus victory twenty years earlier: "Jesse Jackson won South Carolina in '84 and '88. Jackson ran a good campaign. And Obama ran a good campaign here."

I have a world of respect for Jesse Jackson and much of the work he has done. He was a significant influence in the campaigns of 1984 and 1988, and he did run good campaigns. But he was never a front-runner, and his candidacy never reached the level attained by Obama. With his comments, it seemed to me that President Clinton was trying to downplay the magnitude of Obama's South Carolina victory and make it sound like a "black southern event," thereby minimizing it somehow in the cosmic national Democratic perspective. President Clinton was trying hard to control the damage from what had been as much his loss in South Carolina as that of his wife.

Then I looked at the video a little more closely. President Clinton had chosen not just any setting for his television interview and the dismissive Jesse Jackson statement. He was standing at the Meadowlake Precinct in Columbia, less than five minutes from my home. This was no accident or random choice of locations. Bill Clinton wasn't just defining his wife's loss in South Carolina as a "black political event," he was defining it as a "Jim Clyburn black southern event." So this is what he meant when he said he'd show us a fight.

I wasn't much for tying on the gloves in public, particularly against a former president who was about as good a politician and as tough an infighter as I had ever known. But this was getting downright personal. Emily had already struck me rhetorically across the chops as if there had been some equivocation on my part in voting for Barack Obama. My three daughters—and particularly my youngest, Angela—were getting emotional about where their dad stood at this historical moment. Hell, I was getting emotional myself. The last thing I wanted around the household was to be seen as wishy-washy.

I didn't call Bill Clinton in the middle of the night to tell him so, but I concluded that Obama's South Carolina victory was a lot more than just another "black southern event." Whatever might be the outcome of the Super Tuesday primaries, which were only days away on February 5, I was satisfied that Obama was in it for the duration and that the process would be a lot longer than those primaries two weeks hence. Obama had proved that he was not too black for white voters in Iowa and not too white for black voters in South Carolina. His victory in our state proved that he could be a vote getter among white southerners as well. He had gotten 27 percent of the nonblack vote against a formidable candidate, Senator Clinton, and had carried forty-four of the forty-six counties in the state, including all the counties in my congressional district. Obama had defeated Clinton by a margin of 55.4 percent to 26.8 percent, and in so doing he had not only won twenty-five of the forty-five delegates allocated by the primary (John Edwards received eight) but had significantly surpassed the pollsters' predictions of a 41-26 Obama victory. His margin was almost double that.

A Word from Rahm

I returned to Washington a changed man. No one had ever accused Jim Clyburn of being low in self-esteem, but the attention directed toward me and South Carolina because of the primary bordered on ridiculous. Rahm Emanuel, no stranger to the public spotlight himself, offered his congratulations on the effective media blitz and asked if I had planned it that way. I don't think he believed me when I said I had not. My good friend and close political ally, John Larson, overheard the conversation and did believe me. He told me I should have taken credit for it anyhow, truth or not.

At any rate, the South Carolina primary had been successful in one very important sense. National attention had been focused on our state in a positive way, and the televised debates had familiarized worldwide audiences with two of our institutions of higher learning—the Citadel and my alma mater, South Carolina State University—and with one of the state's tourist destinations, Myrtle Beach. The fact that the outcome of the primary was an important one gave our state some political credibility and proved that we had an identity other than being Strom Thurmond's home state and the place where the first shots of the Civil War were fired. We now had a spot on the map as a place with some clout in the Democratic column. We had become important enough for a former president to make an angry, profane middle-of-the-night phone call to complain to an old friend about the outcome of the primary. For all the hoopla, I was still uncommitted, officially at least. But momentum was building in the Obama camp, and there seemed to be panic among the Clintons.

The day before the Super Tuesday primaries, I received another phone call from President Clinton. This one was at a more appropriate time of day, and its tone and manner were more appropriate as well. The president offered apologies for the previous call, and when I did not respond immediately, he said he was not going to hang up until I accepted. I accepted halfheartedly, and the phone call ended.

I suspect that President Clinton was making a lot of those phone calls that day. Seven months later, Bill Clinton and I made our peace, not in a summit-style meeting, but in a small-talk conversational way at the funeral of U.S. Representative Stephanie Tubbs Jones of Ohio. As is often the case in such matters, it wasn't what we said; it was the quiet tone of how we said it.

In those fierce days of the South Carolina primary, the tone was anything but quiet. It was beginning to dawn on a lot of Americans that Obama was here to stay. About the time that the Hillary Clinton bandwagon was supposed to be roaring down

With Mary Steenburgen, friend and colleague Stephanie Tubbs Jones, and Ted Danson at the Martha's Vineyard home of Danson and Steenburgen. Bill Clinton and I made peace at Jones's funeral, held the day after the conclusion of the historic 2008 Democratic Convention in Denver, where Barack Obama was nominated for president.

the highway, it seemed stuck in neutral. From the summer months of 2007 forward, sober-minded Democrats had been viewing President George W. Bush's abysmal approval ratings as assurance that a mainstream Democratic ticket would waltz into the White House in 2009. Now this? A black guy or a white woman heading the ticket? Republicans, fretful over their sad state, may have had heartening visions of a Tom Eagleton or Geraldine Ferraro misstep by the Democrats. And a lot of Democrats must have begun to panic. For all the feel-good rhetoric about having an African American on the ticket, the political reality was that it was still a "heckuva" risk. In a year which was supposed to be a slam-dunk Democratic win, it must have seemed to many Democrats that this was no time for launching a three-pointer from midcourt. For a lot of black Americans who had toiled in the Democratic vineyards for years, including me, there was, just maybe, the making of the impossible dream.

Super Tuesday lay just ahead, and a lot of political strategists may have seen this as a moment of decision. But just the opposite was taking place. Both campaigns lapsed into defensive modes, protecting their flanks, and instead of playing to win they started playing not to lose. The Super Tuesday outcomes were predictably non-decisive. Obama carried thirteen states, Clinton ten. A total of 7,987,274 votes were cast for Obama, 8,081,748 for Clinton. At the end of the day, Obama had 847 delegates; Clinton had 834.

If there was a winner, it was the psychological reality that Barack Obama had passed yet another test in establishing his political credibility, and folks were no longer talking about an African American as simply being "on the ticket." This was no longer just a good political story for the Sunday morning pundits about an underdog candidate making waves. This was the real thing. It was now obvious that the next Democratic candidate for president would not be a white male. In one way or the other, this would be a history-making struggle, and befitting such a momentous struggle, it looked as if it would go right down to the wire.

Neither candidate having come out of Super Tuesday with a clear majority or even a clear advantage, left only two avenues for the selection of a Democratic nominee; one being the withdrawal of one of the candidates. Such likelihood was remote, if not impossible. The candidates had spent millions of dollars, millions of hours, and millions of miles in pursuit of their goals. Giving up on the race a few furlongs from the finish was not in the makeup of either one of them.

2 : *Courting the Superdelegates*

That left the only other apparent course to pursue: courting the uncommitted, or "superdelegates." I knew something about the origins of that convention species. You might say I was in on its creation. It was part of the spillover from the chaotic 1968 Democratic convention, at which the youthful antiwar forces had clashed with party regulars over just about everything, including the means by which delegates were chosen to participate in the convention. A lot of the zeal of these young grassroots forces was aimed at the so-called Democratic establishment, which they felt had blocked the party from taking a strong stance against the Vietnam War. The results of their dissatisfaction made the 1972 nomination of George McGovern possible.

A new process for choosing delegates to the national convention was put in place, aimed at reducing the influence of the party regulars. It required that all Democrats run for the privilege of serving as a delegate to the national convention. A lot of party leaders—state chairs, vice-chairs, governors, congressmen, and other "important" folks—choose not to bother, and the party lost a lot of its power base as a result.

Many of us believed it was wrong, and as a member of the Delegate Selection Commission appointed by Senator George McGovern after the 1972 convention in Miami Beach, I was one of those who set out to make some changes. We had gone too far in reform, I thought, and it was seriously damaging the party. Between 1964 and 1988, Democrats won the White House only once. A lot of those losses were because some of our heaviest political hitters were on the sidelines.

For me the floor fight at the 1972 convention was proof enough of that fact. Under the new rules, the seating of several prominent delegations was challenged, most profoundly that of the Illinois delegation headed by Chicago mayor Richard Daley. Mayor Daley and his troops were sent home, and I remember Willie Brown of California making a stem-winder of a speech in opposition to the seating of the South Carolina delegation, of which I was a member. The state party hired the legendary African American attorney Matthew Perry to defend us, and we were seated. Shirley Chisholm ran for president that year, and she got two votes out of the South Carolina delegation, Florence doctor R. N. Beck's and mine.

Out of all that, and in consideration of the overwhelming defeat McGovern suffered in 1972 at the hands of Richard Nixon, the idea was advanced that the party needed to start the process of healing itself and bringing its power players back into the lineup. Political changes, however, take a long time. It wasn't until 1984 that special

With Shirley Chisholm during her visit to the South Carolina Young Democrats in 1978. I voted to nominate her for president at the 1972 Democratic Convention.

categories were created for party leaders, and it was twelve years after that—1996—that all Democratic members of Congress were given automatic seats as convention delegates. Going into the 2008 convention, there were 4,233 delegate votes, of which about 794 had the special unpledged status of what became known as "superdelegates."

Neither Clinton nor Obama had the committed 2,117 votes necessary to win the nomination after Super Tuesday. That meant that for all the outward profession of transparency and openness in the nominating process, the race would probably be thrown to the superdelegates, those several hundred unpledged party leaders and elected officials who could vote however they pleased and who could determine the outcome of this long, laborious nominating process. It had all the earmarks of the smoke-filled rooms that the party had been trying so hard to avoid, and it could undermine the credibility of either candidate. I frankly worried about how a newcomer such as Obama would fare with the party regulars against a candidate whose husband had served two terms as president of the United States. The process was fraught with danger and could very well doom Obama's relationships with the grassroots voters. It could—in turn—diminish his possibilities of winning the general election.

That's when I decided that my best role would be working with the superdelegates on behalf of Obama. Consequently, when the Democratic Congressional Campaign Committee (DCCC) inquired about my availability to make personal appearances on behalf of congressional candidates in targeted races, I jumped at the opportunity and stated my preference for congressional races in the East, Midwest, and South. I wound up spending a great deal of time in states with critical congressional races and a lot of superdelegates. My main purpose was to help congressional candidates by making public appearances and helping with fund-raising, and I put in a lot of time on those assignments. It was an encouraging experience in many ways. I remember a particular visit to an upstate New York district where I was one of the few black faces among a largely white Democratic constituency. To my surprise these people didn't want to talk about the Iraq war or the disastrous Bush administration. They were concerned about public education, health care, and health insurance, items that Obama was already addressing and I didn't hesitate to reinforce.

The Nonracial Agenda

It turned out that conversations in these predominantly white areas were not so much about race as they were about the well-being of our nation. Despite the fact that I still had not publicly committed to Obama, it didn't hurt that I had become identified with his campaign in the South Carolina primary and that the primary had given South Carolina a high-profile identity in national circles. My plan was working perfectly. I did not have to seek out the superdelegates; they sought me out. They asked my opinions on a lot of things. I was still officially neutral, and my rule was this: I would not volunteer my opinion or preference with regard to a candidate for the nomination. But if I were asked in a private one-on-one conversation, I would express my support for Barack Obama. I got my share of criticism, nasty phone calls, and letters. But I was determined to play a major role in the process of selecting the Democratic nominee when it came down to the votes of superdelegates.

For all the excitement and attention the campaign was producing publicly, it was getting nowhere politically in terms of a conclusive outcome. I kept thinking about my words to President Clinton, that if we're not careful with the way we wage this warfare, the Democratic nomination will not be worth having. And from all the bitterness being fomented as the campaign dragged on, I worried that the party would become incorrigibly divided as we headed into the general election. The degree of anger that President Clinton displayed during our conversation became a nightmarish reminder of the potential dangers that lay ahead.

As we approached the final two primaries, things were still in doubt. The South Dakota and Montana primaries were scheduled for June third, and even though these states carried only a combined delegate total of thirty-one, things were so close that these votes had become pivotal. By my calculations, Obama would still come up six or seven votes short even if he carried those two states by margins of sixty-five to thirty-five percent (which he did not do). I was still publicly uncommitted, and the convention was only three months away.

I had spoken with Obama a few days earlier. Although he made it clear he wanted me to make a public announcement, he didn't pressure me. A day or two later, New Mexico governor Bill Richardson called. He was less subtle. "Do it, Jimmy, and do it now," he said. Bill Richardson is the only person in the world who calls me "Jimmy."

I kept thinking about the unseemly prospect of Obama finishing the primaries a few votes short, and coming to Washington hat in hand or groveling to persuade a few superdelegates to vote for him. In the meantime the Clinton people were putting on a full-court press, and they were not bashful about committing a foul or two along the way. When I hit the campaign trail the next morning, I had already made up my mind that I would make my endorsement as soon as I returned to South Carolina.

The Endorsement

I had a news-media interview that morning in Connecticut, and the question was quickly put to me: When will you endorse? I told the reporter that I would do so at eleven o'clock Monday morning when I got back to South Carolina. It didn't take long for that morsel to get around, and in those supercharged days, even the scheduling of an endorsement made the news.

The unhappy person during all of this was my long-suffering communications director, Kristie Greco. This wasn't the first time I had freelanced a news-media event, and once again she chided me for my indiscretion. With appropriate humility I agreed to stay away from the press for the rest of that week. But during that time I continued contacting superdelegates. From a practical point of view, I realized that Obama needed to have enough of the superdelegate votes sewed up before the South Dakota and Montana primaries closed on that Tuesday evening, so he could say with certainty that it was rank-and-file voters of those two states who had put him over the top.

My work with the superdelegates was going well. Some even said they had been waiting to hear from me before they made a commitment. Then I turned my attention to South Carolina, knowing that I could hardly make a case to other states if I couldn't sway my own. We had eight superdelegates—four Democratic National Committee members, two at large, and two members of Congress: John Spratt and me. Of the eight, six were already committed, leaving Spratt and one other unpledged.

John quickly and graciously committed to Obama. That left one South Carolina delegate to win over, and he was still bearing a grudge from a slight he felt he had received at the state convention from an Obama supporter. I asked him not to hold his grievance with an Obama delegate against the candidate. After some soul-searching, he agreed.

All this was happening on Monday morning, June 2, 2008, the day before the Montana and South Dakota primaries. In the midst of it all came word from my communications director that she had scheduled me to appear on NBC's *Today* show at 7:04 A.M. eastern time from Washington the next morning to announce my endorsement. Perfect! It would still be a couple of hours before the polls opened in Montana and South Dakota, giving plenty of time for whatever impact my endorsement might have.

I got back on the telephone to the superdelegates, knowing now that it was a must that the deal be sealed by Tuesday evening. Things were beginning to have a certain sequence, cadence, and momentum: the morning endorsement, the announcement of the two primary results, and the declaration of victory at the end of the evening.

I was beginning to feel that it was all doable. The fantasy so many of us had harbored for so long seemed less of a fantasy. This might really happen.

A live interview on the *Today* show was nerve-racking enough; doing it at 7:04 in the morning was even more disconcerting. I didn't sleep much. For all my years in public life, television interviews were nothing new, and I considered myself pretty good at them. From my earliest days watching my father preach at his small churches in South Carolina, I had an appreciation and something of a knack for oratory.

As I got older and more political in my delivery, the evangelical part subsided, and I became a little more conversational. But this was different, possibly the most important four minutes in my career. I would be heard by people all around the world, and I would be speaking on behalf of the man who might become the most important person on the planet.

I don't remember exactly what I said but it must have been OK. Responses from family and friends were positive. But the more important responses would be the unspoken action from those superdelegates who were still uncommitted and who might have been swayed one way or the other.

The assumption is usually made that delegates to the convention will vote the convictions of their state or district voters. But you never know, and on that afternoon of the last two primaries in two sparsely populated western states, political fate truly hung in the balance.

Victory in Sight

As the day progressed, I began to get encouraging news. According to my count, it wouldn't take many superdelegate votes to put Obama over the top. By three o'clock that afternoon, I was satisfied that we had done just that. Phone calls from those disparate communities where the nation's political history was being written convinced me that the dream was coming true, that Barack Obama would have enough votes— and maybe a few to spare.

It turned out that we probably needed those "few to spare." In some imprecise calculations, I had projected that if Obama could carry Montana and South Dakota by a 60-40 margin, the combination of delegates from those primaries plus the superdelegates who had committed would be enough to put Obama over the top.

Actually that's not the way it happened. Hillary Clinton won the South Dakota primary by 55 to 45 percent and got nine of the fifteen delegates allocated. Obama carried Montana by 56 to 41 percent and picked up nine of those sixteen delegates. It was almost a dead heat. But we had done better than expected with the superdelegates, and that was what pushed Obama over the top. We had won.

Political victories are not declared with the suddenness of a walk-off grand-slam home run or a fifty-yard field goal. They come slowly and incrementally, and when they happen, it's not always possible to jump up and scream or high-five a neighbor. That's how I was feeling at the moment. An enormous emotional force was building inside me. But nothing was official, and I spent some reflective moments thinking back over my conversations with those superdelegates, wondering which ones had actually come through and made the difference.

I thought about the conversations in the community centers in New York State, the town halls in Michigan, the black churches in Florida, and the hotel meeting rooms in Connecticut. I took a deep breath, knowing that I had spoken face-to-face with many of those people who were making a difference on that historic June day in 2008 and knowing that Obama's support came from the widest possible cross section of the American population.

I knew in my mind and in my heart that it was those South Carolinians who were there at the crucial moments. It was South Carolinians who came to the polls in such overwhelming numbers and sent the message that Barack Obama could win in a southern state. They waited hours and hours to register and vote in places such as my hometown of Sumter, my adopted home of Columbia, and by the thousands in Clarendon County—where courageous black parents had initiated the suit a half century earlier that resulted in the *Brown v. Board of Education* Supreme Court case, which desegregated public schools in the South—and Orangeburg—where people had marched the streets generations earlier to gain the right to vote, to sit at lunch counters, and at the front of the bus. Many of those same people—some in wheel-chairs and with walkers—waited patiently for the opportunity to exercise their hard-won right to vote; this time on behalf of an African American.

People Who Made the Difference

I thought of those good friends in the South Carolina delegation who had agreed in those crucial final hours to make a commitment of faith and trust for the candidacy of Barack Obama. It was not a commitment made out of charity or effusive goodwill. It was a commitment based on what they perceived as the will of the people.

Barack Obama's national television appearance was scheduled for ten o'clock the evening of the Montana and South Dakota primaries. By then it was generally as-sumed that he could declare himself the presumptive Democratic nominee for presi-dent of the United States of America. I was still jittery though. I had gone into election nights before when things looked good and sounded official, only to be disappointed. I remembered specifically a 10:00 P.M. declaration thirty-eight years earlier that did not pan out so well.

I arrived at the National Democratic Club about 9:30 P.M. and joined my regu-lar group at a table in an area where we had a clear view of the television screens. The political junkies were busy calculating and projecting the outcome. As the evening progressed; news reports confirmed my earlier estimates that there were indeed suf-ficient superdelegate commitments to Obama that he would need only a handful of votes from Montana and South Dakota to put him over the top.

Within the next few minutes, results from those states bore out our hopes and projections. Obama had picked up the necessary delegates to declare victory. It was over, and things had gone reasonably close to plan. Obama could publicly thank the voters of those two states for putting him over the top, but we knew it was the reserve of superdelegate commitments that actually made that statement possible. For one of the many times it would happen, I marveled at the effectiveness and precision of the Obama political operation.

Then came an announcement that Obama would be making a speech at the top of the hour. People began positioning themselves to watch the speech. Victory was at hand. I felt a sudden surge of emotion welling up inside me. It had been a long day, beginning with the *Today* show interview and grinding through hours of phone calls and conversations to help build the base for tonight's victory.

I slipped out of the club and went home to watch the speech in the solitude of my apartment. I needed to have some quiet time so I could absorb the magnitude of it all. But there was something else on my mind. I wanted to visit with my parents. Although they had been gone for years, I was reflecting on their many prayers and well wishes. I wanted them to know what had happened, to talk with them like an excited child and tell them about my day.

I wanted them to know that all the toil and courage they had experienced in their difficult and burdensome lives had made a difference, and that subsequent generations had benefited from their struggles. I wanted them to share this momentous occasion, and to celebrate the role they had played in preparing for this historic event, this blessed experience.

But maybe they already knew.

PART
TWO

A Blessed Beginning

"James, you are scheduled to graduate in three months.
Three months of silent treatment is nothing. I believe I could
live in hell for three months if I knew I was going to get out."
And, as if to underscore the lack of manhood I was exhibiting,
she continued, "and I'm a woman."

3 *Inherited Values*

My parents belonged to that generation on whose shoulders the civil rights movement was built. They were the people who endured the oppression and deprivation that came along with life in the Jim Crow South, but who fought back in ways often overlooked by later generations. While black Carolinians by the tens of thousands were migrating to the northeastern and midwestern parts of our nation in search of jobs and better lives, my folks remained, as did tens of thousands of other Carolinians of color.

My parents stayed, I am convinced, for a purpose. They were fighting not just against the racial injustice and economic deprivation that were part of their daily lives. They were fighting against that most insidious of afflictions visited by Jim Crow upon the black populations of the South, the affliction of hopelessness. All around them as they were growing up in the early twentieth century was an air of defeatism born of economic hardship, political oppression, and violent lawlessness against any effort by those of their ilk who attempted to better themselves. From the pulpit my dad preached a positive message of hope and salvation as the rewards for hard work. From her ambitious position as beauty-shop owner and business entrepreneur, my mom showed that there were professional alternatives to what were considered traditional jobs for black women.

There didn't seem to be anything uncommon about my parents' upbringing. Most African Americans in South Carolina lived in small communities dotted through the countryside, eking out a living mostly as sharecroppers or tenant farmers. A few, like my mom's father, John D. Dizzley, owned their own land. He had a good-sized cotton farm near the town of Bishopville, in an area of rural Lee County known as Browntown. My mother, Almeta, was born there on March 22, 1916, the eighth of thirteen children. I came to know Mom's brothers and sisters as close members of our extended family. In fact two of Mom's sisters lived with us for a while before catching the "chicken-bone special" to go up north. I also have fond memories of her mother and father. My grandfather was a strict disciplinarian and a fundamentalist fire-and-brimstone preacher.

There were many stories about John Dizzley, but all that we have been able to verify is that he was the offspring of a Cherokee Indian woman and a white man and that he married a black woman, Everline Grant. She was from Grant Hill, an area off Black River Road between Camden and Sumter, near Spring Hill, where my dad's

My maternal grandfather,
John Dizzley

maternal family, the Lloyds, lived. Although he could have grown tobacco more profitably, his strong faith forbade it. John Dizzley was a pastor in the Church of God, where smoking was a sin.

Browntown and the Lizard Man

Browntown is in a remote part of the rural landscape, but it achieved a measure of notoriety some years ago. A story was circulated that a lizard the size of a man had been sighted there, walking upright. Just as vampires and other fictional creatures had taken their turns occupying our rapt attention, the "Lizard Man" story took the country by storm.

For me this provided good storytelling material, particularly as an ice-breaker opener for speeches. I would tell audiences that I knew the Lizard Man existed, having seen him on several occasions during my childhood visits to my grandparents. The sightings, I would explain, happened on hot summer days just after I had eaten significant numbers of cherries off those trees that were on my grandfather's farm. The story usually caused people to relax, and it always got a good response.

All Mom's sisters left the state, settling in Philadelphia, Baltimore, and New York. I've never been told what caused Mom to remain in poverty-stricken South Carolina, but I've surmised it may have had something to do with meeting a strong-minded older man from nearby Kershaw County. Dad was more than eighteen years older than Mom, and her father had brought him into the Church of God movement.

We never learned much about Dad's early years, except that they were not easy ones. He was born on December 23, 1897, near the town of Westville. According to highway maps there was a community called Clyburn nearby, which may have been his actual birthplace. Dad's birth coincided with some especially bad times politically for black people in America and particularly in South Carolina. The state's Constitution of 1895 had taken away voting rights from most African Americans in South Carolina, and the 1896 U.S. Supreme Court ruling in *Plessy v. Ferguson* had given constitutional authorization for the "separate but equal" doctrine that legalized the segregation of public accommodations in America for the next seven decades.

Dad never said much about his personal experiences in those early years, and what he did say was usually accompanied by the disclaimer, "or so they told me." To me that was a not-so-subtle admission that he had some doubts about the veracity of some of those stories.

Both Dad's parents died before he was three years old, or, as he always said, "so they told me." His father, William, Dad was told, died two months before my dad was born, and his mother, Phoebe, died when he was two years old. I have done a lot of searches and have hired professionals to do searches also. We have found his mother, Phoebe (Pheby), and his brothers, William and Charlie, but no William Clyburn who could have possibly been my paternal grandfather.

Whatever may have been the exact circumstances, Dad was raised on Smyrl Hill in Camden by his mother's sister, Rozena Lloyd, whom we knew as Aunt Rozena. We visited her quite often and felt close to Aunt Rozena and her daughter, Elizabeth.

My paternal grandmother,
Phoebe Lloyd Clyburn, circa 1890

Those visits also made me aware of why Dad may have been circumspect about his origins. It was obvious that Elizabeth was not, as we say, a "100 percenter."

There were other "mysteries" about Dad's background. One of them was his name, "Enos." It is a biblical name. Enos was an obscure figure, the son of Adam and Eve's third son, Seth. According to Genesis, Enos lived to be 905 years, and that's about all we know about him. But my Dad bore the name with pride, and I am similarly honored to carry it as my middle name. Dad had an uncle named Enoch, his mother's brother, and in some of the documents we found Dad listed as "Enoch."

Dad and Mom's dad spent a lot of time traveling together and establishing Church of God congregations throughout South Carolina. Dad's first wife, Rebecca Rembert—who Mom knew—died in childbirth, and Dad remained unmarried for eight years. Mom readily talked about the gentlemanly manner in which Dad had always conducted himself and how she had come to know him as a "good and decent man."

So when this "good and decent man" presented an opportunity for her to leave the hardships and travails of farm life and finish school as well, she did not give the idea much thought. As far as she was concerned, he was a godsend. With her father's blessing, she relocated to Camden to live with and perform house chores for a prominent African American family, the Dibbles, who in return sent her to Mather Academy, which was located across from the Dibbles' home on Campbell Street at the corner of Dekalb Street.

Mom was in the tenth grade when she relocated to Camden. Dad was already living there, serving as assistant pastor of the Church of God on Chestnut Street. Of course she wanted to finish high school before getting married, and Mather, a United Methodist–supported private school, required twelve years to graduate. But across Dekalb Street was Jackson High School, a public school that required only eleven years. So when Mom finished the tenth grade at Mather, she transferred over to Jackson and graduated a year later. Then she and Dad got married.

After a short stint as pastor of the Jenkinsville Church of God in Fairfield County, Dad accepted a call to the Walker Avenue Church of God in Sumter. This was particularly inviting because he and Mom yearned to continue their educational pursuits, and Sumter was the home of Morris College, a Baptist Church–supported, historically black college.

By the time I arrived on the scene in 1940, Dad was established in his pastorate at the Walker Avenue Church of God in Sumter; Mom was emerging as a voice of influence and change in our community; and I was off on an adventurous life that grew out of the seminal convergence of interests of these two remarkable people.

Refusing to Surrender

My earliest recollections of Dad are of his oratorical power within the walls of that small Church of God sanctuary where he held forth. Dad would not tolerate surrender or self-pity among his parishioners. I remember, on one particular evening, a church member either testifying or singing something to the effect that "I have been down so long, getting up never crosses my mind." My dad did not respond with

*My father, the Reverend
Enos Lloyd Clyburn, circa 1950*

sympathy. Instead he lifted his voice to the congregation: "No matter how long you've been down," he said, "getting up must always be on your mind." He then declared that from that day forward such hopelessness should never be uttered.

My father could be stern, and he viewed pessimism as a human weakness with no place in his faith. Hopes for a better life, he believed, applied to expectations here on earth as well as those in the hereafter. I was too young to know the word "resiliency" at the time, but I had already learned the meaning.

I grew up fascinated by the way Dad exerted leadership in the ministerial world. Dad was a preacher of the gospel, a teacher, an orator, and—on occasion—a man of heroic proportions. That's what I witnessed unexpectedly one afternoon during a meeting of Dad's church presbytery.

Dad served for many years as state president of the Presbytery. As happens from time to time in such periods of extended leadership, a group arose in opposition to him and ran a candidate for president against him.

I often accompanied him to church meetings and kept up with things. And while I did not go into the ministry, I learned a lot about political strategies and infighting along the way. And I always admired his reaction when I told him of my decision not to attend the seminary. "Well son," he said to me on that occasion, "I suspect the world would much rather see a sermon than to hear one."

I had heard about the opposition to his leadership and was curious about the development. The church's state meetings always took place at the Church of God on the corner of Lee and Pine Streets in Darlington, and the elections were usually held at the close of the business meeting. When this particular meeting opened, I slipped into the back of the church to eavesdrop on the proceedings.

Dad was presiding, and I loved watching him preside. He was always crisp and concise. He insisted that my brothers and I learn *Robert's Rules of Order*, and he studied them himself, which always kept him head and shoulders above his colleagues. I watched with great anticipation as he opened the floor for nominations for president. Dad's name was placed in nomination first, and shortly thereafter, a member of the insurgent group placed another name in nomination.

Almost immediately, someone moved to close the nominations. Ballots were cast in secret, and when the results were tallied, the vote was tied. Dad announced the tied vote, and one of his supporters quickly moved that all current officers be retained until the next annual meeting. Dad spoke up and reminded the members that the bylaws dictated that in the case of a tie vote, the president could vote, and since he had not voted, he intended to do so.

Thinking the worst, one of Dad's opponents lept to his feet and objected. Dad ignored his attempt to be recognized, and as the clamor in the room grew, Dad shouted out above the noise his emphatic vote. To the absolute surprise of everyone—friend and foe alike—Dad cast the tie-breaking vote for his opponent.

The room fell silent, and Dad continued presiding in routine fashion, asking for further business. There being none, he ended that most memorable annual meeting.

On the way home, I told Dad I had been in the back of the church watching, and he said he had seen me there. When I asked why he had voted for his opponent, he told me that when severe schisms develop in organizations and positions become as intractable as they currently were in the presbytery, it would be difficult for anybody to lead successfully. "They will want me back," he said. And they did. The following year, he was elected without opposition, and he held the position until he retired years later at a time of his own choosing.

Learning about Power

Dad's strategy was more than a political ploy. I realized over time that he was letting his colleagues see the qualities that made him a strong man and a powerful leader. He had lost the election by his own choice, but he gained influence and enhanced his standing in the eyes of those around him, particularly in the eyes of his adoring son.

Dad's mission in life was teaching, first and foremost—whether it was with parishioners from the pulpit, with friends and neighbors in the community, or with three rowdy sons in various interesting stages of development. One of his most basic learning tools was the Bible, but he never made us read it. He simply told us that we had to recite a verse from the Bible at breakfast every morning, and we could not say the same one twice, and on the day he laid down that rule, "Jesus wept" was taken off the table. Dad was also a believer in rendering unto Caesar that which was Caesar's and unto God that which was God's.

In our household that was defined as a dual requirement for the three sons. In addition to reciting a Bible verse every morning at breakfast, we also had share a current event with Dad and/or Mom every evening. Sumter's daily newspaper, the *Item*, was delivered to our door, and we had to read it and be prepared to discuss it. I'm not certain who came out the better in that arrangement—the Almighty or Caesar—but my brothers and I came to understand our dad's deep conviction that we should be the instruments of God's peace here on earth. He had a favorite story to underscore that belief.

It was about a man who every day passed a vacant lot that was overgrown and being used by passersby as a place to toss their empty cans, bottles, and other litter. It was a mess, and after a while, the man decided to clean up the lot and plant a garden. After weeks of hard work at cleaning and tilling and planting and weeding, he finally began to see the results and rewards of his hard work.

One day, as he was weeding his garden, a passerby stopped and remarked that the garden was beautiful and went on to exclaim to the gentleman that the Lord had really been good to him. The gardener agreed and thanked him, but then went on to say to the passerby, "You should have seen this place when the Lord had it all by himself."

A Parable for Life

I am the oldest of three sons. We are spaced two years apart, making us close enough in age to be companions through life and also close enough to make us fierce competitors from an early age. A lesson about that competitiveness came one Saturday morning, when my brothers and I accompanied Dad to the backyard auto-mechanic shop of Mr. Jim Singleton to have some work done on Dad's temperamental 1937 Chevrolet. On this occasion, just as Mr. Singleton started to hoist the front end of that the cranky Chevrolet, my brothers and I began playing near the car.

Dad wasn't certain how strong the pulley's chain was, and he instructed us to move away from the car, and we did so. But in a matter of minutes, my brothers and I got into what I would call a "little physical disagreement" and what others might call a fight. We were around twelve, ten, and eight at the time, good ages for brothers to test out each other's skills in the fine art of self-defense. After watching us for a while, Dad called a halt to our activities and summoned us in that stentorian, ministerial voice of his, which usually meant we were in for some sort of serious exercise in behavioral correction. Expecting the worst, we gathered around Dad, who had taken a seat on a crate. He had a piece of cord string in his hand and handed it to my youngest brother, Charles.

"Break the string," he said. Charles pulled and tugged with all his might, but the string wouldn't give way. Then the string went to John, and he was similarly told to snap the cord. After he failed, Dad handed the string to me, and said, "James, since you are the oldest and strongest, maybe you can pop the string." I tried and failed.

Dad took the string back from me, placed it between the palms of his hands, and began slowly rubbing his hands together. The more he rubbed, of course, the more friction he created, and the more friction he created, the more unraveled the cord string became. It was not long before the cord string had separated into three single pieces of string. Dad gave one piece to Charles, one to John, and the other to me. He then asked each of us to pop the string, and with little effort, each one of us successfully broke the string.

Then came the lesson: "Do not let little disagreements that crop up among you create so much friction that it separates you," he said. "If you do, the world will pop you apart and you may never know why." It was a good message for us at the time and is one of my favorites. I've used it often in speeches and conversations.

I enjoy telling stories, and I've developed a reputation as being pretty good at it. At least people tell me that.

Whatever storytelling skills I may have developed, I trace it back to that day, when Dad gave us the lesson with the strings. It's one thing to tell stories well; it's another thing to have good stories to tell. Dad gave me that. His stories were like parables: simple, easy to understand, and with powerful messages. When I think of the gifts Dad passed on to me, there are two that stand out in my mind. One, the most important, was the example of selflessness and self-confidence when he yielded the state presidency to his opponent. The other was the wealth of stories he passed along.

Not all of what Dad taught us had the nobility of those parables. In some cases it was quite the opposite. I always refer to my dad as having been a fundamentalist minister, but that was not the way he made his living. It would have been next to impossible to provide for a wife and three sons on the church's pay, which was less than a hundred dollars a month. In those days, it wasn't unusual for black professionals to work other jobs.

Dad made his living as a carpenter. I always believed it was another way for him to identify with Jesus. The fact is that Dad was a jack-of-all-trades, an all-round house repairman. He was a very good carpenter and a pretty good bricklayer, although he didn't particularly like laying bricks. He had a working knowledge of plumbing and electrical work, but he didn't consider himself to be very good in either one of those fields.

Some Dirty Experiences

Dad repaired and rehabbed more houses around Sumter than I care to remember. That's because he did not do them alone. I can't remember ever having been too young to help out on his various jobs. Many of them led to some less-than-pleasant memories for my brothers and me. We were his helpers in residence, even when we were too young to do much more than hold a board in place or pass him a hammer or nail. As time passed, the assignments got tougher and nastier.

There was a local white attorney who everyone called Lawyer Shore. He owned scores of what could only be called slum houses in South Sumter. Dad was his renovator of choice, and when time came for some work to be done on these houses, Dad and his young helpers in residence would often be called on for the job.

The toughest assignment I can recall was that of reroofing those houses. You don't know "hot" until you've sat on a tin roof in the middle of a South Carolina summer with the temperature hovering around one hundred degrees. That's hot. And shingled roofs weren't any better. The sun hitting those shingles made them just as hot as a tin roof, and what was even worse than that was the pain of slinging those shingles over your shoulder and climbing a ladder to get them onto the roof. I can still feel those shingles grinding into my skin.

But nothing quite compared with another aspect of "rehabbing" those slum houses. In those days, there wasn't much in the way of sewer systems in South Sumter, and most of these houses had the outdoor form of "plumbing." "Renovation" of these houses often included the relocation of the outhouses. To this day, I can remember vividly digging those new privies next to the old ones and moving the old weather-beaten outhouses over to their new earthen-walled receptors. We used the mound of dirt thrown out of the new hole to cover the old waste-filled privy. The labor exerted in covering the old privy hole with the new dirt, I recall, wasn't the worst part of that exercise, and I won't go into any further detail describing the process. Suffice it to say that the number of these relocations was closer to one hundred than to one.

Even today, every time I attend Jehovah Baptist Church, whose current sanctuary is located on the site of many of those houses we worked on, I think about those character-building experiences.

Discovering Some Secrets

My dad was a complicated man, and I'm not certain I ever really knew the depth of his complexity. Right up until the last days and weeks before his death, I was still learning things that gave me new insight into his values and the struggles of his life. Like a lot of people who put up the good fight against an unfair system, he had a few scars. Some of those scars, he tried hard to conceal. It was a matter of pride and dignity, something he treasured above all else. Occasionally, however, one of the scars would show.

I discovered one of Dad's scars quite by accident one day, many miles from home, during a roadside conversation with a total stranger. It was during my first race for statewide office in South Carolina—and I remember the experience quite clearly.

The year was 1978, and against the advice of family and friends, I was making a run for statewide office at the ripe old age of thirty-seven. The odds of South Carolina electing a black man to one of its constitutional offices in those days—and today for that matter—were pretty long.

On this particular spring day, I was meeting with the Reverend Thomas Dixon, who had invited me to discuss my candidacy with the Hampton County ministerial association. I welcomed the chance.

Since we didn't know each other, we rendezvoused at a designated interchange on I-95 near the town of Yemassee. When I arrived he was already there, and we chatted briefly before heading for the church meeting. As we were getting back into our cars to drive into Hampton, he said, "Clyburn, that's an unusual name. I've only known one other Clyburn in my life, a fellow student at Morris College." Reverend Dixon said he never knew the first name of his friend, but that everybody knew him as "E. L." "Ever heard of him?" he asked.

"Well, yes," I said, "that happens to be my dad, Enos Lloyd Clyburn."

We both smiled at the coincidence. South Carolina is a small state, and such occurrences are not all that unusual. But what he said next caught me completely off guard.

"E. L. was one of the smartest students in our class," he said. "Funny thing, though. He dropped out of school. He didn't show up for our senior year."

I could not have been more shocked. My dad was the toughest-minded, most disciplined man I had ever known. There was nothing about him that would have caused him to quit anything, especially anything as important as getting a college education. He had always pounded that lesson into the minds of my two brothers and me.

As I drove into Hampton that day, I was aware that Dad was in his final months of life. Prostate cancer had taken its toll on him, and—at age eighty—he was spending a lot of time in bed and pretty much confined to the house at 104 Walker Avenue. But I couldn't shake from my mind what Reverend Dixon had told me. After my meeting that night, I drove to Sumter and pulled up in front of the house on Walker Avenue around midnight.

I had called Dad from Hampton and told him that I wanted to stop through Sumter to discuss something with him. When I arrived, he was awake awaiting my arrival and in some pain. He got up to greet me, and after a few moments, I brought up the conversation with Reverend Dixon. Dad's face noticeably changed, and I could see the grief come forth. As he climbed back into bed and began to explain, tears came to the eyes of a man who had never showed me anything but strength.

At that midnight hour, my dad lying on his deathbed told me a grim story out of his past, unlike anything he had ever told me before. It brought tears to my eyes too, and I listened without interrupting him.

Dad had always talked about his early life in terms of family history, names, relations, and locations. He also told about how hard life was, and how hard people worked to survive "in those days." The stories usually contained lessons, and they were lessons that flowed from his sense of pride, wisdom, and self-discipline.

Now he was telling me the other part of his past, the part about which he was not proud.

My Dad's Real Pain

He was telling me about growing up in Kershaw County, where public education in those days was eleven years for white students and for black students only seven. He told me that at the end of the seven years allotted to black students, he wasn't ready to stop learning. He repeated the seventh grade three times. But the teachers finally told him he could not return; he was too far ahead of the other students.

Dad took a job at a bakery, learned how to bake, and continued to educate himself, reading voraciously and devouring every self-help educational program he could find. He took a college entrance exam and passed. He told me that the real incentive for accepting a pastorate in Sumter was because Morris College was there. He then repeated something to me that he had said frequently as part of encouraging me to stay in school and to enter seminary. "Answering the call to the ministry was one thing," he would say to me passionately; "getting oneself prepared to minister was something totally different."

For three years, Dad recounted to me, he pursued a college education at Morris with a passion, befriending people such as Thomas Dixon along the way. Then, he said, his face tightening, "I was summoned to the administration office after my junior year and was told that there was no record of my having graduated from high school. Until I could produce those records, I would not be allowed to enter my senior year.

"And, of course, I couldn't."

Dad sighed, leaned back in the bed, and said, "I never told you about this because I didn't want you to think there was any redeeming value in dropping out, no matter what the reason."

Later that night, after I left Dad, I thought back over the conversation, and I realized he was still only telling me part of the story. He was a proud man, not willing to admit defeat, and he was also a wise man in the ways of people. He never preached to his sons about the injustices he had known or the unfairness in the world around us. He figured we could find out those things for ourselves.

Dad passed away a few months later. Years later I was invited to speak at the dedication of the North Sumter Hope Center, one of three Hope Centers in Sumter that I had a hand in establishing. When I arrived at the Hope Center, I spotted many members of the church my father had pastored for more than forty years.

The North Sumter Hope Center is just a few blocks from the campus of Morris College, and with so many church members in the room, it was little wonder that my thoughts drifted to my parents. I spoke of them in my remarks, and I told the story of Dad's failure to graduate from Morris College. Little did I know at the time that the president of Morris College, Dr. Luns Richardson, was on the stage behind me and would be following me to the podium. If I had, I might not have told that story.

When the program ended, Dr. Richardson came up to me and said that he had never heard the story about my dad and that he was deeply troubled by what he had just heard. He also told me that Reverend Dixon was a member of the Morris College board of trustees.

Three weeks later, Dr. Richardson called to say that the Morris College archives bore out the truth of the story and that he was going to ask the board to grant—Enos Lloyd "E. L." Clyburn—the degree he had pursued.

The board approved Dr. Richardson's request and my dad was awarded the degree of bachelor of theology posthumously at the school's next commencement, 2003.

All the Clyburns were at the commencement. It was a blessed experience for me and a proud moment for all of us.

I tried to envision how my dad would have reacted that day. Unlike me, he would have found a way to hide his emotions and probably grumbled about too much attention being paid to something that happened so long ago, and he would have told us all to get back to work.

4 | *A World without Blinders*

My two brothers and I grew up without racial blinders and without the conditional view of the world that so often characterized black families of the Jim Crow era. Our parents placed no limits on our ambitions. This "no-limits" concept was something we learned instinctively, but it was also something that we came to realize was not all that common among our neighbors and friends. I learned that lesson firsthand one afternoon as I arrived home after school.

Mom operated a beauty shop in the front part of our house. It was a rule that my brothers and I would stop off at the beauty shop when we got home from school and give Mom a report on how things had gone that day. On this particular day, one of the ladies in the shop was a friend of Mom's, who had grown up with her on an adjoining cotton farm in the Browntown community. When I greeted Mom's friend, she exclaimed how much I had grown since the last time she had seen me, and how my voice had changed. I smiled, and she continued with a familiar line of questioning:

My mother, Almeta Dizzley Clyburn, circa 1968

"What do you want to be when you grow up?" she asked me.

I beamed with my best Clyburn self-assured smile and told her of my dreams to finish high school, go to college, and pursue a career in politics and government. By her reaction I might as well have told her that I planned to overthrow the government of the State of South Carolina. Her eyes widened, and her jaw dropped. She then proceeded to tell me in no uncertain terms that I was never to let anyone hear me say that again. Mom was polite and said nothing at the time to dispute the admonishment I had just suffered. Her friend, I am sure, meant no harm. Like my dad's despondent parishioner who had exclaimed "I've been down so long, getting up never crosses my mind," she had been beaten down by the limited expectations of Jim Crow. And she was probably not alone in feeling that a little black boy growing up in Sumter, South Carolina, could find himself in grave jeopardy were it to be found out that he harbored such radical thoughts. But that evening, after Mom closed the beauty shop, she called me to the kitchen table.

A Message of Expectations

"Don't pay any attention to what that lady said," Mom told me firmly, looking me straight in the eye. "Things are going to change. If you stay in school and study hard, you will be able to realize your dreams."

This was not just a mom-and-son pep talk. These were solemn words, spoken with authority and conviction, expressing not just support for me and my ambitions, but also conveying to me a strong message of their expectations of me. Mom and Dad were not just raising children to dream lofty dreams; they were busy organizing a vast conspiracy of resistance to the cruelty of Jim Crow. They were instilling in me the will to carry out a fight that they knew they could not finish. They were pushing me to dream the dreams that they knew they could never realize for themselves.

That's what I wanted to tell them during my private moment of reflection the night Barack Obama captured the Democratic nomination for the presidency. I wanted to tell them that their fight was being won and their dreams were coming true.

In the weeks and months subsequent to Obama's inauguration, history carried us to unimagined heights, and some Americans proclaimed Obama's ascendancy to the presidency as something of a miracle.

It was far from it. This was the triumph of decades and decades of people such as Enos and Almeta Clyburn pushing and driving their children and their friends not to yield to the oppression of the system and instilling in them the will to resist what had been imposed on them. All I knew that evening sitting around the kitchen table on Walker Avenue was that Mom was telling me her family had far outgrown the kind of cotton-field mentality her friend had tried to impose on me a few hours earlier.

Wash Day Society

Mom could make something positive out of the most laborious chores. One of my earliest memories of such duties was an event that was an important part of the rural and small-town way of life in the South in those days: the weekly boiling and washing of clothes.

In the days before washing machines and dryers—even before things like wash tubs with attached wringers became available—clothes were washed entirely by hand. It was an ordeal of drudgery lessened only by making it a social event, and that's what took place every Saturday morning in our backyard. Mom's best friend, Emily Gadson, would join us with her four children—Winifred (Pete), Charles (Bubba), Madge, and Booker T. (Tee Tee). Mrs. Gadson, who everyone called "Ms. Boo," had lost her husband, Winfield, while he was serving in the U.S. Navy, and she was raising the children alone. Single moms in those days were not all that unusual, and there were usually plenty of relatives and friends to help out as part-time parents. It was not unusual for other families in the neighborhood to join Ms. Boo and Mom in the clothes-washing event. Ms. Boo and Mom's friendship naturally led to the formulation of my friendship with Ms. Boo's son Bubba. Bubba Gadson, or "Bubba G.," as he was often referred to, had a great sense of humor. He was one funny guy, and we easily became the best of friends, a friendship that lasted until his premature death in 1980.

Another great friendship that came of our neighborhood social structure was my friendship with Freddy Carter, whom we called "Brother." Brother Carter and Bubba Gadson became my best friends, and remained so until I left Sumter for Mather Academy after my eleventh-grade year. In those days, practically everybody in our neighborhood had nicknames, except my brothers and me.

We were "PKs" (Preacher's Kids), and we were not allowed to have nicknames. But as soon as I left home for Mather Academy I acquired a nickname. My classmates named me "Windy," and in college I became "Senator," which was eventually shortened to "Sen."

I actually looked forward to those clothes-washing days. As a youngster I enjoyed mixing with the neighborhood kids, and our clothes-washing tasks were not that onerous. We poured water into the big, black iron pot, built a fire under the pot to get the water boiling, and then dropped the clothes into the pot and stirred them with a long wooden pole, usually a broomstick.

We would poke and stir to keep the clothes as evenly heated as possible as the boiling process took place. This was how the clothes were cleaned and sterilized. We were sort of human agitators, a term some of my political critics might have later enjoyed picking up in a different context.

Next the clothes were taken out of the pot and placed in one of the big tin tubs to be washed. The clothes were scrubbed on washboards, using homemade lye soap. After washing and wringing the clothes, we hung them on wire clotheslines and fastened them with wooden clothespins to dry in the great outdoors. There was nothing quite as fresh smelling as clothes washed and dried on those Saturday mornings. These were good times for energetic youngsters, and—for all I knew at the time—I was learning an important household skill.

Mom's Ventures

Mom was never afraid of hard work from her days picking cotton in the fields and washing clothes in the backyard. But as her children got older and more self-sufficient,

Mom became restless. She got a job doing shirts at Kirkland Laundry and Cleaners, but she also began to explore other opportunities for personal growth.

Then one day a wagon arrived. It was a beautiful, shiny conveyance that might have been welcomed in most households as a marvelous new toy for the youngsters. That notion lasted only about as long as it took for Mom to explain that the wagon was for her new business enterprise, and not a racing vehicle for her three adventurous sons.

Mom's ambition was to be self-employed and to experience all the personal independence that came with it. As soon as she had saved up the necessary cash to invest, she left Kirkland Laundry and Cleaners and bought a door-to-door distributorship selling Blair and Lucky Heart hair products and cosmetics. The products were delivered periodically to our home by a shipping service. She loaded the products into the wagon and pulled that wagon all over our part of town, selling to friends, neighbors, and anyone else whom she could interest in the company's vast array of popular products. At times when Dad traveled to attend church business, Mom would sit John in the back of the wagon; put Charles between his legs, and a box of products between Charles's legs. I walked alongside.

I still remember that beautiful wagon. It had wooden sides that could be inserted into a metal-base bottom. The wooden sides were adorned with a greyhound dog, similar to the one on the side of Greyhound buses. It would have made a wonderful toy for the three of us, but it probably wouldn't have survived long with the rough-and-tumble treatment it would have gotten from us. It was a good thing it was off-limits.

Emergence of an Entrepreneur

For Mom owning her own business was like economic emancipation. She was a big success in the challenging door-to-door operation, and about the only dissent that came from Dad was based on the fact that he had grown fond of the nicely starched shirts she provided him from her Kirkland Laundry and Cleaners job. As a concession, Mom did his shirts at home, and as a return concession, Dad did most of the cooking. Mom was a good cook and usually prepared the big meal on Sundays. It was an interesting arrangement for the three boys. She never had the time, and Dad never had the patience, to teach us to cook, but we all learned how to iron.

Mom was defying custom in her own way. She was rejecting the traditional paths of black women into domestic jobs or factory employment and was launching forth into self-employment and entrepreneurship. Not only was she setting a nontraditional course for herself, she was encouraging others to join her ambitious and rebellious career path. This made for an interesting household. Little wonder that their three sons grew up with high ambitions and a great deal of self-esteem. No wonder I grew up actually believing I could help change the world.

Mom's venture into "wagon capitalism" was only the beginning of her quest for success in the world of business. She wasn't long into the door-to-door cosmetics business before she met Mrs. Edmona McNeil, the owner of Garner's Beauty School in Sumter, a school founded by Mrs. McNeil's mother to train black men and women in the art and business of hairdressing and the use of beauty aids.

Mom enrolled in Garner's Beauty School shortly after meeting Mrs. McNeil. It was a life-changing decision, and it had the most impact on her entrepreneurial career. She formed a lasting friendship with Mrs. McNeil, graduating from Garner's School on schedule in spite of the daily presence of three rambunctious young boys running around in the beauty-school yard while she was inside getting it done.

Shortly after graduating beauty school, Mom converted the front bedroom of our house on Walker Avenue into her beauty shop.

And that was just the beginning. Mom had further education ambitions, and even as she was managing her own beauty shop and raising three sons, she enrolled as a thirty-four-year-old student at Morris College. The time and effort she put into achieving her goals continue to astonish me to this day. Mom did hair on weekends and between classes, and there were many days—especially during the summer months—when she loaded the three of us into the car and took us to class with her. We'd play quietly—sometimes not *so* quietly—in vacant nearby classrooms or under the window of the room where she was attending class.

It was a memorable day that May when Mom graduated with a bachelor's degree in elementary education as a member of the Morris College class of 1953. By attending school both semesters and every summer, she was able to graduate in three years, all while operating a beauty shop and raising three small boys.

We were all there to observe the graduation ceremony—Dad, John, Charles, and me. While Dad would have forbidden any outward cheering, we were all swelling with pride inside. I was not quite thirteen years old at the time; John was ten; and Charles was eight.

Defying Tradition

As would have been traditional for the time, there were those who expected Mom to close the beauty shop and go into teaching. As a matter of fact, one particular school official at Morris College presented Mom with an ultimatum upon her entering the second semester of her senior year: "Either close your shop so you can graduate and become an effective schoolteacher or leave school and be a 'hairdresser.' You can't do both." Many women of her age and station in life would have succumbed to such a demand, but that wasn't Mom. She defied the ultimatum and deftly but effectively challenged the official's authority to issue it. She graduated with her class, brought that college degree home, had it nicely framed, and placed it on a wall of the beauty shop.

There it hung, almost defiantly telling the world that—yes—she was accomplished enough to earn a college degree, and—no—she was not abandoning her dream of being a businesswoman and entrepreneur. For Mom it was more than the challenge of keeping the business afloat and making a few bucks. For all her devotion to family and community, Mom was a free spirit, and she loved the liberties of being her own boss, earning her own way, and charting her own course in life. For all the restrictive boundaries in place at the time, she was a truly emancipated person.

It was only a few months after Mom graduated Morris College that her college diploma, the entire beauty shop, and most of our home on Walker Avenue were destroyed by an early morning fire. It was one of the coldest mornings of the winter. I watched the fire from the middle of the street, shivering from fear and chill.

My discomfort was made all the worse by the fact that I had run out of the house in nothing but my underwear. Mom had traveled north to visit one of her sisters while the beauticians she had hired operated the shop. There was a freestanding kerosene heater in the shop, and one of the ladies had lit it that morning and left it unattended while she went to the kitchen. That was a mistake. For no reason we could ascertain, the heater exploded.

Dad contacted Mom and told her what had happened, causing her to return earlier than she had planned. I will never forget those slow, silent—but very few—tears trickling down Mom's face as she stood at the front gate to our house, seeing that fire-gutted house for the first time. Not much good can be said about watching your house go up in flames. It was like having a part of my life and my world destroyed, and that's how I remember feeling that morning.

But the Clyburns weren't much for self-pity or self-indulgence. We not only preached, but we practiced the fine art of resiliency. The kitchen had been left relatively intact, although the walls were smoky and blistered. Dad put his considerable carpentry skills to work and was able to make four rooms relatively livable for the five of us.

I can still remember the smoky smell that was part of our lives for a good long while. I have one other memory of an extraordinary experience connected with that fire. Later on the day of the fire, a young man who lived a few doors from us on Walker Avenue came down the street, expressed his sorrow at our misfortune, and presented me with a brown jacket and a pair of beige pants. His name was Albert Montgomery. He was a couple of years older than me and not particularly a friend. But he became one that day, and his extraordinary gesture of kindness left a lasting impression on me. To this day I try to repeat his kindness every chance I get.

One of those chances presented itself some years later under similar circumstances, after I had begun my tenure in Congress. A colleague, Representative Gene Taylor of the Fourth District of Mississippi, had lost everything when Hurricanes Katrina and Rita swept through his home on the Gulf Coast at Bay St. Louis.

Gene was one of those independent-thinking souls known as "blue dog Democrats," and I think he was a little taken aback when I offered him a Tulane green jacket after his devastating loss. He was reluctant to accept it until I explained to him my own experience. "This is not only something to help meet your own need," I told him, "but to carry out what has become for me a lifelong feeling of heartfelt obligation." Once he realized it was a personal gesture, he accepted my offer graciously.

There is one other lingering connection with Albert Montgomery. He had a sister named Easter. Almost fifty years after the fire, on the occasion of my becoming chair of the Congressional Black Caucus, I was being interviewed by a young Washington reporter who told me that she had family roots in Sumter.

My parents with me and my brothers, John and Charles, at John's wedding in 1964

She told me of a grandmother she had visited often as a child. When I asked the grandmother's name, her answer was, remarkably, "Easter Montgomery." The world got a lot smaller for me that day.

Adversity and Energy

The fire on Walker Avenue seemed to energize my family. Far from dwelling on the loss, Mom became more ambitious and aggressive in her career pursuits. Dad had a more ambitious plan. He bought the small lot adjacent to our house and got permission from city officials to build a beauty shop on the lot.

After we had begun the layout for the new construction, Dad was told by city officials that the placement of the building had to be closer to the house where we lived. So, he moved it, only to be told later that the new building had to be actually connected to our house. This was neither possible nor desired, as the house where we lived was the parsonage, belonging to the church next door, where Dad was pastor.

The city officials' unexplained demands were eventually suspected to be a designed effort to frustrate the building project. We completed the construction, anyway, and Dad rented it out as a single-family residence.

If the city officials' objective was to deter my parents, they had not brought their best game to the contest. During the period of the back and forth "it's OK; it's not OK" with the city officials, Mom had located an available single-story, three-unit building two blocks from our house, at the corner of Walker and Liberty Streets, and she proceeded to rent the entire building.

Within weeks of her frustrated efforts to build her own shop, she had relocated her business to the middle unit of the newly acquired building. The Clyburn Beauty Shop was back in business. Relocating the shop to its new location was something of a gala event for black Sumter. With her keen powers of persuasion, Mom had arranged for the reopening to be announced on the radio, a rarity in those days. It was announced on a fifteen-minute rhythm-and-blues program hosted by "Jiving Joe" Anderson. I can still hear "Jiving Joe" telling his Sumter listeners about my mom and saying, "You can't keep a good woman down." He got that one right.

Mom opened a launderette in another of the three units at her new location and a restaurant in the third. Part of her plan was to create jobs for my brothers and me as well as to make a profit. On both counts we didn't do very well. The best part of the restaurant operation was the daily offering of small sweet-potato pies that Dad baked. The worst part was probably the work done by my brothers and me. Working in that restaurant, I believed at the time, was worse than picking cotton.

The launderette was somewhat profitable for a while and probably could have been extremely successful had any of us been more mechanically inclined. The washing machines and dryers required constant attention, and after a while it became too much of a burden to find someone to fix them. The restaurant and eventually the launderette were closed, a rare instance of failure of one of Mom's business ventures.

For Mom the restaurant and launderette experiences were only momentary setbacks. Her beauty shop flourished and soon outgrew the facility she was renting. She found two pieces of property at 645 and 647 West Liberty Street, a block down the street from the three-unit building she was renting. Mom contracted with Lincoln Brock, a local black building contractor, to erect a large enough building to house a beauty and barber shop on the lot at 645. Before she began construction, she approached a talented up-and-coming young barber by the name of Morris China, and asked him if he wished to establish his own business at her newly planned beauty center. He eagerly accepted, and at the time of this writing he is still operating his barbering business there.

Once the new building was completed and the beauty and barber shops opened for business, she opened a beauty-supply business in the little house that was situated on the lot at 647.

Along the way Mom found the time to branch out into the ice-cream business. Not long after she opened her first shop on Liberty Street, she became acquainted with the owner of a bicycle shop and ice-cream parlor down the street and across from where the beauty shop is now located. His name was John McElveen, the father of Joseph T. McElveen Jr., the current mayor of Sumter.

In addition to operating the ice-cream parlor, John McElveen had several ice-cream carts, and during the summer months he hired youngsters to push those carts throughout their neighborhoods selling his ice-cream products.

Still seeking gainful employment for her three sons, Mom struck a deal with Mr. McElveen for my brothers and me to sell ice cream from the carts during the summer.

I was the first of the brothers to be employed under the arrangement. I pushed ice-cream carts around the neighborhood all summer long. That arrangement, however, lasted just one summer.

Before the following summer came around, Mom the entrepreneur had bought her own ice-cream cart and renegotiated the arrangement she had with Mr. McElveen. Under the new arrangement, Mom would own the cart, and Mr. McElveen would supply the ice cream and the dry ice to keep the ice cream cold. It wasn't exactly high finance, and it didn't really change things much for my brothers and me, but Mom became the classic middleman. By the time it was all over, she owned not only the cart but also the ice cream, which she bought from Mr. McElveen and Borden's Ice Cream Company. Mom had truly become an entrepreneur, and quite a successful one, at that.

Do unto Others

Mom was not a selfish entrepreneur who considered the bottom line the only measure of success; she was also an entrepreneur maker. She and Dad had always been keen on self-employment, self-enhancement, and holistic personal development. In that vein, with Dad's approval Mom often brought young women from her childhood home community of Browntown and other nearby rural areas to live in our home and enroll at Garner's Beauty School under her tutelage.

She also encouraged young girls who lived in our neighborhood to make cosmetology their career. When they graduated from beauty school, they often trained under Mom in her shop until they were equipped to venture out on their own. Many of them opened their own beauty shops and related businesses, becoming entrepreneurs in their own right.

Two of the neighborhood girls, Ida Lawson Smith and Dolly "Butchie" Harvin Swinton, started with Mom in 1953 and 1954 respectively, when they were just teenagers. They later became managers at the shop and eventually co-owners of the business after Mom's passing. Ida retired from the shop in 2010 after fifty-seven years, but as of this writing, Butchie is still there.

A Moment of Awareness

It had never occurred to me to inquire about how Mom was financing these enterprises. I discovered the answer to that unasked question in a surprising way.

After my 1970 election loss, I was still harboring thoughts of opening a business. I contacted the Small Business Administration (SBA) about assistance in financing my proposed venture. I was informed of a workshop the SBA was planning at Morris College, and Dad and I attended the session. We were surprised to find the meeting so sparsely attended, and of those in attendance, there were only two black people besides Dad and me. During the question and answer session, I asked about the number of loans made to black businesses, and I got what I considered an evasive, unsatisfactory answer.

After the meeting, one of the two SBA officials conducting the meeting came over to me, and somewhat apologetically said he realized his answer to my question had not completely satisfied me. He went on to say that he was reticent to answer the question openly because the agency had made only two loans to a black person in Sumter. Both of them, he said, had been to my mother.

This revelation reminded me of a conversation Mom and I had several weeks before Mignon's first Christmas. Mom's was attending a cosmetologists' meeting in Charleston, where Emily and I were then living, and we invited her for dinner. After dinner she asked Emily to excuse the two of us for a minute, and we walked back to the bedroom where Mignon was sleeping in the crib I had recently bought after a profitable evening of "pot" bowling. "James," she said to me, "you need to get out of this apartment, buy a house, and make a home for your growing family." I told her I would, just as soon as I could see my way clear. She looked me and very sternly retorted, "Son, let me tell you something, if you wait until you can see your way clear before attempting anything, you will never get anything done." The admiration I had for Mom was kicked up to another level and several notches.

Bracing for the Fight

Sumter was an edgy town in the mid-1950s. The *Brown v. Board of Education* decision of 1954 had not only widened the already deep divide between white and black South Carolinians, it had also created distinct fissures among blacks. Even before the issue of school desegregation had become a viable public and political issue, cautious black families were drawing back from the brink of confrontation over racial matters, and the younger risk takers were beginning to step forward.

Some of these transformational moments have been nicely recorded in an oral-history paper by a graduate student, Elinor Rooks, the daughter of Professor Pamela Rooks of Francis Marion University in Florence, South Carolina. Elinor conducted interviews with families whom I knew growing up, people such as Lorin Palmer, Frances and David Singleton, and Ralph Canty, and they told her the story of Sumter's becoming a focal point of demonstrations in the 1960s. It was a place where Freedom Riders stopped on their way farther South, where black boycotts of white businesses were organized, and where a great cross section of people, including Morris College students and what were called "middle of the roadies," participated. It became one of the early places for lunch-counter sit-ins in 1960, about the same time I was active as a South Carolina State College student leader in the Orangeburg sit-ins. Ms. Rooks quoted Frances Singleton as recalling that "we took that glorious walk about two blocks [from the Kress variety store lunch counter where they sat in, to the city jail] with pride."

I wish Mom and Dad had been here to be interviewed by Ms. Rooks. They would have had a lot to say. They would have said that it was no accident that Sumter became a prime place for such activity. They would have said that the sit-ins, boycotts, and other demonstrations were not the actions of what some liked to call "outside agitators." These were events that sprang directly from the heart and soul of the communities themselves, from people tired of oppression and willing to take the inherent risks that went along with such uprisings. Mom and Dad had spent their lives lifting the spirits of their fellow travelers in Jim Crow South Carolina, challenging them to reject the old ways and set forth on new and uncharted paths to the future. They lived to see at least part of their dreams come true.

Mom was fifty-four, and Dad was seventy-three when John West took office as governor and I joined his staff as assistant to the governor for human resources. It was a moment for all of us to pause and sniff the roses. It was, however, still a time of some professional uncertainty on my part. This was during the time when a South Carolina governor could serve only one four-year term. Emily and I were beginning to build a family, and that family would have every right and reason to look to me as a productive breadwinner four years hence and thereafter.

For Mom and Dad, however, this had to be a moment of triumph. It wasn't so much that their son had become something of a public figure, it was the fact that the opportunity for any black South Carolinian to achieve such status was a tribute to them as leaders of the revolution that was overthrowing Jim Crow in the state. It was another step down a road they had begun to travel more than thirty years earlier.

The Dreaded Moments

It turned out to be a short-lived triumph for Mom. She had been complaining of an intensifying pain in her lower back, pain she had been suffering since her return from a Christmas trip to Baltimore to visit with her sister Louise. Mom attributed it to a fall she had taken during her visit, but I suggested as a precautionary measure that she come to Charleston, where my family and I were living at the time, to undergo a thorough and complete physical examination at the medical center there.

She came to our home in Charleston on a Sunday to begin tests the next morning. I returned to Columbia on that Monday afternoon, leaving Emily to keep watch over things. The next day Emily called me at my office and left a message. When I returned the call, Emily explained to me, quite calmly, I might add, Mom's medical condition using terminology with which I was not familiar. Emily was never one to show undue emotion in stressful moments; she could keep her cool when I was losing mine. When we concluded our call, I placed a call to my brother John and shared with him what Emily had told me. He was familiar with the medical terms and knew the news was much more serious than Emily had allowed me to realize.

After speaking with John, I called Emily back. She admitted that she had spared me the dire news. Mom was suffering from multiple myeloma, and in 1971 that was virtually a death sentence. I was going to be returning home that evening, and Emily did not want me driving to Charleston bearing the burden of the full import of Mom's condition. The next day the doctors informed us that she only had about eight months to live.

We all knew how she dreaded the thought of contracting cancer. During those days in the black community, cancer was anathema, and the stigma associated with it was unforgiving. As a matter of fact, people loathe uttering the word; it was more often referred to as "the Big C." Not so much because of this uninformed stigma, but out of respect for Mom's dread, we decided to spare her that fearful piece of information. So we made a collective decision not to tell her the full gravity of her condition.

It was hard to keep anything from Mom, but to my knowledge, everyone cooperated, and we never used the word "cancer" in her presence or spoke of the terminal nature of her illness. Mom's condition was not easy for Dad, and his keeping with our little subterfuge as a willing participant was not any easier. He was a man of naked truth and honesty. But he knew that revealing the truth of this matter to Mom would serve no purpose beyond a self-serving devotion to truth.

Dad never lied to Mom about her condition; he simply kept quiet. Mom's pain and weakness did not keep her mind from staying busy. One evening, as we were gathered in her room, she asked everybody to leave the room except me. I had the distinct feeling that we were approaching a moment of truth, as had happened on a few other occasions in our lives. I was right.

The first question was one I had heard from Mom before. For whatever the reason, she had always taken quite seriously a question posed by one of her customers at a moment when she was expressing pride in her three sons. The customer had asked Mom what she would do if she learned that I had fathered a child out of wedlock. Despite my strong and absolute denials, Mom returned to the question on more than one occasion afterward, and on this evening, as she lie only a matter of weeks before dying, she asked me again.

This time, however, she put it a different way. Mom let me know that she wasn't sure that she was going to get any better, and if that were the case, she did not want to die having a grandchild she had never met. I guess I had not done a very good job convincing her by my previous answers. So I told her the truth, one final time: "Mom, there is absolutely no reason for you to be concerned. You know and love all your grandchildren. There are no others."

She seemed satisfied this time. But she had another—more difficult—question for me too, and it caught me a little off guard. She asked me to tell her the truth about her condition. "Son, I do not want you and your father spending what little savings I have on me unless I really have a chance to get better," she said, her voice still strong enough to remind me of the earlier difficult decisions she had helped us to make.

I was momentarily torn between leveling with Mom and doing what I could to make her final days as comfortable as possible. I chose the latter. I lied to Mom about her condition and assured her that there was a chance she would be getting better. It was a very, very difficult thing for me to do, but I still believe it was the right thing to do. Mom died on August 23, 1971, five months beyond her fifty-fifth birthday and two days short of the eight months the doctors had given her to live.

Her eight months of lingering pain and suffering had given me some time to prepare myself for life without her. Her passing became a merciful end to her ordeal. But nothing could have prepared me for the emotional outpouring at her funeral. It was the moment when the Sumter community she had known so well and loved so dearly could pay tribute to a woman who had been such a powerful force in leading us into new and uncharted directions.

Mom had spent her entire adult life as First Lady, Sunday-school superintendent, and an otherwise active member of the Walker Avenue Church of God. It was clear to everybody, however, that the sanctuary of our church was not large enough to accommodate the number of mourners expected. Consequently we requested—and were granted permission—to hold the service at the larger Jehovah Baptist Church on South Harvin Street.

As anticipated, even that large sanctuary was overflowing with people who wished to say good-bye to my mom. She was eulogized as a "renaissance woman," and I guess that described her well. Mom was a woman of strong faith, but—like my dad—she also believed in the worldly aspect of things. As the definition of the word "renaissance" states, Mom helped us to experience "a rebirth and a rededication" of our hearts and souls.

Sitting in the pew directly behind me was the Reverend I. DeQuincey Newman, who always considered himself family. As Mrs. Dorothy Dawkins was singing an unbelievable rendition of Mom's favorite hymn, "May the Work I've Done Speak for Me," Reverend Newman belted out a loud and elongated "amen." It precipitated a chorus of "amens" and sighs throughout the church. That had a profound impact on me.

The stoicism I had been taught as a part of my Christian faith could no longer be maintained. For the first time since that private conversation I had with Mom as she lay on her deathbed, the tears flowed. And flowed.

5 | *The Young Clyburns*

My brothers and I are close and always have been. I'm not sure I can explain it in any rational way. We're three distinctly different types and personalities, and we've led three separate and independent lives. But every year, during that week between Christmas and New Year's Day, our families gather at Hilton Head Island, South Carolina, where we discover and rediscover that we're as close as we've ever been.

A lot of people tell me they're envious of how close my brothers and I are, and I have to admit, I'm damned proud of my brothers and proud of how close we are. But I also have to admit that I would have difficulty explaining why we're so close or what we did over the years to make it that way. All I know is that we helped to shape each other's lives growing up on Walker Avenue in Sumter.

In my mind, it goes back to that day of the cord-string lesson from my dad. He wasn't preaching or lecturing to his young sons that day, but his message to the three

With my brothers, John (left) and Charles (right), in 2010

rowdy brothers could not have been more direct. It was a message about family and the bonds that tie families together. These bonds are formed around the threads of human loyalty, unqualified and unconditional. The loyalty that became my political standard began with the loyalty that my brothers and I felt—and still feel—for each other. Dad's cord-string illustration is the foundation upon which we built our brotherhood and has become an allegoric recitation in our families whenever we talk to our children about loyalty. While my brothers and I at the time may not have understood all the meanings and implications of Dad's analogy, it was sufficient to show three strong-willed youngsters the benefits of togetherness.

I can't imagine our relationship being any other way. There have been moments, for sure, when we tussled, particularly as youngsters competing and brawling on a regular basis. And there were things at times that caused us to be pitted against each other. Whenever there are three of anything, there will be times when two will be pitted against one; it's a natural division. In our case those divisions tend to change from time to time and from issue to issue. We are evenly spaced two years apart in age, making us natural rivals with each other at times and natural allies whenever somebody else picked on one of us. That is how it was then; that is how it is today.

I was born on July 21, 1940; John was next, born on October 22, 1942, and Charles arrived on December 19, 1944. Although John's social sphere during our early years was closer to my own, I tended to be more protective of Charles when disagreements arose. For one thing John looked more like Mom's family—the Dizzleys—and Charles and I looked more like Dad's family—the Clyburns. I guess that accounted for some of that alignment. I'd like to think it was not as shallow as that, but it's a thought.

Whatever may have caused us to be divided on occasion, there was far more energy and force that drove us together. From our earliest days, we had the feeling that there was something special about us and that there were expectations that we would amount to something more than just the ordinary. Those expectations created pressure. But somehow that shared pressure among the three of us converted those expectations into sources of energy for each of us.

Growing Up as "PKs"

I guess my first sense that being a Clyburn was a little out of the ordinary came from the fact that we were "PKs," or "Preacher's Kids." Most of the children in our neighborhood attended church on Sundays. But my brothers and I did not stop there. Aside from Sunday service, we were required to go to Wednesday and Friday night prayer services every week as well, and that—in itself—set us apart from many of our friends. It made growing up a little more complicated. In time the only exception to those Wednesday and Friday evening prayer services was when the high school band was performing. Our parents expected us to be faithful to our church upbringing, but they also wanted us to be well-rounded. Music was an important part of our cultural development.

We weren't just any ole PKs, either, as we would learn over time. In conversations with other preacher's kids, I never came across anyone who grew up with the strictures that we did. E. L. Clyburn was no ordinary minister or father, as we learned during our earliest years. He was a no-nonsense man who was highly regarded in our neighborhood by young and old and religious and secular alike. We were this man's PKs, and that—in and of itself—made us special in our own eyes.

There was something else distinctive about the Clyburn brothers. At a time when educational opportunity for black children in South Carolina was very much a hot political topic, each of us was enrolled in school at age five, at least a year ahead of most of the state's children, black or white. How it was done remains to this day an absolute tribute to Mom's ingenuity and determination, and in some cases, just plain stubbornness.

As the oldest, I was the first to arrive at the first-grade door. Mom had enrolled me in the small kindergarten she had established at our church a year earlier, and she was able to convince the public-school authorities that my experience in the Church of God kindergarten qualified me as being academically and socially ready for first grade. It may have been a great leap of faith on the part of the school folks, but there I was in September 1945, a little more than five years and one month old, setting forth on my formal education career at Lincoln School in Sumter. World War II had just ended, and a lot of black veterans were returning home. Their military experience helped to fuel the civil rights charge that would change all our lives forever. But at that moment in my short little life, I was worried mostly about keeping up in class with kids who were a bit older.

John was next to step forward for early enrollment, in the fall of 1947, and he was even younger than I had been when I entered first grade. John was actually only four, and the school rule was that a child had to be six no later than October 1 of the upcoming school year. Even Mom knew she couldn't bend the rule that far, but she was not to be deterred. Lee County was not as strict as Sumter about the minimum age rule, so she sent John to Bishopville to live with her parents for a year. He enrolled at Browntown School at age four and was so advanced that they moved him to the second grade partway through the year. He came back to Sumter a year later and was put back in the second grade. Still, five years old in the second grade—not bad.

Charles, the youngest, also did not adhere to the October 1 rule. He didn't turn six until December 1950, so Mom had to find a creative solution to get him started at age five. St. Jude Catholic School was across the street from our house; and, because St. Jude was not a public school, they could take certain liberties with their enrollment criteria. The minimum enrollment age was one such liberty. So, Mom enrolled Charles in St. Jude Catholic School at age five for the first grade, and a year later she enrolled him as a six year old in the second grade at Liberty Street Elementary, a public school that had been recently built in our neighborhood.

A New Urgency

It's a story that still amazes me. Here were two people—E. L. and Almeta Clyburn—who spent their entire lives overcoming the hardships and impediments that lay in the way of the educational attainment they desired. Their zeal in giving my brothers and me a head start to achieve educational success at a level they themselves had never known is still astonishing to me. My parents' collective zeal and Mom's wit in particular made for an impacting story, but it was a story being played out elsewhere in South Carolina and throughout the South.

Black parents were assigning a new urgency to achieving educational equality for their children. One such place where this urgency was felt was Clarendon County, just twenty-two miles from Sumter. In 1947, the same year Mom enrolled my brother John in the first grade in Lee County, twelve courageous parents in Clarendon County signed their names to a lawsuit known as *Levi Pearson v. Elliott,* challenging the racial inequality of public-education offerings in School District 22 of that county. As was the norm during that period in our history, when a black man filed suit against the system of "Jim Crowism," that lawsuit was thrown out on a technicality. Not to be deterred, another parent, Harry Briggs, a service-station attendant in the Clarendon County town of Silver—the birthplace of tennis trailblazer Althea Gibson—stepped forward as plaintiff and filed another suit. This challenge became known as *Briggs v. Elliott,* the first of the five combined cases that made up the landmark case of *Brown v. Board of Education* (1954), a lawsuit attacking public-school segregation by race in America. Mom's restlessness and impatience with the lack of educational opportunities available to her children was not an isolated instance of resistance to the status quo. It was part of a widespread rebellion designed to overturn Jim Crow laws throughout the southern United States.

Just as she had fought stereotypes in her business career, she was energizing the movement to remove from her children the barriers of racial injustice she and her generation had been forced to suffer. Of course my brothers and I didn't know all that at the time.

Music, Music, Music

In our early years, a lot of our attention was paid to the pursuit of music. Mom and Dad both loved music, and they were convinced that not only was it important for us to appreciate music, but it was also important that we learned to play and perform it.

The Clyburn brothers brought mixed feelings and abilities to that proposition. Charles, the youngest, was by far the most creative and artistic of the three of us, and he quickly displayed the kind of genius that made him a lifelong musician with great skills. Even as a child, he learned to play all the brass instruments, and he was good at all of them.

John, the scholar, was the least musically inclined among us. His talents lay in the intellectual world and not in the pursuit of the harmonies and disciplines of music. He struggled to learn to play the cornet for a while, but he never really liked the instrument and soon lost interest. Then he tried the French horn. Well so much for that one too.

Mom started me out playing the piano, an assignment that I truly and deeply disliked. For one thing, when I was seven and eight, playing the piano seemed to be something for girls, a misguided notion prevalent among boys even to this day. I discovered early that I really did enjoy music, but piano was definitely not for me. Whether my feelings were misguided or not, piano lessons were torture for me—and for my teacher, Mrs. Pleasant. This tortuous experience finally ended when Mom acceded to the idea of my learning to play a horn.

In those days of postwar South Carolina, Jim Crow still reigned, and there was not much in the way of music education for "Negroes" in our "separate but equal" school system. Music lessons were all private, and there was an interesting, informal arrangement for black youngsters in my hometown. Richard Sumter, a local grocer, was a good instrumentalist, and he provided private music lessons for black kids in the back of his grocery store. Mr. Sumter also doubled as an informal "band director" in the days before there was a high school band in our "separate but equal" Lincoln High School. He had some kind of arrangement with the school district that his students would play for school functions, all fifteen or twenty of us, ranging in age levels from elementary school on up to senior high.

There is a certain instrumentation required to attain some semblance of balance and fullness in the orchestration of a band. To achieve this, Mr. Sumter persuaded some students to learn particular instruments in order to fill places in his little musical organization. My brother, John, for example, wanted to learn the trumpet, but Mr. Sumter needed a cornet player. So the cornet became John's instrument.

I wanted to learn the alto or tenor saxophone, but Mr. Sumter needed a clarinet player, so that became my instrument. I liked the clarinet all right and actually became quite proficient at it. I was good enough in fact that by my eleventh-grade year in high school, I was offered a band scholarship to attend Alabama State University in Montgomery, a fact in which I still take some pride. Montgomery was about 360 miles from home, however, and I still shudder to think what might have happened had I accepted that scholarship. By my junior year in high school, other interests were interceding in my life anyhow.

Changes of a Sort

A lot of things were changing in South Carolina. It was the late 1950s, and the folks in Clarendon County had won their lawsuit some years earlier, in May 1954, when the U.S. Supreme Court issued its *Brown v. Board of Education* decision, striking down the segregation of public schools in the nation.

But Jim Crow was dying a slow death in South Carolina. As early as 1951, the state had set about making cosmetic changes in its black schools to give them the appearance of being equal to white schools but not improving educational quality. I was not yet fourteen years old when the *Brown* decision was handed down, but I was thirty years old before South Carolina made real efforts to desegregate its public schools.

In the meantime, however, the cosmetic changes were coming to Sumter, and the state was doing everything it could to head off school integration. Liberty Street Elementary School was built "out West," as was called the black community in the western part of Sumter where I was born and reared. Lincoln High School was extensively renovated and the state established a formal band program at the school. Robert Sanders was hired as band director, replacing Richard Sumter as the back-of-the grocery-store "community" band director. A real high school band was being formed, and we were excited and ready to show our musical and marching skills. But it was a long time before the newly formed high school band got uniforms. In the meantime the girls wore blue skirts with white blouses, and the boys wore blue pants and white shirts. This ad hoc solution was our "uniforms" for a very long time. But we were taking our place as members of the new Lincoln High School marching band. And that is what counted the most.

We were even accepted to march in Sumter's 1955 Christmas parade, a decision that set off great ecstasy among the young men and women who had labored to make the band an element of pride for black families in our city. We would be able to march and play right along with the other bands and floats in the parade, strutting our stuff tall and proud in our blue and white "uniforms"—although Lincoln's school colors were blue and gold. To speak of a curious irony, one of the tunes in our repertoire was "Dixie." Go figure. We were excited and eagerly looked forward to the actual manifestation of the thought that our friends and families would line the streets and cheer as we marched by. What a great way to welcome in our Christmas season.

Then some memorable realities set in. On the day of the parade, we arrived at the designated place where the parade formed up at the "foot of the bridge" at the Manning Avenue overpass. It was then that we learned of our placement in the procession. We were not mixed in with the other bands and floats as we had expected. We would not be sharing the cheers with the rest of Sumter's holiday-minded parade contingent.

We were placed dead last in the parade. That placement was not only demeaning in comparison to where units from the other schools and organizations were assigned; it carried another particularly demeaning distinction.

Santa Claus was traditionally the final unit in the parade, and he was followed by mounted horses. The horses were last in the parade for obvious reasons: They left deposits along the street that made walking behind them hazardous and sickeningly unpleasant. That's where the Lincoln High School band was placed to march that day, right behind the horses and their white riders. It was a two-and-a-half-mile march through the muck and the stuff left behind by the horses. Jim Crow had not died in Sumter; he was standing off to the side, chuckling and still finding creative ways to insult black people.

Years later, I still harbored resentment about that incident. People asked why I simply didn't "just get over it." All I could remember was marching in my starched white shirt, freshly pressed blue pants, and freshly shined shoes and carrying my brand new clarinet, stepping around the puddles of horse waste that had been deposited in our way and fighting off nausea as I struggled to inhale sufficiently enough to play my clarinet. I can still smell the aroma of the "oats" those horses left along the route in front of us.

That was in December of 1955, the winter of my junior year at Lincoln High School. By then, my brother John was attending Mather Academy, the boarding school in Camden that Mom had attended. He and I were talking about my transferring there for my senior year. It was an appealing option for me for several reasons.

I was not exactly covering myself with glory at Lincoln High School in those days. I had had some very good teachers at Lincoln, including Ms. Josephine Stallings;

Mrs. Fannie Ivey, who also gave me private typing lessons in the basement of her home; Mrs. Betty Logan Stover; and Mrs. Agnes Wilson, who later became South Carolina's 1969 teacher of the year. But I had gotten myself off on the wrong track. I started cutting classes like a crazy person and spending most of every day in the gym. For what? Who knows? I wasn't even a very good basketball player. My friends and I had drifted off into some pretty bad antisocial behavior, and I was not exactly upholding my status as the PK of a highly respected minister.

And then there was the thing about losing out in my pursuit of a particularly appealing young lady. She had made it clear that she preferred the company of a star football player to that of a relatively talented band member. This was devastating to a guy who considered himself pretty cool. Amid the pain and the shame of teen rejection, I looked toward Mather as a place of social refuge.

There was actually a good contingent of Sumter people at Mather at the time, including quite a few of John's friends and classmates from Lincoln. One of them was Joyce McCain, whose aunt had been my first grade teacher and whose father, James "Nooker" McCain, had been my Pony League baseball coach. "Nooker" McCain was a prolific unsung hero of the civil rights movement, and one of several political activists outside the religious community that my dad greatly admired. A few short years later McCain played a major role in my life and my introduction to civil rights work.

Joyce McCain's roommate at Mather was Harriett Ercelle Hill, who had become one of John's best friends. During one of my frequent trips to visit John at Mather he introduced me to Ercelle, and she and I sort of clicked. John started using her as an enticement to get me to transfer to Mather, and I was becoming comfortable with the atmosphere at that small school.

After a few visits and after listening to John's arguments at Thanksgiving and Christmas that year, I was sold on the idea of transferring to Mather and ready to give it a try. Given the way things were going at Lincoln, what did I have to lose? My social stock was on the decline, and after that Christmas parade experience with the band, I was less enthused about that segment of my life. And of course there was Ercelle.

There was, however, a major problem: Mather was expensive. And the cost of raising three teenage boys was stretching the Clyburn family budget to the limit. Mom, who had already lost confidence in Lincoln after a negative episode I had had with the assistant principal, agreed to my transferring to Mather but only if we could solve the money problem. Dad also supported my transfer but confirmed that we couldn't afford it without some financial help. That's when Mom, the problem solver, applied her wizardry.

During Mom's days as a student at Mather, she had come to know a fellow student named Eddie McGirt from Camden and a woman named Evelyn Giddings, who was an employee at the school. McGirt had graduated college and had become the football coach at Mather, and Ms. Giddings had become dining room supervisor. Among the three of them, they cooked up a plan that would make it possible for me to transfer to Mather for my senior year of high school.

I would become a member of the football team, and while I wasn't very good, it would help Coach McGirt fill out the squad with enough players to hold good practices. I would also work for Ms. Giddings in food service by running the dishwashing machine after each meal. I had developed passable machine-operating skills during the days of my mom's restaurant and launderette on Liberty Street in Sumter, so I was of considerably more value to Mrs. Giddings than I was to Coach McGirt.

Football was a lot of fun though, even in practice. I was actually a pretty good second-team linebacker, and John and I enjoyed playing the linebacker positions together. We enjoyed gang tackling running backs, John cutting below the knees and me grabbing the runner around the waist and holding on for dear life.

A real thrill of my high school football experience was getting to know Eddie McGirt. He had played football and basketball and was on the track team as a student at Mather. After graduating, he went on to play football at Johnson C. Smith University in Charlotte, North Carolina, where he earned his degree.

After graduating from Johnson C. Smith, he returned to his high school alma mater to become football coach. Then, after coaching at Mather for several years, he returned to Johnson C. Smith as head football coach, a position he held for twenty years with great success. As a testament to his personal integrity and gridiron success, Coach McGirt was inducted into the Central Intercollegiate Athletic Association (CIAA) Hall of Fame, and the football field at Johnson C. Smith was named in his honor.

John and I never got to play in a football game together during the 1956 season at Mather, but it was a learning experience just being on Coach McGirt's squad. To John's credit, by his senior year he had developed into a formidable high school football player. He was first-team center and the team's offensive play caller, receiving the most valuable player trophy his senior year. So thanks to Coach McGirt, Ms. Giddings, and my innovative mom, I made it to Mather for my senior year, and thank goodness for that. It not only rescued me from my doldrums at Lincoln High, it proved downright transformational in many ways.

Some New Acquaintances

For one thing attending Mather provided me my first real opportunity to get to know and interact with white people over a sustained period of time. Up to that point, my only interactions with white people occurred during the times I went with Dad to the Church of God national convention in Anderson, Indiana, which was held in June every year. In fact I developed a friendship with two young white guys with whom I hung out several summers, and we maintained written contact for several years. As strange as it may seem, there were few opportunities for white people and black people to have anything other than a very casual acquaintance in Jim Crow South Carolina. For all practical purposes, we were strangers to each other and sometimes viewed each other as alien beings.

Two white teachers at Mather helped me overcome that debilitating complex inherent in the social fallacy of nonengagement between black people and white people. Mrs. Barbara Van Landingham was my English grammar and literature teacher, and

Ms. Edna Lukens was my Bible teacher. Both of them helped me through that awkward phase of making actual personal contact across racial lines, and they made it a positive experience. I've often wondered since then how many people have crossed those racial lines for the first time and did not have such a positive, and maybe even blessed, experience. I've wondered, and still wonder, how many people formed long-term negative opinions because their only contacts across racial lines were negative and or confrontational. It's a troubling thought.

In my case Mrs. Van Landingham and Ms. Lukens made the transition for me a pleasant and natural experience, and I have thought often of their influence on my life. They prepared all of us in those classes for life in a multicultural society. They showed us that good faith and common decency can go a long way in building a trusting society. I would have my share of ugly racial incidents, a very frightening one at age 15. But when I was sixteen, those two ladies provided me a good foundation of tolerance and understanding. In fact it was Ms. Lukens who disabused me of the notion of seeking my future at some stop on the "chicken-bone special," the name given passenger trains and buses that carried black families—bearing their fried chicken dinners in brown paper bags and shoe boxes—from South Carolina to the big cities up North in search of jobs and opportunities.

I once wrote an opinion-editorial piece about my feelings for Ms. Lukens, who left Mather and married shortly after I graduated. That op-ed piece came to the attention of Mrs. Barbara Boltinghouse, who at the time of the piece was superintendent of Boylan Haven/Mather Academy, which had become the name of Mather Academy after its merger with a Florida School. Mrs. Boltinghouse called to tell me that she had shared the piece with Ms. Lukens who, after leaving Mather, had become Mrs. Kuker. By this time Mrs. Lukens-Kuker had retired to the United Methodist Church Home in Asheville, North Carolina.

Mrs. Boltinghouse told me that Mrs. Kuker said she remembered me favorably. I was quite moved by that. Frankly I was impressed that after all those years she remembered me at all. And when Ms. Boltinghouse gave me the phone number of the retirement home, I immediately called Mrs. Lukens-Kuker.

The conversation was very moving. So moving in fact that I packed up the family one Sunday, and we all drove to Asheville to see her. I wanted my wife and children to see the white woman who had helped me come to know members of her race who were fair-minded and caring human beings.

The meeting was emotional for all of us. It let Mrs. Kuker know what an impact she had on a teenager who was looking for guidance at a critical stage in his life. And it let members of my family know where the seeds of racial understanding had been planted in my heart—and who had put them there. In the face of the racial realities of the time, my parents had instilled in my brothers and me a high sense of tolerance, reasoning, and resilience. But racial understanding could come only from the experience of personal engagement. The fact that my first sustained experience across racial lines was a positive one is to the credit of these two wonderful women.

I spent only a year at Mather, but it was a time in which John and I grew closer; not just as big brother and little brother, but as young men forming opinions about each other on a mature basis. Two particular incidents played a major role in bringing out these qualities.

The first was a crucial one for me, and it had to do with my qualifying for graduation. As a senior transfer student, I was dependent on some of my cocurricular activity at Lincoln High School counting toward my credits for graduation at Mather. My thinking was that I would be able to use my vast experience in music toward the mandatory music-appreciation credit required of every Mather graduate. To my considerable shock and distress, I learned that all the years of music I had taken with me from Sumter would not be counted toward my diploma requirement at Mather, and there was nothing I could do about it at that late stage of my preparation for graduation.

The issue was settled with the decision that I would be allowed to graduate only if I passed the final exam in music appreciation. If I failed, I would have to come back the next year, and the course was offered only in the second semester. It was pressure I had rarely felt to that point in my short life.

A Test of the Brotherhood

That's when the Clyburn brotherhood grew a lot stronger. The music exam came in two parts: essay and multiple choice. I had no trouble with the essay, but to answer the multiple-choice questions successfully one would need to have been a part of the classroom discussions, in which, of course, I had not participated. John, God bless him, was not much of a musician but he was a scholar, and he had taken music appreciation. Through much timely and creative maneuvering, he helped get me through the ordeal. Without his brotherly attention I would not have graduated from Mather with my class. That much I know without question.

The second moment in which John's brotherhood came to the fore was a sentimental one. And I guess in all our years of careening through the Clyburn family experience, we had not taken much time for such expressions. This one struck me powerfully. It was at graduation, and it was that ritual by which memory books were issued to the graduates for us to gather little personal thoughts and messages from those we wished to remember from our Mather days. On his page, John wrote a short, simple statement: "It is by chance that we are brothers, but through understanding we can be friends."

Over the years John and I have had our share of tussles. One of them became so serious that in the midst of that lengthy disagreement, John called a "time out" and suggested that we leave the subject unresolved since neither of us was going to change the mind of the other. That decision still holds. But in other instances John's note in my memory book remains a definition of our deep and abiding feeling for one another. It's one thing to be brothers; it's another thing to be friends.

But my graduation almost didn't happen. One day Mather superintendent Eubulus Marsh happened upon Ercelle and me in an area that was off-limits to students. We assumed that we would be called before the disciplinary committee and either be suspended or expelled. After several days of seeing Mr. Marsh every day and hearing nothing from the committee, I decided I couldn't take the silence anymore and called my mom to come get me. She came the following Sunday afternoon.

When she arrived I was standing out front waiting. She stayed in the car, rolled the window down, and asked for a full explanation. She listened in silence and when I finished, she rolled up the window and started to leave. I asked her to wait for me to get my clothes which were packed. She rolled down the window and said, "James, you are scheduled to graduate in three months. Three months of silent treatment is nothing. I believe I could live in hell for three months if I knew I was going to get out." And, as if to underscore the lack of manhood I was exhibiting, she continued, "and I'm a woman." With that she drove off. Several days later I was called before the disciplinary committee, which was chaired by Ms. Lukens. My punishment was so mild that I don't remember it.

The next year proved to be a different experience for the Clyburn brothers. I was starting my first year at South Carolina State, John was entering his junior year at Mather, and Charles was in his first year at Lincoln High in Sumter. For the first time we were all in different locations. And there was a different dynamic in place as well.

John and I were away, and Charles was still at home with Mom and Dad. John and I were not only away from home, we were outside the regimen that PKs are forced to pursue. In addition Charles was trying to face the challenges of developing a mostly secular music career while still being a PK in an evangelical home environment.

Each of us in our own way was beginning to put on the cloak of the secular world. John and I were even quitting regular church attendance, and Charles was allowed to skip Wednesday and Friday night services, at least sometimes. Our parents were adjusting to life with three strong-minded teenagers, and they were becoming more tolerant of our newly forming lifestyles and habits. Charles was even allowed to play in a dance band. We were testing our wings and easing ourselves literally and psychologically out of the only nest we had ever known.

Something else was going on among the three of us. We were no longer accessible to each other on a day-to-day basis to exchange ideas and experiences. These were days before cell phones, which maddeningly seem to keep people in hour-by-hour and minute-by-minute contact. There were only a few miles separating us, but, whatever the distance, we were becoming independent of each other and independent of our parents as well.

It made each of us begin to wonder who we were and what we stood for. Were we still PKs, within that moniker's encompassing definition? Would we begin rebelling against the strictness with which our parents had exerted so much influence on the shape and substance of our lives? Would the "secular" world prove damaging to the morals and values we had gained from our religious upbringing?

These questions really had no immediate answers. It was years before each of us reached his own accommodation. For my part I came to treasure the role of the church and the Bible in my life, and I realized early on that those hours of learning Bible verses and those mornings and evenings spent in the sanctuary of my dad's church laid a foundation for my life that was virtually unassailable. I may have left the church for stretches of my life, but I have come to realize that the church never left me. Of perhaps a more sensitive nature was the matter of the relationship among the brothers. We had been virtually inseparable growing up, sharing triumphs, troubles, comforts, and discomforts on a daily—and almost hourly—basis. But as we grew older, more independent-minded, and finally separated physically, the closeness and contact lessened. It was a time for us to decide whether the cord string of Dad's profound illustration would come unraveled, or whether we could find ways to sustain the bond of brotherhood over the long haul.

Loyalty and Its Complexities

I guess that's when I began to form in my own mind the notion of loyalty. It's one thing to help each other through times of school challenges or personal crisis, but it's another thing to find ways to overcome disagreements and forge bonds that can withstand days and miles of separation. It was during that challenging time of contemplation and introspection when I realized that "loyalty" is not such a simple word. In fact it can be downright complicated. It doesn't mean constant and blind agreement on everything. It doesn't mean acceptance of flaws and mistakes without question. It doesn't mean faith in each other to help solve each other's individual problems. Sometimes I think unrealistic expectations can be wedges that drive families—and particularly siblings—apart.

My notion of loyalty is one that almost defines itself. It evolves from the experience of knowing people—family members and others—long enough and well enough to have a realistic sense of what makes things harmonious and workable. It's like my brother John calling "time out" that day when he realized that furthering our argument could possibly damage our relationship as brothers. We came to know each other's limits and accepted them as part of our brotherhood. Being right or wrong on a single issue, or winning an argument in a fit of angry combat, was hardly worth the danger of letting the cord string come unraveled.

In time loyalty in that same sense of human tolerance came to define my own sense of human values and political expectations. I've always winced when someone in the news media throws around the term "Clyburn machine," as if there is in existence somewhere in South Carolina a highly disciplined mechanism that functions in support of my political interests and positions. Nothing could be further from the truth.

I do not, however, resent references to "Clyburn's network" or "Clyburn's political family." If I did not have some sort of personal following by now in my political career, then I must have been some kind of fool, wasting a great deal of my, and other people's, time and effort over all these years. Of course there are people on whom I am dependent and from whom I have expectations. There is human and personal loyalty involved, and that loyalty works both ways.

It's too bad that "loyalty" seems to have fallen out of favor these days. Use the word in some circles and you'll be accused of operating a "good ole boys club," or functioning in a "smoke-filled room." If there are imperfections in the personal exchange of ideas and beliefs, then it's a function of human nature and human behavior. I'll take those imperfections any day over the kind of monolithic polarizing mechanisms by which all members of certain political organizations are expected to think and vote exactly the same way on every issue all the time. That's a real political machine, and that's what has driven us to the kind of polarization that paralyzes our nation's politics and public policy today.

We are not robots, and when the rights of people to think freely and independently are sacrificed for political conformity, our system of governance as well as our social maturation is in grave danger. One of the great things about democracy is that it's the only system that gives people the right to change their minds. I tremble when I think of how that single act of rethinking is viewed as a weakness by so many people these days.

My experience with my brothers in shaping a sense of loyalty to each other is the basis of my political beliefs and expectations of those with whom I share loyalties. I've got my own cord string, and while I am still not very good at duplicating the trick my dad performed in Mr. Singleton's backyard that day, I think I got the message, and I've always felt blessed by the experience.

I know my dad would like it if he could see how my brothers and I have remained close—and how his lesson of shared values and expectations has shaped an entire sense of political loyalty for his oldest son.

PART THREE

Finding
My Way

*Our troubles, we began to realize, were not just with the
segregationist political elements in Columbia or with the
closed-minded officials in the City of Orangeburg. Our troubles were right there on campus under a dictatorial president
still practicing the worn-out dicta of the nineteenth century.
The question facing us was whether we would continue to
accept that kind of treatment. It was time, we decided among
ourselves, to challenge that system. It was time to step forward where previous classes had accepted the status quo. It
was time to make a major gesture to indicate our dissatisfaction with that status quo.*

6 | *Into the Streets*

To the outsider's eye, my hometown of Sumter would have appeared to be just another sleepy southern community during my childhood. At that time its population was around 10,000–12,000 people—about half white and half black.

Most of Sumter's jobs came from a low-paying furniture-manufacturing plant and a large U.S. Air Force base nearby. The town is named for a Revolutionary War hero named General Thomas Sumter, who was nicknamed the "fighting gamecock," and the city proudly took on that moniker as well. Sumter, the "Gamecock City," lies forty miles to the east of Columbia.

When I was growing up, there were only a few who could claim celebrity status outside our little community. Mary McLeod Bethune, from nearby Mayesville, was one. She had attained international status as a civil rights pioneer and an insider with First Lady Eleanor Roosevelt. Sumter's real place in history lies with courageous people such as Osceola McKaine, J. T. "Nooker" McCain, J. Herbert Nelson, Ernest Finney, and Fred James, all of whom stepped forward to give public leadership and visibility to a civil rights movement that had been building for years.

My first direct exposure to that issue came while I was still a teenager. Mom was active in the NAACP, and the local chapter was being sued by a local attorney named Shepherd Nash for defamation of character. He was claiming that the executive committee of the local chapter had damaged his reputation by claiming he had pressured signers of a petition calling for school desegregation to remove their names from the petition. The Reverend Fred James, pastor of Mount Pisgah AME Church in Sumter, was president of the Sumter NAACP at the time and a member of its executive committee. He later became a bishop of the AME Church. Another member of the executive committee was the Reverend I. DeQuincey Newman, a legendary leader of the state NAACP. They seemed unlikely practitioners of character defamation.

I later learned that the Nash suit was part of a "counterattack" by southern white leaders in South Carolina and four other states designed to put the NAACP financially out of business.

The Making of a Giant

Despite the weighty implications of the suit, Mom wanted me to visit the courtroom with her. The word was out that there was a black lawyer in town who was really

*Reverend Isaiah DeQuincey Newman,
a South Carolina civil rights legend.
Clyburn Papers, South Carolina
State University.*

special. Mom came home to get me and said, "I'm taking you down to the courthouse so you can see what you can be when you grow up."

That was my introduction to Matthew Perry. The courtroom was filled, and everyone, including me, was mesmerized by his demeanor and overall performance. He was a young lawyer at the time, thirty-three years of age, and was only beginning to establish himself in the realm of civil rights litigation. Harold Boulware, the Columbia attorney who had been instrumental in earlier NAACP work, was pulling back from the practice, and he was turning over much of the organization's work to fellow Columbian Lincoln Jenkins Jr. As the suits mounted, Jenkins called on his boyhood friend Matthew Perry, who was practicing in Spartanburg at the time.

Over the next half century, I knew Matthew Perry in many roles: friend, colleague, fraternity brother, mentor, and outright champion of heroic proportions. But as many times as I experienced his presence, I was never as awed as I was that day as a teenager sitting in that Sumter courthouse.

As it turned out, Matthew Perry did not win the case. He chose to settle rather than run the risk of costing the NAACP an even larger financial loss in a trial before an all-white jury. Winning or losing the suit seemed a secondary matter that day in the Sumter County courthouse. What really counted was that Matthew Perry had won over the hearts and minds of everybody in that courtroom and throughout the community.

Sometimes you can lose in a manner that can make you much better off than you would have been had you won. In the overall scheme of things, Matthew Perry was a winner that day.

For all the skill and courage of attorneys such as Matthew Perry and the people they represented, the NAACP was hurting in the 1950s. It was a time of political madness. In addition to court actions designed to damage the organization financially, South Carolina was carrying out a legislative vendetta. In a special session of the General Assembly, later dubbed the "Segregation Session," the state legislature enacted nonsense statutes designed to combat the effects of *Brown v. Board of Education* and other court rulings to desegregate the dual public-school systems in the South. One of those measures provided that no state employee could be a member of the NAACP. While courageous people such as Septima Clark and many others refused to capitulate —subsequently losing their teaching jobs—others yielded to the economic pressures and gave up their memberships.

The NAACP at Risk

Between 1956 and 1958, the NAACP lost 246 branches in the South—50 of them in South Carolina—and membership regionally fell from 128,716 to 79,677. These were devastating losses, and although I am not sure that this declining membership was the reason, the NAACP became less aggressive in its strategies, largely limiting its activity to the courtroom.

If the white southern power structure thought it had won the civil rights battle by weakening the NAACP, however, it had another thought coming. The Congress of Racial Equality (CORE) entered the fray. Many people, including me, believe that civil rights efforts actually became stronger with the involvement of newer, more aggressive organizations.

CORE's leader in the South at that time was James T. "Nooker" McCain of Sumter, who had been my Pony League baseball coach in Sumter and whose daughter, Joyce, was the roommate of my friend Ercelle at Mather Academy. McCain was a good family friend and a man whose leadership abilities were well known in local circles. He was a Morris College graduate and served for seven years as its dean. From there he went to Marion County, where he served for five years as a supervising principal.

When the "Segregation Session" of the South Carolina General Assembly banned membership in the NAACP for state employees, McCain was fired. He moved over to Clarendon County, where he became a high school principal, only to lose his job again when his membership in the NAACP was revealed in a Charleston newspaper.

The Emergence of J. T. McCain

I reflect on those days of vengeance and madness in our midst, and I wonder that anyone could retain a measure of sanity or stability about them. James McCain emerged as a giant regionally and nationally in the civil rights movement and became a lifelong hero in the mind of this Sumter teenager.

Under the leadership of James Farmer, CORE began to look for opportunities to grow and expand, and it viewed the South as the place to do so. After losing his teaching jobs and after a couple of years with the S.C. Human Relations Commission, McCain caught the attention of CORE, and he became the first field secretary of the organization.

By then South Carolina had built a solid record of resistance and success in civil rights, particularly in the struggle for equal teacher pay, school desegregation, voter rights, and even desegregation of public transportation. A year and a half before Rosa Parks made her famous and courageous refusal to give up her seat on that bus in Montgomery, Alabama, a suit was filed in Columbia, South Carolina, against the operator of the city's bus system. Matthew Perry and Lincoln Jenkins eventually became the attorneys in *Flemming v. S.C. Electric and Gas Company.* The case involved a black rider, Sarah Mae Flemming, who charged that she was forced to the back of the bus and struck by the driver. This suit formed part of the case law on which the Montgomery suit was adjudicated in Rosa Parks's favor.

In the spring of 1961, CORE organized the now-famous Freedom Riders to dramatize the unlawful segregation of public transportation facilities in southern cities. Two buses left Washington—one Greyhound and one Trailways. The Trailways bus was scheduled to pass through South Carolina on its way deeper south to Birmingham.

As it turns out, it was in our state that the riders encountered their first violence after a relatively peaceful journey through Virginia and North Carolina. On that Trailways bus was a young man whom I had met during the second meeting of the Student Nonviolent Coordinating Committee (SNCC) at Morehouse College, in October 1960. At that time John Lewis, who became my close friend and colleague in the U.S. Congress years later, was a student activist from the American Baptist Theological Seminary in Nashville, Tennessee.

Things got violent almost immediately after the bus crossed the state line into South Carolina. Several of the passengers, including John Lewis, were beaten during a stop at Rock Hill, and further brutality ensued thirty miles down the road at Winnsboro, where three of the riders were arrested. McCain quickly organized a rescue team of CORE supporters, including local civil rights attorney Ernest Finney, to secure the release of those detained in Winnsboro, and all were reunited under the care of McCain in Sumter. Lewis, who had sustained a badly split lip in Rock Hill, left temporarily for an important trip back to Philadelphia to interview for a two-year foreign-service internship. He rejoined the group in Birmingham two days later.

Sumter and the Freedom Riders

There was no violence in Sumter for the Freedom Riders, and they spent two days with McCain and local chapter members, recovering from the brutality at Winnsboro and Rock Hill and mapping plans for their harrowing visits to dangerous destinations farther south. John Lewis didn't visit my hometown on that occasion and didn't meet my friend and mentor James McCain until much later. But John told me on many occasions of the high esteem in which he held James McCain and the role he played

in the civil rights struggle. John Lewis and James McCain are two of the most courageous people I've ever known, and I think constantly of how much our entire society
owes to these men.

Sometimes important things get overlooked in our rush to record history and
identify the people and organizations in these major events. We overlook the larger
picture and the deeper historical perspective. Sumter and Orangeburg, South Carolina,
didn't suddenly emerge in the 1960s as centers of protest activities. They were places
where the confluence of historical resistance, church influence, college involvement,
and just plain human will created the atmosphere where change could happen.

It was actually on college campuses where the movement came together in the
1960s. And unlike what may have been perceived as just a bunch of rowdy and un-
ruly young college students, this was a movement populated mostly by thoughtful
and energetic people who had been prepared for the experience by parents such as
E. L. and Almeta Clyburn.

I became a CORE guy. I had been a member of the NAACP in Sumter, but it had
been outlawed on the S.C. State campus. So McCain invited me and others to become
a part of the budding CORE chapter on the Claflin campus. It was made up of a lot
of the same people, but by then CORE had become a direct-action organization, and
we suspected we would probably become involved in marches and demonstrations.
We were right.

The Coming of the Sit-Ins

Historians have said that the Greensboro, North Carolina, demonstration at Wool-
worth's was a "spark that had ignited a raging prairie fire," as the sit-ins spread across
the South in a matter of days. That wasn't exactly right. There was not much spontaneity about any of this. The Greensboro lunch-counter demonstration had been actually planned before Christmas of 1959, but it had been rescheduled for after the New
Year so that the protests would not lose momentum during the holiday break.

What seemed to be a "wild fire" to some was actually the sustaining of a sequence and momentum that was planned and anticipated. There was in place a
CORE rule for action, a training regimen that spelled out the nonviolent resistance
tactics, and we had all undergone that training. There was a close network of communication among the colleges, and we were not relying on the news media to keep
us informed. In fact many years later I came to know about a conspiracy between the
State newspaper of Columbia, South Carolina, and the governor of the state. That
knowledge helped me explain to some of my colleagues why the wall of the Rosa
Parks museum in Birmingham, Alabama, showed the route of the Freedom Rides going through South Carolina, but the only newspaper accounts on display were from
the *Charlotte (N.C.) Observer.*

If there was a "raging wild fire" taking place at the time, it was the white political reaction. Pretty soon, legislators had tied the sit-in movement to everything from
outside agitators to socialism to communism. Somehow the act of ordering a cup of
coffee at a lunch counter had become identified with many evils and was of a magnitude roughly equivalent to an act of treason. The South Carolina Senate even passed

a resolution criticizing Winthrop College for inviting a distinguished North Carolina U.S. senator, Frank Porter Graham, who was sympathetic to the sit-in demonstrators, to speak on campus. All this was over a cup of coffee and some doughnuts.

A Big Day in Orangeburg

On February 25, 1960—three weeks after the Greensboro demonstration—it was our turn in Orangeburg. I was in my third year at S.C. State, and about forty students from State and Claflin marched to the downtown Kress store, only to find the lunch counter closed and the stools removed.

Then, on March 15, we staged one of the biggest demonstrations anywhere in the South. More than a thousand students from S.C. State and Claflin assembled to march downtown. Seven of us, who came to be known as the "Orangeburg Seven"—including me, my roommate Clarence "Duke" Missouri, our classmate Bobby Doctor, and Lloyd Williams—planned the march. Our meetings were held on the Claflin campus, and the four of us, along with Claflin's student council president Tom Gaither and several other Claflin students, were joined later by S.C. State students James Curry, an army veteran, and Charles McDew, a first year student from Massillon, Ohio.

We were careful to plan our march from the neighboring college campus across the railroad tracks toward downtown Orangeburg so that we could not be accused of blocking traffic or clogging the sidewalks. For a thousand marchers, that took a

Addressing the reunion at Claflin University of the March 15, 1960, march in Orangeburg. On my far right is James Gilliard, and immediate right, Clarence "Duke" Missouri. Bobby Doctor is on my left.

lot of planning, and we chose several routes into town, being careful to travel in two-by-two columns so that other pedestrians could pass us on the sidewalks. One group went down John C. Calhoun Drive; a second group marched along Russell Street; and I led a group down Amelia Street, which runs parallel to Russell Street, about two blocks to the north. It was early in the morning and it was bone-chilling cold, particularly for March in midlands South Carolina.

We were following as best we could the dictates of CORE and the instructions of James McCain. We were well dressed, and we conducted ourselves well. We were practitioners of the nonviolent creed of Mahatma Gandhi and Dr. Martin Luther King Jr., although I'm not sure all of us knew who Gandhi was at the time. I am not sure that all of us had fully bought into the concept of nonviolence either.

For all the distress and violence of the 1960s and 1970s, I actually thought that by the end of the twentieth century, we might have passed into an era of racial tolerance and even understanding. But those thoughts were put aside a half century later while I was serving in Congress and President Barack Obama was seeking the passage of a key health reform bill. Many of its opponents, representing various fringes of the political underworld, apparently decided the legislation amounted to a racial issue. During that time I heard again that vicious chorus of racial slurs and witnessed those egregious, demeaning gestures and actions.

On that grim March 1960 day in Orangeburg, things got progressively worse for us as we marched toward the center of town. Even as we were enduring the wrath of the white tormentors, we were told by the local police to turn back, that we were disturbing the peace and violating city ordinances. As I looked over at the cordon of detractors who had formed along Amelia Street and were pursuing us, I wondered why it was that in our quiet, orderly march we were being accused of disturbing the peace, but that loud and boisterous crowd following us was somehow not being accused of "disturbing the peace."

As the three groups drew nearer to downtown, still walking in double—and sometimes single—file down the sidewalks, another indignity awaited us. In the worst tradition of southern law enforcement, many of us were assaulted by the powerful fire hoses of the Orangeburg Fire Department. There we were, dressed in our Sunday best, being driven into the ground, up against trees and walls, the hoses soaking and drenching many of us in freezing weather.

We had planned to sit-in at the S. H. Kress Five and Dime store, the bus station, and the Rexall drugstore, which was across the square from the Kress store. We expected the drugstore to be particularly resistant. It was rumored to be the favorite hangout for the local powers that be, where many of the "meetings before the meetings" took place. So when we reached the square, as previously planned, Bobby Doctor, Duke Missouri, and I proceeded across the square to sit in at the drugstore.

To this day, that episode stands out as the most intense encounter I have ever experienced. It was also the episode that brought into high relief the limitations of the impact Dr. King's preaching of nonviolence was having on some of us.

Evidently the proprietors of the drugstore knew, or had been tipped off, that we were coming because within minutes of our entering the premises the police arrived, and all hell broke loose. They had their nightsticks in hand. We were grabbed and taken out of the store forcefully and slammed against the police cruiser.

Their language was very threatening, but they never lifted their sticks to hit us. Even this was too much for Bobby, however, who was one of those who insisted that he was not then—and never could be—a disciple of nonviolence. He resisted the treatment and, fearing where that was going to lead, Duke interceded and saw to it that Bobby ceased his rebellion and got into the cruiser. If the language and tactics of the police were intended to engender anger and resistance, it was having the desired effect, and things were close to getting out of hand. I was having trouble with Dr. King and Mr. Gandhi's teachings myself.

At that moment, I could understand what drove many young men and women into the ranks of the aggressive organizations with tactics such as those later advocated by Rap Brown and Stokely Carmichael. It was all I could do to hold fast to our instructions and remain focused on the mission.

Things Get Pretty Raw

Of the more than 1,000 students who started the march that morning, 388 were jailed. Our destinations on that long, cold, and dreary march turned out to be the county jail for some and the city jail—a building whose seedy look earned it the ironic nickname the "Pink Palace"—for others. But even those destinations were not the end of our distress.

There were too many of us to be accommodated indoors in the decrepit old Orangeburg County and city jails. The final insult that day for hundreds was being herded in soaking clothes into an outdoor stockade, where the only heat came from a nearby burning pile of garbage and the cigarette lighters many passed among themselves to warm their hands. The students who could not be accommodated in the jails and stockade were ordered back to the campuses.

What happened next stays with me even today, although I didn't internalize it until a year later during an incarceration in the Columbia city jail. Many of the students who were sent back to the dormitories cleared their beds of linen and blankets and returned to the stockade and threw those blankets over the fence so that those cold, wet students could have some modicum of warmth. Other students who were not incarcerated, or did not march because of threats to their student-aid jobs—found ways to help as well. Those who worked in the dining hall and cafeteria fixed sandwiches and sent them down to the stockade. Later that day, I found out about those sandwiches in an interesting and lasting way.

Those who were indoors were not having a good time of it either. Our cell had a leaky radiator hanging from the ceiling. We were stuffed like sardines in that cell making it impossible to avoid the hot water that the overhead radiator was leaking. We actually took turns enduring that discomfort as we maneuvered around the cramped quarters.

It had only been four years earlier that I had been stepping around the piles of horse droppings in the Sumter Christmas parade, and I wondered what new kind of fresh hell was awaiting us. Bond was set at two hundred dollars per student, and the adult black community rallied to our defense, putting up their homes and property. They raised more than seventy-five thousand dollars to get us out of that miserable stockade and those rancid cells back to the warmth and security of our dormitory rooms. But the wait to be released on bond from those various hell holes was an absolute eternity.

As fate sometimes has a way of doing things, the day proved to be a life changer for me in an unexpected way. After hours of extended discomfort in our various places of confinement—the county jail, the "Pink Palace," and the stockade—we were all reunited in the main courtroom of the county courthouse to await our fate for the evening. Some students who were not under arrest and had not experienced the remarkable "hospitality" of the city and county had come to the courthouse and were allowed to mingle with those of us who were under arrest and waiting to be bailed out.

For my part I was famished, and I spoke rather loudly of my condition. It turned out my words found their way in the direction of a cute, ninety-two-pound coed who responded by thrusting toward me one of the sandwiches she and some of the other students had brought to the courthouse. I reached for it, and with an impish grin, she drew it away, broke it in half and we shared the hamburger. It was my first unguarded moment of that long day.

It was well after darkness when we were finally released on bond. A group of us walked back to campus together, and the petite coed who had teased me with a hamburger took the stroll with me.

That was my introduction to Emily England, and fifteen months later, on June 24, 1961, we were married. I found out later, as we celebrated our tenth wedding anniversary in Charleston with Bobby and Joan Pharr Doctor, Elijah and Jean Doctor Rogers, and John and Vivian Hilton Clyburn that what I thought was a chance meeting during that incarceration was not really the case. Weeks earlier Emily had observed me walking across the campus with the young lady I was "holding hands" with at the time. She told her roommate, Eleanor Sims, that the two of us would make a much better couple, and she intended to do something about it. For the first of countless times over the years to come, Emily proved to be right.

The student demonstration on that ides of March day in 1960 did a lot to bridge the gap between the generations. Those who may not have favored the original idea of the protest march were appalled at the shameful treatment we received and found ways to express their support for us later. The Reverend Matthew McCollom—another great NAACP leader from Orangeburg and pastor of Trinity United Methodist Church—said: "There was no schism between the adult community and the student community in Orangeburg."

The sacrifices by older black families, including the posting of bond money to secure our release from jail, were taken as a vote of confidence by those of us in the student population who endured that dreadful day. It was also a down payment on the eventual overturning of the verdicts issued against us by the Orangeburg magistrate. That's when I had my next interaction with Matthew Perry, the brilliant young lawyer whom I had seen six or seven years earlier in the Sumter County courthouse defending the NAACP against the unhappy school-board attorney.

This time I was the defendant, and I remember well the conversations I had with Matthew Perry as he tried to prepare me for the ordeal of that courtroom experience. We sat in the small witness room off the larger courtroom, the same one from which I was released from custody a few weeks earlier. All of us were being asked questions about the march and what we had in mind when we planned it.

We were also asked questions about our family backgrounds. Calculations were being made about everything. What we might say during questioning, how we might stand up under cross-examination, and what kind of repercussions might be visited upon our families should our names be published in the newspaper. Matthew Perry did not know me or anything about my background.

But the Reverend I. DeQuincey Newman did; in fact he knew me and my family very well. "Deak," as everybody called Reverend Newman, suggested to Matthew that I should be the first one to take the stand. Not so much because of my intelligence in answering Perry's questions, but because my family was insulated from any significant reprisals. Dad was not preaching to any white people, and Mom was not fixing any white people's hair.

My memory fails me on a lot of the details of that courtroom event. But I do remember that I was nervous, and I knew a lot of people had a great deal at stake in how well I performed on the witness stand. I have read the record of my testimony several times and am pleased with my performance.

There was one black person on the six-person jury that found us guilty, an elderly black man who asked for a recess just as I was asked a very difficult question to which I was not sure I could offer a beneficial answer. I was very relieved that when we returned from recess, the solicitor did not revisit the question. Although that elderly black gentleman voted us guilty, he did me a big favor and may have made a timely and significant contribution to the entire process.

The outcome of the trial was inconsequential and a little discouraging. We were found guilty and were fined fifty dollars apiece. The Orangeburg experience proved to be something of a dress rehearsal for the protest in Columbia about a year later.

Then, as had been the case in Orangeburg, all 187 of us were found guilty of "breach of the peace." Columbia city judge Frank Powell fined us one hundred dollars each. Our convictions were appealed to the S.C. Supreme Court, and, as in Orangeburg, the convictions were upheld. This time, however, the attorneys took our arguments to the U.S. Supreme Court. Two years later, on February 23, 1963, the U.S. Supreme Court issued its landmark decision *Edwards v. South Carolina*, overturning our convictions.

Justice Potter Stewart said the words that made the whole miserable experience worthwhile: "The circumstances of this case reflect an exercise of those basic constitutional rights in the most pristine and classic form. The Fourteenth Amendment does not permit a State to make criminal the peaceful expression of unpopular views." That's what I had been trying to tell them that day in March 1960 in that courtroom in Orangeburg. I said to the attorney that we could assemble at "any place we decide." Justice Stewart of course had a much richer vocabulary.

7 : *Back to the Basics*

There was something impersonal about the way the public perceived the civil rights movement of the 1960s. Aside from a few high-profile leaders, demonstrations were reported in terms of masses of humanity surging against the walls of those defending the status quo. Protestors came across as being some sort of faceless force recruited for a tour of duty in the streets.

The shame of it all is the utter misrepresentation of the courageous young men and women who made those marches. Each of them was there to express a strongly held opinion and to risk personal safety and security to make certain those feelings were heard and felt. Their motivation went back days, weeks, and months prior to the actual demonstration, and it endured long after the event itself actually passed.

As far as the March 15, 1960, march into downtown Orangeburg was concerned, history will probably be told in terms of the numbers of marchers, their collective ordeal of public indignity, their arrest and confinement, and the eventual outcome of the legal cases. But, if that is all that's remembered, there is a vast untold story about the origins of those brave marchers. It's a story that began with some remarkable individuals who decided they could do something to change things and improve their lives. It had to do with that particular group of young men and women who arrived on the S.C. State campus in September 1957.

I guess I sensed at the time that there was something different and special about my class, above and beyond the normal human characteristics. We took ourselves seriously and had a sense of mission. Even as a student myself, I could feel it. But I could never put words to it or define it.

That came some years later, after I had graduated from S.C. State and was serving as director of the Neighborhood Youth Corps in Charleston. One day I had an unexpected visit from a man who had been very important to me during my years at S.C. State, Mr. Paul Webber. He just dropped in unannounced at my office in the Old Citadel Building on Marion Square, and in a matter of minutes, he revealed and illuminated some undiscovered truths about that unusual aggregation of human spirits.

"In all my decades of experience with S.C. State and the Orangeburg community," Paul Webber said to me, "the class of 1961 was the only group of real nonconformists I had ever known." His words shocked me, at least partly because I had never put our role on campus in any kind of historic perspective. I never thought we viewed ourselves in that context.

He and I talked for a long time, and I was moved by our conversation. Paul Webber was one of the people I had come to know and respect greatly at S.C. State. I was a regular customer at the soda shop he owned and operated near the campus, and he taught me the only South Carolina history course I ever took. After Mr. Webber left that day, I thought back to what he said, and I tried to figure out what made our class different. I wondered what it was that caused generations of students to accept things as they were, and then for one class—the class of 1961—to say, "Enough!"

A Tradition Unchanged

A lot of it, I realized, went back to the very origins of S.C. State itself in 1896 and the purposes that had been defined in its earliest days. In his fine book *Black Carolinians: A History of Blacks in South Carolina,* I. A. Newby described the school as having been "established by white Carolinians to serve their purposes. Its function was to segregate blacks, provide them with an 'acceptable' education and fit them into a social order of white supremacy."

We looked around us and wondered how much had changed over the six decades of the school's existence. We had an all-white board of trustees and a black college president who had been hired in 1950 with the understanding that trustees did not want a president "sympathetic to desegregation." President Benner C. Turner had lived up to that mandate. In 1955–56 he worked to suppress student and faculty support of petitions calling for enforcement of the 1954 *Brown. v. Board of Education* and the subsequent *"Brown II,"* which ordered desegregation of public schools "with all deliberate speed." Dr. Turner's resistance to those efforts and his use of discipline against those protesting students and faculty, according to S.C. State historian William Hine, earned him the gratitude of white citizens and the acrimony of black students.

It was only about a year later that we arrived on campus as freshmen, and it was clear to me from the start that we were considered to be wards of the state under an autocratic president. People external to S.C. State may have had difficulty understanding the extent to which our lives and our actions were regulated and controlled by the administration. A fence was erected between our campus and neighboring Claflin College to discourage the two student bodies from interacting.

Campus elections were a sham. They were more like exercises in a Third World republic. Students were required to vote for a slate of officers who had been nominated by the administration. You can imagine that there would not be too many dissidents or "prodesegregation" activists on that slate. Students were nominated on the basis of their academic standing and on enough other subjective criteria to assure the election of student government officers to the liking of the administration.

Our troubles, we began to realize, were not just with the segregationist political elements in Columbia or with the closed-minded officials in the City of Orangeburg. Our troubles were right there on campus under a dictatorial president still practicing the worn-out dicta of the nineteenth century. The question facing us was whether we would continue to accept that kind of treatment or whether we would try to do something about it. It was time, we decided among ourselves, to challenge that system. It was time to step forward where previous classes had accepted the status quo. It was time to make a major gesture to indicate our dissatisfaction with that status quo.

As a clearly recognizable step in that direction, we undertook to offer an alternative slate of officers in the upcoming student-government elections. While such a move might not be considered so unorthodox today, it was viewed as nothing less than revolutionary in 1960. Among our criteria for the selection of candidates was first and foremost that the candidates would be chosen by the students and only the students.

There would not only be no involvement of the administration in the selection of the slate, our candidates would be clearly and deliberately antiadministration. Knowing that the administration had opposed our organizing and carrying out the marches into downtown Orangeburg, we decided further that our candidates would come only from those who had participated in the march. "Where were you when the water blew?" became our campaign slogan, and it was plastered on stickers and signs all over the school.

Just to make things even more rebellious, we discovered that there had never been a woman president of the student body. So we nominated Catherine Peppers of Columbia, a courageous young woman who had endured the fire hoses and jailing on that miserable day.

Once our candidates were announced and the campaign got under way, all hell broke loose; but we won, and we assumed a role not as flunkies for the administration, but as voices from within the ranks of the students themselves. We began to instill in our fellow students not only a sense of rebellion and resistance to the world around them, but also a role in—and even responsibility for—what lay ahead in their lives.

The pattern of docility that may have been the intended product of the administration's heavy-handed treatment of students would be replaced by a demand for student freedom. The quest for learning would go beyond the traditional fare offered to young black men and women to prepare them for a role in a segregated society. The educational experience would be one of trying and testing new ideas, new thinking, and new ways of shaping the expectations we would bring to our lives.

Exceptional and Menacing

In the late 1950s and early 1960s in South Carolina, it must have been a worrisome message coming from the state's largest black college. Black men and women who demanded freedom on college campuses might also demand their full and equal rights as citizens once they left campus. What a frightening thing that must have been to the establishment leaders of the time. No wonder Paul Webber thought we were exceptional. We were.

In looking back on those times, I place Paul Webber and his wife, Clemmie, among those who dared to associate with us. I do not know at what risk those friendships may have been extended; faculty and students had been disciplined only two years earlier for defying President Turner and participating in antisegregation demonstrations.

Most of the faculty members, in fact, were cautious, and I could understand why. They would say little to rebellious students, but they could clearly demonstrate their sympathies by enthusiastic salutations in the hallways and by the tone and substance of their lectures. Besides Paul and Clemmie Webber, others who inspired us with some caution at the time were Paul Sanford, Frank and Valeria Staley, and Geraldine Zimmerman.

Some other faculty members prepared us from our freshman year for what lay ahead academically and otherwise, and I am particularly mindful of lectures and reading assignments from some of them. Ernestine Walker, who taught me history, was one of my favorites. She insisted that I read and internalize John Hope Franklin's great history of the African American people, *From Slavery to Freedom*. Marguerite Howie taught my advanced sociology course, and Bill Howell introduced me to sociology studies. One of his lectures, titled "We Are but the Sum Total of Our Experiences," has stuck with me for life and is the foundation on which I develop more than half of my speeches today—as well as this book. There were other younger faculty members who were a little bolder, including Grace Brooks, Diane Harper, and Marianna W. Davis, with whom I developed professional and social relationships that still exist today. What a strange world it was to realize that faculty members had to be careful, and even a little secretive, about how fully they could afford to educate their students.

My First Smoke-Filled Room

One faculty member who later came forward openly with those of us who had chosen the rebellious role was Paul Sanford, who often visited our dorm. He left impressions on us in many ways. The most immediate was the fact that he was an inveterate chain smoker who had a distinctly eccentric way of enjoying his habit. Even though we provided him an ashtray, Paul let ashes fall to the gray tile floor, and he extracted every possible puff from his unfiltered cigarettes. When there was nothing left but a fragment, he extinguished the remaining ember between the sole of his shoe and the floor. When we weren't listening with rapt attention to his comments, we were scrambling to make certain Paul Sanford wasn't setting fire to our dormitory room. After he left, we worked into the wee hours of the morning to sweep up cigarette butts and mop up tobacco stains.

But Paul Sanford did light some real fires of intellectual curiosity and political inquiry among us. He spoke with us as colleagues and friends—not as students—and imparted some real-world wisdom about a revolution underway not far from our shores, the Cuban revolution of Fidel Castro against the American-supported dictatorship of Fulgencio Batista. Paul Sanford spoke about the people of Cuba and the conditions of their lives that made revolution possible and feasible for so many disadvantaged people. It was a topic of great interest to those of us so deeply involved in dissent on the campus of S.C. State College.

Paul Sanford was a great student himself, and he was constantly studying and analyzing events elsewhere in the nation and the world. It was a characteristic I found inspiring, and it has become an important part of my own world. There is no part of my life or my career that is not enhanced by a daily exposure to life elsewhere on the planet and conditions and experiences we may share with others. If I have not learned a new lesson every day, I have fallen short of a personal goal. You can blame all that on my dad and Paul Sanford, I guess.

Paul was one of the first people I ever heard to speak of some major concerns about the conditions in Southeast Asia, about the defeat of the French colonial forces in Vietnam, about the perils of American involvement there, and about the dangers that lay ahead for us in that region. What he foresaw was later played out in tragic proportions by our nation and by the young generation that paid so dearly for the disastrous course of U.S. policy. His wisdom extended our learning experience far beyond the books and the classroom.

There was another aspect of Paul Sanford's influence for me. He knew of my religious background, and we spent a lot of time discussing religion and politics. His views were much less orthodox than mine, and I became intrigued with the world he was introducing to me, a world of faith that went beyond the strict beliefs I had known growing up. He started telling me of the writings of Bahá'u'lláh, the founder of the Bahá'í faith, which he had embraced. I was fascinated, and on one occasion I agreed to go to Augusta with him to visit their "church." I even thought of affiliating.

A Stretch of Faith

As it turned out, we never made the trip to Augusta. Something came up that caused him to cancel, and for whatever the reason, we never discussed the Bahá'í faith again. It may have been fortunate; I don't know. I do know that the whole experience of learning about another faith, a faith that teaches tolerance, broadened my mind and helped me understand the world around me a lot better.

My brief exposure to the Bahá'í faith did serve me well on one unexpected occasion. During the summer of 1960, Duke Missouri, my brother John, and I made our way to Paterson, New Jersey, as we usually did during the summer months, to find work. During this particular summer, things were not going well, and it took us a while before we finally found jobs with a construction company renovating dormers. The job required some carpentry skills, which John and I had acquired in our many experiences as Dad's helpers. Duke's skills were pretty much limited to handing up boards and that sort of thing, but we got the job.

It was a tough summer financially for us, and we were surviving on peanut butter and jelly sandwiches for the most part at lunchtime because we always seemed to be short of cash. Just as things were really getting tough, however, fate seemed to intervene, and we were sent to a job in Englewood, New Jersey. For a while the homeowners whose dormers we were repairing were a little distant. We kind of figured it had a little bit to do with having three black guys spending the day up in their attic.

One day though, as I was passing through a room on the second level of the house, I saw a familiar looking picture on a table. "Isn't that Bahá'u'lláh, the founder of the Bahá'í faith?" I asked the lady of the house, who was standing nearby. Her face registered pure shock. How on earth could this guy who was doing day-laborer's work on her house know anything about this fairly remote and highly intellectual faith? I proceeded to discuss with her some of the things I had learned from Paul Sanford, and we had quite an interesting conversation. We had found a common ground, and her coolness toward us vanished. From that day forward, no more peanut butter and jelly sandwiches at lunch. She provided refreshments to help us cope with the summertime heat in that New Jersey attic, and we had a full lunch awaiting us when noontime arrived. I don't think she was all that pleased with the work we did on her dormers, but she seemed very pleased to have found a person conversant with the faith she practiced. My "extended" S.C. State education was already coming in very handy.

The Hazards of Good Music

It's important to keep in mind that those of us who were registering our dissent with the powers that be at S.C. State were young people in our late teens and early twenties. We were getting a lot of fun out of life, and not all our dissent on campus was of a deeply serious, political nature. Some of it may have even come under the heading of "mischief," but the administration took it all with the same grumpy heavy-handedness. Our first act of nonconformity was in fact a matter of pure innocence, or so we thought.

It came only a few months after we had arrived on campus, when we decided to enter a float representing the freshman class in the homecoming parade. It seemed to catch the administration a little off guard, and we were quickly informed that we would be required to submit our theme and the design of our float for approval. Fair enough.

The 1957 freshman class float at S.C. State College. I'm on the left with childhood friend Emma Wilder. "Duke" Missouri and Rosemary Bland are at right. Photograph from the S.C. State yearbook.

We had already given the topic some thought, and we decided it would be great fun to concentrate on the music that had become so popular in the 1950s. These were days when we were listening to people such as Sam Cooke, Johnny Ray, and the Platters. It seemed the most natural thing in the world that our theme for the freshman float would be "rock and roll," and that's what we submitted for approval.

The administration wasn't pleased. Rock and roll was a little wild for the taste of those square, sedate folks, I guess. "Motown" music was coming out of Detroit, and goodness knows that was a place of real danger for our small-town South Carolina minds. They asked that we "reconsider" our theme and "modify" our plans. We were having none of that and decided to go with our original idea.

It took us all night to build and decorate the freshman float, but there it was in the homecoming parade the next day, a "rock and roll" float for the freshman class with Jim Clyburn and his roommate, Duke Missouri, riding on it, smiling and waving to the crowd. My homegirl and May Day dance partner throughout grade school, Emma Wilder, was my dancing partner on the float. It must have been a pretty good float. We won second place for theme and design, and our friends in the administration must have choked on their homecoming dinner that evening. Little did they know that the homecoming float was just a sampling of what lay ahead from this group of dissenters who hit campus that September 1957.

Dissatisfaction with restrictive student life and lack of academic freedom at S.C. State was a major point of contention for our class during our four years at Orangeburg, and the seeds of dissent we planted continued with future classes. Things came to a head in the spring of 1967 under the leadership of my friend, and later district aide, Ike Williams of Charleston, who was president of the senior class at the time. Ike and his fellow class presidents mobilized a classroom boycott that was almost 80 percent effective and virtually shut down the college for a matter of days. In May of that year, Dr. Benner Turner, the symbol of autocratic rule at S.C. State, submitted his resignation and concluded his seventeen years as president of the college.

For the frisky young men and women who had entered S.C. State some ten years earlier, the event was a time-delayed triumph, but a triumph nonetheless. We remembered what it took: the boldness to stand up to authority, the spirit to introduce to staid administrators the notion that rock and roll was a part of their lives, and the shared human ordeal that made a permanent bond of the question "Where were you when the water blew?"

Paul Webber was right. We were a damned remarkable group of people.

PART FOUR

The Charleston Shuffle

I was emerging with something of a hybrid political identity. I was the S.C. State graduate who had been jailed for student protests. But I was also the classroom teacher who had been head of the eleventh-grade level at C.A. Brown. I had gotten college scholarships for hundreds of needy high school graduates. I had also been heavily involved in the Medical College hospital strike, and the City of Charleston garbage workers' strike. And I had coordinated St. Julian Devine's successful campaign for City Council. People were having trouble putting me in a pigeonhole. And I liked it that way.

8 | *Two Steps to the West*

May 27, 1961, kicked in a phase of my life that is probably best described by that popular line dance that seems to get everybody up and on the dance floor. No, not the electric slide. The steps to that one are rather straightforward and do not offer as many opportunities for missteps as the one I have in mind: the Charleston shuffle. What was supposed to be one of the best days of my life was one of the worst days of my life. And it shouldn't have been.

It should have been a day of triumph, a day when I should have been able to celebrate with the other members of my class the completion of the academic journey we had begun together in September 1957. It should have been the day on which we would recall all those things that had made us a special class: those moments of joy, those moments of pain, those things that bind people together.

The members of the class of 1961 looked good in their caps and gowns, and as they took their final march to receive their diplomas, they filed pass me. I was not in the procession; I was seated in the audience. I was wearing a hat but not the cap and gown I had envisioned four years earlier. I was watching it all in misery, embarrassed that I had not qualified for graduation with the rest of my class.

I wasn't accustomed to failure. Nothing in my background or life provided for that kind of experience. Most of it could be chalked up to things such as too much attention to things outside the classroom—theater productions, social activities, and, yes, civil rights. I had lost track of things such as classroom attendance.

As I sat there, I glanced over at Lowman Hall, where I had spent my freshman year getting into situation after situation and causing Dean Myers heartburn. In fact, Dean Myers decided my roommate, Clarence "Duke" Missouri, and I were causing too much trouble, so he split us up. I spent the second semester in room 215 alone. Duke had a more sinister explanation for the move. His take was that Dean Myers was more interested in having me in the room alone than in punishing him. At any rate, Lowman Hall was the freshman dorm. The next year, we moved into Bethea Hall, the upperclassmen dorm, and a year later Duke and I arranged to become roommates again. But Duke was marching, and I wasn't.

The first two years at State were rather uneventful, except for the administration's announcement at the end of our freshman year that a new and stricter grading system would be implemented in September 1958. The impact was felt at the end of the first semester of our sophomore year, and a lot of my friends did not survive that change. I almost didn't.

Duke was a pretty good running back when we were at Mather. I was not very fast, so I concentrated on defense and was a pretty good linebacker. But because of a knee injury, I got to play in only one game for one play at Mather, and that was a game where everybody of any consequence was too hurt to play. Both of us felt, however, that we were good enough on our side of the ball to make State's team, although we had no illusions about getting much playing time. In fact we were not particularly interested in playing much. We were mainly interested in the social side of being on the team and traveling to other college campuses.

So we decided to try out for the team during the 1959 spring drills. Our tenure did not last long. Almost half the football team had fallen victim to the new grading policy, which was the real reason our classmate David "Deacon" Jones transferred to Mississippi Valley State University. After a few practice sessions, it became apparent that we were going to make the team and even have to play. It was not what we had in mind, and we were not on scholarship; so, one day after a particularly tough practice session, we decided that we had had enough.

We did not even bother to tell Coach D. D. Moore of our decision. We just did not go back. I even left a brand-new pair of sneakers in my locker that accrued to somebody's benefit. Coach Moore found out that we were no longer on the team when he happened on the two of us walking across the campus with cigarettes in our mouths. He issued a stern reminder of his "no smoking" rule, admonishing us that he did not allow anybody on his team to smoke. We assured him that we were well aware of his "no smoking" rule. He got the point. After leaving State, Coach Moore became very active in the North Carolina Democratic Party, and—to his credit—every time we were together, he referred to me as one of his boys.

My best sport, however, was baseball, and we had a pretty good baseball team at Lincoln. It was one of the things I hated to give up when I went to Mather. In addition to being in the band for many years, I was the starting second baseman on Lincoln High School's baseball team for three years. I was not a good hitter, but I made only one fielding error in my high school playing career, and it came in the last inning of my last high school game, at Emmett Scott High School in Rock Hill.

During my junior year at State I decided to try out for the baseball team. This was precipitated by a visit to the campus by Elston Howard, the first black player for the New York Yankees, which, if my memory serves, was next to the last of the major league baseball teams to desegregate. I made the team at State, but not at my favorite position of second base. Coach Martin made me a third baseman because he needed one and a homeboy of mine, James Scarborough, who had replaced me at second base when I left Lincoln, was placed at second. I was never comfortable at third base, but I had made the team and would be getting a chance to travel. That was the main thing for me. But things did not work out quite the way I had planned.

The first game of the season was against Denmark Area Trade (now Denmark Tech), over in Denmark, South Carolina. It was on a Tuesday afternoon and conflicted with my social-sciences seminar course, which all social-studies majors were required to take and pass. The teachers in the Social Studies Department took turns teaching that course, and as fate would have it, it was Ms. Marguerite Howie's turn. Because of the game, I missed the class. A day or two later, Ms. Howie summoned me to her office and inquired as to why I had missed her class. When I told her the reason, she asked whether or not I was planning to play professional baseball in the future. I told her that I did not think that professional baseball was in my future, and then Ms. Howie sternly informed me that if it were not, she would advise me not to miss her class again. That conversation ended my college baseball career.

I joined the debating society in hopes of sharpening my argumentative skills. Arguing was a significant pastime at State in those days. We called it "holding court." Our little group had a campus-wide reputation of being hard on each other and doing so in a manner that provided great entertainment for the student body.

When it comes to leaving a mark, I suspect for me it probably was through the campus theater. I was a hit in my high school senior play, *Spooky Junction,* so I decided to join the Henderson Davis Players at State. I had leading roles in three productions, *Our Town, An Inspector Calls,* and *The Rainmaker,* as well as supporting roles in *Down in the Valley, Julius Caesar,* and several one-act plays. All this was in addition to being pretty active in campus politics, the 1960 presidential campaign, and spending a lot of time across the railroad tracks at the College Soda Shop and around on Goff Avenue at Lamar's Tavern. These activities were not conducive to attendance at 7:30 A.M. classes, and I missed quite a few of them.

Posing with fellow Henderson Davis Players Clarence Missouri, Hiram Spain, and James Gilliard during a scene from Julius Caesar at S.C. State. Photograph from the S.C. State yearbook.

With Emily on our wedding day, June 24, 1961

I wasn't all that bad a student, but I was not managing things very well. I must have thought—using the language of Wall Street—that I was too big to fail. Well Wall Street and I learned a painful lesson along those lines.

So, there I was, sitting in the folding chairs on the front lawn of White Hall that spring day in 1961, wishing the graduation ceremony would speed up, and hoping that the earth would swallow me up in the process. I had a hard time smiling that day.

Ever since the "hamburger" incident at the Orangeburg jail a year earlier, Emily England and I had become quite serious about one another, and sometime during the weeks leading up to her graduation we decided to get married.

We set the date for June 24, and because I had spent summers in Paterson, New Jersey, we decided that would be the setting. I was still harboring thoughts of a life in the public sector, and New Jersey seemed a lot better place than South Carolina for a young black guy with political ambitions.

We kept our decision to get married quiet for quite a while. We informed our parents by telephone. Emily's sister, Mattie, my brothers, John and Charles, and our mothers were in attendance. Our fathers did not attend, and Emily's uncle, Joseph H. Washington, gave away the bride. The service was performed by the Reverend Joseph Thompson, who was a member of the Chaplain Corps at S.C. State College.

The ceremony took place in the living room at 39 Carroll Street in Paterson, the home of Rose Wilder, whose sister, Bertha Wilson, was a close friend of Mom's. I always stayed with "Bert," as we called her, during the summers I worked in Paterson. This arrangement was the manifestation of an unspoken friends-of-the-family commitment: Bert had stayed with us in Sumter for a short while before "going up north."

Emily's Uncle Joe had an apartment in Greenwich Village, and he offered it to us for our honeymoon. He had another treat in store for us as well. Our first night as Mr. and Mrs. James E. Clyburn would be spent—on his dime—at the historic Teresa Hotel in Harlem. It was known as the lodging place for such celebrated people as Lena Horne, Duke Ellington, Dorothy Dandridge, and Sugar Ray Robinson. Someday, I thought to myself, they may remember that Jim and Emily Clyburn spent their wedding night there as well. Of course it has since fallen victim to "urban removal."

A week after our marriage, Emily reported for work at Fairwold (W. G. Sanders) Middle School in Columbia, South Carolina. I moved in with her Aunt Ida Washington in New York and shared a room with her cousin Elijah "Bootsie" McCants. I landed an evening job as night shipping clerk in a textile mill in Hackensack, New Jersey; my hours were between five in the afternoon and two o'clock in the morning. The first bus back to New York was at five o'clock in the morning, so I had three hours to kill before dawn every morning in beautiful downtown Hackensack.

This was not only a bad way to start a marriage; it was a bad way to live. The commute to Hackensack was unbearable, and Emily was back in South Carolina. For all my hopes for a good life in New Jersey, one day I hopped a Greyhound bus and was back in South Carolina for the July Fourth celebrations. I spent the rest of the summer painting Mom's beauty shop in Sumter and doing odd jobs for her while awaiting the start of the fall semester at S.C. State.

A New Beginning

Emily and I were both fortunate to have grown up in two-parent households. But the atmospheres in our respective families could not have been more different. As children we learn from watching our parents interact with each other and with us and our siblings. In the Clyburn household, things often began and ended with biblical and moral lessons. With Peter and Mattie England, one learned the power of patience and the value of silence.

My return to S.C. State was strange. Most of my friends from the class of '61 were gone; so with a lot of time on my hand, I decided to do one last play at State:

The Rainmaker, which had been popular on Broadway about ten years earlier. It told a story about people looking for relief from drought on a midwestern farm during the Depression era. I took the whole thing to heart. I was dealing with a personal drought myself, and goodness knows I was ready to find some relief in my own life.

That relief began to appear in unexpected ways during the second half of the semester. Part of my class load was something called going "on the field." It was an exercise in directed (practice) teaching, where we gained classroom experience in an actual school setting. The teaching experience was a good addition to my life, but there were two significant challenges.

My directed-teaching assignment was at Carver High School in Spartanburg, about as far from Orangeburg as you can go and still be in South Carolina. Not having a car created a regular logistical challenge for me as I prepared for my directed-teaching assignment at Carver High. I was not only entering the early stages of marriage; we had found out only a few weeks before my teaching assignment began that our honeymoon in Greenwich Village had been a little more than blissful. Emily was pregnant.

Realization of my responsibilities as a husband and future parent delivered a message as powerful as any I had ever received. Life was coming at me full speed, ready or not. No more college plays, and although Dr. Algernon Belcher, who was chair of the Social Studies Department, and others were encouraging me to consider law school, that was out of the question for the time being. It was Moment of Truth time.

Unfortunately moments of truth do not always come with instruction manuals. About the time I was pondering my new role in life, I was informed that in order for me to complete a degree that would qualify me to teach social studies, I would need to successfully complete a course in geography, a course I had not taken during my academic ramblings through the college's curriculum.

The course was taught only on Saturday mornings. So began my first exercise in shuffling up and down Interstate 26, from Orangeburg west to Spartanburg with an intermitted slide over into Columbia. I would then shuffle from Spartanburg east to Orangeburg, repeating the intermittent slide into Columbia. I made the Spartanburg-Columbia-Orangeburg shuffle on a weekly basis for six weeks so that I could do directed teaching Monday through Friday, and take a Saturday morning geography course back on campus during what I hoped would be my final semester at S.C. State.

To prevent my having to hitchhike the 130 miles from Spartanburg to Orangeburg every Saturday, Mom—once again—came to the rescue. She loaned us her car. She had a way of coming through at critical junctures in my life.

Though I had tried not to be assigned to Carver High School for my directed teaching, it did have some bright moments. One of my classmates, Freddie Middleton, with whom I had a good relationship, was also assigned to Carver, and we roomed together. Several other classmates had found teaching jobs in the area; one of them was Hiram Spain with whom I had and still have a very pleasant relationship.

But the biggest thrill was that Matthew Perry's office was across the street from the school. I would often go over after school, and we would spend hours talking about the state of affairs in South Carolina and the nation and our dreams and aspirations for the future. Invariably the conversation would turn to my going to law school. We both knew that with Emily expecting in March, law school was out of the question for the moment, but that did not stop us from discussing it. And doing my shuffles back and forth between Spartanburg and Orangeburg, I would have long reflections on our discussions and would mentally prepare for the next one. Matthew Perry was always a gentleman in public, but in many of our private discussions he would share some of his frustrations, disappointments, and tribulations. I always looked forward to our next conversation.

During one of those weekend trips back to the campus I was told that my lifelong friend and classmate, Emma Wilder, was trying to contact me. Emma and I had grown up two blocks from each other in Sumter, and my dad was her mother's house repairman and renovator of choice. We had started first grade together, and we were always paired during May Day exercises. That was really a big day for us each year, and our partnership had continued at S.C. State, when she had been my dance partner on that notorious freshman class rock and roll homecoming float.

Emma and I were both fifth year students in the fall of 1961, and we were both looking for teaching jobs in Sumter or Columbia. When I heard she was trying to reach me, I assumed it was to tell me she had found a job. My assumption was correct, but there was more to the story. An administrator from Charleston School District 20 had been on campus and had offered her a job, and it came up in their conversation that the district had an emergency and needed a social-studies teacher. Emma had told him I might be available. She gave me his name and phone number, and I proceeded to make what turned out to be one of the most important phone calls of my life.

Going Gullah

Wilmot Fraser was the "Supervisor of Negro Schools" in District 20. He and I met about a week after I called him, and we talked about the job. We hit it off well, and it became clear that this was a case of supply and demand. They were in dire need of a social-studies teacher, and I was in dire need of a job.

We reached an agreement almost immediately, and within two short weeks, I successfully completed the directed-teaching work and passed the Saturday geography class, thereby completing South Carolina State's requirements for the bachelor of arts degree. Things were looking up. I was a family man, and we were expecting a child; I had a college degree and a teaching job. I could take a deep breath and exhale. My career—whatever it might turn out to be—was underway. So I shuffled east down Interstate 26 to Charleston.

9 | *Two Steps to the East*

Charleston, South Carolina, had not been on my radar up to that point in my life. Pure fate took me in that direction. The event that created the job opening for me in Charleston School District 20 was that Ms. Maggie McGill Magwood, the incumbent social-studies teacher, gave birth to a child during the 1961 Christmas vacation. She had chosen not to inform school officials that she was pregnant, a violation of the school district's policy.

As it turned out, her decision was a blessing for both of us. She was blessed with a child, and I was blessed with a job. It would have prompted my dad to refer to a verse in the book of Isaiah, a reference I often heard him cite, that says our steps in life "are ordered." It is also the source for one of my favorite spirituals. My immediate concern was the difficulty of taking over a class in midyear and not losing a lot of time and continuity for the students. I had two good helpers in that regard. Ms. Magwood obviously cared a lot for the students and could not have been more gracious. She counseled me, instructed me, and provided me invaluable guidance. As though she had not already done enough for me, she was one of my earliest financial supporters when I ran for elective office some eight years later. I count my relationship with Ms. Magwood as one of the most blessed experiences of my life.

My main support in my new pursuit, however, came from James B. Coaxum, a fellow teacher whom I came to regard as a real pro in the unusual setting where I began my teaching career. James Coaxum was a native Charlestonian. Simonton's student body consisted of all black eighth graders in Charleston, doubtless a grand exercise in "separate but equal" public education in South Carolina, in spite of the fact that this was eight years after *Brown v. Board of Education*. There were twenty sections of these pubescent youngsters, and they were grouped according to the outcomes of aptitude tests. The highest achievers were placed in 8-1 and 8-2; the lowest achievers were in 8-19 and 8-20; all the others were placed somewhere between, as determined by their test scores.

Coaxum and I had sections 8-17 and 8-18, which made for some exciting classroom adventures. I kept expecting the prototype of Morgan Freeman as Principal Joe Clark in *Lean on Me* to come striding down the hall at any time. The Morgan Freeman prototype never showed up, but James Coaxum did. He was a mentor and good friend. He did not seem fazed by the challenges of trying to teach these kids, many of whom seemed to have little interest in school.

Coaxum and his wife, Doris, helped introduce me to Charleston and the quirky nature of its society. I spent a lot of time at their home in Washington Park, and I listened intently as they told me of the special living environment in which I had found myself. We became good friends, and I was impressed with their grasp of things in such an unsettling time of social and political change. The Simonton experience turned out to be a good one for me.

Besides James Coaxum, I became friends with Nathaniel "Rip" Bennett and Cornell Hicks, who taught the 8-19 and 8-20 levels of the curriculum. The four of us taught the boys and girls considered the least likely to succeed. We represented something of a "Fearless Foursome." It was our job to team teach English and social studies, and math and science, while trying to maintain some semblance of order in the classroom. Before the day of things such as cell phones, Twitter, and Facebook, communication was usually carried out by loud exclamations across the schoolyard or piercing shouts down the hallway. It was probably good preparation for my service in the U.S. Congress some years hence.

There was another dimension to my experience at Simonton. Rip and Cornell, along with another good friend and fellow teacher, Joseph Moore, were members of Omega Psi Phi Fraternity. For as long as I could remember, I had the ambition to be a member of that fraternity, largely because so many of the important men in my earlier life in Sumter had been Omegas—my principal at Lincoln High School, J. H. Kilgore; my band director, Robert Sanders; my baseball coach, Robert Jenkins; and Eddie McGirt, my football coach at Mather.

Perhaps a word would be in order here about the extraordinary importance of fraternities and sororities among black Americans. While fraternity members at schools such as the University of South Carolina, Clemson, or Wofford, may have viewed their membership with solemn gravity, the role of those organizations was largely social. Among black people, it went far beyond that. Black men at the time were not invited to be members of the local Rotary, Lions, Kiwanis, or any of the other civic clubs. Outside the church and Masonic orders, fraternities and sororities were the main vehicles by which secular civic activities took place in the black community.

The value of fraternities and sororities went far beyond college days; they were lifetime associations and alliances that helped us not only to define our own social spheres but also to mobilize coalitions of community activities that cut across religious, professional, and business lines. Even though it was five years after my college graduation before I submitted to induction into Omega, I was already paying attention to which Greek letter organizations were identified with which individuals in my life.

Another Omega man I came to know and appreciate was the principal at Simonton School, Nathaniel L. "N. L." Manigault. He was well-liked, a competent administrator and a man of considerable intellectual capacity. He was also known to have a weakness for demon rum, a factor that some feared might cost him an opportunity to become principal of the new all-black high school scheduled to open in September 1962 on the east side of the Charleston peninsula. Its original name was Eastside High School, but it was later decided that the new school would be named for

Charles A. Brown, the chairman of the all-white school board, a fact that tells you something about the racial and educational climate in the "separate but equal" South in those days.

At any rate there was much speculation about N. L.'s fate; which teachers would be chosen to staff the new school; and which teachers might find employment at Burke High School. Burke was the fifty-six-year old school on the west side of the peninsula, which had been the alma mater of many notable South Carolinians, including Harvey Gantt, who broke the racial barrier to desegregate Clemson College in 1963 and later became the first black mayor of Charlotte, North Carolina.

For my part I was looking elsewhere at the time. I had been offered a teaching job at Robert Smalls High School in Beaufort, a historic coastal town south of Charleston. Beaufort was appealing to me because it was rich in black cultural and political history. I also liked the idea that the school was named for a heroic former slave whose bold efforts during the Civil War had gained him his freedom; he was later elected to five terms in the U.S. Congress. To make things even more appealing, Emily had been offered a librarianship at St. Helena School on nearby Lady Island. It seemed a perfect arrangement for us.

We drove to Beaufort one Sunday afternoon to "check out" what I thought would be our new home, and to my consternation, things just didn't click for Emily. She had been dubious from the beginning, but she became more negative after our Sunday drive. So much for the charms of Beaufort, Robert Smalls High School, and Lady Island; we were staying in Charleston or going back to Columbia.

As fate would have it, my fraternity brother to be N. L. Manigault, did become principal at C. A. Brown and offered me a job at the new school as a world-history teacher. He dressed up the job offer by telling me how "uniquely qualified" I was to teach world history to tenth graders. I had already heard, however, that none of the more senior social-studies teachers wanted to teach world history.

But I didn't mind being told I was "uniquely qualified" for anything, and teaching world history was for me like throwing Br'er Rabbit into the briar patch. It was one subject I thoroughly enjoyed. My conversations with Paul Sanford at S.C. State had helped me develop an appetite for the other political worlds and the other civilizations that shared our planet and influenced our own daily lives. In later years I had opportunities to travel widely, and I gained particular insight from my visits to the Soviet Union, other European countries, several Asian countries, and various nations on the continent of Africa.

Some of the worst political figures I encountered in my various positions of public service were those who never traveled, who never understood that the world was a complicated place, and who believed that the sun rose and set every day only along the borders of their own particular bailiwick.

In the spring of 1962, I was just glad to have a job for the coming year. We were doubly blessed when Emily was offered an assistant librarianship at Burke High School. It probably worked out just as well that we did not make the venture down to Beaufort. As things turned out, Charleston became a good home for us, and it offered a good base of operation for this aspiring young politician.

Of all things, however, my belated graduation from S.C. State College was proving to be complicated. While I had completed all my course work during the first semester, the college was allowed only one commencement per year, and it came at the end of the spring semester. And supposedly there was a requirement that all graduates had to march in the commencement procession or they did not receive their degrees. The graduation was scheduled for a Monday, three weeks before my Simonton school year ended, which meant that I would have to take a day of unpaid leave from my teaching job to attend the graduation exercises. Believe me, a day's pay in those tightly budgeted times was not to be taken lightly.

So, as I prepared for my day of destiny, with cap and gown rented and leave time arranged, what would arrive in the mail on the Friday before the Monday commencement but my S.C. State College degree, with all the "whereases" and "wherefores" proclaimed and the name James Enos Clyburn prominently displayed somewhere in the middle.

I quickly cancelled my plans for a Monday trip to Orangeburg, notified the school that they would not need a substitute on Monday after all. As it turned out, however, my final paycheck of the school year had already been reduced by the amount of one day's unpaid leave. When I explained that I had actually taught that day, I was told nothing could be done because the paperwork had already been submitted. So there I was, a victim of "paperwork already submitted," and to this day Charleston School District 20 owes me a day's pay. But I had my college degree, a year late and a few dollars short as it was, but mission accomplished all the same.

Step to the Line

One of the drawbacks of teaching public school was the nine-month nature of the job although Charleston spread out the annual salary over ten months. Even so, two and a half months of summertime living with no income, unlike what the Gershwin-Heyward song proclaims, were not easy. And on March 22, 1962, our first daughter, Mignon, arrived, both as a blessing and as an economic challenge. As a couple of relative youngsters setting off on life's adventures, we were not equipped for ten weeks without pay. So the three of us squeezed into our new 1962 Ford Falcon and headed up North to visit relatives and look for a summer job.

Our first stop was Baltimore, where my favorite cousin on my mother's side, Delores Nichols, and her husband lived. Delores is the daughter of my mother's sister Louise. As we were proudly showing off our addition, Delores and her husband invited us to spend the summer with them and seek summer employment there. It was a generous and welcome offer for cash-strapped young parents, and we gratefully accepted. We were also the recipients of more generosity during our summer in Baltimore.

Another of my mother's sisters, Hattie, who also lived in Baltimore, presented us with a portable foldaway crib, which fit neatly in the back seat of our Falcon. When unfolded it made a perfect bed-away-from-home for little Mignon, and subsequently for our daughters Jennifer and Angela. Even later, after they had all outgrown its baby-size dimensions, we made a point of lending it to younger couples for their own new arrivals. That crib and Mignon's first bassinet became family treasures and heirlooms. They were just recently discarded because of current safety strictures.

Every day that I went out in search of a job, Emily kept the Falcon, and I rode the bus. The plan seemed a good one as far as it went. But it was a very hot summer in Baltimore, and I was not exactly relentless in my pursuit of a job. On one particularly hot day, I sought relief off the steaming sidewalk in what seemed to be a cool refuge: a bowling alley.

I had never been in a bowling alley before, but it proved to be one of those moments when fate seemed to take matters into its own hands. As I cooled off, sipping a midday soda, I looked around the place and saw people seemingly having a lot of fun at what appeared to be a fairly simple game. So I rented a pair of shoes, got some instructions about the rules, staying behind the foul line, and score keeping, and decided to try my hand. After I rolled a couple of gutter balls, the attendant showed me the four-step approach, which is really three steps and a slide. Before my first game was over, I had made a spare and had bowled two strikes. In the second game I bowled a 169. Not bad for a guy from South Carolina who hardly knew what the game was all about.

I was hooked. For the next few days—in what will be my true confession on the subject—I spent more time in that bowling alley than I did looking for a job. At the end of two weeks I gave up looking for a job, and Emily, Mignon and I took a few more days to visit relatives in New York, Philadelphia and Washington, D.C. We left Baltimore without a job or any new income, but we had a new baby crib. And I had a new pastime, which turned out to be more than just a hobby.

After two weeks and, as we were running low on money, we navigated our way back to South Carolina. We stopped in Rowland, North Carolina, to visit relatives on my dad's side, and Bennettsville to visit some Church of God members, Sarah Blackmon and Ona Gay. We finished our itinerant summer with family trips between Charleston, Sumter, and Moncks Corner. In the course of things, my mom and Mignon grew quite fond of each other. It probably didn't hurt that they had the same birth date, March 22. The fact is, Mom was never really sure if her birthday was March 22 or 23; there were records of both dates. But when Mignon was born on the twenty-second, that settled it; Mom was born on March 22. She had always known it was the twenty-second anyway.

Stepping Up

As much as I enjoyed teaching world history, I realized that what really motivated me was the opportunity of engaging young people in the education process, whether they wanted to participate or not. My experience with the 8-17 and 8-18 eighth graders at Simonton had a profound impact on me. For all the behavioral menaces those days presented, the real challenge was to break through barriers of resistance and open potentially rich and fertile minds to the joy of growing and learning. In two short years I had become devoted to the job of teaching, and I believed, with some admitted prejudice, that N. L. Manigault was probably right: I was "uniquely qualified" to teach tenth grade world history.

My teaching strategy was based on two experiences of my earlier life. One, my own recollection of world history as a classroom subject was not a good one. I remembered it as being boring and filled with memorizing dates and events. Two, my own experience of clipping news articles from the *Sumter Daily Item* every day as a boy probably taught me more about the world around me than any classroom or textbook exercise. So I combined the two experiences to produce a basic format, which went something like this:

The students would be required to learn only two dates, 476 A.D. and 1066 A.D. Those were dates that shaped our civilization beyond what most high school teachers recognized at the time. The first was the year the "barbarians" were truly "at the gates." That's when the Germanic tribes overran Rome and ended the western Roman Empire. The second was the conquest of Anglo-Saxon England by the Norman French nobleman who became William I of England, which led to the beginning of the hybrid language, culture, and political heritage handed down to us as the basis of much of our own American civilization.

Each day I would scour the newspapers looking for items that related to the planned lessons for the next day or week ahead. Part of my teaching method was to let current events dictate my weekly lesson plan, if not the daily ones. To carry that notion one step farther, occasionally I selected a student to teach the class. I gave the student a week's notice, and I helped with preparing the lesson plan.

I got a kick out of watching students come to life and take a genuine interest not only in the academic subject but in the real world that lay around them. In October of 1962, for example, there was the event that came to be known as the Cuban Missile Crisis. The Russians were building missile installations on Cuban soil, about ninety miles off the American shore. That's what was in the newspapers and on the radio- and television-news programs every day. That's what was on people's minds. It was an unbelievably important moment in world history.

So I put aside the world-history books and their descriptions of Peter the Great and the Fertile Crescent, and we kept up on a daily basis with the Cuban Missile Crisis, which was happening right before our eyes. The chapter on Cuba in our textbook became our point of historical reference. It made for good classroom discussions and good student interest and engagement. It's what I thought education was all about. It didn't always make for good conversations in the faculty lounge, however. Some of my colleagues were not enamored of my innovations, and they thought I would find trouble with the administration.

As it turned out, quite the opposite proved to be the case. In May of 1964, as I was completing my second year at C. A. Brown, N. L. called me into his office. We had met there several times before, usually after faculty meetings. We would discuss things that had taken place at the meetings and how and why he had handled things the way he had. This time, however, the meeting was not about faculty. What N. L. had in mind was for me to assume more responsibility in the school. "You have great promise," he said, "and I want to put you on the road to becoming a principal." I was flattered but not really surprised. I had grown comfortable and confident with

N. L., particularly knowing that he had probably deflected some of the criticism of my teaching methods from older faculty members.

On that day, I was made the chair of the junior level at the school, and although I would continue to teach five sections of tenth-grade world history, I would have an eleventh-grade homeroom and would be in charge of eleventh-grade activities such as the junior-senior prom. I was not yet twenty-four years old. It hadn't really been all that long ago that I was going to the junior-senior prom myself. Things were moving along pretty fast for a guy who had been something of an academic casualty only a few years earlier.

Charleston was proving to be a good place for the Clyburns. Emily had been right about staying there, as she usually was. My expanded role at C. A. Brown was taking me into some other areas of particular interest to me. I spent a season as assistant football coach and even announced the home games for the Panthers football team. I was not only doing well in my job, I was having fun.

I was also beginning to discover other worlds outside the hallways and classrooms of C. A. Brown High School. One of those discoveries began with a knock at my classroom door one afternoon as I was attending to some after-class paperwork. My visitor was a Catholic nun dressed in a traditional habit. She introduced herself as Sister Mary Anthony; director of the nearby Our Lady of Mercy Neighborhood House. I actually recognized her because my stations for recess and school-bus duty were right across the street from the Neighborhood House. We had never spoken, however, and I knew little of the operation she managed, except that it seemed to attract a lot of youngsters during various times of the day.

She proceeded to describe the Neighborhood House and its mission and explain why she had come to visit me. She had observed, she told me, that several of the habitual class cutters who hung out at the playground adjacent to her center would leave the playground and reenter the school building around the same time every day. On inquiry she was told that the students were on their way to attend my world history class.

I smiled and explained to her the special teaching methods I was applying to actively engage my students in the learning process. She acknowledged her suspicions that I must be doing "something right" to attract students who otherwise would have been loitering in the playground and becoming prime prospects for dropping out of school completely in the not-too-distant future.

"That's why I came to see you," she said. "You and I have similar missions, motivating young people." She then invited me to become a volunteer at the Neighborhood House, and a few days later, I accepted. I threw myself into it, recognizing the opportunity to work not only in the classroom, but outside it as well. Sister Anthony was right; we did have the same mission, and before the year was out I had established the first Big Brother program (currently Big Brothers Big Sisters) for black children in South Carolina.

Sister Anthony's visit opened vast new areas of interest for me outside the classroom. I became the adviser to a social club of several remarkably bright male students, who organized to study together and tutor less-motivated students. Through

With the Corsairs (standing third from left). James Gadsden is on my right; Ralph Dawson is seated second from the right; Charles Foster is seated on the far left. Photograph from the C. A. Brown High School yearbook.

these new activities I was beginning to see life from many perspectives—the potential dropouts who were finding some motivation in my classroom, the development of mentors for promising young men and women in the community, and the nurturing of leadership skills in a select group of inspired young male students.

The group named themselves the "Corsairs Club." They were remarkable in many ways. I never knew what brought them together with such a noble mission in life. I do know that becoming their adviser was a life changer for me. They needed a faculty adviser in order to qualify as a school-sanctioned activity, and the fact that they chose me was gratifying in itself. But that was only the beginning.

At once-a-month Monday meetings in my apartment, we explored the world together, the potentials and limits of our shared universe. I conducted trips about the globe, as Paul Sanford had done for us at S.C. State. Like Paul Sanford, I engaged those young men in discussions about world events, including Vietnam, where signs of an impending international crisis were appearing; and Cuba, the political anomaly that lay only ninety miles off the Florida coast. These topics found ready curiosity among them, and rich conversations ensued. But this was not a one-way transaction by any means. I was exposed to the minds, hearts, and souls of young people who had a clear and unshakable view of their future and the role they intended to play in making the world we discussed a better place.

They were serious about life, and in our monthly conversations I realized that they were implanting in me a new seriousness about my own life and the role I would play in events as they unfolded around me. I had walked the streets of Orangeburg, and I had taught in the prickly hallways of Simonton and C. A. Brown. But now I was seeing where it all led, what outcomes there were to be won in a world that looked beyond the traditional boundaries and limitations as defined by race and prejudice.

Here truly in the lives of these young men was the making of a new society for anyone who would pay attention and give it a chance.

And I was right. From that small group of students emerged some remarkable individuals, most notably the young man who became the first black graduate of the Citadel, a future U.S. ambassador to Iceland, and a politically influential Wall Street lawyer.

Stepping Proudly

Charles Foster was the courageous pioneer who broke the color line at the Citadel. He bore all the abuse normally heaped on the first-year Citadel "knobs" with grace; and with amazing fortitude, he bore the additional abuse reserved for a black man. Some of the stories he told me about his treatment at the Citadel were truly grievous, and I'm not certain I could have been as tolerant as he was of the wretched experiences he was forced to endure. But Charles's tolerance was born of the huge reservoir of internal strength and self-worth I had seen in the Corsairs Club. I can still picture him striding proudly down Rutledge Avenue, head held high, in his Citadel uniform. I was proud too.

The Charles Foster story did not have a happy ending. He died in a house fire in Nashville, Tennessee, some years later. But to its great credit, the Citadel did not forget him. A scholarship was established in his honor, and I was honored to deliver the address that commemorated the occasion. Future cadets will remember the example he set for courage and forbearance. I will remember the great promise he showed in those Monday night meetings of the Corsairs Club.

Stepping Beyond Our Shores

From the beginning James Gadsden was curious about world affairs, and our conversations were more than just idle inquiries on his part. On finishing C. A. Brown, James departed for Harvard, where he graduated cum laude with a degree in economics. Two years later, he earned a master's degree from Stanford in East Asian studies and set forth on a career in the foreign service. We stayed in touch—mainly by telephone—and as my career in Congress progressed, I began to get messages from him through other House members who had met James while visiting his various stations. During twenty-five years of service, he served in such disparate places as Hungary, France, and Taiwan, and for five years he was an economic and political officer at the European Union in Brussels.

During my third term in Congress, James was assigned duty in Washington with the State Department, and we began to communicate more frequently. We talked about a lot of things. Then one day I got a phone call from him that meant more than all the others combined. The call affirmed for me that he had not forgotten his days in Charleston with the Corsairs Club and was about to build on that experience. James told me he wanted to design and implement a program for at-risk students at Anacostia High School, a school near the navy shipyards in Southeast Washington, and he wanted me to help kick it off. In those few moments of conversation, I realized that the baton that had been passed from Paul Sanford at S.C. State to Jim Clyburn at

With former student James Gadsden (left), after he was sworn in as U.S. ambassador to Iceland, 2002

C. A. Brown High School was being extended for yet another lap to James Gadsden at Anacostia High School in Washington, D.C. The world seemed to me to be a lot better place after that phone call.

The James Gadsden story does not end there. Some years later—in 2002—another phone call brought the extraordinary news that James Gadsden, whom I had once known as the little black boy from Coming Street in Charleston, was going to become the U.S. ambassador to Iceland. He invited me to the swearing-in ceremony at the State Department. It took some rearranging of my schedule to be there, but this was one event I would have flown halfway around the world to attend.

Just before the program began, I was ushered to a special place on the floor to stand during the ceremony. Probably for the visitor from Congress, I figured. James was sworn in by a deputy secretary of state. When the time came for James to speak, he recognized family members, schoolmates, and others in the room who had influenced and inspired him. Then he thanked me for being there and spoke three sentences I will never forget. I was credited, in his words, for "introducing me to a world far beyond our shores. I wish all of you could have spent time in his classroom. You would never be the same." I was glad I wasn't called on to say anything after that. I couldn't have spoken a word.

The Wobbler

Not all the members of the Corsairs Club were what you might call "model students." They were smart, hardworking, and highly motivated. But they had distinct styles and personalities, and some of them could be downright troublesome at times. One such case was Ralph Dawson, a good student who did not mind challenging authority. I guess I saw a lot of myself in him, and while I admired his traits, some other teachers felt differently. One day, a few months after I had left C. A. Brown, I got a call from one of his classmates telling me that Ralph had been kicked out of school. I immediately left for the school, visited with the teacher, and found out that Ralph had indeed gotten out of hand. But I negotiated some terms under which Ralph could return. Then I headed for Ralph's house.

I told Ralph that I was there to take him back to school, but only on the terms I had negotiated with his teacher; he would have to stand in front of the class and apologize to the teacher.

Ralph was having no part of that, and he summarily refused. That's when I went to Plan B. I told him that he had a choice: he could go back to school with me and apologize to the teacher or—using my best Charleston street dialect—he would have to "whip my ass."

I heaved a sigh of relief when Ralph took option number one. He grudgingly got in the car. We did not speak during the short ride to C. A. Brown. His apology, accomplished only after some bobbing and wobbling in front of the class, was hardly a thing of beauty and conviction, but it was good enough to get him back in school that day and set him back on the road to graduation.

Ralph Dawson wound up at Yale University, where during his freshman year he roomed with another strong-minded individual, a white guy named Howard Dean, who went on to become governor of Vermont and a Democratic candidate for president. While I can only imagine the exchanges between those two men, Ralph later provided an account of some of their conversations for an article in the January 12, 2004, issue of the *New Yorker:* "When it came to race," he was quoted as saying, "Howard was not patronizing in any way. He was willing to confront in discussion what a lot of white students were not willing to confront. He would hold his ground. He would respect the fact that I knew forty-two million times more about being black than he did, but that didn't mean he couldn't hold a view on something related to civil rights that would be as valid as mine." I can just hear those conversations now. Howard Dean and Ralph Dawson going toe to toe would have been something to watch.

Ralph Dawson went on to Columbia University Law School and is now a partner in the prestigious New York labor law firm of Fulbright and Jaworski. He also became prominent in the New York State Democratic Party, and when I was working to swing superdelegates toward the Obama camp prior to the 2008 convention, Ralph Dawson, my Corsairs Club friend, provided one of those crucial last-minute commitments.

Who would have imagined men such as Foster, Gadsden, and Dawson coming from those Monday meetings in the Clyburns' apartment? But then, it might have been an even longer shot to predict a world history teacher from Charleston's C. A. Brown High School winding up in the U.S. Congress.

Three Steps and a Slide

My life in those days was hardly pointing toward a career in Congress. One morning while I was apartment hunting in Charleston, I noticed that there was an announcement of a bowling alley being opened in downtown Charleston that would cater to black bowlers. That announcement was riveting to me, and I quickly sought out the owners and passed myself off as an experienced bowler who would be willing to work full time or part time when the new establishment opened. For all the nobility of teaching the rising generation of young men and women, there was the economic reality of supporting a family on a teacher's salary. I was open to a more lucrative career opportunity, and besides I loved bowling.

The job interview consisted of bowling a three-game set with Johnny Williams, who was representing the owners, Eugene Skinner and Kenneth Renken. Some years later I got to know Renken's daughter, Peggy Renken Hudson, who became governmental relations director for two trade associations in Washington. As for the job interview with Johnny Williams, I bowled well enough for Johnny to offer me a part-time job organizing leagues and developing young bowlers at the new all-black facility, Fun Bowl, which was due to open in September 1962, about the same time as school started.

I accepted the job. Bowling was a fairly new thing for black people at the time, but I was able to organize adult leagues for four nights a week and Saturday morning leagues for children. I became a certified bowling instructor as the only black person at a "whites-only" bowling alley in Savannah, Georgia, and I was making forty dollars a week, thirty-two after taxes. I also got the benefit of bowling for fifteen cents a line, which was considerably better than the fifty cents a line it cost the paying public.

The real benefit, however, came from what we called "pot bowling," which was the gambling side of the sport. While the forty dollars a week was good supplemental money for a teacher's salary, "pot bowling" was even better. In addition to betting among ourselves at Fun Bowl, several of us spent one weekend a month traveling a circuit between Charleston, Augusta and Savannah, Georgia, and occasionally Ocala, Florida. I didn't always win, but I won much more often than I lost. For a while I was pocketing more at pot bowling in a month than my teacher's salary. Besides I was having a lot of fun, and some of the money that came from these gambling activities went into my work at the Neighborhood House and refreshments at the Corsairs Club meetings. I was becoming, in certain ways, a professional bowler, you might say.

I was also coming into contact with the wide variety of people who were frequenting the new Fun Bowl lanes. I was getting to know all manner of people—students, teachers, lawyers, sheet-metal workers, beauticians, barbers, doctors, plumbers, and many more. For a guy who had it lodged in the back of his brain that someday he might want to enter the political world, it was a priceless educational experience.

I was also learning a little about human nature and the fine art of personal and public relations at a rather basic level. These were days when the American Machine and Foundry (AMF) Company was asserting itself as leader in the manufacturing and marketing of bowling equipment. They held weeklong sessions around the country to train people in promotional strategies and tactics. An AMF representative was sent to Charleston to invite Fun Bowl's ownership to send someone to a training session in Chattanooga, Tennessee. As Fun Bowl's leagues promotions manager, I was the likely candidate. But, for whatever reason, I was never brought into the conversations. Word was spread that I would be the choice, but no one ever bothered to tell me. I guess that's what you'd call "management by indirection." At any rate an exit conference was called with the AMF guy for one Saturday morning at 9:30. I heard about the meeting from Leroy "Teaky" Russell, the guy who oiled and polished the lanes.

The meeting time happened to coincide with the time I was planning to pick up my tenth-month paycheck from C. A. Brown and Emily's from Burke High School. Emily was in Atlanta attending a summer session for a master's degree program at Atlanta University. I guess I could have arranged to pick up the checks at another time. Although Teaky and I were very good friends, I didn't like the idea of learning of the meeting from him, and I told him what my plans were for that Saturday morning. It was not a matter of status differences that bothered me; it was a matter of the pecking order. Teaky was not the human-resources manager. So, while I was out retrieving Emily's and my checks from our respective schools, I intentionally took my time getting to Fun Bowl. When I got to C. A. Brown around 9:45, there was a telephone message that I was needed at the bowling alley. When I got to the bowling alley around 10:15, Johnny Williams, Eugene Skinner, and the AMF representative were waiting for me and had been since 9:30. As I walked toward the table where they were sitting, I waved at Teaky who was pretending to be busy oiling the lanes but was intently observing the episode. When I reached the table I apologized for being late and explained that I hadn't been told of the meeting. There was some squirming around the table and exchanges of glances among the three of them. Then we got on to the meeting and discussed the training and my availability to attend.

As the meeting ended, Eugene Skinner turned to me and said that he understood that Emily was attending Atlanta University for the summer and I would pass through Atlanta on the way to Chattanooga. He suggested that I might want to leave early enough to spend the weekend before the conference in Atlanta with Emily and handed me a hundred dollar bill. I readily accepted the offer.

He also told me he understood why I was late and appreciated the message I was sending up the management chain. Sometimes it takes gestures like that to get attention, I realized, and to prevent being taken for granted.

Later that day, Teaky said to me that if he had not seen it, he would not believe that I "would have the nerve to keep two white men waiting." I also tucked away a lesson for my own future reference: don't play games with people. Be direct and be clear. In my own mind it became my "Teaky Rule."

10 | *Two Steps Forward*

For all the good outcomes I was beginning to feel in the various aspects of my life, I was becoming restless. I wasn't sure that I wanted my goal in life to be a high school principal or a bowling alley manager. I wasn't sure that the satisfaction of my volunteer work would sustain me or get me to where I wanted to be. That was the decision-making table among the power brokers. I was beginning to wonder how to get to that table and which doors needed to be opened for me to get started on my trip.

One day I got a call from my S.C. State classmate and lifelong friend Elijah "Baby" Rogers, who was living in Columbia, teaching in Winnsboro, and hating every minute of it. Baby was spending every waking minute looking for opportunities to escape the classroom, and I was beginning to share his anxieties. He told me that the South Carolina Employment Security Commission was about to implement a new program under the Manpower Development and Training Act (MDTA) of 1963. They were going to establish two Youth Opportunity Centers (YOCs), one in Columbia and the other in Charleston.

The Employment Security Commission had never been known as one of the more racially enlightened and progressive agencies of state government, and when I went to the local office to inquire about the new program, I was told stiffly that I would need to be on a register to qualify, and to be on a register, I would need to take and pass an aptitude test. That clerk seemed to be saying that such would be enough to disqualify a wretch as lowly and vile as me. With persistence, however, I smiled the smile of a South Carolina State graduate and holder of an "A" teacher's certificate and filled out an application to take the test.

The test—of course—would be administered in Columbia, more than a hundred miles away. And of course the 1960s were not known to be good times for stirring entrenched agency interests in "customer service." The welfare agency was known to close its doors promptly at five o'clock every day, no matter how many people were standing in line. In the case of the Employment Security Commission, if you wanted to apply for a job in Charleston then—of course—you would be required to drive to Columbia. But by now I had gotten the steps of the Charleston shuffle down pretty well so shuffling to the west on I-26 one more time would not be a problem.

That's what I did—probably to the surprise and consternation of my officious friend at the Employment Security Commission. I was informed by mail that I had met the qualifications to be an "employment counselor" and a "youth opportunity specialist," whatever that meant. I was granted an interview with J. Graham Altman Sr., the manager of the Charleston office of the Employment Security Commission, a remarkable man who, I was told, had only a high school education. He promptly told me I was going to be hired.

The news was met with very little fanfare down the hallways of the Employment Security Commission. Baby and I were the only two black people to apply. He got the job in Columbia, and I got the job in Charleston. The director of the YOC, a Mr. Ed Beasley, seemed less than pleased about the whole business. He gave me less than two weeks to report for work, thinking, as had the clerical woman some weeks earlier, that the short notice might serve as a deterrent. But N. L. Manigault was once again my champion. He said he would "handle it." And he did. I was finding those Omega men to be pretty good people.

And thus it was that I embarked on my state-government career. As it turned out, Mr. Beasley wasn't the only unenthusiastic soul as I took my place on the YOC staff. There were a few welcoming folks—three of them, I believe—and I actually made a couple of good friends in those early, chilly days. J. Bradley "Brad" Fowler became a very good friend and reintroduced me to the game of golf as my sport of choice after my heavy indulgence in bowling. His wife at the time, Sandra, remains a close friend and confidant.

Then things really began to wobble in the Clyburn household. A few months after I started at the Charleston YOC, my friend Baby Rogers was accepted into graduate school at Howard University. About that time, Emily got offers for librarianships at the Veterans Administration Hospitals in Augusta and Columbia, and she wanted to accept the one in Columbia. So Baby and I orchestrated things so that I could be transferred from Charleston to Columbia to take over his old job. It was time to shuffle back to the west so we shuffled up Interstate 26 to once again settle our family in the state's capital city.

Neighborhood Youth Corps and New Careers

For all the good prospects of jobs and career opportunities in Columbia, however, I missed Charleston. It's a city that can do that to you, and the political bug was beginning to bite as well. I did not feel that Columbia was the place for me to launch a political career. I wasn't sure that Charleston was either, but at least I could count a few agreeable souls there who might listen to my hopes and dreams.

Not only did I have aspirations for public office, but I was missing the stimulation of the community work I had found with Sister Anthony and others. There was a connection between my volunteer work and my political ambitions. If I was going to solve the problems and meet the needs of those I was helping in my community work, what better way was there to do it than through public office? At age twenty-five, I was beginning to feel some rationale and direction in my life, and the timing seemed right.

My experiences with the Youth Opportunity Center and the work with the Neighborhood House and the Big Brother Program had begun to get some attention from community leaders. In fact Vice President Hubert Humphrey had cited me and my work with the Big Brothers Program in a Sunday newspaper insert. Those were the days of Lyndon Johnson's presidency, and the Great Society was in full blossom. Despite political grumpiness from some state leaders in South Carolina, the War on Poverty was not only providing new programs and services for low-income families in the state; it was also opening new jobs and career opportunities for black professionals.

Three months after leaving Charleston I began getting feelers as to whether I would be interested in taking over a new program in Charleston that would be administered by one of the Great Society's mainstay local organizations, the Community Action Agency (Programs), or CAP. It would be a county-wide job training project administered and funded by the U.S. Department of Labor.

This would be the second major program overseen by the Charleston CAP. The first—Head Start—was administered by a white woman. Conventional wisdom of the progressive 1960s suggested that the second CAP program would be therefore managed by a black administrator, and my name had become prominent in local conversations.

The main backers of my candidacy, I learned, were the folks who were connected to Our Lady of Mercy Neighborhood House, where I had volunteered while teaching at C. A. Brown, and St. John Mission Center, a similar activity on Charleston's East Side under the sponsorship of the Episcopal Church. Wasn't that an interesting development, I thought, this Church of God evangelical guy from Sumter being promoted by the two "high" churches in Charleston—the Catholic and Episcopalian? I'm not sure how my Dad would take to that. My guess is he would never think twice about it. He was pretty ecumenical when it came to programs to help people in need.

I was not aggressive in pursuit of the job, but during the next few weeks, I came to know two influential Charlestonians who would play important roles in my life. One was Father Henry Grant, the Episcopal minister who was director of the St. John Center and chairman of the board of the CAP agency. Father Grant and I had lived in adjacent apartment buildings, but we did not know each other well. The other was Marybelle Howe, the wife of a former solicitor for the Charleston Circuit, Gedney Howe Jr., who was the city's most prominent politician at that time. Mrs. Howe was involved in just about every community-based program in Charleston and was an active member of Church Women United.

Whatever ambivalence I may have felt about my interest in the job were erased about eleven o'clock one night early in January 1966, when I returned home from one of my frequent trips to the bowling alley. There was a note that Father Grant had called and wanted me to call him back, no matter how late. Not knowing the nature of the call, I sat on the side of the bed and returned the call.

To my surprise and some dismay, Father Grant wanted to know if I was interested in becoming director of the Neighborhood Youth Corps. He was insistent—as Father Grant could often be—in getting answers. But I was sitting only a few feet from Emily, whom I had not told about any of the possible job opportunities. My answers to Father Grant's insistent questions were pretty awkward, and I promised him we would resume the conversation the next morning. "We are interested in you," he concluded the conversation, "and if you are interested in the job, you need to apply right away."

The next morning, I wasted no time getting to the office and calling Father Grant. He was a little miffed at what he thought was my lack of forthrightness the night before, thinking I was playing "hard to get." Far from it, I assured the hard-driving priest, I was just not ready for my wife to learn of the job opportunity by way of an overheard phone call. I assured him, in fact, that I would not only be applying for the job, but I would also be delighted to accept it—if offered—and would be looking forward to a return to Charleston.

And so in April 1966, after only six months in Columbia, I became director of the Neighborhood Youth Corps, and we pointed the Ford Falcon back down Interstate 26 and returned to Charleston, the next step to the east in what was becoming an energetic "Charleston shuffle" for our family. Our absence from Charleston was so brief that a few of our acquaintances hardly knew we had left.

The Neighborhood Youth Corps job turned out to be something of a leap of faith. The U.S. Labor Department had funded the program for only seven months, and that's all the time I had to prove that the program should be refunded. The salary for the seven months was forty-nine thousand dollars, more than double what I was making for a full year at the Youth Opportunity Center. I figured it was a gamble well worth taking, and besides I had always been a pretty good gambler.

My appointment got quite a bit of coverage in the local press, and it wasn't long before I was on the receiving end of a rather painful lesson in Charleston black culture. Shortly after accepting the position, I was visited by a native Charlestonian I had considered a friend. But this was not a courtesy or congratulatory call. She told me that she had applied for the job and felt that she should have gotten it. Then she proceeded to give me two reasons. First, she said, using an old Gullah term, I was a "cumya," meaning not a native Charlestonian, and she was a "benya," meaning she was. Second, she noted, her skin tone was lighter than mine. The job should have been hers because as a rule such positions in Charleston always went to mulattos. She even cited Wilmot Fraser as an exception to the rule.

Still reeling from that surprising piece of information, I was subsequently contacted by a Charleston blue blood of the Caucasian persuasion. Her name was Mrs. Rowena Tobias, and she also gave me some introductory wisdom about Charleston. Hers was quite a bit more pleasant but no less surprising. She invited me to her home on South Battery, a street where black people were traditionally told to enter through the back door. I was greeted out front, and quickly discovered that this was not a meeting of several scions of old Charleston, this was to be just the two of us—Mrs. Tobias and me—over tea of course.

She began by telling me that she had been following my career and was impressed with me and the potential impact I might have on Charleston and the state. She then gave me a brief history lesson, recalling that the Charleston port, at some distant time in its past, had been the center of commerce for the East Coast. The city's strength, she said, had always lain in its ability to address and solve problems by discussing them openly and working together until a solution was found. That approach seemed to work, Mrs. Tobias said, on all the city's problems but one—the problem of race. She said that, whenever the issue of race came up, people stopped talking. Until Charlestonians were willing to address race with the same openness and candor that they discussed other issues, she told me with deep conviction, the problem would continue to be vexing and damaging to the city's well-being.

Then Mrs. Tobias got direct with me, and I came to understand how she could value the qualities of candor and openness. "I appreciate the frankness with which you seem to deal with these issues," she said, "and I want you to make me a promise. Promise me that when the issue of race comes up in our city, you won't stop talking." I made her that promise, and I think I have kept it.

Even though I had lived in Charleston for four years as a schoolteacher and community organizer, I guess this was my official greeting to a position of some influence. Within a few days, I had been criticized by a black woman for taking a job she had wanted and thought she should have gotten because of the differences in our pigmentation, and I was praised by a white woman and told to keep discussions on the issue of race alive in the city. Charleston is a place I will always love but have never been able to figure out.

As it turned out, Charlestonians were perfectly capable of discussing race, just not always in a very productive way. Most of the new community-based programs in which I was either professionally involved or personally interested carried with them nondiscrimination clauses and policies. That meant the Head Start program had to be racially integrated, and the same was true of the Neighborhood Youth Corps, which I had just been hired to supervise. My staff was racially integrated. This didn't suit a lot of old Charleston of course, and I began to understand and appreciate the words of wisdom from Rowena Tobias. Moving from the sheltered confines of all-black schools into the bright light of newly desegregated community programs was a bit more contentious than I had expected. But I had promised Mrs. Tobias that I would stay at it, which is what I intended to do anyhow.

One day I looked up and saw Marybelle Howe coming through the door of my office. Wondering what new hell she was bringing to my attention, I braced myself. She handed me one of those display-size cards, which bore the Latin phrase "Illegitimi non carborundum"—translated into English as "Don't let the bastards grind you down." Charleston was a place of unending puzzles and contradictions. For all its racial polarization, there was no city in America with a greater history and tradition of black pride and tradition. All of Charleston society—black and white, below Broad Street and above—was stratified, I was learning, and had an air of exclusivity and elitism about it. The kid from Sumter would have a tough time cracking either side of it.

The Neighborhood Youth Corps was a jobs program for at-risk youngsters, and it had two components. One was for in-school students and offered fifteen hours a week of work in part-time jobs. The other was for high school dropouts and provided thirty-two hours of work. Both programs were scaled at $1.25 per hour, the minimum wage. It was a good concept, and I found myself dealing with some of the same

With Laura Martinez (on my left) and two Neighborhood Youth Corps students leaving Charleston to attend Wilberforce University in 1967. Clyburn Papers, South Carolina State University.

population of young people I had come to know at Simonton, C. A. Brown, and Sister Anthony's outreach programs.

But Charleston being what it was, it was hard to find agencies willing to hire these young people. One day, out of frustration, Laura Martinez, my job developer, who happened to be white, lamented the shameful attitude people had toward these young people and offhandedly exclaimed, "It would probably be easier getting these kids into college than finding them dollar and a quarter an hour jobs."

It got me to thinking. Why not look into the possibility of getting them into college?

The next morning, I dispatched Laura and another employee, Martha Hook, to the Charleston library, and they spent a week researching grants and scholarships for low-income high school graduates. As it turned out, Laura had been right. It was easier to get these kids into college than it was to find them minimum-wage jobs in Charleston. This research also led us to apply for a Talent Search grant shortly after I left the Neighborhood Youth Corps, and we were successful.

We created a Talent Search program and wound up placing hundreds of high school graduates in colleges and universities all over the nation. Our flagship school was Wilberforce University, near Xenia, Ohio, one of the oldest African American colleges in America and a place of refuge over the years for many distinguished South Carolinians. We got a lot of good attention throughout the lowcountry and beyond the borders of our little state. Maybe Jim Clyburn was becoming known in Charleston as something other than a racial trouble maker I thought, and maybe Rowena Tobias was noting that I was keeping my promise to her. Maybe I was even getting some attention among black Charlestonians, as well, despite the fact that I wasn't a mulatto.

The political unrest of the summer of 1968 throughout the country was being felt in Charleston and extending into the human service community itself. The top job at CAP came open. It was a big deal. The CAP organization was in many ways the signature agency of the Great Society program. It was the local implementing agency of the many programs of the Office of Economic Opportunity (OEO), and as such it was the front-line unit of the War on Poverty.

I was being encouraged to apply for the CAP director's job by some of the same people who had paved the way for my taking the job at the Neighborhood Youth Corps. Father Grant and Marybelle Howe were on the governing boards of both agencies, which made for some interesting political dynamics. I informed them that I would apply for the job, knowing that it would be a long shot. Neither one of them discouraged me from doing so, but neither encouraged me either. I soon found out why.

In the meantime things were stirring elsewhere in the Charleston human service community. One of the agencies I came to know during my work with the Neighborhood Youth Corps was a nonprofit, the S.C. Commission for Farm Workers (SCCFW), which worked to improve conditions for migrants and seasonal farm workers. The commission had hired as its executive director Dewey Duckett of Columbia, a man I had gotten to know during my brief career in Columbia with the Youth Opportunity Center there. A few days after he took the job with the Commission for Farm Workers, I dropped by to pay a courtesy call and to welcome him to Charleston.

What I found was a little unsettling. The attitude and demeanor of several employees seemed troublesome to me. I mentioned it to Dewey, but he seemed oblivious to what seemed obvious to me. I had a strong gut feeling that Dewey Duckett was in for some tough times at the Commission for Farm Workers.

It turned out that I was correct in my assessment. It wasn't long before he was under siege, and things were not made easier by the fact that he had decided not to move his residence to Charleston. He continued to commute from his home in Columbia. I had been around Charleston long enough to know that if there's one thing Charlestonians can't abide, it's having a Columbian running a Charleston agency.

That—and other transgressions—made Dewey's stay with the farm workers agency a short one. All this was transpiring while CAP was looking for a new director. So it wasn't long before there were two openings in the Charleston area, one for a CAP director and the other for someone to succeed Dewey Duckett at the Commission for Farm Workers. My interview for the CAP director's job did not go well, and part of the problem seemed to be coming from my friends. For example, during the interview, Mrs. Howe asked me if I had ever fired anybody. When I answered "no," she asked me if I had the guts to fire anybody. Hardly a friendly question, I thought. When I said that I did, she seemed unconvinced.

There seemed to be three factors working against me: they thought I was too young; they thought I wasn't tough enough; and they thought the community was not ready for a black person in the position. It didn't take a genius to figure out that the third factor was causing a lot of the unrest in the community and among board members, and when the final decision was made, the job went to David Wesley Clark, a white minister from Columbia.

Father Grant and Marybelle Howe were conflicted over the CAP director hiring, and I let them know how disappointed I was. Shortly thereafter some interesting political dynamics kicked in, and I was offered the position Dewey Duckett had recently vacated at the SCCFW. I took the job as something of a consolation prize and began the process of making myself an advocate for decent living and working conditions for the seasonal migrants and area farm workers who picked crops across the lowcountry farmlands.

The Communists and the Klan

This new position didn't prove to be a walk in the park. Dewey Duckett had never gotten control of the agency, and when he left things were in disarray. But there were other foreboding issues. It seemed there were communists on Johns Island, or at least that was the contention of SCCFW's bookkeeper, who was reputed to be a member of the John Birch Society. He was feeding information to longtime First District congressman L. Mendel Rivers, a communist fighter if there ever was one. There was a call for an investigation of my hiring and the agency's activities. I had been called a lot of things in my young life, but "communist" was not one of them. As for the other activities, I hardly found anything sinister about providing workers with self-help housing, health care, and adult-education programs. But then I never did know much about the thinking of those who worried about communists on Johns Island. In the end there was no investigation.

If a communist conspiracy was not high on my list of worries, however, the Ku Klux Klan was. It seemed that our agency's adult-education program for seasonal farm workers was being housed in a building owned by a man who was purported to be either a member of or a sympathizer with the Klan. The building was near the intersection of U.S. 17 and S.C. 162, and I remembered that the first cross burning I ever saw was on that property. Having a part of our operation located where a KKK cross had been burned just wouldn't do, and it bothered me even further that one of the staff members knew about it and was not inclined to act on it. The staff member, Al Fields, was a good guy and a fellow Mather graduate. Al had served as interim director of the agency, and as I took over as full-time director, he made it clear he wanted to stay on as my deputy. His indifference to the KKK-related property worried me, though, and I was learning that while he was good at things that were process driven, he was limited in other areas of management. Using the "Teaky Rule" I had developed in my other life as a bowling-alley guy, I went directly to Al, told him of my concerns, and then pointed him in another direction. I made him housing director for the agency, and his first assignment was to terminate our rental arrangement on the property whose owner was identified as being connected with the Ku Klux Klan.

Al's next project was finding an alternative site for the adult-education program. Such a site soon became available on property next to a small rural church in the area, and we used the self-help process, which was employed in erecting housing for the seasonal migrant workers, to construct a building for the adult-education center on the property next to the church. I was off to a good start in my new job, and Al was becoming quite good in his role as housing director. It was not an easy job, and I became impressed with how well he was doing in finding good, scattered sites for our self-help housing programs in Sumter, Williamsburg, and Dorchester Counties. But Charleston County was presenting significant problems. In every board meeting the issue of the lack of progress with the Charleston component of the self-help housing program occupied a significant amount of time and discussion. I knew that my success or failure at the SCCFW would in large measure be determined by how well I did with this component.

We needed an acre for each house to accommodate septic tanks, and organizing seasonal farm workers to move from site to site was a complicated problem. I decided it could be solved by creating a self-help community, and I dispatched Al to meet with Arthur Ravenel, a Republican activist, to get his assistance in finding a fifteen- to twenty-acre site that could become a small self-help housing community.

Calling on Arthur Ravenel for help was not all that big a deal. I had identified as a Republican in my early days. My dad was a Republican, as were most politically active black people in the pre-Goldwater, pre-Thurmond days of the party. I had actually taken Richard Nixon's side in a debate during my college days, and that's all that was needed to get Ravenel's favorable attention. He was in the real-estate business, and in little time he found us a good twenty-acre site on Yonges Island near Adams Run, and we bought it.

The new site helped me with another problem, that of morale among the self-help families. Things had been sort of half-hearted around the agency for a while, and morale problems were building. With the purchase of the new site, I was able to negotiate with the federal government (the Farmers Home Administration) for a new and special plan for constructing self-help housing. Under the plan, the worker families would dig the foundation of the new housing community, and our agency would contract with a private company with expertise in the prefabrication business to "dry in" the houses, a term of the trade that meant they would wall in the buildings and put on the roofs. The families would then earn their "sweat equity" by finishing the rest of the houses.

It turned out that the Farmers Home Administration liked the novelty of the plan and approved it. A self-help housing community was born on Yonges Island, and the SCCFW was establishing itself as a credible organization in the lowcountry of South Carolina. I was pretty damned pleased with myself and with the way things were turning around with the SCCFW, particularly after their earlier missteps with the previous director.

Breaking Ground

I felt so good about getting this done I decided to reach right to the top of the state's political structure and invite Governor Robert E. McNair, to officiate at the ground-breaking ceremony of the housing project. My call to the governor's office was referred to a staff member, Phil Grose, who became a very important professional and personal friend in the decades to come. Phil called back a few days later to let me know that the governor was otherwise occupied that day. But, he asked, "How about the lieutenant governor?"

I was aware that Lieutenant Governor John West was planning to run for governor in 1970 and that Phil was helping to lay the foundation for the run. West, a Democrat, understood that the black vote—which, because of the 1965 Voting Rights Act, had grown tremendously since the last general election—could be crucial to his success. I issued the invitation, and he accepted. The date was set for August 16. That proved to be a date, I would later reminisce, on which I not only met the second-ranking political officer in the state, I made an acquaintance—and initiated a friendship—that endured until John West's death some four decades later. My dad would have probably said that our meeting was "ordered."

Before my link-up with John West, however, an even more important event took place on that date, one that took precedent over everything else. The night before the ground breaking, I stayed up late planning and fretting over the big event and worrying about things that could go wrong. I had just drifted off to sleep when Emily awoke me with the news that the arrival of our second-born child was upon us. Suddenly, the thought of John West, self-help housing, and seasonal farm workers in general vanished from my consciousness, and Emily and I headed for the hospital.

As it turned out, our newcomer, Jennifer Lynn, arrived in good time, 8:00 A.M. to be exact. Jennifer's well-timed birth allowed me to welcome her into the world, dash home, take a quick shower, get dressed, and head out to Yonges Island in time for the 11:00 A.M. ceremony. The short trip allowed me to refocus on the event and some of its details. John West would no doubt be pleased to see in attendance one of my prominent board members, Marybelle Howe, whose husband, Gedney Howe Jr., was considered to be "Mr. Democrat" in Charleston County.

I had to remember to make sure that West and Mrs. Howe got together for a conversation. I also had to mention to West that this self-help housing project was a really big accomplishment for the Commission for Farm Workers, and by inference James E. Clyburn. It was something the organization had been trying to do for years, and it was something the new director, his board, and his staff were getting done.

And then I began to worry about the task of actually getting the housing community built. It was a long way from a ground-breaking ceremony to actual completion of the project; in fact that was the hard part. A lot of people had a lot at stake in the successful completion of the project—our board and staff, the workers' families who would be occupying the homes, the farmers who employed the workers, the Farmers Home Administration, which was funding it, and not the least of all, James E. Clyburn himself, who had people such as Rowena Tobias and the Charleston "benyas" keeping an eye on him. As I pulled up to the site, I saw that people had already begun to arrive. I greeted them with the really important news of the day—that I was a father again—and there was much good cheer over that event.

Then the black sedan bearing the lieutenant governor arrived with John West himself at the wheel. It was a good gesture for the beginning of a program concentrating on self-help, and I quickly greeted him with a handshake and an expression of appreciation. He took me aside and asked for some details on the event.

Aside from mentioning the arrival of our new daughter, I explained what the housing concept was all about, and he listened intently. A few minutes later, I introduced him to the group as the next governor of the state, and he followed through with a speech that not only made me and the SCCFW look good, it also made low-income housing sound like one of the major issues facing the state of South Carolina. He sounded as if he had a thorough familiarity with our housing concept.

I was not only relieved at his presentation, I was floored by his grasp and comfort with the topic. He was a "quick study" if there ever was one, and I was beginning to understand what would make him a good leader and a remarkably strong governor. It wasn't a shallow performance either. In a few months, John West was elected governor, and low-income housing was one of the major items in his inaugural address.

As we worked our way back to his car, he told me how impressed he was with what I was doing. He also told me that he definitely planned to run for governor the next year, 1970, and if he got elected, he would like for me to consider coming to work for him. I thanked him for the gesture, but never gave his comments any serious thought.

Breaking ground for the self-help project was only part of what was bringing the SCCFW to a position of prominence. Overarching all that we were doing was the Talent Search grant we received, which allowed me to bring my star performers from the Neighborhood Youth Corps—Laura Martinez and Marty Hook—over to the SCCFW. They hit the ground running, and in no time they were generating college opportunities for the children of seasonal farm workers from our service area that had been made available to low-income high school students in Charleston. In a three-or-four year span, we were able to send around four hundred of these students from the lowcountry and Sumter and Williamsburg counties to college.

I realized that I was beginning to take on a role of "rainmaker" among certain segments of the population, and it was stirring in me some long-held ambitions. My eyes were being opened to the vast array of opportunities that lay out there for positive and productive work in such critical areas of education, housing, and employment. It was also opening my own eyes to the notion that maybe I did—after all—have what it took to be a good politician and a successful publicly elected officeholder. I could feel the fire burning in my belly.

11 | *One Step to the Rear*

A lot of things were making the late 1960s a time of crisis in America and a time of growing tension in South Carolina. In 1968 state law-enforcement officers opened fire upon students on the front lawn of South Carolina State in Orangeburg. Three of the students, who had been protesting a segregated bowling alley, died in the incident, which became known as the Orangeburg Massacre. That same year, Dr. Martin Luther King Jr. and Senator Bobby Kennedy were assassinated, and a little later that summer thousands of protestors turned the Democratic National Convention into a chaotic event.

A year later, hundreds of black hospital workers at the Medical College of South Carolina and scores of City of Charleston garbage workers went on strike over wages and working conditions, and I immediately identified with their cause. I had come to know many of the workers and their families, and I knew firsthand of the abuse and discrimination they were suffering. The Medical College at the time was a bastion of old-time racial prejudices, and the strike seemed almost an inevitable outgrowth of those realities.

Charleston was split into several camps. Most white families opposed the strike, and they became worried about issues of public safety as the strikers took to the streets. Among black Charlestonians there was reluctance among older conservatives to take sides, at least early in the strike. There was no reluctance, however, among my friends and associates, who had been fighting for change for years before things came to a head at the Medical College.

Father Henry Grant took a leading role. He had been made chairman of the bi-racial Community Relations Council a year earlier, and he told the Charleston Rotary Club to get ready for "a long, hot summer." The involvement of the Southern Christian Leadership Conference (SCLC) and the AFL-CIO in support of the strikers' new union, local 1199-B, brought national attention to the strike. It also brought new divisions.

As the strike materialized, I became acquainted with its leaders, including Mary Moultrie, its undisputed leader, and William "Bill" Saunders, its top spokesman. The hospital and garbage workers' strikes ended with some concessions on both sides and with a feeling of relief on the part of Charleston in general. There was no appreciable violence, and the settlements were worked out with state and city governments and local leadership. In fact I played the role of chief negotiator with the city on behalf of

With Senator Ernest "Fritz" Hollings at a Young Democrats barbeque on Johns Island.
Clyburn Papers, South Carolina State University.

the garbage workers. Out of it all, there emerged a new sense of unity among Charleston's black political leadership, and for Jim Clyburn there was a new sense of urgency about running for public office.

I was twenty-nine years old. I had established myself professionally in the classroom and in a broad range of community responsibilities and volunteer activities. Since leaving the classroom, I had joined the Charleston County Young Democrats and was active in an organization known as the Charleston County Political Action Committee (PAC). These were days when J. Palmer Gaillard was the powerful mayor of the city, and Charleston politics was dominated by the tightly organized downtown power structure known by some as the "Broad Street Gang." PAC, headed by Herbert Fielding and advertised as an independent organization, was considered the black arm of that downtown group.

As black political influence was increasingly being felt in the city, Mayor Gaillard made it known that he would endorse a black candidate for city council in the upcoming citywide elections. His choice was a prominent businessman, St. Julian Devine, the owner and operator of a moving and hauling company. When the PAC also endorsed his candidacy, his election became virtually assured.

Even so a group of us decided we needed to organize a campaign for Devine, and we started holding meetings to figure out what needed to be done. In a meeting one evening I mentioned that we should adopt a campaign slogan, and when asked for one, I suggested, "Devine for Ward Nine," referencing his home precinct, which rhymed with his name and of course it was 1969. The slogan caught on, and before the meeting was over I had been drafted to be the campaign coordinator by Richard Fields, who was considered to be Charleston's most influential black attorney (and in whose office we were meeting, as we often did).

The designation actually gave me a good feeling, however, particularly being this young guy from Sumter. The "benyas" were listening to this "cumya." When I told Emily later that evening with a little pride what had happened, she let me know—to my utter surprise—that St. Julian Devine was a relative of hers.

The next morning, I paid a call on the candidate at his Cooper Street home, and I relayed the conversation I had had with Emily the night before. He asked her maiden name, and when I told him, he yelled to his wife, "Mr. Clyburn is married to P. J. England's daughter." It made quite a difference in my status almost instantly. At the next PAC meeting, St. Julian Devine announced to the group that he and I "were family." From that moment on, I was much less of a "cumya" around crusty old Charleston.

Devine won the election, becoming the first black member of Charleston City Council since Reconstruction, and I was given some of the credit. It was considered something of an "establishment" victory for Charleston, since Devine had the mayor's endorsement, and I guess it was good for me to be associated with the "power structure."

I was beginning to realize that I was emerging with something of a hybrid political identity. I was the S.C. State graduate who had been jailed for student protests. But I was also the classroom teacher who had been head of the eleventh-grade level at C. A. Brown, and I had gotten college scholarships for hundreds of needy high school graduates. I had also been heavily involved in the Medical College hospital strike and the City of Charleston garbage workers' strike, and I had coordinated St. Julian Devine's successful campaign for City Council. People were having trouble putting me in a pigeonhole. And I liked it that way.

Down deep, the rebel in me was still very much alive, and although I was proud of Devine's victory and the role I played in it, something was gnawing at me. During all the marching and singing, it began to dawn on me that the social activism in Charleston County seemed to be centered on Johns Island. All the singing and shouting was taking place in various churches throughout the city, but I noticed that much of the real planning was being led by Esau Jenkins and Bill Saunders. Mary Moultrie was our heroine. She was articulate, fearless, and strong, but even she seemed to be getting her activism from those who frequented the Progressive Club on Johns Island.

I had met Esau Jenkins and had begun hanging out at the Progressive Club, which was the home base of his activities. Although she was old Charleston and lived on the peninsula, Septima Clark was making contributions at the Progressive Club, teaching citizenship, conducting voter registration, and encouraging community empowerment. Esau Jenkins started the CO Federal Credit Union, and I became a charter member. I started voicing my concerns in the PAC meetings because it seemed to me that registering people to vote was only half the challenge. Giving people reasons to vote was the other half, and I did not think that we were connecting those dots. Time and time again my thoughts were dismissed. Although I could often count on St.

Julian Devine and Richard Fields—who had become a political mentor—to second my emotions, I was always being told that I was too much the social activist and not enough the practical politician.

Feeling that I was getting nowhere fast, I began thinking about ways that black people could get elected to public office without having the approval or endorsement of the white power structure. The full-slate voting requirement was in place at the time, meaning that if there were ten open positions, voters were required to vote for ten candidates. Single-shot votes were not counted. That meant that you voted for your choice one time and against your preferred candidate nine times. In the days before single-member districts, it meant that white majorities ruled, and without the special attention of a white leader such as Palmer Gaillard, black candidates stood very little chance of winning.

Birthing the UCP

It began to occur to me that the time may have arrived for a third party to develop a socioeconomic platform and provide special support for black candidates in state and county elections. I began talking up the idea with some of my good friends, including Bill Saunders, my new friend from the hospital strike, and Ike Williams, who had been a student activist at S.C. State and had led a successful student boycott in 1967. Ike had served two years in the military and returned to South Carolina to succeed I. DeQuincey Newman as field secretary of the NAACP. Also involved were John Harper, whose father taught at Mather Academy and who had enrolled at Fisk University after completing the tenth grade in high school. Allard Allston, a Darlington native and Yale graduate living in Columbia, was joining in the conversations, as was Ed Francis, a young minister from Moncks Corner. These were young political activists who were associated not only with local causes but also with the larger picture of building a political environment in which black people had more than a secondary role.

I learned from some unique experiences—the hospital and garbage worker strikes and the St. Julian Devine campaign in particular—and we decided that the 1970 elections would be our first venture into elective politics. One major problem presented itself, however. We didn't intend to run write-in candidates. We figured that would be a waste of time and effort. We intended for our candidates to be on the ballot, and that required that we be certified as a legitimate political party. We named ourselves the United Citizens Party (UCP), and we set out to acquire the ten thousand petition signatures necessary to be certified.

For the relative few of us involved, it became a monstrous—and perhaps impossible—task. Things were not going as well as we had hoped. I was beginning to understand firsthand what Theodore Roosevelt must have been feeling when he wrote the piece to which I often refer, "In the Arena." Then one day I got a call from I. P. Stanback of Columbia. He was an insurance executive with the North Carolina Mutual Insurance Company and seemed a little unhappy and concerned about our venture. I had gotten to know I. P. during my short stay in Columbia. I met him in a bowling league that I had joined, and we developed a pretty cordial relationship.

I. P. Stanback was a conservative Democrat from the earliest days, and he let me know that the last thing he wished to see happen was anything that could damage the candidacy of his old friend John C. West, who was running for governor. West's opponent was segregationist Republican Albert Watson, and West would need the full and enthusiastic support of black voters to beat the Republican. I assured Stanback that I too supported John West for governor and that I was not interested in doing anything to damage his chances.

Stanback invited me to Columbia to discuss the UCP and our plans, and I assured him that our plans were to select candidates in seven or eight counties to run for local and legislative offices. I would not only avoid any harm to West's candidacy, I told him in no uncertain terms, I would do everything possible to see that John West won the governor's race.

Once assured of my allegiance to West, Stanback seemed to like the idea of a political party to provide a wake-up call to Democrats who might be taking black voters for granted. He not only supported the idea, he offered to help us with the petition drive.

And with that, I learned a good political lesson. I. P. Stanback was serving at the time as Most Worshipful Grandmaster of Prince Hall Free and Accepted Masons, and his offer of help meant not only the involvement of his network of insurance agents, but also his network of Masonic lodges. Within weeks we achieved the ten thousand signatures we needed, and the UCP was born. A footnote to the story came from the fact that, not long after we got the party certified, a black attorney, Thomas Broadwater, filed to run for governor as a UCP candidate. True to my promise to I. P. Stanback, however, he got no support from any of us involved in the founding of the party, and wound up with only 3,500 votes, hardly enough to disturb the impressive vote total John West polled to defeat Albert Watson.

For all my work in founding the United Citizens Party, however, I was still a Democrat in pretty good standing in Charleston County. Jim Clyburn, the political hybrid, was still in business, and I was listening attentively to my good friends among the Democrats who were pushing me to run for the legislature. Herbert Fielding was going to run again for one of Charleston's eleven seats in the South Carolina House of Representatives, and up in Columbia there would be two black candidates—I. S. Leevy Johnson and Jim Felder. So I decided to go all in and give Charleston an opportunity to also elect two blacks to its House delegation.

In 1970 full-slate voting was one of the creative devices used to neutralize the impact of black voters. Anyone who voted for fewer than eleven candidates would not have their votes counted. I won the Democratic nomination for one of the eleven seats, and we had a grand celebration. The next morning I found a note on my bathroom mirror that had been left there by Emily. It read: "When you win brag gently; when you lose weep softly."

In the general election, I went to bed thinking I had won—as was announced on the 11:00 P.M. news. I was awakened at 3:30 A.M. by a TV reporter, who told me that I should get down to the courthouse, something was wrong. When I arrived at the courthouse I was told that instead of having won by five hundred votes, I had lost by five hundred.

Besides wondering about the validity of that late-night shift, I felt anger and bitterness. Then I remembered how my dad had handled such a moment. It also helped that I remembered that note Emily had left on my mirror the morning after my primary victory several months earlier. Now I don't know how gentle my bragging was after that victory. But on that day of defeat, I walked into that same bathroom; looked up at the mirror where that note was still stuck, and I wept softly.

As disappointing as the loss was, there was one gesture I have never forgotten. We had called ourselves the "Democratic Action Team." We pooled our resources and divided the media time equally. Herbert and I were the decided underdogs and, according to conventional wisdom, would need more media time than the others. Joe Riley, a House member at the time and the long-serving mayor of Charleston, was on the eleven-member team running for reelection. There was little doubt that he and about six others would win. Also there was a tradition that the highest vote getter would be designated delegation chair.

At one of our team meetings, Joe announced that he felt certain he could get reelected without any media advertisements. Consequently he wanted all his media time divided equally between Herbert and me. He noted that it would probably cost him first place in the field, but he felt that it was more important for Herbert and me to get elected.

For a black candidate to win in a full-slate race, it was necessary to get not only a big black turnout but also strong support from the white political establishment. Many white politicos were clearly and publicly helping black candidates because it was a way of getting black voters to the polls for John West. Up in Columbia, banker Hootie Johnson, in fact, was serving as I. S. Leevy Johnson's finance chairman.

In Charleston, however, things were being done a little bit differently. One might say they were a little less social and a bit more political. Herbert had run in 1968. He was chair of PAC, which had been a reliable vote getter for the Broad Street Gang for many years. There was also another element that would allow the power structure to avoid being accused of tokenism. Lonnie Hamilton, the popular and able band director at Bonds-Wilson High School in North Charleston, had decided to challenge the long-standing notion that teachers were not to involve themselves in politics. He ran for Charleston County Council—with help from the Broad Street gang—and had successfully withstood a legal challenge to his candidacy.

With Lonnie running for the Democratic nomination to County Council, the powers that be had a real good chance to elect two black candidates to county-wide office and to simultaneously extend an olive branch to the voters of North Charleston. I became the odd man out. I knew it but was not discouraged. I knew that the voters out on the Sea Islands would be with me. I also had the Charleston Young Democrats, of which Bernard Fielding, Herbert's brother, and I were the only black members, and there was that small crop of new white progressives in Charleston who were socially active but not politically well connected. Among them was Charles

*With University of South Carolina president Harris Pastides and Bud Ferillo, who is holding up
his Travelstead Award, given by the University of South Carolina Education Foundation in 2012.
Bud and I have remained lifelong friends and activists for equality and social justice. Photograph
courtesy of the University of South Carolina.*

"Bud" Ferillo, who had just returned from Vietnam. He decided that before getting
serious about looking for real work, he would run my campaign. And a very sophis-
ticated, highly emotional campaign it was. I came close, but unfortunately this was
not a game of horseshoes. Herbert captured one of the seats, becoming the first black
person to represent Charleston in the General Assembly since the nineteenth century.
Lonnie Hamilton won also, and became the first black member ever on the Charleston County Council.

I. S. Leevy Johnson and Jim Felder both won also and joined Herbert as the first
black House members in South Carolina since the post-Reconstruction era. I guess I
will never really know the real reasons for my having lost. Maybe my activist days at
South Carolina State and my involvement in the hospital and garbage workers strikes
made me appear too "militant" for some white voters. Maybe my role in the founding of the United Citizens Party made me seem disloyal to the Democratic Party.

Or maybe, as I told Barbara Williams of the *Charleston News and Courier*, I just
didn't get enough votes. Or maybe it was just time for my next step in the Charleston
shuffle.

PART FIVE

Making History

*. . . the governor wanted to play golf on Saturday morning, . . .
since Phil thought nobody on the staff played golf, he asked
for a volunteer to sacrifice his or her Saturday morning. I got
great joy out of informing him that I played golf. I got the
Saturday morning assignment. The episode got better when we
walked into the clubhouse. They were expecting the governor
but not anyone who looked like me. The governor acted
oblivious as we signed up to play. Maybe he didn't know that
the Santee Cooper Country Club had a whites-only policy. I
sure did. It gave me great pleasure to watch the guy behind
the desk nervously taking our money and handing us some
score cards.*

Governor West plucked me off the political battlefield, wounded and defeated, and offered me a history-making position. It was a position I enjoyed and sought to use as an opportunity to make significant changes for citizens of South Carolina who looked like me.

I lobbied the governor incessantly for the creation of the South Carolina Housing and Finance Commission, and he responded favorably. Although the South Carolina Supreme Court ruled our efforts unconstitutional twice, the third time proved to be the charm.

I played a significant role in the creation of the South Carolina Human Affairs Commission and pretty much selected the entire governing board of its predecessor agency, the Governor's Advisory Commission on Human Relations. Governor West appointed his confidant and former campaign manager, Harry Lightsey, to chair the

At a 1971 meeting about creating the Governor's Advisory Commission on Human Affairs (second from right in foreground), with Lieutenant Governor Earle Morris, Governor John West, and fellow aide Phil Grose. Clyburn Papers, South Carolina State University.

commission and instructed me to find eighteen members, three from each of the six congressional districts. It was done and with little fanfare.

But my serving as the first African American executive on a South Carolina governor's staff presented a learning curve for everyone.

White Knuckles?

A few weeks after his inauguration, Governor West invited Emily and me to be among the staff members and their spouses accompanying him to the 1971 National Governors Conference in Washington, D.C.

Of course we accepted and were thrilled to take our first trip on the state plane. Even back then, although not as much as now, Emily was not very fond of flying. The governor noticed that, and asked whether or not she was a member of the white-knuckles society. I remarked that for Emily that would be rather hard if not impossible. The governor immediately recognized the faux pas and turned beet red as the others laughed nervously. It got even funnier when we landed.

Seeing Ain't Believing

Upon our arrival I was to deliver a funding proposal to the Office of Economic Opportunity. Two cars had been ordered to pick us up; one for the governor, his security, Mrs. West, and the governor's executive assistant and his wife, the other for Phil and Ginny Grose and Emily and me.

The governor and his party were whisked off as we waited for our car and driver. It seemed a bit unusual for only one driver to be there and we started looking around the place, to no avail. Then I remembered seeing a black gentleman walking away as we entered the terminal, and he was now standing across the room from me. I walked over to him and inquired as to who he might be waiting for. He told me that he was waiting for some staff members of the governor of South Carolina. I told him that that would be us.

When we got into the car, I told him that some of us needed to be dropped off at the hotel and I needed to be taken to a downtown office building. After dropping Emily, Ginny, Phil, and the luggage at the hotel, we continued to my destination. Once we were alone, the driver apologized profusely. He told me that when he saw Emily and me getting off that plane he just knew we could not be the staff of a South Carolina governor.

Finally a Win

Shortly after we returned from Washington, a group of young Democrats approached me about running for the state presidency of the South Carolina Young Democrats. I had become active in the group several years earlier and had played a pretty critical role in electing Donald Fowler president, which launched his very successful political career. Don went on to become state and national Democratic Party chair. I ran; Don returned the favor, and I won. During that contest I developed quite a few lifelong political friends, and a few political enemies who have lasted just as long.

Tee Changes

The governor decided to hold our first staff retreat during the 1971 Christmas holidays. Phil Grose, who was in charge of assigning staff duties and responsibilities for the retreat, announced that the governor wanted to play golf on Saturday morning, and since Phil thought nobody on the staff played golf, he asked for a volunteer to sacrifice his or her Saturday morning. I got great joy out of informing him that I played golf. I got the Saturday morning assignment.

The episode got better when we walked into the clubhouse. They were expecting the governor but not anyone who looked like me. The governor acted oblivious as we signed up to play. Maybe he didn't know that the Santee Cooper Country Club had a whites-only policy. I sure did. It gave me great pleasure to watch the guy behind the desk nervously taking our money and handing us some score cards. Twenty-five years later, Emily and I became property owners in the Santee Cooper Resort, which granted us automatic membership in the Santee Cooper Country Club.

In addition to creating the State Housing Authority and the Human Affairs Commission, there were several other policy initiatives and political situations that I was proud to be part of during my tenure in the governor's office. Three of them involved personal heroes, the Reverend J. A. De Laine, Ms. Septima Clark, and Mary McLeod Bethune. The results were mixed.

A Homecoming Lost

Shortly after taking the oath of office, Governor West handed me a letter he had received from Reverend De Laine. Reverend De Laine, an African Methodist Episcopal (AME) minister, was the organizer of the efforts in Clarendon County that resulted in the *Briggs v. Elliott* lawsuit, which was the first of the desegregation cases folded into *Brown v. Board of Education of Topeka, Kansas*. Reverend De Laine and his family were terrorized. His house and church were burned, and his life was threatened. During an attack, Reverend De Laine retaliated, and a warrant was issued for his arrest. He was smuggled out of the state and later surfaced in New York.

In his letter Reverend De Laine related the prospect of not having much longer to live and expressed his wish to return home and be buried in South Carolina soil. The governor gave me the task of facilitating Reverend De Laine's return and organizing a homecoming program, which Governor West felt could help turn a page in South Carolina history.

I shared what the governor wanted done with Chief J. P. Strom of SLED, and Chief Strom approached the only person still living who had signed the arrest warrant against Reverend De Laine about dropping his action. He refused to do so. Consequently it was impossible to promise Reverend De Laine his freedom if he were to return to the state. I was distraught, and so was the governor. Reverend De Laine returned to the South but stopped in Charlotte, North Carolina, where he died and is buried.

Partial Payment

Not long after it was announced that I would be joining the governor's staff, I was contacted by a group of ministers on behalf of Septima Clark, who had been fired from her job as a public schoolteacher because she refused to denounce her membership in the NAACP. She had also lost her pension, and they wanted it restored.

I had worked very closely with Septima during my years in Charleston, and I have quite a few fond memories of her, particularly one I mention often. As part of a weekend retreat of the Penn Center board, we took a boat ride to Daufuskie Island. My daughter Mignon accompanied me. When the water got a little bit choppy, Mignon got very excited and started running back and forth from one side of the boat to the other.

In asking her to sit down, I raised my voice a few decibels. I did not realize it, but Septima was observing me. After a while our eyes met. She beckoned me over to her and patted the seat next to her, a gesture I understood to mean "have a seat." When I sat down, Septima slowly but sternly said to me, "Isn't it strange how we sometimes react when we see so much of ourselves in our children." I have never forgotten that brief conversation, and I thought helping get her pension restored would be a good way to show my appreciation. The governor was on board, but we were never able to convince a majority of the legislature to go along. We did get a modest lump sum payment. A few years later Representative Robert R. Woods got the legislature to revisit the issue and got several additional payments but not full restitution.

Hanging Tough

I will always consider getting the portrait of Mary McLeod Bethune hung in the State House a seminal achievement. One day I shared with Governor West how lonely I felt walking throughout the capitol building, seeing all those portraits and statutes of South Carolinians and none of them a black person. I told him that it was an oversight that should be corrected. He agreed, and appointed a committee to find an appropriate South Carolinian to honor.

The committee submitted three names from which the governor was to make the final pick. Although I was familiar with all three, I told him that we should go with somebody much more widely known and suggested Mary McLeod Bethune. A few days later Governor West rejected the committee's recommendation and decided to go with Ms. Bethune.

Getting the portrait done and hung was no walk in the park. A legislator from Spartanburg County, Richard Hines, took to the floor and lambasted Mary McLeod Bethune as a socialist and communist and someone who should never be honored by the legislature. He had a field day and got a lot of press. I feared John West would be upset. But he did not relent and suggested that we bring another House member from Spartanburg into the fray. Sam Manning, who was a very learned legislator, reluctantly got involved and became a counterbalance to Richard Hines. In spite of Representative Hines's vitriol, Representative Manning hung tough. Governor West hung tough too, and the legislature took a tough vote. I was very proud, and my mother

Speaking at the unveiling of the Mary McLeod Bethune portrait in the South Carolina State House in 1976. Clyburn Papers, South Carolina State University.

would have been happy, when Mary McLeod Bethune's portrait was hung above the first landing of the west staircase of the State House on July 10, 1976.

Affirmative Steps to Right Past Wrongs

Probably my proudest moments in the governor's office came when the governor held a series of meetings with state agencies to inform them they needed to take affirmative steps to implement fair employment practices. Many of them did not like it, but Governor West stood firm as he did so often in the face of adversity.

One of those times cemented our relationship. Early in my tenure I was invited to address a West Columbia Optimist Club. Unbeknownst to me, Governor West was addressing a Rotary Club in downtown Columbia at the same hour. During my remarks, I highlighted how far we had to go to make things equitable in South Carolina. During his remarks, the governor was highlighting how much progress South Carolina had made in race relations. That night WIS television reported on both speeches, using a split screen to highlight the contradictions. When I saw the report, I feared the worst.

The next morning the governor summoned me into his office. He told me that he had seen those news reports, and it looked as if the two of us needed to get on the same page. I apologized for the embarrassment my comments had caused and offered to resign. Governor West replied by calling my attention to a twelve-ounce glass on his desk that contained about six ounces of water, and said: "To me that glass is half full, you probably see it as half empty. The difference in our descriptions is our experiences. You and I are fine. Go back to your office and let's get to work." Some of the good old days were really good, and so were a few of the good old boys.

13   *Myth Buster*

When I accepted Governor West's offer to head the State Human Affairs Commission (SHAC) in 1974, I didn't expect to remain in that position for more than seventeen years. At the time my life was in a state of flux, and I was pondering several career options.

But there were some compelling reasons for me to take over the agency. The 1969 Medical College hospital strike down in Charleston and reactions in Lamar and Columbia to a 1970 letter from federal officials ordering the state to take significant steps to desegregate its public schools by September made creating a state agency to deal with racial issues seem like a good idea. But not everything had gone well. While he had continued to articulate his progressive goals and had initiated steps to introduce affirmative action and equal employment opportunity strategies among reluctant state agencies, other important components of the governor's campaign were in some jeopardy.

SHAC, created in 1972 with the virtually unanimous approval of the General Assembly, had fallen on hard times. The agency was losing favor with the legislature and was suffering from weak management. It had overspent its budget and was not even aware of it. There were more than one hundred bills in the General Assembly to abolish the commission, and one had come within four votes of passage.

These were particularly unsettling developments for me. I had been active in the creation of SHAC and felt I had a personal stake in its success. The last thing I wanted to see was an ignominious end to the institutional symbol of racial progress in South Carolina.

There were other problems with the enlightened and ambitious visions West had articulated to a hopeful state when he was inaugurated. At the time, in addition to appointing me to his staff, he had named two other African Americans to staff the Governor's Advisory Commission on Human Relations, which he had created by executive order prior to the establishment of SHAC. West's immediately organizing a human-relations agency was impressive and seemed a good faith follow-up to his pledges to promote racial justice in the state. The three of us were assigned a highly visible space, which became known as the "Ebony Suite," and we all enjoyed the good-natured acceptance this bit of humor indicated. When the Human Affairs Act of 1972 became law, staff members assigned to deal with those issues left the office to take up residency in a suite across the street from the capitol.

I, too, left the Ebony Suite shortly thereafter. When I joined the governor's staff, I made a commitment to stay only one year. My intention was to return to Charleston, a city I had grown to love and where my family was still living. However, the governor asked me to stay and encouraged me to go to law school. Here was the governor joining forces with Matthew Perry and Emily Clyburn, both of whom had been urging me to go to law school since before I graduated college. So I decided to give it a shot.

When I enrolled in law school, I became a part-time employee on the governor's staff. Consequently I and my staff assistant, Margaret Purcell, were assigned office space in the Wade Hampton state office building. Suddenly there were no black faces in the governor's office, and it did not go unnoticed.

Ike Williams, who at the time was serving as field secretary for the State Conference of NAACP branches, put it most succinctly. In a caustic letter to Governor West, he lamented that "what was once the Ebony Suite in the Governor's Office had become a lily white flower garden."

A Wake-up Call

The letter underscored more than the visible evidence that black people were missing from the governor's office. Black influence had been diminished as well. I discovered that I and some key colleagues were being consulted less often about things at the executive level. Staff meetings were being taken up more with reports from the funding gurus and less with open discussions and debates. Ike Williams's letter became public, and it came as a wake-up call to John West. He could see the entire vision he had advanced for racial progress in the state crumbling. Shortly thereafter, the Human Affairs commissioner resigned, and there was indecision and division among board members as to a successor. West felt the agency he had helped to create and nurture was drifting away from him. He and I had remained close and on good terms, and when we discussed my taking over the agency, it was with the same kind of candor and trust we had known almost four years earlier.

I was not particularly enjoying law school, and my ten years of the rough and tumble of politics and government had started an itch that I felt needed to be scratched, so I agreed to put my name in the hat. With the help and support of a persuasive young commission member from Columbia, Jean Toal, a longtime friend who later became chief justice of the South Carolina Supreme Court, and a community organizer and tenacious cohort from Charleston, Bill Saunders, who later became a member of the State Public Service Commission, I was chosen in October 1974 to head the agency, once and for all ending my pursuit of a law degree.

Only three months remained in the West administration, so I knew any major repairs to the agency would require some immediate attention from him, as well as the friendship of his successor, whoever that might be. My good friend Bryan Dorn was the Democratic candidate for governor, and James B. Edwards, a Charleston oral surgeon who was something of a newcomer to statewide politics, was Bryan's Republican foe.

I made it clear to John West that, while I had no long-term career interests in the Human Affairs job, I saw my role as more than patching up his damaged relations in

With former Republican governor Jim Edwards at a Martin Luther King Jr. event at Morris Street Baptist Church in Charleston. Clyburn Papers, South Carolina State University.

certain parts of the black political community. I wanted to stabilize the agency for a long-term role in pursuing racial justice in state government and South Carolina. He understood and agreed, and as a step in that direction, he authorized ten new staff positions under the Comprehensive Employment and Training Act (CETA) to shore up the agency's lagging staff resources. As it turned out, Jim Edwards defeated Bryan Dorn in the governor's race a month later, and South Carolina had its first Republican governor of the twentieth century. "I was so surprised at the results," Edwards joked some years later, "that I felt that I should demand a recount."

Edwards and West developed a good friendship in the months between Edwards's election and his inauguration, and the Republican proved to be a good friend of SHAC as well. He renewed the ten CETA slots for the agency. I also developed a pretty good working relationship with Edwards's executive assistant, Carroll Campbell, who later became governor in his own right. The actions of Carroll and of Roger Kirk, the governor's education assistant, allowed me to conclude that there still existed some of what made my father a Republican.

Proving a Point

In 1974 I not only wanted to advance the interests of black people in the state, but I wanted also to be "Exhibit A" in the case for including more African American executives in state government in South Carolina. I wanted to prove that Governor West's dream of a "colorblind" administration meant more black people in the corner offices of authority as well as elsewhere in government. I wanted more "Ebony Suites" not only as places of public and political visibility but also as sources of influence, leadership, and pride.

With the SHAC staff in 1992. Courtesy of Paul Beazley.

In terms of SHAC it meant building a staff with both professional competency and personal commitment. It meant having on board people who would "walk the walk" as well as "talk the talk." It meant showing to the public that we understood and cared about people's troubles and that we could also do something about them. It meant destroying some long-held myths.

When I got to SHAC, I found some really good people and committed public servants, such as Bobby Gist, Paul Beazley, Clay Gompf, Virginia Newman, Jesse Washington, Earl Brown, and Herb Langford. With that CETA money I brought on others: Margaret Purcell, Pat Hartley, Sam Selph, Dalton Tresvant, Judy Weesner, Ray Buxton, Judy Hodgens, Eilene Irving, Sally McMaster, and Mary Snead. These new people melded beautifully with the older staffers and together became a formidable force for "firmness and fairness." They helped to build an effective, cohesive staff that could show to the world men and women from diverse backgrounds working in an atmosphere of harmony.

What we developed at SHAC, I told an interviewer from the *Palmetto Post* in 1985, was a staff that was "very cohesive, very professional, very upbeat, energetic and aggressive." It was a major step in the right direction and made my job easier and more pleasurable.

Governor Edwards appointed Alan Code, a retired educator to chair the commission. I did not know Mr. Code personally, but he was from Seneca, the hometown of my dear friend Ercelle from Mather Academy. I called Ercelle, and she provided me with some significant insights that were very useful in my getting off on a good foot with Mr. Code. It was also helpful that he was originally from Sumter County, had attended Morris College, knew my dad, and had spent a summer supervising an adult-education program that employed my sister-in-law Vivian. We established a positive relationship, and I admired him greatly in spite of the differences in our political allegiances, he a ruby red Republican and I a yellow dog Democrat. I have every reason to believe that the feeling was mutual.

My first order of business at SHAC was to rescue the agency from political harm and to restore its credibility and stability. The next step, I realized, was to meet the expectations Governor West and legislative leaders had placed in the agency when it was created. For all the altruism we liked to attribute to its founders, I realized there were other, more basic political motives. By creating their own civil rights agency at the state level, legislators were told, we could "keep the feds out." While that premise may have had some grounding in logic and legal possibility, it was not an automatic result of establishing SHAC. The Equal Employment Opportunity Commission (EEOC) was still the federal sheriff in those enforcement jurisdictions and would continue to be for the foreseeable future.

I realized that, once the agency and the staff achieved some stability, our future relevance would depend largely on developing a good working relationship with federal enforcement agencies. If we couldn't realistically "keep the feds out," we might be able to partner with the feds in a way that would give the state a role in these matters.

The major problem was the relative weakness of our statute. The feds had the authority to grant "deferral status" to state agencies, but their practice was to do so only with states that had statutes "substantially equivalent" to the federal law. South Carolina did not have a statute of such strength, nor did most of the southern states. Elsewhere in the nation, EEOC had granted deferral status to states with legal authority it deemed equivalent to its own enforcement power. Chances of our upgrading our statute to be equivalent to federal law seemed slim, so it would probably be some time—if ever—before we would be taking over jurisdiction from EEOC on South Carolina cases.

Finding Some Allies

There was another avenue, however, which I thought might be explored to provide some relief from what seemed to be an absolute position the feds were taking on this matter. I had become active in the National Association of Human Rights Workers (NAHRW), an organization of individuals with long-standing reputations for activism and influence within the civil rights community.

I had also joined the International Association of Official Human Rights Agencies (IAOHRA), an agency membership organization that had great influence with the federal fair employment practices and fair housing agencies. In time I became president of both groups. My thought was a strategic one and involved the building of relationships among a coalition of states without deferral status. What we couldn't get done as individual states, we might be able to do on a collective basis.

I found a section of the EEOC enabling statute that I thought would help our case. I argued that section 709 of Title VII of the Civil Rights Act of 1964 empowered EEOC to enter into contracts with any state or local agency "charged with the administration of fair employment practice laws." Our coalition of southern and midwestern states within the membership of NAHRW believed that this section gave EEOC more latitude than it had been exercising. Our argument proved effective, and we ultimately carried the day, changing the contract funding policies and the method of designation of "deferral agencies."

Unlikely Brothers

One day I was sitting at my desk contemplating my next move when I felt a presence at my door. I looked up, and I. DeQuincey Newman was standing there. Deak asked could he come in for a moment, and after I invited him to do so, he asked if he might close the door. I sensed that something significant was on his mind.

Deak told me that he thought I had a tremendous future in South Carolina, but he also thought that I had a problem that I needed to work on. His explanation set me back on my heels. He told me that he thought I was very gifted and had great promise as a politician, but that I was too much of a loner. He told me that if any black person wanted to be successful in South Carolina politics, he or she needed to have an entree into the white community, and he suggested that I get myself a white brother.

He went on to say that any white person wanting to be successful in South Carolina politics would do well to have a black brother. I did not know what to think about Deak's comments, and I did not feel all that good about them. Yet those comments stayed on my mind, and the more I reflected on them the less I felt insulted by them. In fact, I decided, I needed to put some of that concept into practice to get SHAC's authority expanded.

Before I took over the helm of SHAC, the commission had lost a court case involving a complaint that had been lodged against the City of Columbia. In its decision the court held that SHAC had the authority to investigate any complaint of discrimination, but its enforcement authority was limited to state government agencies.

That decision was demoralizing to the agency, and there was no question that I was sailing against the wind. It was not just about the City of Columbia. This argument was about jurisdiction over every city, town, and incorporated area in South Carolina, and I was not going to win it without significant assistance. So I set out to find some white brothers. I found a few in the state legislature and a few more in the private sector.

I was particularly successful developing allies in the banking community. I had enjoyed a friendship with Hugh Lane Sr., chairman of Citizens and Southern (C&S) National Bank, during my community activism in Charleston. In fact he had selected me to chair a low-income housing initiative he started on Charleston's east side.

Codifying the procedural relationship we had developed with the federal EEOC would elevate our stature among the national civil rights groups and could assure our legislative and political backers that we had achieved status and stability. We developed an inside game and an outside game working with the friends we developed in the legislature and banking industry. This unlikely brotherhood got legislation passed that was determined to be "substantially equivalent" to the federal law, and SHAC was granted "deferral status."

The agency's qualification for "deferral status" came up again after the passage of the new and improved federal Fair Housing Act of 1988, designed to crack down on discrimination in the housing business. South Carolina responded with its own Fair Housing Act, signed into law by Governor Campbell a year later.

The icing on the cake came when we attempted to investigate a discrimination complaint against the sheriff of Chester County. Sheriff Robert H. Orr Jr. had refused to cooperate with us. Citing the City of Columbia case, he filed a lawsuit challenging our authority. This time the result was different. In somewhat of a landmark decision the South Carolina Supreme Court ruled in the case of *Orr v. Clyburn* that the legislative changes to our law had given us sufficient investigative and enforcement powers to carry out our mission.

All the while, I knew that we as an agency, and I as the commissioner of that agency, were undergoing our own trial and judgment exercises in the forum of public scrutiny. We knew that race was still a matter of great delicacy in South Carolina, no matter how far along we may have thought we'd moved politically. As we did our job of investigating and making our findings known, we knew that parties to our cases—state agencies, corporations, aggrieved individuals, anyone who felt mistreated—were applying their own sets of judgments to us. They were wondering whether we, in fact, could be "colorblind."

I set out to test that notion in 1978, when I decided to run for statewide office. In a three-way race for secretary of state, I led the ticket with 43 percent of the vote. Although I lost the runoff two weeks later, I received more than 47 percent, which meant that I got a good number of white votes along the way. I refused to accept the defeat as being racially motivated. I preferred instead to admit again that I did not get enough votes and to think that the notion of electing a black man to statewide office was "an idea whose time had not come." I always knew that the job at SHAC had another dimension that could eventually bring me and the agency higher visibility than all the organizational and legal work we were carrying out. For all the efforts that had gone into building racial peace in South Carolina, our state was not immune to outbreaks of dangerous racial controversy.

Firming Things Up

Within a few weeks of its creation, SHAC's forerunner, the Governor's Advisory Commission on Human Relations, was thrust into a dispute over the segregation of a city-owned golf course in Greenville. The limitation of an advisory commission was the issue that led the court to conclude that their role was just to advise. But what kind of advice does one need about such policy? This issue factored greatly in the discussions and debates over the creation of SHAC. So after its creation and the decision in *Orr v. Clyburn,* SHAC became the place where racial disputes were referred for resolution. I would like to think that was a sign of the confidence and credibility we had built as a state agency.

I was very proud of the fact that my mantra of being "firm, but fair" had been internalized by the staff and recognized by the public. One of the best testimonies of that accomplishment came one night when I was sitting in the Charlotte airport waiting for the flight to Columbia. A gentleman approached me and introduced himself as the human resources director of a national company that had a plant in Greenville. He told me they had recently been the subject of a discrimination complaint that we investigated.

I reacted to his overture the way I usually did in those kinds of situations, by expressing the hope that everything came out to his liking. He responded, "not exactly." He told me that we had ruled against them, but that he really appreciated how we conducted the investigation and issued the determination. That gentleman really made my day. It was confirmation that I had been pretty successful with what I was trying to accomplish at SHAC.

I sincerely believed that my day would come, but I had no idea what trials and tribulations I would soon have to reckon with in order to get there. In fact if my family name did not begin with the letter "C," I would probably consider it the one letter of the alphabet I could very well do without. As if the City of Columbia and County of Chester were not enough, consider the not-so-blessed experiences I had with the Citadel, Conway, and the Confederate battle flag.

My experiences in these disputes added a considerable number of new gray intruders among the darker growths of hair that had populated my head for a decade.

PART SIX

A Racial Arbiter

. . . a big pickup truck drove up shining a big spotlight in our direction. Two white gentlemen jumped out. . . . They had a hook and steel cable attached to the front of the truck. . . . one of them hooked the cable to the bumper of our car, and they pulled us to safety. . . . They adamantly refused to accept any pay, jumped into their truck, and drove away, proclaiming that there might be others out there who needed their help. I don't know what made me gaze at the rear of that truck as they drove away, but I did. . . . The back window of that pickup was covered by a screened rendition of the Confederate battle flag. When we got into the car, I turned to Emily and said, "Just when I thought I had this flag thing all figured out."

14 : *The Chester Controversy*

On May 11, 1979, Chester County was thrust back into my life. A young black man was found dead along a Chester roadside. An autopsy determined that his death had been caused by a hit-and-run driver. Rumors circulated that the young man—Mickey McClintock—had been murdered for dating a white girl. Things reached a fever pitch when allegations were made that he had not only been murdered but had been castrated. SHAC was asked to investigate.

Public attention to the incident escalated, and in time considerable interest was generated among black people throughout the area. That interest became much more intense with the arrival of the Southern Christian Leadership Conference (SCLC) from Atlanta. The SCLC president, the Reverend Joseph Lowery, who later became a good friend and fierce supporter, called for a state investigation of the allegations and threatened to organize a march from Chester to Columbia. As things escalated, requests were made to exhume and reexamine McClintock's body. Reverend Lowery supported those calls and sent an SCLC field organizer to Chester.

Golden Frinks, the SCLC field secretary, with whom I was well acquainted, was good at arousing passions and motivating crowds. He started spending lots of time in Chester doing just that. He organized a group of local ministers, many of whom had supported me in my race for secretary of state the year before. They spent evening upon evening speaking to overflow crowds at churches throughout the county. Like so many racial disputes, the matter was boiling down to the advocacy of a civil rights organization as opposed to the role of a quasi-judicial agency seeking to resolve the issue administratively. I attended many of those mass meetings, and Mr. Frinks took to making me the target of many of his taunts. Advocacy was carrying the day.

Golden Frinks made good on his threats and started leading a march from Chester to Columbia. Things were spiraling out of control. I tried everything I could to restore calm. I went so far as to offer a cash reward for any information that would be helpful and deposited five hundred dollars in a local bank to hold in escrow.

At the height of the controversy, I received a visit from Chief J. P. Strom of SLED. He told me that he thought we should exhume the body, which was fine with me. But then he said that the governor was out of the country, and his staff had instructed him to coordinate his activities with me.

I agreed to a second autopsy, and when the protestors and SCLC insisted that a black medical examiner perform the procedure, we brought in an African American pathologist from Washington, D.C. The result was the same as had been determined six months earlier—no castration, no murder, simple hit-and-run—a terrible tragedy for the family but no racial crime.

It's easy to get swept up in the spirit of the moment and allow rational judgment to be overwhelmed by emotion. I understood that. I probably didn't satisfy my political supporters or make a lot of new friends by taking the dispassionate route, but I insisted that facts should determine SHAC's outcomes.

Once the facts had been determined, I charged Golden Frinks with misleading the Chester community and lying about the castration and murder. When a reporter asked Frinks for his response to my charges, he shrugged his shoulders, looked directly into the TV camera, and said: "So what? Everybody tells a little lie every now and then."

Such an outcome is never satisfying. I don't know if anyone was ever arrested in connection with the young man's death. Much pain had been inflicted on the Chester community for no good reason, and there seemed to be little remorse for it all. I came away with the consoling thought that SHAC, battered as it was by all the outcry and controversy, had survived a serious test. Our reputation for firmness and fairness, even in the face of difficult conditions, remained intact.

15 : *The Citadel Confrontation*

The Citadel is a Charleston, South Carolina, military college, where student behavior is regulated by strict rules of conduct. These rules are outlined in a student handbook known as the "Blue Book." An important element of the regulations is the fourth-class system, which allows upperclassmen to exercise their leadership abilities upon fourth classmen (freshmen). The system denies certain privileges to fourth classmen while giving upperclassmen the authority to conduct special inspections and issue special instructions.

According to the Blue Book, the fourth-class system is intended to "train, develop, and motivate each Fourth Classman—not to eliminate." The regulations further state that "the Fourth Class System must provide the upperclassman with positive leadership opportunities associated with training, developing, and motivating newcomers toward becoming first-rate cadets." A basic tenet of the system is to "develop within a cadet a sense of dignity, pride and honor." The system normally functions reasonably well, but in the case of a black fourth classman, Kevin Nesmith, the system was abused to the point that it may have had the opposite of its intended effect.

On October 23, 1986, at approximately 12:30 A.M., five white second classmen (juniors) were gathered in their barracks discussing matters at the Citadel. The five cadets did not think Cadet Nesmith was "pulling his weight," and they decided he needed more motivation.

At about 12:45 A.M., one of the five second classmen suggested they pay Mr. Nesmith a visit. They had to be secretive because it is a violation of Blue Book regulations to bother a fourth classman between "all-in" and reveille. They decided to conceal their identities by wrapping themselves in white sheets to give the appearance of Ku Klux Klansmen. On his own, one of the cadets constructed a small paper cross (8½" × 7") and burned the edges of it. Not all the other four cadets were aware of this cross.

At about 1:00 A.M., the five cadets entered Mr. Nesmith's darkened room chanting, "Nesmith, Nesmith, get your shit in a pile." This aroused Mr. Nesmith's roommate, Michael Mendoza, who was in the bottom bunk. Mendoza later testified before a commandant's board that he thought he remembered them also chanting "Nesmith, Nesmith, we're going to get you," but he was not clear on this, and the five cadets denied saying it.

Mendoza got out of bed and reached for the light switch but they held him back, telling him to "go back to bed, this doesn't concern you." At that point Mendoza "took a swing at" one of the cadets and threatened to "beat every one of your asses." As the five cadets started to leave, Mr. Nesmith woke up. As the last cadet was leaving, Mendoza grabbed the sheet, which had been wrapped around the cadet's head and body. Underneath, he was wearing a shako and pom-pom with a towel wrapped to give the appearance of a pointed hood. Mendoza took a swing at the cadet hitting him on the head, causing the towel and pom-pom to fall to the floor in the hallway. Mendoza picked them up as the cadet ran away with his hands over his face. The entire episode lasted about ninety seconds.

Mendoza did not see the burned cross until he returned to his room. At this point he and Nesmith realized that this was a "serious incident" and reported it to their corporal and their company clerk. The clerk told them to give him the towel, shako, pom-pom, and cross, and let him proceed through the proper channels. The towel was an important piece of evidence because it was marked with a serial number that could identify the guilty party. Mendoza later contacted his tactical officer because he wasn't sure the corporal or company clerk would follow through.

Before reveille, someone went into the company clerk's room and removed the towel; however, the thief later returned it because stealing is an honor-code violation that results in automatic expulsion and because the absence of evidence would wrongly implicate the company clerk in the incident. By the next evening all five participants had been identified.

Meanwhile Alonzo Nesmith, Kevin Nesmith's brother and a member of the Citadel's board of visitors, contacted Citadel president James Grimsley and requested that the offending cadets be expelled. General Grimsley told Mr. Nesmith that the matter was being investigated and that it would be handled in accordance with standard procedure. Mr. Nesmith then reported the matter to Delbert Woods, president of Charleston's NAACP branch. News of the incident soon began to spread throughout Charleston's black community.

On October 29, 1986, a commandant's board hearing was held to gather the facts and make a recommendation to President Grimsley regarding punishment. All members of the commandant's board were white. After a hearing that lasted approximately four hours, the board recommended that the cadets be suspended for the remainder of the academic year but that the suspension be set aside with the proviso that it would be enforced against any of the five who committed a class 1 or class 2 offense during the school year. The board also recommended that the rank-holding cadets be reduced in rank to the grade of private, that all cadets be transferred to other battalions and be awarded sixty demerits and 120 tours for gross poor judgment and major violations of the fourth class system, and, that no amnesty, tour cuts, or work tour credit be authorized. The 120 tours (fifty minute marches at a pace of 120 steps per minute in full-dress uniform with rifle in proper shoulder position) was the maximum allowed in the rules and regulations.

On October 31, 1986, President Grimsley reviewed the board's recommendations. He concurred with them, but added 75 more tours and ordered that each cadet be restricted to campus for six months. Each cadet accepted the punishment without appeal.

On Monday, November 10, eight Charleston area religious leaders met with General Grimsley to urge him to reconsider the punishment order. The same group later requested Governor Richard Riley's assistance. On November 13, Alonzo Nesmith resigned from the Citadel board.

In the weeks that followed the announcement of punishment, the Nesmith incident received nationwide coverage by the news media. On November 14, the Citadel board of visitors discussed the matter with Governor Riley and invited the governor or his representative to receive a full briefing on the complete facts of the incident. Governor Riley suggested that the SHAC commissioner would be the proper individual to receive such a briefing and requested that I review the situation to determine the "appropriateness" of the punishment.

I sent three staff members to Charleston the following week and on November 21, I presented our agency's findings to SHAC's governing board. Our review of past commandant's board hearings revealed that the school's discipline of the five cadets represented the most severe punishment ever given to any cadet—with the exception of several expulsions, dismissals, and suspensions, which were the result of physical hazing, possession of drugs, or multiple/repeated code violations. There was no history of punishment for racial hazing, and no previous record of any cadets having been so charged. Consequently I recommended that the racial climate at the school be reviewed to determine if a widespread problem existed. That was easy; but what about the hard stuff?

Appropriate v. Adequate

Now I never thought for one minute that Governor Riley was intending to elevate my status by drawing me into this controversy. It was a hot potato, and as SHAC's commissioner, I was the most adequate and probably the most appropriate fall guy.

I was between a rock and a hard place. I knew that at least two of my board members felt that the students needed to be expelled. I also knew that the attorneys for the Citadel knew that the section of the Human Affairs Law under which we were carrying out this investigation did not give SHAC enforcement authority. It was clear to me that no matter what I or my board might say, the Citadel's board was not going to expel those students.

As I often do in these sorts of situations, I retreated to that portion of our house that I now call my library. I spent long moments contemplating the situation I was in and the ramifications that would flow from whatever decision I might announce. I read and reread my staff's findings and reflected again and again on what we were asked to do. All of a sudden, there it was—my escape hatch. I was asked to determine the "appropriateness" of the punishment, and one could argue that it probably was.

But was the punishment adequate? I suspected that for those two or three board members, the NAACP, the group of ministers, and the Nesmith family, it probably wasn't. At the public meeting announcing my finding, I punted. I found that the punishment was appropriate and left it up to the governor to decide if it was adequate.

16 · *The Conway Crisis*

Three years after the Citadel controversy, we encountered probably the toughest racial conflict of all my years at SHAC. It involved a white high school football coach and a black quarterback at football-happy Conway High School. The dispute was absolutely incendiary. It began in April 1989 with the decision by Coach Chuck Jordan during spring drills that his starting quarterback from the previous season, a black rising senior named Carlos Hunt, would be replaced as quarterback by Mickey Wilson, the son of a white assistant coach who had played sparingly the year before. Hunt would be moved to defensive back at least partially, as it was explained, because college scouts were more likely to offer him a scholarship at that position. The decision was fraught with enormous racial implications that went far beyond the football field, and for months the entire Conway community was rocked with protests, demonstrations, and boycotts.

On September 1, 1989, more than four months after the dispute had arisen, Governor Carroll A. Campbell asked SHAC to investigate the matter. He had become sufficiently concerned about the potential danger not only to those directly involved in the controversy but to the state as a whole. While decisions about football players and the positions they were assigned on the team did not normally fall under the purview of SHAC, we were charged by law with "fostering mutual understanding" among the people of the state. That meant wading into the middle of a racial dispute in which there wasn't much "mutual understanding" existing at the time.

By the time we arrived in Conway, all but five of the team's thirty-six black players had gone "on strike." The Reverend H. H. Singleton, the Conway NAACP president, who coordinated the strike, had been fired from his teaching job at Conway Middle School, and prospects for elevated tension as the school year got under way were palpable. The uproar was getting national attention. In an article published in the November 27, 1989, issue of *Sports Illustrated*, Reverend Singleton was quoted as calling the decision to move Carlos Hunt from quarterback "callous and racial intolerance that seems to border on racial bigotry." Coach Jordan—who had started a black quarterback in three of his six years as head coach and had compiled a record of 51-18 along the way—was quoted as saying, "I have the right and obligation to make personnel decisions."

I assigned two staff members to the controversy, and they spent four days in Conway conducting a wide-ranging investigation, which included interviews and examining statements, conversations, and relevant records. After reviewing their report on their findings, I issued a statement. It came as no surprise to me that it did not please a lot of people.

I said: "My staff informed me that they did not find sufficient facts upon which this agency could legally make a determination that race was a motivating factor in Coach Jordan's decision toward Carlos Hunt." I was quoted in the *Sports Illustrated* article as saying that the incident "was as far from racism as anything I've been involved in." I did not dispute that quote.

Almost immediately a member of my own commission attacked my decision vigorously. Dr. William F. Gibson, a Greenville dentist with whom I had had some previous disagreements, said, "Mr. Clyburn may live in a society different from the one I live in. He may live in a race-neutral society . . . but I personally believe this incident was racially motivated."

Dr. Gibson, who was state chairman of the NAACP and chairman of the national board of the NAACP, went on to attack the agency, saying "It's regrettable that a state agency that is steadily losing its credibility among a large segment of the people it is supposed to protect, would present such a biased finding."

I was taking a lot of heat, in many ways tougher than any I had felt as SHAC's commissioner. I commented, "People have said you ain't thinking like a black person, and I tell them they're exactly right. I'm thinking and acting like an administrator. I expect doctors to think and act like doctors, lawyers to think and act like lawyers, and reporters to think and act like reporters. I don't think black or white; I make administrative decisions based on facts, not race." I went on to say, "I'm sorry Dr. Gibson has felt it necessary to personalize this issue. It's unfortunate that people can't understand that as head of a state agency, I can't let emotions guide me."

If I was catching heat on the racial front, I was getting some words of support from normally conservative newspapers. One of them, the *Greenville News*, wrote:

> This is the same Jim Clyburn who has argued eloquently against flying the "Gone with the Wind" version of the Confederate flag atop the state capitol and who, as a state official, has ferreted out overt and subtle vestiges of racial controversy in this state.
>
> Clyburn's integrity is an admirable personal quality and an asset to South Carolina. It's ironic that some black leaders seek to discredit him for a sense of fairness they have often found lacking in white officials.

My college-town paper, the *Orangeburg Times and Democrat,* was similarly supportive: "Finding courageous public officials is not an easy job, but S.C. Human Affairs Commission head James Clyburn fills the bill. Clyburn issued his finding knowing that it wasn't what much of the black community wanted to hear, but he went ahead with what he knew was right. That takes courage, and for that, Clyburn should be saluted."

For all the back and forth, there were no winners and lots of losers in the Conway affair. For my part I worried that Carlos Hunt and the other black members of the football team would be losing a year of experience and costing themselves possible opportunities for scholarships that would permit them to go on to college.

I was not satisfied with simply conducting an investigation, issuing a finding, and returning to Columbia. My role, I felt, had a deeper dimension that dealt not so much with the law and the legal facts of the case as it did with the human factor and the destructive consequences of human discord. I returned to Conway a few days after the Human Affairs Commission investigation was closed, trying to negotiate a settlement that would make it possible for the black players to return to the team.

Things were not improving in the community, however, and on Saturday, September 9, 1,000 to 1,500 people marched in Conway to support the black players' strike and protest Reverend Singleton's firing. In that atmosphere of unrelenting tension, I met at length with various parties to the dispute and their attorneys, including Coach Jordan, Carlos Hunt's mother, Reverend Singleton's attorney, and the principal of Conway High School.

I drafted several proposed compromises that would make it possible for the black football players to return to the team. Compromises, however, require a degree of good faith among the parties, and in this instance there was virtually no good faith on the table. On September 12, my proposals were rejected, and the stage was set for more public tension and acrimony. The football season was lost, but Reverend Singleton was reinstated to his job.

A Calmer Day in Conway

A few months later, on January 26, 1990, I was invited to speak to the mostly white Conway Rotary Club, an invitation that I took as an important step by the community toward healing its wounds. As I concluded the speech, which contained a lot of rhetoric about restoring stability and racial peace to the area, I said:

> We learn painful lessons from Conway, and the pain takes a long time to leave us. But if the result is a reaffirmation of the good faith and trust among the leadership of all aspects of our community, then the pain has been productive and beneficial.
>
> Today, by your inviting me to speak, I feel we have taken a step in that direction. I sense that there are those in this audience who do not agree with everything I have said. There may be those who do not agree with anything I have said. But you have agreed among yourselves that you will hear me out, and that you will weigh my judgments and my comments in your future deliberations.
>
> That's all I can ask. That's all that can be expected from the leadership of a community which has been jolted badly by division and exploitation. I cannot take away the pain, nor can I prescribe instant solutions for the future. I can only say that there are those throughout this community who yearn for the type

of dialogue and communication which can bring about long-term, beneficial solutions for all those involved.

My references to pain were not all rhetorical. I carried my own share of scars away from the Conway experience.

I wrote in 1991, "Human relations cannot be measured by a ledger-sheet type of accounting. It's more likely to be imprecise, uneven and imperfect. Reaching levels of progress may even occur quietly, and may not set off bells and whistles. It's something that is more likely to be defined in terms of the old generalization, 'When you get there, you'll know it.'"

What If

In the cases of Chester and Conway, the only sense of accomplishment or closure was intuitive, at best. The combatants backed away from the brink of confrontation, but neither side conceded much of anything. In each instance there had been those fomenters who manipulated the public emotion and exploited racial fears and suspicions. As the combat eased, they retreated from the fray, but they never admitted any wrongdoing. Even though the charges that set off the original disputes were proved false or exaggerated, the damage they did took years to repair. Acting as an investigative agency and seeking to establish true accounts of what was taking place, our commission generally found itself wedged squarely in the middle between the combatants, taking fire from each side. For all the grief associated with such a role, however, the job of Human Affairs commissioner produced its own special kind of rewards.

A lot of it, admittedly, was private and personal and generally came at the end of a hectic day when the combatants put off their war for one more day. Some of it came retrospectively, as I pondered my role—perilous though it may have been—and tried to give it some historic perspective. In a way I welcomed the opportunity to step into the full-blooded disputes in Chester and Conway because I knew that we had the opportunity of preventing something far worse from happening.

I have wondered what might have happened if there had been a Human Affairs Commission to listen to the complaints of college students against the City of Orangeburg in 1960. I have wondered most profoundly if innocent young lives might have been saved had there been a Human Affairs Commission to hear unhappy college students who were being deprived of their legal right to go bowling at an Orangeburg establishment in 1968. I have wondered what might have happened if there had been a Human Affairs Commission to hear the grievances of unhappy employees at the Medical College Hospital in 1969. We will never have those answers.

But I've been prompted to wonder on the other hand—as I recalled my own experiences at Conway, Chester, the Citadel, and elsewhere—if we had indeed succeeded in preventing something far worse from happening in those tension-fraught settings. And if the answer was "yes," even a speculative and tentative "yes"—that human danger had been diminished and racial justice had been promoted—then I was satisfied that we had made a contribution to making our state a better place to live.

We were a long way from achieving John West's vision of a "colorblind" state, but we may have helped to bring something tangible—some actual shape and dimension—to what previously had been a vision. John West himself, speaking on the twenty-fifth anniversary of the commission's founding in 1997, said the commission "has brought South Carolina out of the dark years of suspicion, mistrust and division and has created an atmosphere of wholesome and healthy human understanding."

I'm not sure I would have gone that far. But I was satisfied, after almost eighteen years of bruising and battering as commissioner, that we had created an imperfect reality where there had previously only been an idealistic dream.

17 | *The Confederate Battle Flag*

The year was 1962. I was teaching eighth grade youngsters at Simonton School in Charleston. I wasn't paying a lot of attention to the fact that up in Columbia, the all-white General Assembly was hoisting a Confederate flag atop the State House to celebrate the one hundredth anniversary of the state's participation in the Civil War.

Our classroom discussions were directed elsewhere in those days. I was trying to energize those young minds about the world around them. I was more interested in preparing those students to look forward and anticipate what the next one hundred years might bring to our planet.

Although I have not found anything in writing, Governor West told me that it was understood that the resolution authorizing the flying of the flag was to be for that legislative session; but, somehow at the end of that two-year period, the flag was not brought down. No one bothered to raise the question, and year after year, the flag fluttered there beneath the American and state flags. Over time I guess people came to accept it as one of those things "that's always been there" and didn't question the political propriety of it or the message that it sent. Tourists noticed it and took pictures. Postcards on sale at the Capitol Newsstand, a half block away from the State House, displayed it as an identifiable part of the state's culture of resistance.

A lot of people, I think, believed that the flag had been there since the days of the Confederacy and therefore represented some kind of historical linkage to the state's past. Even when it became known that it was a fairly recent addition to the flagpole, there was relative indifference toward it. It was a hundred feet in the air, and people had to crane their necks to see it. What's the harm?

Civil rights leaders were busy with other important issues at the time, flexing their political muscles over things such as desegregation of public schools and the right for black South Carolinians to cast ballots in local, state, and federal elections. The presence of "that" flag atop the State House seemed almost incidental by comparison.

Once, during his second term in office during the late 1960s, Governor Robert E. McNair decided to see what kind of reaction he would get if the Confederate flag was not raised one day. By midday the furor was so great that he quickly put it back in place, telling callers that it had been "sent out to be cleaned."

It was about then that people began to realize that the flag's presence atop the State House dome was not so casual or incidental to a lot of people. And it was about then that many black South Carolinians began to wonder why a flag they felt symbolized slavery and oppression was flying atop their State House.

A Lonely Vigil

That flag did not enter my consciousness until a few days after I became a member of Governor John West's staff in January 1971. I was sitting in my makeshift office just off the lobby of the governor's office when a reporter walked in and asked how it felt to be sitting under a dome that was prominently flying the Confederate battle flag. I had never given it a thought and was at a loss as to how to answer the reporter's question. I don't remember exactly how I did.

In 1977 my good friend and neighbor Kay Patterson, who was serving in the S.C. House of Representatives, decided it was time to address the flag issue head-on and at full speed—which, by the way, was the only way Kay Patterson ever did anything. But while he was one of twelve black legislators serving in the House at the time, the issue didn't generate much political "traction." People had other things on their minds, and Kay's vigorous calls to action seemed like a voice in the wilderness.

Well the flag didn't come down; the issue didn't go away; and Kay Patterson didn't back off. Year after year he renewed his protests, gaining a little support as he went along. I agreed with Kay and had my own strong feelings that the flag should come down. But I was also a state agency head who had to navigate an annual budget through a mostly white General Assembly, and I decided that the well-being of SHAC took priority over expressing an opinion about the flying of that flag over the State House dome. Over time I began to realize that my friendship and creditability with the likes of Kay Patterson might also come into play if I insisted on a neutral role in the matter.

So in 1987, ten years after Kay had begun his lonely fight, I decided to join the fray, legislators' furor or not. But I did not want to do so without having a thorough knowledge of the flag and its history, so I did some research. I made several visits to the Confederate Relic Room.

Among other developments, Attorney General Travis Medlock, who was the son of a Methodist minister, issued an official opinion that the flag could be taken down, and while the attorney general's official opinion prompted no immediate action, it had the effect of broadening the base of support for the issue. By then Kay Patterson was in the South Carolina Senate, where he was joined in the flag fight by fellow senators and my longtime friends John Matthews of Bowman and Herbert Fielding of Charleston. In announcing my decision to take a stand on the issue, I also wrote a rather lengthy op-ed piece exploring the various Confederate flags that had been used from time to time during the war. As I said then, "It is amazing how many people would rather worship a proven myth than face the simple truth. The truth of the matter is there were three flags of the Confederate States of America, but the flag which flies over the State House was not one of them. 'That flag,' as I prefer to call it, is an elongated version of the Confederate battle flag and is actually the Confederate

'Navy Jack' which flew over the bow of Confederate ships." I also explained how small the Confederate Navy was, limiting the likelihood of many South Carolinians ever having fought under this "Navy Jack."

I went on to explain that South Carolinians were much more likely to have fought under a flag that was a modification of the state flag that Sergeant William Jasper raised over Fort Moultrie during the Revolutionary War. "Twenty years after the Civil War," I wrote, "the United Daughters of the Confederacy (UDC) rejected the battle flag and the 'Navy Jack' and voted to adopt the original 'Stars and Bars' as the appropriate flag to serve as a lasting memorial to the brave men and women who fought and died during that war."

My purpose in all this was to suggest that the flag flying over our State House was not an official Confederate flag. It was instead a flag that had been rejected by the UDC and had actually risen to prominence and popularity as a symbol of the Ku Klux Klan. Nathan Bedford Forrest, the founder of the KKK, was a Confederate general from Tennessee, and he and many Tennesseans had fought under "that flag," which in addition to being known as the "Navy Jack," was also called the Tennessee flag.

I wrote in my op-ed piece: "The KKK resurrected the battle flag. They flew it at all of their rallies and displayed it on their vehicles as they terrorized black neighborhoods in the 1920s and 1930s. It was during this reign of terror that black folks were driven from their land and homes and sought refuge and safe harbor in the North."

My purpose in this discussion was to explain why the flag atop the State House was so onerous to black South Carolinians. Black people didn't see "that flag" as a symbol of the Confederacy as a nation, as the "Stars and Bars" flag might have been. The flag they saw was one that adorned pickup trucks and Klan rallies and was a symbol of the raw terror of the KKK. AME bishop John Hurst Adams put it well when he said that supporters of flying the Confederate flag "talk about heritage. It is a heritage of slavery."

For my part I was beginning to understand the intensity of the issue. My position on the flag, moderate as I thought it was, provoked some intense responses. While most of the letters and phone calls were positive, a few were decidedly not. One caller, a lowcountry businessman I knew quite well, asked for the names and addresses of the board members of SHAC so he could tell them what he thought of my "sticking [my] nose into areas where it was not needed or wanted." I gave him the names and addresses and—for his convenience—threw in the phone numbers as well. A few of the letters were of such a nature that they had to be turned over to law enforcement officials, and the threats became so frequent and intense that SLED assigned an agent to me and the agency. It was the second time I had been assigned such protection. This time, it lasted for all five of my remaining years at the agency.

I don't know why people thought black South Carolinians had no stake in this. One upstate editor, who I also knew, said he had spoken with fifteen young black people in his community, and none of them found the flag insulting. He scolded me and other black leaders for not spending enough time on "positive relations between the races." One of the few unsigned letters suggested that it was "blacks who were guilty of racial descrimination [sic], not the whites." It was about that time when I realized that the Confederate flag issue would not be settled on a rational base. History certainly proved me right on that one.

Elsewhere around the South, rational minds were taking hold. Alabama, under the leadership of Governor Jim Folsom, lowered the Confederate flag from its capitol dome in Montgomery in 1994 and put it at a nearby war memorial. Consequently South Carolina became the only state still flying a Confederate flag above its State House for the balance of the twentieth century.

An early compromise involved the point I was trying to make about the legitimacy of the various Confederate flags. That proposal was to replace the Confederate battle flag with the Stars and Bars atop the State House, and it had support from some white and black leaders. But the compromise lost out to the element that favored no action at all, and that position carried for the moment.

Incomplete Compromises

Then came more compromises, most of which were centered on the proposition of "Taking the Flag off the State House Dome and Putting it Somewhere Else." The "somewhere else" ranged from the Confederate museum to an unspecified location somewhere on the State House grounds. The South Carolina State House grounds, it should be pointed out, is a veritable showplace of statues honoring heroes of the state's segregation past—men such as "Pitchfork Ben" Tillman, who engineered the 1895 constitution that disenfranchised black South Carolinians; James F. Byrnes, who carried the state's effort to retain its segregated schools to the U.S. Supreme Court; and Strom Thurmond, whose opposition to the various civil rights acts in the 1950s and 1960s was legendary.

Except for an African American history monument dedicated in March 2001 and a small monument honoring Governor Robert E. McNair, it was difficult to find anything on the State House grounds that did not in one way or the other reflect the state's racially divided past. As people mulled over an appropriate location for the flag once it was taken down from the State House dome, there seemed to be more than a few likely options.

Even so the issue was claiming some political casualties. David Beasley, the Republican governor who had surprised people of the state in 1996 by advocating the removal of the flag from the dome, was defeated in his bid for reelection in 1998 by Democrat Jim Hodges. Beasley's stance on the flag, which attracted national attention, was speculated to have been one of the causes for his defeat. The Beasley plan, another of the "Put It Somewhere Else" proposals, did have the effect of rallying forces on both sides. The state Chamber of Commerce, thinking racial division was bad for business, sided with Beasley in support of taking down the flag. So did four former governors, two Democrats and two Republicans. One of the governors in that antiflag number was my friend Governor West, whom I had asked as early as 1971—his first year in office as governor—about taking down the Confederate flag. West later said he regretted deeply not having taken steps to remove the flag during his administration, and he considered it a missed opportunity of his governorship.

West, who was serving in the state Senate in 1962, was among the legislators who voted for the original resolution calling for the flying of the flag atop the State House. Almost forty years later, he helped to organize a reunion of many of those same legislators, who now called for the removal of the flag they had placed on the dome. Retired Clemson University president Robert C. Edwards, who had helped orchestrate the peaceful desegregation of Clemson with the admission of Harvey Gantt in 1963, wrote an impassioned op-ed piece for newspapers in the state, urging that the flag be taken down.

One of the more moving declarations was written by Columbia attorney and longtime state senator Heyward McDonald. "No matter what reasons we give for keeping it up or bringing it down, there is an overriding reason to bring it down. As long as it flies on the dome, it is the center, the flash point of misunderstanding, controversy and even hatred between the citizens of this state. Let us put aside our divisive political and racial confrontation about the flag and adopt the statesmanlike approach, as together we begin this new millennium without prolonging this new civil war." It was one of the last things ever written by McDonald, a longtime advocate of racial peace and civil rights progress. He died on January 5, 2000, and the op-ed piece was carried in the *State* newspaper a few days later.

The Flag, First and Last

For all the powerful urging to take down the flag and settle the issue, it seemed to have a life of its own. In a 1996 survey legislators ranked the flag issue the least important of thirty-two issues to be taken up for consideration that year. And yet, in terms of time, political combat, and public interest, it was becoming the issue that seemed to have the rapt attention of the entire state.

In July 1999 my friend and fraternity brother James Gallman, who was state president of the conference of NAACP branches, announced that a national boycott would be initiated by the NAACP to place pressure on the state to lower the flag. The boycott was aimed at the state's tourism industry and was designed to keep groups from bringing meetings, conferences, or conventions to South Carolina.

While the boycott had some immediate effect, it was not ruinous to the state's economy. As much as anything it upped the ante politically for the state to search for a solution, and it led to some creative proposals. Governor Hodges pushed for a Martin Luther King holiday and the creation of a heritage museum to showcase the state's diverse cultures. The state's largest religious denomination, the Baptists, joined the second largest denomination, the United Methodists, in urging removal of the flag. Even Bob Jones III, president of the conservative evangelical college in Greenville that bears his grandfather's name, joined a rapidly growing coalition of business, professional, and educational organizations supporting the removal of the flag.

Bumper stickers saying "TAKE IT DOWN" began to appear, and Governor Hodges included the appeal for removal in his 2000 State of the State speech. A few days later, forty-six thousand people gathered at the State House to show public support for removing "that flag" from the State House dome. The governor asked Alex

Sanders, president of the College of Charleston, and me to work together in finding an acceptable compromise.

Alex, who had been a state senator from Richland County for many years and a judge before accepting the College of Charleston presidency, said, "I have no great ambition to do it, I already have a job and that sounds like a hard job to me." I was serving in Congress by that time and agreed with Judge Sanders's assessment. Furthermore I knew the real deal, or so I thought, until I had another blessed experience.

Just When I Thought I Had Things All Figured Out

It was a cold rainy night, and Emily and I had just changed planes in Atlanta, headed to Columbia from what was for us a pretty extended period of time away from home. As we sat on the plane waiting our turn in a long line of planes waiting to take off, the pilot announced that he had just received an advisory that icy conditions had forced the closing of the Columbia airport, so we would be returning to the terminal to await an update. Back inside the terminal we were informed that the flight was being cancelled, and the airline was making arrangements to put us up overnight. Neither one of us found this a very happy situation. We were ready to sleep in our own bed.

As we pondered our situation, I shared with Emily that I remembered passing a gate with a flight to Charleston posted at it. With a little help from the gate attendant, we found out that the Charleston airport was open and there were seats available on that flight. As we rushed to the gate, I whipped out my cell phone and called Emily's sister Mattie Wadley. She and her husband, Bob, agreed to leave their cozy home in Santee and pick us up from the Charleston airport. This was pre-9/11, and it did not matter to the airline that we and our bags would be on separate flights. And it did not matter a whole lot to us that we would not be spending the night in Columbia; our Santee home was the next best thing.

Things were working out just fine. We made the flight, and the Wadleys arrived at the Charleston airport at about the same time as we did, around 11:00 P.M. It was raining and a bit colder than we usually like it in South Carolina, and as we rode toward Santee, sharing the highlights of our trip with Mattie and Bob, the temperature started falling, the rain started turning to sleet, and the road conditions changed dramatically.

It appeared to me that Bob was driving too fast for the conditions we were beginning to encounter, and I suggested that he slow down a bit. He retorted with assurances that his years of driving around Cleveland, Ohio, in similar conditions rendered him fully capable of handling the situation. Minutes after he uttered his assurances, we hit an icy spot. The car skidded off the highway and did not stop until we were deep in wet and icy brush and slush. We were very lucky that the embankment ran slightly uphill and was not one of those deep drop offs that have claimed the lives of many people traveling west on I-26 between U.S. 17 and I-95.

Bob made a few attempts to back out of the dilemma but to no avail, and the icy precipitation made it very unpleasant to stand outside of the car for long. As we sat contemplating our next move, I could see a mile marker and knew we were in Dorchester County. It occurred to me that although we were of different political persuasions, I had had some recent interactions with the Dorchester County sheriff that were rather cordial. So once again I whipped out my cell phone and asked the operator to connect me with the county sheriff's department. The sheriff answered the phone himself. I told him who I was, what kind of situation I was in, and where I could be found. He assured me that help would soon be on the way.

About fifteen minutes later a big pickup truck drove up shining a big spotlight in our direction. Two white gentlemen jumped out and asked if we were all right. We assured them that we were. They could see what kind of help we needed. They had a hook and steel cable attached to the front of the truck. Brushing aside any assistance from any of us, one of them hooked the cable to the bumper of our car, and they pulled us to safety. I thanked them profusely and asked that they pass along my thanks to the sheriff. I noticed that the two of them looked rather befuddled at my request, so I asked whether or not they were from the sheriff's office. They assured me they were not.

They told us that they were from Georgia and were working a construction job at one of the cement plants nearby. They went on to explain that they had been sitting in their motel room watching wrestling on television and just felt that there may be somebody out on the icy roads who needed some help. I thanked them and offered to pay them. They adamantly refused to accept any pay, jumped into their truck, and drove away, proclaiming that there might be others out there who needed their help. I don't know what made me gaze at the rear of that truck as they drove away, but I did. Sure enough, it bore a Georgia license plate. But much to my chagrin, the back window of that pickup was covered by a screened rendition of the Confederate battle flag. When we got into the car, I turned to Emily and said, "Just when I thought I had this flag thing all figured out."

Snatching Defeat from the Jaws of Victory

There were a few other things I had failed to figure out about this issue. In my wildest imagination I could not have imagined that I would ever find myself in dispute—in absolute combat—with the NAACP.

Here was the organization my mother so proudly embraced and which—according to Reverend Newman—had recognized her as its first South Carolina Woman of the Year, the organization within which I held my first elective office as president of the Sumter branch's youth council. Here was the organization that Septima Clark considered so important that she defied state law to remain a member and lost her teaching job and state pension as a result. Here was the organization that Matthew Perry represented so skillfully in the state's courts and that provided the painful avenue to justice for so many black Americans. Here was the organization that the Reverend I. DeQuincey Newman so courageously and diplomatically led down the streets of protest and into a position of political influence and respect in South Carolina.

And yet, in some ways, it was not the same organization. I learned that the hard way.

Passions had been building on the flag issue for years, and the legislature found itself divided in ways that might not have been unexpected. It was far more complicated than the black-white division that might have been expected on such issues.

On the proflag side there were groups such as the Sons of Confederate Veterans, an organization that called the Civil War the "Second American Revolution." There was a legislatively led coalition of loyalists who were making Confederate history and nostalgia a cottage industry and had already secured millions of state dollars to raise and restore the Confederate submarine *H. L. Hunley.* There were others who just naturally fell in line with the notion of a South Carolina rebellion against the federal government, a sentiment for many which seemed to be as alive in the year 2000 as it had been 140 years earlier.

Over on the other side—favoring the removal of the flag from the State House dome—was an interesting aggregation of politically motivated and conscience-driven establishment types who saw the flag as an embarrassment to the more "respectable" elements of the state. Charleston mayor Joe Riley led a march from the Port City to Columbia. My three daughters and I joined the march as did my political mentor John West. Even many South Carolinians who had little interest in politics or the operation of state government had an opinion about the flag.

As all the various interest groups erupted with their strongly held feelings and positions, South Carolina's political arena became a place of passionate and emotional combat. It was a place where the views and values of the one million descendants of slaves clashed with the views and values of the one million descendants of Confederate veterans in a battle over whose heritage would be represented in the state's historic capital. In terms of the operations of state government, there was really nothing at stake, no programs, no budgets, and no services. But in terms of the state's sense of self-esteem and the image it projected to the rest of the nation, everything was at stake.

For its part the NAACP, which had been somewhat indifferent in its support of the flag-removal efforts over the years while Senator Patterson and I were earning police protection, suddenly became hard-nosed. In 1999 the NAACP passed a resolution that specifically condemned "the Confederate Battle Flag being flown over the State Capitol and within the House and Senate Chambers" and called for "its removal and relocation" to "a place of historic rather than sovereign context." The language was ambiguous, I thought, in describing a new site for the flag.

As the issue was coming to a head, time was running out. As the deadline for adjournment of the General Assembly approached, and as a compromise bill awaited a crucial second reading on the floor of the state Senate, opponents of moving the flag let it be known that they would filibuster if they were not satisfied with the final proposal. To block the filibuster, supporters of moving the flag would need to hold together thirty-one votes out of the forty-six-member chamber. That was quite a tall order for a General Assembly that started the session saying they would rather not address the issue that year.

We knew the proflag folks would expect the relocation site to be a prominent and visible one, and after exploring several options, we came up with a compromise we thought would satisfy all involved. The Confederate battle flag would be taken down off the State House dome and out of the legislative chambers, and be placed next to the equestrian statue of Confederate General Wade Hampton in front of the state office building bearing his name. The statue had been moved from a place underneath trees just east of the State House several years earlier and commanded one of the most scenically attractive sites anywhere on the grounds. Not a perfect solution, but it clearly seemed to meet the NAACP's requirement that it be moved to a place of "historic, rather than sovereign context."

Everyone signed off, including the NAACP. On the morning that we gathered on the State House grounds near the proposed site to announce the agreement, word came from the governor's office that the NAACP had changed its mind and was no longer supporting the compromise. Despite the wording of its own resolution, the leadership of the organization had apparently decided that its position was now that the Confederate flag had to be removed not only from the State House itself, but from the State House grounds as well.

Such a position, at that stage, was impossible to accommodate politically, and it created all manner of political awkwardness for many of us. We had negotiated in good faith to reach a compromise in which all parties yielded something and to which all parties could agree. When the NAACP withdrew from that compromise, it seemed to be a breach of faith to many who had labored not only to get the flag down, but also to negotiate a settlement that would accomplish that purpose.

Adding Insult to Injury

The legislators who were involved were especially incredulous and responded with legislation to place "that flag" where it is today, a place of absolutely conspicuous presence on a flagpole thirty feet high directly behind the Confederate soldier monument at the north front of the building. Visitors no longer need to crane their necks to see the Confederate flag seventy-five feet in the air; it now greets them right in the front of the capitol building at the top of a thirty-foot pole.

James Gallman called the plan "an insult," and I agree with that assessment. But that did not have to be the case. Mr. Gallman announced that the NAACP would keep the boycott in place. His statement at the initiation of the boycott had been that the NAACP was in it "for the long haul." That haul was getting a lot longer.

I was torn. I felt that our compromise had met the conditions of the NAACP resolution, and I knew that many people—Governor Hodges, Alex Sanders, legislative leaders, my friends John Matthews and Kay Patterson, and others—had worked long and hard to reach a settlement. We felt disappointed and even betrayed. Charges and countercharges flew briskly, and some of us set out to quiet things down.

In July 2000 I wrote a column that was published in several daily newspapers. It was titled "It's Time to Take a Deep Breath." In it I praised the NAACP for bringing the flag issue to the political forefront in South Carolina. But I was critical of what I considered to be the "unfortunate and unfair" comments of national NAACP president and CEO Kweisi Mfume about the outcome.

I even said I "regretted" that my friend Kay Patterson had chosen to respond to Mfume's comments. I was trying hard to be a peacemaker in all of this, because

I treasured my two fully paid life memberships and longtime relationship with the NAACP. I also valued my friendships with all those who had worked so hard to reach the compromise that brought the flag down.

I held out hope that, at some point in the future, we could revisit the issue and find a less objectionable solution. In the meantime, I wrote that "we should step back from this issue and take a deep breath. All sides should declare a moratorium and give our state and neighbors time to heal from this bruising battle and reconcile with each other."

Apparently such was not to be. The NAACP stepped up its vigilance in the anti–South Carolina tourism boycott, and chose to single out Kay Patterson and me for special attention.

About two years after the flag settlement—April 16, 2002—I received a troubling letter from Julian Bond, chairman of the NAACP's national board, whom I had known since my SNCC days. Julian had a rather distorted view of several important facts and wrote to me as if I had been on a distant planet at the time. The NAACP, it seemed to him, had been in the forefront of efforts to have the flag removed for years, and had stood for placing the flag "in a museum, as the historical artifact it is." It was the first time I had seen such language—and the reference to museum—used with regard to the NAACP's position, and I give Julian a lot of credit for some imaginative historic revisionism. Julian went on to request the rescheduling of a fundraising function I was hosting for the Congressional Black Caucus Institute (CBCI) in Charleston, calling it a "golf tournament."

At that point I began to question seriously the motives and the quality of informed leadership the NAACP was giving to this issue. I responded to Julian's letter rather bluntly, telling him that I was "absolutely amazed at the attitudes and actions you are employing in South Carolina." I informed him that Senator Patterson and I had fought through death threats and police protections for fifteen years, advocating removal of the flag while "the NAACP was content to sit silently on the sidelines." As far as the placement of the flag was concerned, I related the succession of events under which the NAACP accepted—then rejected—the settlement. "There is nothing in the NAACP resolution calling for the flag to be placed in a museum," I wrote, "and there is no way under the sun that South Carolina black legislators could have gotten such a compromise."

With regard to his request that I relocate the "golf tournament" outside South Carolina, I think my friend Congressman Bennie Thompson, who was chairman of the CBCI, put it best. In response to a letter from Kweisi Mfume, with whom we had served in the Congress, he wrote, "It is not a golf tournament. It [golf] is a sidebar to our Health and Environmental Justice [conference]. It is being sponsored by Congressman Jim Clyburn to benefit the Congressional Black Caucus Political Educational and Leadership Institute. The participants are his South Carolina constituents and supporters and the funds they contribute will be used to support our political education and training programs." Bennie, from the Mississippi Delta, came to Congress in 1993, the same year I did. He went on to tell Mr. Mfume, "It is very clear to me that there is a significant lack of support for the sanctions among the NAACP's rank and file."

All the accusations emitting from Julian Bond and Kweisi Mfume in the spring of 2002 were in the context of an elaborate excommunication event that the NAACP was orchestrating against Kay Patterson and me for misdeeds such as the "golf tournament." James Gallman, the state conference president and my fraternity brother, proclaimed that the NAACP "should not offer any positions of honor to those individuals [Kay and me] at our Freedom Fund Banquets or public programs while their stance is counter to that of the NAACP."

And what were our crimes? In Gallman's words, I was guilty of "acting with local agents of the tourism industry who gave misinformation to the managers of tennis star Serena Williams to come to South Carolina in violation of the economic sanctions. Her visit to the Family Circle Cup proved embarrassing for her and her family."

For all the conspiracy-sounding language of Mr. Gallman, I was rather open about it all at the time. I was aware that Serena had contractual obligations to play the Charleston tournament but was looking for a mitigating activity to honor the NAACP boycott. I suggested—through a mutual acquaintance, her accountant Larry Bailey, with whom I occasionally played golf—that she consider donating some much-needed laptops to students at the nearly all-black School District One in Clarendon County and sponsoring the juniors and seniors of Scott Branch High School on a field trip to the Family Circle Cup. Clarendon County is the birthplace of Althea Gibson, the women's tennis legend who was one of Serena's idols, and Scott's Branch in Clarendon County was at the vortex of the legal action that led to *Brown v. Board of Education*. Serena agreed, and my campaign committee chartered buses to get the students down to Charleston.

As for other transgressions, Gallman wrote: "Both Clyburn and Patterson had a hand in persuading the rap group 'OutKast' into performing at the Three Rivers Festival in Columbia." This "display of disunity among African Americans brings dishonor to our efforts." In this instance both Kay and I were guilty as charged. In my response I wrote: "I did speak with representatives of OutKast . . . , at the request of several constituents. Most memorable among them were three young African American women—one of whom was a young, single mother—who appealed to me as their elected representative. They informed me that their jobs grew out of the Sumter/Columbia Empowerment Zone, the $10 million a year for 10 years economic development program that I had worked to get for my two hometowns, Sumter and Columbia. They felt their continued employment turned on the success of the event for which they had worked so hard."

Kay was a little more colorful (as he always is) in his response to Gallman's declaration. "Ain't it 'bout time for y'all to stop lookin-up the Confederate-soldiers-rears at the Confederate-flag and help us with some issues of substance lak 1) educate our children; 2) get a good job; 3) access to health-care; 4) live in a good-house & safe-neighborhood and 5) be treated with respect-and-human-dignity! YOU WON'T DO NUT'IN AND GIT MAD WITH THOSE OF US THAT DO! Ain't that a beach?!!" Kay always expressed himself a lot better and much more colorfully than I did.

While I was encouraged by the outpouring of support I received from local branches and rank-and-file members of the NAACP, it bothered me that we were splintering over issues in which I was a central figure. I was deeply grateful by the action of the Sumter branch, for writing to express its "displeasure, disapproval and dissatisfaction with your [Mr. Gallman's] decision to direct the branches to take action against the above-mentioned African American elected officials [Kay Patterson and me]."

I found myself in agreement also with the branch's opposition to "you [Gallman], assuming the single authority to issue directives to the branches." In the middle of this controversy I received an invitation from the Rock Hill branch to keynote their Freedom Dinner. I declined, citing the controversy. They responded that they were aware of the controversy and still wanted me as their speaker. I accepted.

I have known since childhood that NAACP branches unite around causes, but stubbornly assert their independence when it comes to matters of their own positions and directives. Kind of like my dad at the Church of God meeting that day in Darlington. Politics is about leading people to decisions, not telling them what to do.

It was also troubling to read in the documents from Bond, Mfume, and Gallman that the NAACP boycott should take precedent over service to my constituents. In that regard I answer to no one except the constituents in my district. As I told an NAACP Freedom Fund dinner at Hilton Head in 1999 (before my attempted excommunication), "I usually wear a green tie on St. Patrick's Day, and I join my Jewish and Muslim colleagues and my Italian and German American friends in celebrating their days of heritage observances, and I respect the right of Confederate soldiers' descendants to recognize their own place in history. I love the NAACP and consider it to be a vital part of my own heritage. But I will not let it dictate to me the nature of my service or behavior with regard to my responsibilities as a U.S. Congressman representing some of the most neglected communities and needy people in America."

The pain of the Confederate flag incident remains with me. The result was not only the selection of an objectionable location for the Confederate flag, but worse than that was the role the NAACP played in disrupting what could have been a high point of South Carolina political maturity. It was a slap in the face to people such as Jim Hodges, Dick Riley, John West, John Matthews, Kay Patterson, and, yes, Jim Clyburn.

George Will, the conservative columnist whose work was carried regularly in the state's daily newspapers, put it aptly in a December 1999 column when he wrote:

> This state had an aptitude for disgruntlement. It may have suffered more than any other state from the Civil War, but it deserved to, having done more than any other to ignite it. And even now, when it is a full participant in the prosperity of the country's southeast quadrant, it finds itself driven by an utterly optional argument.

While most Americans are too busy making money to wage culture wars, South Carolinians find time to be at daggers drawn with each other over a symbol.

We were locked into a test which by now was not so much a matter of finding an acceptable political compromise; it was a matter of which side was more disgruntled.

In that kind of atmosphere there wasn't much chance of a good solution, and in fact the final outcome was a wretched one. Twenty-three years earlier, as he began the struggle to bring the flag down from the State House dome, I cannot imagine that Kay Patterson believed that it would be brought down from the dome and placed right in the front yard of the State House.

So there, not more than fifty feet from the statue of archsegregationist Benjamin R. Tillman, stands the battle flag whose memory he did so much to impose on South Carolina culture and civilization. Sometimes hard work and good intentions produce very little in the way of benefit. Sometimes a compromise turns out to be no compromise at all. At a time when so many good people in South Carolina meant to send a good message of the state's good intentions, the outcome was in many ways the exact opposite.

This photo was taken at a rally in Charleston in July 1967. Dr. King (at the mic) did not miss a beat while the other stage participants including me (second from left) react to the sound of an explosion we thought was a gunshot. It was actually a photographer's flash bulb smashing on the floor.

PART SEVEN

Coming to Grips with Reality

I had gotten sidetracked by an episode of self-doubt and some irritating challenges that I had allowed to distract me. I still saw myself completely dedicated to a life of politics; that's where my skills lay, and that's what energized and motivated me. My dreams and hopes were still built around the prospect of my being elected to public office. Two losses in that arena in 1970 and 1978 might seem to make such a prospect rather remote, but I promised myself that I would just redouble my resolve and run again for secretary of state the following year, 1986.

18 | *A Day of Reckoning*

Dayton, Ohio, was hardly the place where I would have expected to confront some difficult realities of my life and reach some crossroads decisions. But that's where I was on October 31, 1985, when the world seemed to be converging on me from several directions at once.

For one thing I was completing my tenth year as commissioner of the State Human Affairs Commission (SHAC), and while I was pleased with the professional progress and public status of the agency, I did not expect it to be the final resting place of my political career. I had run for the State House from Charleston County in 1970 and had not gotten enough votes.

Then, in 1978 I ran for South Carolina secretary of state, a true leap of faith considering that no African American had held a constitutional office in South Carolina since Reconstruction. It was an enjoyable and in many ways blessed experience. Traveling to every nook, cranny, curve, and corner of our beautiful state accorded me rewards whose true value can never be measured. I met people of all persuasions, ilk, and status, who all in their own ways expressed an unquestionable, unconditional love for our state. Some of these expressions were favorable to my candidacy; some were not. I was bent on the idea of my state moving forward, but I was not so naïve as to deny the fact that some things and some people are steadfast in their persistence to maintain the status quo. In spite of all the rewards of my candidacy, the ultimate prize eluded me. I fell short . . . again. I felt like giving up on my long-held dream of elective office.

But what does a person do after quitting?

I have always had an inherent need to contribute to advancement, to make a difference, to act as a spoiler for status quo agendas, and to do so from a platform of progressive thinking against prejudice, contentment, and stagnation. For all the challenges of policing and promoting racial justice in South Carolina, I was beginning to feel the grind of administrative and management responsibilities. I had always considered myself a high-energy, high-profile guy, not a grinder.

Ten years as commissioner of a controversy-prone agency was also taking something of a personal toll on me. A Columbia attorney had filed a complaint with the Equal Employment Opportunity Commission accusing an agency deputy and one of our investigators of improprieties during an investigation, and he charged that I did not have the best interest of the charging parties at heart. A federal judge had just

With the source of my strength, my wife and daughters, circa 1974:
(front) Jennifer and Angela, (back) Mignon and Emily

dismissed a sexual harassment case brought against me by a young woman I hardly knew and to whom I could not remember ever speaking. A grievance panel had just ruled against me in the firing of an employee whose work record was replete with oral and written reprimands, an unpaid suspension, and a prior mutually agreed-upon resignation. The committee chose to ignore written documents, the employee's own admissions during her testimony, and corroborating testimony of more than a dozen of her former and current coworkers supporting my decision. What kind of life was this? Is this what I had marched down Amelia Street to achieve? I was in a slump and I wondered—at age forty-five—if this was a time for me to change directions, maybe even leave South Carolina.

I was in Dayton in my capacity as president of the International Association of Official Human Rights Agencies (IAOHRA). I was to participate in a program designed to address in a diplomatic way the growing rift between our member agencies who promoted racial justice and the White House, which had declared its opposition to Affirmative Action. President Reagan was completing his first term and had made the termination of the program a goal of his administration. Our host in Dayton, Jerald Steed, believed it would be beneficial to bring together appropriate spokesmen from both sides to discuss the issue. As the director of a state Fair Employment Practices (FEP) agency from South Carolina, I would make the case for Affirmative Action, including a defense of specific goals and timetables that program opponents found so onerous. Representing the opposing view, that of the Republican administration, would be the four-year chairman of the Equal Employment Opportunity Commission, a gentleman who would become much better known a few years later when he was nominated to be an associate justice of the U.S. Supreme Court, Clarence Thomas.

The discussion would not have the format of a Clyburn-Thomas debate. Our hosts were too savvy for that. While part of our purpose was to bring attention to Affirmative Action and to rally state human rights agencies to its defense, there were other less visible issues at play. The occasion for our gathering was the annual meeting of the Dayton Intergovernmental Equal Opportunity Commission, and we were anxious to demonstrate that for all the differences we might have on issues, we could conduct ourselves in a civil and deliberative manner. While program presenters and host staff worked hard to sustain that atmosphere, some of the participants may have gotten a little zealous in their support of affirmative action and may have expressed their views to Clarence Thomas privately in rather direct ways. For the most part, however, we were anxious to prove that all of us were part of the "system"—the orderly process of government that allowed for disagreement and dispute in a peaceful and civilized manner.

Another "off-the-agenda" issue on our minds was the fate of Clarence Thomas himself. While those of us advocating for Affirmative Action had had our share of disagreements with Clarence over the years, we knew that his reappointment to the EEOC position in the second term of Ronald Reagan's presidency was somewhat in jeopardy. We also felt that the leading candidate to replace him would be even less acceptable to us, so we tried to keep our criticism of Clarence Thomas somewhat muted and well within the bounds of civility. We were quietly hoping he would be reappointed, a sentiment in which history seems to have proved us wrong.

And there was of course a personal agenda of my own, the future of Jim Clyburn and whether that future could best be spent at SHAC. Dayton actually proved to be a good place from which to take something of a long-range perspective, both figuratively and geographically, on that future.

Our luncheon speaker was Don Crawford, who had been elected the first black city commissioner twenty-four years earlier from a population that was only 16 percent black. Quite a pioneer in the civil rights cause himself, Don had welcomed Dr. Martin Luther King to the city twenty-one years earlier, at a time when his white fellow commissioners were less enthusiastic about Dr. King's presence in the city. Don had made the occasion memorable by presenting Dr. King a key to the city and noting that in Dayton, Ohio, "there are still some doors in this city that neither this key nor my persuasion could open for you."

Dayton had improved its racial stance considerably over the years, and Don's rhetoric had not lost a beat. Clarence, Jerald Steed, and I agreed that none of the three of us was up to that level of oratory.

Similar but Very Different

Earlier in the day, the program had gotten off to a civil, if somewhat unusual, start. Clarence Thomas spoke first, and he put things on a personal basis, describing his upbringing in Georgia by a grandfather as a devout Catholic and his education at Holy Cross College and Yale Law School. As he spoke, I marveled at how different our lives had been, even though we both grew up in the segregated South.

I recalled this episode years later while watching an interview Clarence did on *60 Minutes*. He told a painful story about how his grandfather admonished him never to look a white woman in the face. It reminded me of a parallel incident early in my own life. My dad had taken me with him to a meeting of ministers at the Church of God campground in Augusta, Georgia. He was introducing me to several of his fellow ministers, and one of them extended his hand to shake. I stuck out my hand somewhat indifferently, and cast my eyes downward. My dad grabbed me by the shoulders, spun me around, and smacked me with a very memorable clout. In his sternest, ministerial voice, he instructed me that whenever I spoke to or shook a person's hand, I should look them squarely in the eyes. It was a lesson from the practical text of E. L. Clyburn, and it is one I carry with me vividly—and practice faithfully—to this day. It also rather dramatically describes the different worlds of Clarence Thomas and Jim Clyburn.

Bridging Differences

Clarence described his position on Affirmative Action that morning in narrow terms, calling his opposition to the goals and timetables of the program as matters of "personal philosophy." His beliefs on the subject were as much a part of him, he said, as his arms and legs. That made it tough to attack him, although there were so many hands raised for questions as he finished his presentation that Jerald deferred them until later.

Jerald then brought me to the podium. The first thing I noticed was that Clarence immediately left the room. I didn't know if it was an urgent restroom call or whether he decided there was something more important for him to do with his time than listen to my presentation. It was a little unsettling for me because there were parts of my presentation I wanted Clarence Thomas to hear. I did some mental reshuffling of my talk, knowing all along that I had the advantage of not only discussing an issue I knew well, but also speaking from the side of the issue that was favored by most of the people in the audience. I was preaching to the choir, and I took advantage of it.

I began by spending a little time comparing as discreetly and carefully as I could the different philosophies Clarence Thomas and I brought to the issue. I knew I was speaking to a national audience, and I wanted people to understand that just because Clarence Thomas and I both grew up black in the Deep South, we had known a different set of experiences and viewed many things—including Affirmative Action—in a different way. Unlike Clarence, I chose not to go any further into my childhood and upbringing and turned next to the differences in our respective jobs. Mine, I explained, was as the chief executive officer of a state agency that was empowered by statute to develop and implement procedures to "eliminate and prevent" discrimination. Clarence's was at the federal level with a more restricted range of authority, I said. Having thus prepared the audience in a polite way—and in Clarence's absence—for a discussion of our differences, I launched into an aggressive advocacy of Affirmative Action.

I stressed the dual role of my agency, that of elimination *and* prevention, and I acknowledged that in the first endeavor—elimination of discrimination—our office worked under the watchful eye of the EEOC, operating under the guidelines and procedures developed and implemented within its interpretation of court decisions and understandings of Title VII of the Civil Rights Act of 1964. It sounded bureaucratic but as I looked out over my audience, I saw them nodding, and I realized that those choir members to whom I was preaching were bureaucrats too. Besides, it felt good to be citing statutes in support of my cause, instead of hearing that great litany of statutes against my cause as had been the case so frequently earlier in my life.

It was in the area of prevention of discrimination where we parted ways with the EEOC, I said. Without making any reference to arms and legs—as had Clarence Thomas—I offered a recitation of what I considered a rather remarkable experience of Affirmative Action in my Deep South home state. In South Carolina, I said proudly, we had not only developed procedures; the General Assembly had promulgated policies requiring Affirmative Action plans from all state agencies and their subdivisions. I saw a few jaws drop among those audience members who had been nodding in bureaucratic assent only a few moments ago. Legislative support for Affirmative Action in South Carolina, the state that led secession from the Union 125 years earlier and set off the Civil War? How times had changed!

Clarence Thomas was still not in the room to hear my stirring comments, but I ascended my soapbox anyhow and launched into a downright patriotic declamation about Affirmative Action. It was something I had first used a year earlier to close out our South Carolina Human Affairs Forum in Columbia, and I liked it so well I decided that my Dayton, Ohio, audience should hear it, as well. Here's what I said that day:

> Affirmative Action is an experiment. Affirmative Action is America in action. We are an experimental nation toying with the idea of individual rights as opposed to collective control and tyranny. So far, the experiment has worked no doubt to the surprise of many who witnessed its birth over two hundred years ago.
>
> It is interesting to speculate why not only has the nation survived, but also its ideals and principles. Let me hazard a few guesses as to why America and its ideals have worked over all these years. First of all, I do not believe America is perfect. Neither did the Founding Fathers of the nation. No sooner had our Constitution been written than the first ten amendments were presented and adopted. They were called the Bill of Rights, and we can all be thankful that they were included in the package.
>
> Americans have never tried to conceal or ignore their imperfections. For the most part, they have tried to recognize and correct them. When the enslavement of a race of people created a conflict which threatened the very foundation of our Constitution, the nation went to war with itself to resolve the conflict and ensure the integrity and sovereignty of the Constitution. And, a century later,

when it was found that discrimination still prevented millions of Americans from participating as full-fledged citizens, our nation moved to correct the flaw with wide-ranging civil rights legislation.

While it is common to say that no nation in the history of the world has granted more individual freedom, it is just as valid to say that no nation has ever tried harder to correct the flaws and impediments in its system. We are still imperfect; and, we are still trying to live up to the principles to which the Constitution has committed us. The important message is that this nation has never stopped trying. And, we would do well not to stop NOW.

On that triumphant note, I swelled with some self-satisfaction and was prepared to let those high-flung words conclude my speech. Then I noticed that Clarence had returned and from the look on his face, he was anything but serene. I later learned that he had been cornered by some zealous pro–Affirmative Action folks outside the conference room who apparently were not content to wait for the question-and-answer session to have their time with him. Not a good thing.

It would not be a good thing either for me to conclude the speech with a scowling Clarence Thomas sitting at the head table. The last thing any of us wanted was for him to feel we had set him up. From a political point of view, it was not very smart. From a personal point of view, it was not very polite. And from a professional point of view, for those of us whose agencies were so dependent on good relations with EEOC, it would be disastrous to make the boss unhappy.

So I did not conclude my speech at that moment. I was thinking quickly and if there was one thing my political campaigns had taught me, it was thinking on my feet. I remembered that Jerald Steed, our host, had used as a theme of the whole conference that we build bridges among the various elements of disagreement in our midst.

At that point, the great bridge builder Abraham Lincoln came to my rescue. It was a passage that still hangs on the wall of my office in Washington. It's titled "Duty as Seen by Lincoln." I had actually considered using it to start the speech, but Clarence wasn't in the room at the time. Besides, it made a better closing comment under the circumstances. I recited it by heart: "If I were to attempt to read, much less answer, all the attacks made on me, this shop might as well be closed for any other business. I do the very best I know how—the very best I can; and I mean to keep doing so until the end. If the end brings me out all right, what is said against me won't amount to anything. If the end brings me out wrong, ten angels swearing I was right would make no difference."

I finished and noticed there was a slight smile on Clarence's face. The audience was more enthusiastic, and on that happy note, I decided to conclude my presentation. I wasn't sure how good a case I had made for Affirmative Action or how successful I had been in putting Clarence Thomas at ease. I only knew with some certainty that I was getting a little weary of the balancing act of what was beginning to feel like my own "Dayton Peace Accords" about ten years before the better-known version that ended years of ethnic wars in the Balkans.

Gloom and Doom

Later that afternoon, I spent some quiet time in my motel room. The gloomy November Ohio weather was doing nothing to improve my own gloomy mood. Ugly legal and political battles awaited me once I returned home to Columbia, and Clarence Thomas would be waiting back at the convention center in about an hour for a joint press interview to resume our conflict over Affirmative Action. And then, as if to make things seem really personal, an alarm went off in the motel, and there was an announcement on the intercom for all occupants to evacuate the building to help test their emergency system. I suddenly became a forty-five-year-old rebel. I decided that I would carry out my own act of personal defiance and civil disobedience and not leave the building.

A few minutes later, having successfully defied authority and remained surreptitiously in my room, I decided to walk a few blocks to a department store to buy a belt because I had left home without one. My mind was thrashing all over the place by then and lurking into some dark corners of my past. Walking down the street in Dayton, Ohio, I was reliving some of the crises of my earlier life.

I thought about how uneven and disorderly things had been during those years of my life. For whatever heroic image I may have had of myself as a crusader for equal rights on the streets of Orangeburg, Rock Hill, and Columbia, I also knew that my third year at State was an academic disaster because of overindulgence in campus politics and theater projects. I remembered the pain a year later of watching my friends and classmates graduate in June of 1961, knowing that I had to put in an extra semester because I had cut too many classes and changed my major one time too many.

All this from a guy who grew up in the relative happiness of a family of two loving and nurturing parents and two proudly supportive brothers. How could that have happened? What kind of guy had I become? I thought about the instability that carried over into the early years of my marriage. On June 24, 1961, we got married in Paterson, New Jersey, because that's where we thought we'd live. I had good memories of my summers there, and for all the nobility we may assign to South Carolina's later civil rights transformation, prospects for a young black family in 1961 were probably better in New Jersey than they were in my home state.

As it turned out, we stayed in South Carolina, but things were far from stable for us. Upon my graduation from State, we began an odyssey of shuttling back and forth on Interstate Highway 26 in pursuit of job opportunities—Orangeburg to Columbia in 1961, Columbia to Charleston in 1962, back to Columbia in 1965, back to Charleston in 1966, and finally back to Columbia in 1971.

My catharsis on the streets of Dayton, Ohio, was suspended long enough for me to enter the department store and buy the belt that I needed to wear that evening. Then I spotted a tie nearby and for some reason thought about my good friend Phil Grose, who was my partner in this project before he passed away. Phil and I actually met in November 1970, although we had talked by phone prior to that time. He was my supervisor when I served on Governor West's staff, and we developed a friendship which continued until he transitioned. We often talked about our experiences in the governor's office and how much fun it would be to write a book one day. We felt very strongly that many things we were doing were not being adequately and accurately reported. We knew a lot about how South Carolina worked and who made state government work.

I bought the tie and stepped out onto the street to begin my walk back to the motel. The sun had broken through the Dayton gloom by then, and I was beginning to feel better about things. I was standing at the corner of Third and Jefferson Streets in Dayton, Ohio, but I was beginning to realize that I was standing at a crossroads of a larger nature of my own. The internal thrashing I was experiencing had left me sobered to the realities of my world. I had to make some tough decisions about this crossroads in my life, and I had to make them pretty soon.

The walk back to the motel was more upbeat. I reflected on the meeting of the previous evening with C. J. McLin, another Dayton civil rights champion, who was serving his twentieth year in the Ohio House of Representatives. As a younger man, he had filed suit against a dime store in downtown Dayton for its refusal to serve him, and during his service in the army he had protested for equal treatment of black servicemen. In later years he had been a catalyst in mobilizing black political strength at the state and local levels. I had met him at the 1972 Democratic Convention in Miami when I was president of the South Carolina Young Democrats, and I had stayed in touch with him since then, regularly seeking his advice and help when venturing into political thickets outside the South. I also knew that he had close ties with U.S. Senator John Glenn, with whom my brother John had developed a close political relationship.

Jerald Steed and I called on C. J. at his funeral home that evening to get his opinion of our strategy to get Clarence Thomas reappointed as EEOC chairman. A lengthy discussion ensued in which we agreed that we all had serious differences with Clarence in many areas of the civil rights world. But we also agreed that as Reagan entered his second term, the nation was swinging politically to the conservative side. What we needed most in light of the impending political storms at that time was stability and continuity at EEOC. Clarence Thomas gave us both. I also knew that we were having a press conference the following day, and I wanted to make sure that our statements were in sync with local civil rights leadership.

C. J. reluctantly concurred in our strategy to support Clarence's reappointment and agreed to help us in that effort. I figured a good word with Senator Glenn and others in the Ohio political orbit would broaden the credibility of our effort. Time with C. J. McLin was always well spent, and I remember this evening particularly. C. J. died three years later and was succeeded in office by his daughter, Rhine McLin, who went on to serve as mayor of Dayton.

I got back to the motel remarkably weary. But my mind had cleared, and I spent a few moments preparing for an evening in which I knew I would be playing second fiddle to Clarence Thomas. He was the out-of-town celebrity from Washington; I was just this guy from South Carolina.

Sure enough, the press conference quickly developed into a one-man forum for Clarence to express his view against Affirmative Action. I fielded my first question only after Clarence had left for another interview. I was caught up in what must have sounded like some political equivocation. I said I opposed Reagan's position on Affirmative Action, but that opposition didn't necessarily apply to all his policies.

The answer wasn't satisfying to one particular reporter, who must have been looking for the print equivalent of a sound bite. So he asked me again, using slightly different words. I answered him again, also using slightly different words. I pointed out that Affirmative Action didn't represent all that big a part of the overall operation of our work, and even Clarence himself had said it constituted "less than one percent of EEOC's work." I said, "I tend to feel that we should not allow a one percent area of disagreement to occupy one hundred percent of our discussions. I feel obliged to leave that area alone and to concentrate on building a relationship with the EEOC on that other 99 percent."

I was working hard on our enterprise of being friendly to Clarence Thomas, but it was becoming complicated, and the local press was looking for something more combative. At a later presser, Clarence was asked about procurement "set-asides," which were something of the business equivalent of Affirmative Action and had become a hot topic locally. Clarence ducked it, noting that EEOC had no jurisdiction in such matters. Finally came a question—perhaps something of a "softball"—that gave him a chance to talk about enhancing the relations between EEOC and the state agencies. It probably didn't make the morning papers or the TV news reports, but it made Jerald and me feel better, and it gave Clarence a chance to show he was agreeable to finding some peaceful territory in which all of us could be comfortable.

Mixed Feelings

The good feeling carried over to the dinner that evening, which was a celebration of the twenty-third year of the Dayton Human Relations Council. Dayton had a heritage of progressive relations between the races, and it showed that night. There were 550 people in attendance, and for a city that's just a little larger than Columbia, that's quite a turnout. Mayor Paul Leonard greeted us, and I was introduced by the local Urban League director to make a few remarks and introduce Clarence Thomas. I kept to the high road, repeating some of the material I had used earlier in the day, and it was clear that our strategy was working. When Clarence took the podium, he was pleased and comfortable, and we heard an oration about his childhood and growing up in Georgia, the importance of education to black people, and his broad philosophy of life. He stayed away from the contentious spots, and when he finished, we were all smiling. Jerald and I could feel good that we had accomplished our purpose for bringing him to Dayton in the first place.

The program ended on a high note with the recognition of Ed King for his twenty years as director of the Dayton Human Relations Council. I had gotten to know Ed four years earlier, when the International Association of Human Rights Agencies held its annual meeting in Dayton and I had spoken as president of its sister organization, NAHRW. Ed was honored that night by James McGee, who had succeeded Don Crawford on the City Commission and became Dayton's first black mayor, serving from 1970 to 1981.

King and McGee had been successful in dealing with that most delicate of political issues, the expectations that follow the election of a black man to a major political office. Some say such an election is proof that there are no racial problems after all. Others acknowledge that racial problems exist, but they expect the black man to solve them instantly. Somehow King and McGee had managed to help guide Dayton carefully through that tumultuous decade of the 1970s, using great political skill and diplomacy, and that evening was a tribute to their rare accomplishments. It was also verification in my own mind that important political movements and decisions are not matters of bludgeoned outcomes in winner-take-all fights to the death. Jerald and I had learned that much firsthand in our nuanced work with Clarence Thomas that day. Ed King brought the evening to a fitting close by quoting the well-known Victor Hugo passage that says in essence that more powerful than the invasion of mighty armies is an idea whose time has come.

The powerful idea of promoting a good racial climate in political and economic matters was an idea whose time had come—and successfully—to Dayton, Ohio, and I was pleased to help celebrate that reality. Another idea whose time had come with me that night was the almost instant need to turn in for the night and rest up for the trip back home the next day.

Alas even that was not to be a simple proposition in what was becoming my endless—and maybe even my sleepless—day in Dayton. As Jerald, Clarence, and I were leaving the conference center, we were greeted by two very serious-looking police officers who ordered us back inside. I decided one act of civil disobedience was enough for one day, and I meekly and wearily complied, along with my two companions. Once back inside the door, one of the officers asked, "Is there a Mr. Clarence Thomas around?" Jerald pointed out Clarence, and the officers proceeded to give us some information I could really have just as well done without.

It seemed that during the banquet, authorities had discovered a roomful of automatic weapons in our motel. They had not been able to determine the occupants of the room, and they were at a complete loss to figure out any purpose for the weapons. There were a couple of theories, though. One was that there was a gold show in the convention center and there may have been a plot to rob the show. Did that take a room full of automatic weapons? That seemed to be quite a bit of overkill, but what did I know?

Another theory, and this one sent chills through all of us, was that there might be an assassination attempt on Clarence. Once again, such an enterprise would hardly seem to require a roomful of automatic weapons, but at that point I was not thinking too clearly. Clarence seemed offended at the notion of a plot against him and dismissed it, saying that he saw nothing controversial about himself. Clarence opined, only sort of tongue in cheek, there might have been some confusion of his name with that of Clarence Pendleton, who was President Reagan's chairman of the U.S. Civil

Rights Commission, and had been traveling around the country making some pretty caustic racial comments.

All the talk about who was and was not controversial was a little academic at the time. I was tired and ready to get to the motel and go to bed. It was finally agreed that we would be allowed to do so, but with a twenty-four-hour watch on Clarence Thomas's room. After spending a few minutes watching the television news in Clarence's room, we all turned in for the evening.

19 | *Reaffirming My Goals*

After returning to my room I was visited again by visions of Jim Clyburn's past, present, and future. I rummaged through my past in some more detail, wondering if there was another good career I had missed. I thought back to the joy I had gotten working with young people as a teacher of English and history at Simonton and C. A. Brown Schools in Charleston and wondered if I had jumped too quickly into other fields. I thought of my moves to the South Carolina Employment Security Commission, the Neighborhood Youth Corps and New Careers programs, and wondered if I had changed jobs too quickly. I thought about my encounters with controversy as I took over as director of the Commission for Farm Workers in 1968 at a time when the agency and its previous director were the objects of public criticism over management of the commission's finances. I recalled with some pain my decision to choose appointment as SHAC commissioner over continuing in law school, a decision which caused a real family crisis which lingers to this day.

Happier thoughts crowded in, and I began to notice a pattern. I had felt comfortable and effective in my capacity as president of the South Carolina Young Democrats, and I was energized in my roles as president of the nation's two leading fair employment practices associations. I enjoyed the political byplay, the public aspect of my jobs, the feeling that what I was doing made a difference in people's lives. I had enjoyed visiting with people such as Don Crawford and C. J. McLin and seeing firsthand how people could influence the course of history around them.

But I was beginning to feel some loneliness in that dreary Dayton hotel, six hundred miles from home. As I had felt so often, I was missing my dad—my great partner in life, E. L. Clyburn—who had transitioned seven years earlier, in 1978, and I was missing the wise counsel I would have gotten from my mom, Almeta Dizzley Clyburn, who had left us fourteen years earlier in 1971. I drifted off to sleep that night without having resolved the major personal dilemmas that had occupied my long day in Dayton.

The next morning I awoke surprisingly well-rested. Somewhere along the line, I had found some guidance. I could still conjure up imaginary visits with my parents, and I could hear my dad's stern admonition. "Stop feeling sorry for yourself, partner, and get on with your life," he would have said to me. And I could hear Mom repeating what she had told me so many times in the past, "You can make of yourself anything you want, if you just work hard enough." That's exactly what they would have said. I knew that beyond any shadow of a doubt.

Things got a lot clearer after that. What I would have told Mom was that I still had the same ambition I had articulated in her beauty shop thirty years ago. I wanted a career in public life. And to Dad, I would have nodded in agreement sheepishly and would have admitted that I had begun to find excuses for not facing up to what needed to be done.

My day in Dayton had not produced any new thinking. But it had brought some focus to what I knew had been my ambition all along. It was just that I had gotten sidetracked by an episode of self-doubt and some irritating challenges that I had allowed to distract me. I still saw myself completely dedicated to a life of politics; that's where my skills lay, and that's what energized and motivated me. My dreams and hopes were still built around the prospect of my being elected to public office. Two losses in that arena in 1970 and 1978 might seem to make such a prospect rather remote, but I promised myself that I would just redouble my resolve and run again for secretary of state the following year, 1986.

I acknowledged to myself that it was not exactly a superhighway leading me to that ultimate goal in life. But I accepted the reality that whatever obstacles might seem to lie in my path would be addressed and removed. Anything short of such determination would disappoint my friends and doom me to failure.

On that morning after my day of reckoning in Dayton, Ohio, I wrote myself a mental memorandum and gave myself four assignments:

1. Get back to South Carolina and confront my detractors. Not to do so would be caving in and sacrificing the public credibility I had worked so hard to build.
2. Take control of my own destiny in a positive and aggressive way. It's what my dad would have expected of me.
3. Defend SHAC against its detractors and continue my mission of making it a "firm, but fair" arbiter in the difficult world of racial conflict.
4. Recognize the reality that my goal in life was to achieve the kind of record and reputation that would qualify me for my lifelong dream of being elected to public office.

I boarded the plane later that morning with a new belt and a new resolve about my life. I also had a new tie. The one I had bought for Phil, I decided, would go well with my outfit. I'll get him something else one day, I promised myself.

PART EIGHT

The Dream Realized

About the time the Rotarians were checking their watches and wondering where I was going with all this, I pointed out that with the new district lines splitting Lee County, all but one of my relatives lived—and would be voting—in the Fifth District, and I felt certain they would be voting for John Spratt. "I fully expect, and I am absolutely certain, that John Spratt will be treating my family members, with the utmost dignity and respect," I said. "By the same token, you can be absolutely certain that I will treat you, sir, the members of this club, and all other white voters of the Sixth District with the same dignity and respect I expect John Spratt to extend to my family members in Lee County."

20 | *Deciding to Run for Congress*

When Winston Churchill became prime minister of Great Britain, he said that he felt all his past life "had been but a preparation for this hour."

On a much more modest scale, I knew that feeling. In spite of the fact that I had suffered my third election loss in 1986, when the lines were drawn following the 1990 census to create a black-majority congressional district in South Carolina, I had the unmistakable and undeniable feeling that my life had indeed been spent preparing for that moment. I was almost fifty-two years old at the time, hardly an age to be taking personal, professional, and financial risks, particularly with three daughters in the formative stages of their lives. Angela Denise had arrived on July 27, 1973.

But what the heck, Churchill was sixty-six when he became prime minister of Great Britain and he didn't do too badly. Maybe South Carolina could endure a fifty-two-year old running for a freshman seat in Congress. I know I didn't feel fifty-two; I felt like a kid. Suddenly everything seemed to make sense. Everything seemed to be part of the preparation process—the more than seventeen years of racial mediation and enforcement at the Human Affairs Commission, the nearly four up-and-down years with John West, the work with migrants and seasonal farm workers at the South Carolina Commission for Farm Workers, three wonderful years at the Youth Opportunity Center and the Neighborhood Youth Corps and those fruitful years of class-room experiences at C. A. Brown High School.

There was more than that too. It went back to that day on Amelia Street in Orangeburg, and controlling myself as I was being slammed into that police cruiser at the Rexall drugstore while high-pressure fire hoses were pelting my fellow students with water. It went back to the time spent with Matthew Perry and understanding what it took to win and not just fight. It went back to James T. McCain and the will he instilled in a lot of youngsters from Sumter, South Carolina, to fight with peaceful means in the face of physical danger and human abuse.

It went back to my three political losses—and the lessons gained from those defeats. I had learned to become more realistic about my aspirations, a little more analytical about what was happening, and a little more practical about my expectations. In those three elections, I had been an underdog, looking to pull a political upset. I was fired up with some sense of pioneering and trailblazing, and it may have blinded me a bit in light of the historical and political facts of life around me.

For all that wisdom, however, there were some immediate realities. "Tip" O'Neill, the great Massachusetts congressman and Speaker of the House, said it well when he suggested that all politics were local. He was correct to a point, but to that statement I would add another: all politics are also personal. Those political folks who try to soothe damaged friendships by saying "There's nothing personal in all of this," could not be more mistaken. It's all personal. In some cases, politics can be more personal than any other aspect of life.

I had taken to heart the various conversations I had had with my good friend and traveling companion Rudolph Canzater, who often urged me to run for Congress. His reasoning was very personal. I thought about what it could mean to other friends and acquaintances, not to mention members of my family. My wife, siblings, and children could become targets. All those deep thoughts were converging in those formative days of June 1991, when it became clear that states covered by the Voting Rights Act of 1965 and its 1982 amendments would be required by the U.S. Justice Department to create congressional districts in which the minority population would be in the majority. For once I realized I would not be the long-shot candidate. I remembered the famous words of the Texas congresswoman Barbara Jordan, who once said, "When they wrote the Constitution and began with the words 'We, the People,' I was not included in that 'We, the People.'"

Well I would say to Barbara on this occasion, thanks to your work and the work of many, many others, I felt as if I were included in "We, the People." There was something tangible and visible that said to black Americans, and particular to many black southerners, there is some degree of fairness and reason in your world. For once, as we ran for public office, it would not be as automatic underdogs.

I confess that the prospect of a majority-black congressional district in South Carolina intrigued me and drew my attention. As the plans were being drawn and debated, I monitored those activities, and when the district was finally established in eastern and central South Carolina, I was encouraged. It included several places where I felt I could do well, including Sumter, my hometown, Orangeburg, my college town, Charleston, my first "adopted" home where I had run a good race for the South Carolina House of Representatives, and Columbia, my "new" home for more than twenty years. The district included a good sector of middle-class black neighborhoods and historically black colleges. In addition to S.C. State and Claflin in Orangeburg, there were Morris College in Sumter, Allen University and Benedict College in Columbia, and Voorhees and Denmark Technical Colleges in the town of Denmark.

There was also a sizable population of white residents in the district. Unlike some of the more urbanized black majority districts in the eastern and midwestern portions of our nation—where the black population ranged upward to 90 and 95 percent—the new Sixth District of South Carolina was about 42 percent white, and included all or most of the county seats of Florence, Marion, Colleton, Dorchester, Williamsburg, Clarendon, Sumter, and Bamberg.

These were the counties that fell along the north-south corridors of U.S. Highways 17 and 52 and Interstate 95, which provided many of the low-wage employees for resorts and high-end developments in places such as Myrtle Beach and Kiawah and

Seabrook Islands. The Sixth District would be one of the economically poorest congressional districts in the entire country. Many of these workers traveled several hours every day by bus from their homes in places such as Lake City, Kingstree, and Hemingway to the expensive beachfront and golf resorts many miles away. It was a tough and not very rewarding existence, and for a prospective congressman, it would prove to be one of the most perplexing of many perplexing problems of the newly fashioned district.

But before any thought of serving the people of the district could be entertained, there was the business of putting together a campaign to run for election. John West had another piece of advice that applied here. The two most important rules of politics, he said, were (1) to get elected and (2) to get reelected. Since rule number 2 was not applicable—unfortunately—I concentrated on rule number 1.

As I set out on that goal, I realized that I had good potential bases of support in several locations around the district, but Columbia would be my headquarters and would be crucial to my chances to win. Columbia, the state capital, was the political mecca of the state, and it's the place where black politics was a particularly powerful and mature force. Black families in Columbia had been active politically for decades, and there was reportedly a Columbian at the first U.S. meeting of the Niagara Movement at Harpers Ferry in 1906. It was in Columbia that one of the nation's early NAACP chapters in America had been organized. My quest for a congressional seat would begin in Columbia, and if things didn't go well there, it could well end there.

There were three politically important people in Columbia whom I needed to have with me for my campaign even to get under way. Two of them were powerful within their own communities—Kay Patterson, who represented the state Senate district where I resided, and Ike Williams, the longtime NAACP field secretary who had been an activist in the civil rights movement almost as long as I had. The third was Bill DeLoach, a savvy strategist and insider in political circles around the state. I had come to know Bill in 1974 during a heated gubernatorial race, and that's when I began to recognize his considerable political instincts and abilities.

Bill had actually been among the early people encouraging me to run for the congressional seat, and his interest meant a lot to me. But I had a bigger role in mind for him than that of friend and political adviser. I wanted Bill to run the campaign. He had been a lowcountry teacher representative for the South Carolina Education Association when we first met while trying to elect S.C. Congressman Bryan Dorn to succeed Governor West. We had become friends, and when I was asked four years later to recommend an African American to join the long-shot campaign of Dick Riley for governor in 1978, I suggested Bill DeLoach.

Riley won in a major political upset, and I knew that Bill DeLoach had had a lot to do with it. He went on to serve as a key member of the Riley administration for eight years, and when it ended, Bill set up a highly successful consulting business in South Carolina. He had everything I needed for that top spot in my campaign. Few people knew the political terrain in our state as Bill did. Few people knew the upper echelon of Democratic Party politics better than he did. And no one knew Jim Clyburn— political baggage and all—better than Bill DeLoach did.

Between Bill and me, it was something of an open secret that I was interested in the congressional seat. But before the "secret" became public, there remained the conversations with Senator Patterson and Mr. Williams. If—for whatever reason—they couldn't support me, the race would be badly handicapped for me.

Kay Patterson was a dedicated educator, community leader, and civil rights activist, and he had been a good political friend of mine for years. Kay Patterson could also be a fearsome adversary. He wrote a weekly column for the influential Columbia weekly *Black News,* and people cringed at the prospect of having their names appear in Kay's column. He was a highly educated and literate man, but his writing style was an exaggerated street slang that could be—and often was—uncompromising and brutal, particularly on his black readers. I kept a copy of the column Kay wrote the week after I lost my 1978 primary election for secretary of state, in which he described black voters as "sharecroppers" on the Democratic Party "Plantation." Noting my loss, he asked his readers, "If you is a Sharecropper, then where is your share?" He chided them and wrote, "Sometimes I wonder—yes I duz. You wuz so mad with me, all worried and wanting to fight 'bout which one of those four good white men folks [Bryan Dorn, Brantley Harvey, Dick Riley, or Tom Turnipseed] would be the next Guv'ner—you ain't had time to elect a good Blackman [Jim Clyburn] to Secretary of State in 1978."

I heaved a sigh of relief that I had escaped Kay's wrath that day, and I vowed I never wanted to run any risks with him—ever!

Ike Williams represented a different set of issues. High-profile and outspoken, he was a few years younger than I, and we had both grown up as admirers of the great NAACP leader Reverend I. DeQuincey Newman, who had died in 1986. Like me, Ike championed causes of academic advancement and student rights during his years at our alma mater, S.C. State, and he led an effective classroom boycott in 1967 to advance some of the issues my colleagues and I had addressed years earlier. Ike went on to succeed Newman as field secretary at the NAACP, and he and I maintained a good but sometimes strained friendship.

In those early days of my exploratory thinking, Bill DeLoach carried out his first major act as unofficial manager of my unofficial campaign. He contacted both Ike and Kay on my behalf, "feeling them out" as to their inclinations toward my candidacy. He reported back that he felt comfortable that they would be with me. That was encouraging, but I told Bill I needed to hear it directly from each of them.

The next day I received a phone call from Ike Williams, and with no hesitation he pledged to me his "unwavering support." While I had hoped Ike would be with me, such a strong pledge was something of a pleasant surprise. As a former NAACP executive, Ike understood that his role as arbiter of civil rights disputes was different from mine as Human Affairs Commissioner, and that we would have disagreements, some of them public. But he had stood with me in one of my most difficult decisions, the Conway controversy. It took some courage for Ike to support me when other NAACP leaders were opposing me. He was a good political operative—a savvy street fighter—and his encouragement in my race for Congress was critical.

The next morning I got a call from Bill DeLoach asking me to drop by his office at lunch time if I had no other plans. I did so, and there was Kay Patterson. To my relief, I learned that Bill had already cleared the way for a good conversation with the senator by confirming with him that Kay had no plans to run for the seat himself. Then came the clincher, and it became a goose-bump moment etched permanently in my memory. Kay Patterson pulled out his checkbook and wrote me a check for one thousand dollars, which at that time was the federal limit for individual contributions. Nothing could have thrilled me more than knowing that the senator was not only with me, but that he was with me big time. My campaign was off to a good start.

There remained the question about Bill DeLoach himself. For all the conversations we had been holding, Bill was still helping me out only as a friend. I had yet to see if he would come on board as captain of my team. As things turned out, the conversation with Bill went beyond my best hopes and expectations.

As had been the case with Ike Williams and Kay Patterson, Bill required no selling job at all. In fact he was several steps ahead of me. He informed me that he would be glad to manage the campaign on two conditions. The first was that we would need to hire a campaign director who would be in the office every day. This was a really good situation for me because Brenda Lee had been organizing meetings with black women on my behalf, and this allowed me to hire her on a full-time basis. But I thought Bill's second condition, that he not be paid was a little bit strange. I would have paid Bill the maximum to get his services; to get him free was too good to be true, and as is often the case, it did prove to be too good to be true. I found out later that Bill was setting me up big time. His management of my campaign would come at a cost, but the benefits of his political foresight and astuteness were worth it.

Having cleared the first three hurdles, it was time to address the big one. It was time to tell Emily England Clyburn what was on my mind. She held the ultimate veto power and wasn't bashful about complaining to me that she was always the last to know what I was doing. Although she would not admit it, Emily had a high degree of cynicism about politics, a quality which justified—I thought—my not listening to her as much as I should have.

Bill knew me well enough to know my apprehension about telling Emily. There was an upcoming trip to Philadelphia to attend the annual meeting of IAOHRA. I had served as president of IAOHRA and its sister organization, NAHRW, and regularly attended their annual meetings. It would be a good time, I told Bill, to break the news to Emily of my plans to run for Congress.

Well, as it turned out, it just didn't seem to be a good time to talk with Emily about my plans. I woke up every morning telling myself that this would be the day, and I went to bed every night not having done so. Weeks later, as speculation began to appear in the news media around South Carolina, I finally broached the subject with Emily. Of course she had known all along what I was thinking and doing and had just decided that she was going to make it tough for me. Our conversation was upbeat—not nearly as dreadful as I had expected—and with the green light from Emily, it was full speed ahead.

There was a formidable field lining up for the race. Aside from the ten-year incumbent, Robin Tallon, there were five black candidates in the Democratic primary race, and all of them were veterans of political activity in the past:

John Roy Harper of Columbia was legal counsel for the South Carolina Conference of Branches of the National Association for the Advancement of Colored People (NAACP) and had served on County Council in his home county of Richland.

Frank Gilbert was the state senator representing Florence and Marion counties in the geographic heart of the old Sixth District.

Kenneth Mosley of Orangeburg was a college professor at my alma mater, S.C. State University, and had been the Democratic nominee for the old Second Congressional District in two previous cycles.

Herbert Fielding was serving as a state senator from Charleston.

Of the four black adversaries, Herbert was my only regret, and it was a real one. We had been political soul brothers for a long time and had become best friends. In the 1970 election, which had been such a disappointing loss for me, Herbert had been a winner.

Political friendships are tough to sustain, but I decided that whatever the outcome, Herbert Fielding would remain my friend. And over the years, we have done just that.

Personal feelings are one thing. But there was another reality burdening me as I pondered the commitment to run for Congress. I was carrying a lot of political baggage. I had lost three straight elections—two statewide races for secretary of state in 1978 and 1986 after my 1970 loss in the Charleston County House race. For whatever reasons those losses occurred, they could raise serious questions among people who might be asked to support me. It was suggested on occasion that there was a "three-strikes-and-you're out" rule. I usually responded that life is not played by baseball rules.

All that, however, was still not my biggest concern. Unlike my four prospective opponents in the congressional race, I had spent the last eighteen years of my professional career in one of the most controversial jobs imaginable. As Human Affairs commissioner I was the arbiter of racial, gender, and other kinds of discrimination disputes, and as anyone who has spent a lifetime—or less—in South Carolina, there is nothing more sensitive than people's feelings about their civil rights. For all the public policy pronouncements of goodwill and great hopes, there was just beneath the surface of citizens, black and white, the simmering of deeply held human emotions. When those emotions did flare up, and when troubles did erupt, more often than not you'd find Jim Clyburn in the middle of things.

Controversy-laden public issues—including the Conway, Chester, and Citadel incidents and the Confederate battle flag debate—had cast me in the role of mediator in a forum of exploding human emotions.

Along the way, as a long-standing agency head—a card-carrying bureaucrat—I had withstood my share of audits, lawsuits, and random public criticism, all of which "went with the territory," but which did little to enhance the resume of a prospective congressional candidate.

It had been hard on me personally, and in many ways it had been even harder on my family. I wondered, at the very heart of my thinking, whether I should subject the Clyburn family to more of that ordeal.

Bill DeLoach and I argued over those matters, and he laid out the other side of the issue, telling me with great conviction how many reasons he could put forward for me to run, including what a good guy I was, how many people liked me, how widespread my support was, and so on. After all the smoke had cleared from the room, Bill's smooth-talking rhetoric prevailed (as he knew, and I hoped, it would), and by the time he had finished his argument, I had decided to move on to the next steps, political baggage and all (as I knew I would).

Nobody's perfect, I guess.

21 | *Adventures in Campaigning*

A lot of the time spent in election campaigning runs together like something of a blur. It seems to be one continuous string of dinner speeches, "meet-and-greet" gatherings, fund-raising phone calls, long automobile rides, and power naps.

There's no way to avoid those experiences. I had learned from my earlier campaigns that there is no good alternative to the grind of hard work. Some candidates believe they can escape the ordeal by raising a lot of money, buying a lot of technology, and engaging in mass communication—things such as flashy television advertising, automated phone calls, heavy direct mail, and so on—believing that these things substitute for hard work. I guess I never raised enough money in my early campaigns to indulge in that kind of luxury. Local politics is personal. And your approach to obtaining voter support had better be personal as well.

So what I did indulge in was a heavy application of "retail" campaigning, the old face-to-face style that leaves your throat sore, your right hand aching, and your jaws tired from too much smiling. But amid all that marathon activity, certain moments stand out in my memory, especially as I worked my way through my first campaign for Congress. I had gotten a good boost from important friends and colleagues, and I was starting out in a good frame of mind. But there were several defining moments.

Going Pro

The first one came very early when my brother John, who had settled in Washington with his family back in 1965, and our S.C. State schoolmate Elijah "Baby" Rogers put together a luncheon for me. They invited some friends of theirs, and a few other S.C. State schoolmates. It would be an introduction for me to the Washington way of doing things, and before the luncheon was over, we had raised fifteen thousand dollars. That was a pretty good day's work, I thought.

John asked me to stay for a moment as the luncheon was breaking up. He wanted to introduce me to Diane Feldman, a Washington pollster who had worked with John and Baby on several D.C. political campaigns. She and I had a brief but remarkably productive conversation. I was impressed by her credentials and professionalism, and I had an intuitive confidence that she could be of tremendous benefit to my campaign. In the months ahead that confidence was more than borne out.

The big question at that moment, of course, was whether this candidate from South Carolina could afford a professional political consultant. I had hardly even put together a campaign budget, and here I was launching into what would certainly be a major expenditure. But John, who had just helped me raise fifteen thousand dollars at a small lunch, smiled and assured me in his best Clyburn-brotherly way that with the funds available among the D.C. cadre of family, friends, and S.C. State schoolmates, the Feldman fees "would be no problem." In a matter of moments, my confidence shot upward. I was already dealing on a high level with a Washington campaign pro.

The Field Opens Up

A second defining moment came several weeks later just a few moments before I started an interview with the *Berkeley Independent* in the town of Moncks Corner. I was handed a message requesting that I return a phone call to Robin Tallon, the incumbent Sixth District congressman, who had held the seat for five terms. Robin had already announced plans to seek reelection.

I decided to return Robin's call before starting the interview. Robin told me that he was withdrawing from the race. He said he had a pretty big war chest of campaign funds, but he didn't "have the stomach for the kind of campaign [he] would have to conduct in order to secure the win." Robin was a nice guy and had always done well with black voters. I could understand his hesitancy to get into a primary race with five black candidates in what could be a political free-for-all. He went on to say that— although he would not be making a public endorsement—he felt his withdrawal would make me the odds-on favorite to win. I thanked him for the call and told him how much I appreciated his encouraging words.

I immediately called Charlene Lowery, who had been on Robin's Florence staff for almost ten years. When I told her about my conversation with Robin, she pledged support and reminded me of how close our families had been over the years.

Charlene had twin aunts, Delores and Delares, who were longtime operators at the Clyburn Beauty Shop in Sumter and who considered my mother to be an important mentor of theirs. Their feeling of indebtedness to the Clyburn family, Charlene explained, gave her the cover she needed just in case Frank Gilbert, one of my opponents in the Democratic primary, made trouble for her. Gilbert represented Florence and Marion Counties in the state Senate, and he and Charlene had been longtime members of the same church. Things were starting to look good. In a matter of weeks, I had brought on board a big-time consultant from Washington and had gained a big time supporter from Florence.

Faith Restored

Defining moment number three was one of those experiences that can be described only as a refreshing and restorative shock to the system. It gave me a fresh insight into human nature and let me know that there are some good guys out there after all. I was already feeling good about the early stages of the campaign when I was invited to visit a sewing plant in the town of Andrews to meet with the plant owner, who was also the day-to-day manager. A sewing plant in Andrews, a town that was having its share of economic troubles, was hardly a place to feel upbeat. Sewing plants are fairly fundamental, low-wage types of operations.

The town of Andrews straddled the county line between Georgetown and Williamsburg counties in an economically disadvantaged part of the state. The plant actually sat on the Georgetown County side of the line outside the Sixth District. I called on the plant manager one spring morning and after exchanging a few pleasantries he presented me with a five hundred dollar check. I thanked him, and as I stood to leave he motioned me toward the far end of his office, which overlooked the production floor of the plant, where several hundred people were busy at work, most of them African Americans.

He turned to me and said, "I know that this plant is not located in the Sixth District, but most of the workers down there live in that district." He said that he was convinced that I was going to be the next congressional representative from the Sixth District. In that context, he said, one of the early issues Congress would address would be raising the minimum wage.

"As the owner of this plant," he said, "I will be asking you to vote against increasing the minimum wage." Then came the shock, and to this day, I do not think I've ever been more thoroughly surprised. "All of those people down there are going to want you to vote for it," he said. "Now none of those workers can afford to write you a check, as I just did. But they are representative of the majority of the voters in your district. You would do well to never forget them."

On that spring day in that grim sewing plant in Andrews, South Carolina, I had my faith reinforced in the basic goodness of a single human soul. I never saw that man again, and I realized that he had nothing to gain in offering me such advice. But in that moment, he had showed me a generosity of spirit much larger than the five hundred dollar check he had handed me. I left believing that there was some kindness and decency in unsuspecting places out there, and I suddenly found new energy to pursue my ambition to become a congressman for "the least of these."

Things Get Nasty

There were also some defining moments of a not-so-pleasant nature. As my candidacy began to take an upswing, some of my opponents decided it was time to sling some mud in my direction. The most vicious such effort came in the form of a document entitled "ABC" (Anybody But Clyburn), and it nearly ruined my longtime friendship with Herbert Fielding.

The document appeared at a news conference held by Ken Mosley at the real-estate office of State Representative John Scott of Columbia. It highlighted a scurrilous litany of whispers and innuendoes that had been circulating during the campaign. It also highlighted some legal troubles my brothers had recently experienced, and there was a list of women with whom I had been rumored to be romantically involved. The document even regurgitated some of the vicious accusations made by my detractors accusing me of mismanagement of SHAC. While some people might shrug off things like that as "politics as usual," I could not be that casual. I took the document to be a personal insult directed not only against me but against my family, as well.

Herbert Fielding called me—our first direct conversation of the campaign—because he had heard I was holding him and his campaign responsible for the "ABC" document. He vowed he would never stoop so low. I wanted to believe him because I never knew Herbert to have that kind of mean streak in him. But I also had it on pretty good authority that the source of the document was a former employee at SHAC who had been terminated by her supervisor and whose appeal had been rejected by me. That employee was working in Herbert Fielding's campaign office.

Perhaps the worst part of the entire "ABC" document was the fact that it reached our household through the hands of a neighbor, who gave it to one of my daughters, who gave it to Emily, who presented it to me. Campaign hardball was one thing, but attacks that reached into my family life were way, way below the belt.

Later I found out that my detractors were trying to bring my four opponents together in something of a joint effort to discredit me. It was even reported that two of them were trying to work it out so that whichever candidate got into a runoff with me would be supported by the other three. Bill DeLoach, a tireless worker of the information grapevines, kept me posted on these deeds, and we were able to proceed without much diversion of effort.

Herbert swore that he was not involved in these efforts, and I really wanted to believe him. Our friendship meant as much to him as it did to me, I felt, and I chose to think he just might not have been paying as much attention to the work of his staff as he should have been. At any rate I survived this shameful episode, which I dismissed as a childish and foolish act of desperation. I freely admit though that it caused me a few sleepless nights and I grew much more appreciative of Emily's steadfastness and my daughters' understanding during the whole ordeal. Their devotion, along with Bill DeLoach's political astuteness, got me through it, somewhat bloodied but no less determined to keep myself focused on the real issues of the campaign.

Losing Support

There was another defining moment involving my friend Herbert Fielding, and I believe this was just a plain old political miscalculation. Herbert had made it clear that a major part of his campaign attention would be concentrated in Williamsburg County, a vast rural area with a large black population, and he established a major campaign office in the county seat of Kingstree. The undisputed political chief in the area was a Baptist minister, B. J. Gordon, with whom Herbert had served in the South Carolina House. Based on that friendship, Herbert was enjoying B. J.'s support, and it was a source of considerable strength for the Fielding campaign.

B. J., however, had been ensnared in an extensive "sting" operation known as "Lost Trust" two years earlier in 1990. The sting, carried out by the U.S. Attorney's Office, brought charges against twenty-eight legislators, lobbyists, and others—including B. J. They were accused of accepting bribes in exchange for their vote on a piece of legislation supporting pari-mutuel betting.

For whatever the reason, Herbert Fielding chose to distance himself from B. J. Gordon with some remarks made during a visit to Williamsburg County. My Williamsburg County coordinator, Veronica Cooper, made sure the word got back to B. J. He was furious, and immediately began to reassess his support for Herbert.

As it turned out, some of B. J.'s supporters were quietly helping me anyhow, including his sister and Selma Conyers, who was the Democratic Party chair for the county. They were also happy to suggest to B. J. that he switch his support from Herbert to me. B. J., whom I had known pleasantly for years, agreed, and he went even further to demonstrate that support. He leased one of his large recreational vehicles to the campaign. It was a visible symbol that my candidacy had the B. J. Gordon seal of approval.

He helped me in other ways as well. Through his service as moderator of his Baptist association, he invited me on several occasions to speak at church meetings. He also made calls to his friends and associates throughout the Pee Dee and was even effective in Colleton County, which is fifty miles to the south of Williamsburg.

I guess I should thank Herbert for whatever he said that offended B. J. Gordon, but that would be too cruel. I'll simply say it was another defining moment—a very positive moment—in my expedition toward a congressional seat in Washington.

Winnowing the Field

One by one my opponents seemed to be falling to the side, some by mistakes—such as Herbert's distancing himself from B. J. Gordon—and others through opportunities afforded me in one-on-one encounters. As my golf buddy Johnny Kinloch would say, I was "cutting them out of the herd one by one."

Ken Mosley was an early target of mine, at least partly because of his role in the "Anybody But Clyburn" business. He offered me an opportunity for an initiative on my part when he criticized my handling of the Human Affairs contracts with the Equal Employment Opportunity Commission and the U.S. Department of Housing and Urban Development. Both these agencies were major enforcers of antidiscrimination statutes, and I had worked long and hard to develop "deferral status" for South Carolina and its antidiscrimination agency—the Human Affairs Commission—so that we could handle complaints at the state level when those complaints originated in South Carolina. Ken Moseley had chosen the wrong area in which to attack me. I knew these federal agencies well, and I had been active in the national organizations of state civil rights agencies. He laid this pitch right into my wheelhouse, and I knocked it out of the park.

I then decided to turn the aggressor myself, and I began raising questions about the time Ken was taking away from his duties as a faculty member at S.C. State. I knew the investment of time it would take to be successful in this campaign and had resigned my position with the SHAC to focus my attention on campaigning full time. Wherever Ken showed up on the campaign trail, I would wonder out loud how much the parents of S.C. State students were getting for their money.

I reminded them that this was Ken's third run for Congress, and I soon heard that the attacks were hitting home. Over time I began to see less and less of Ken Mosley on the campaign trail.

Frank Gilbert was my most formidable foe. He had served eight years in the General Assembly, the last two in the Senate. He represented a portion of Florence County, an area with a large concentration of white voters and a place I considered to be up for grabs. My opportunity to square off with Senator Gilbert came somewhat unexpectedly during a forum conducted by the mostly white Florence Rotary Club. Four of the five candidates participated. By then Ken Mosley had effectively been cut out of the herd.

The format provided that each of us could make brief opening comments, and there would be questions from the floor. Except for the fact that there were four black congressional candidates appearing before a mostly white audience, the first part of the program seemed unremarkable and inconclusive. It was during the Q&A that things got interesting.

A Great White Hope

One of the members rose and asked each of us to respond to the same question, reminding us that the Sixth District was now majority black and considered to be overwhelmingly Democratic. With the withdrawal of the white incumbent, Robin Tallon, all the remaining candidates in the primary were black. Whichever of us won the primary, he acknowledged, would probably become his next congressman.

In that eventuality, he asked, "How could white voters, who account for over forty percent of the voters in the district, be expected to be treated by a black congressman?"

It could have been considered a "loaded question," and two of the candidates seemed uncomfortable and verbally squirmed with their answers. Frank Gilbert was not bashful, however, and he offered a rather direct answer, talking about the history of black people in government and the paucity of black representation in the district, state, and nation. He concluded that the time had come for a black person to serve.

For all the truth in Frank's response, it didn't seem to leave much of an impression on our white listeners. I had anticipated such a question and welcomed it. What could be a more forthright concern for these members of the white establishment in Florence, South Carolina? For years Florence had been the economic and political center of the Pee Dee, and it represented the largest concentration of white voters in the district. Unlike some of my fellow candidates, who may have found the question to be abrupt or even hostile, I took it to be thoughtful and honest.

When I spoke, I did not challenge or disagree with Frank directly. But I sensed that it was a chance to "cut him out of the herd" in his own home county. I also saw the chance to speak directly to a constituency that had been largely unaddressed in the fight among the five of us for black votes in the district. My answer was not specifically designed to cater to white voters; it was intended, however, to let them know their hopes and dreams were as much in my thoughts as those of black voters.

I began with some indirect comments about the geographic boundaries of the district. Lee County, I noted, had formerly been entirely in the Sixth District, but redistricting had split it 50-50 between the Sixth and the Fifth Districts. Such a distinction had important family and political implications for me. I told them that my mother was born in Lee County, and I still had many relatives there.

About the time the Rotarians were checking their watches and wondering where I was going with all this, I pointed out that with the new district lines splitting Lee County, all but one of my relatives lived—and would be voting—in the Fifth District, and I felt certain they would be voting for John Spratt.

"I fully expect, and I am absolutely certain, that John Spratt will be treating my family members, with the utmost dignity and respect," I said. "By the same token, you can be absolutely certain that I will treat you, sir, the members of this club, and all other white voters of the Sixth District with the same dignity and respect I expect John Spratt to extend to my family members in Lee County."

I sensed that it was not the kind of answer they expected; but, from the spontaneous applause that followed, I could tell I had convinced them that they could trust me to be fair and evenhanded. I had bridged the black-white issue directly but tactfully. I had also probably cut Frank Gilbert from the herd.

The experience with the Rotary Club emphasized a growing concern for me as the campaign progressed. The five black candidates in the primary were being largely seen and heard in black venues, and we were scrambling among ourselves for that 60 percent of the district voters. The big prize, however, the one that would separate one candidate from the rest, lay in white communities, where—like the questioner at the Rotary Club—people were wondering how they would be treated by a black congressman. Our polls were showing that about half the voters in the district were undecided, and most of them were white.

Bill DeLoach concurred that it was a major problem for us. I mentioned further that my speaking schedule was not exactly being filled up by invitations to speak to white groups, and I wondered how we could reach white voters. My brief comments to the white Rotarians, however well received they might have been, hardly constituted saturation coverage. Bill's answer was simple and complicated at the same time: "We will reach them in their living rooms," he said.

The Big Gamble

Television advertising was nothing new in the early 1990s, but it was expensive, and it was used largely in statewide or national campaigns. For us to commit a large portion of our mission—reaching white voters—to television was a major gamble and an expensive one at that.

We had limited our media buys to radio. But our radio messages were for the most part concentrated on smaller constituencies and had narrow purposes. How would we craft a message with a mission as broad as outdoors—a message to white people? And how could we pay for it?

Bill had answers to each. To question number one, he said, "We will use a values piece," whatever that meant. To question number two, he said, "You will go to the bank." It was then that he reminded me that he had agreed to work the campaign with no pay. The other, unspoken, part of that commitment, he said, "that working without pay was my financial commitment to the campaign. Now it's your turn to make your financial commitment."

It was a moment of truth for me, and it was probably the determining moment of the campaign. For all the encouraging feelings I had gotten from the early burst of fifteen thousand dollars from my brother John and his Washington friends, fund-raising had not come easily, and I had even been attacked by a local minister for receiving twelve thousand dollars in contributions from some local bank officials. Of course that minister did not bother to mention that I had been a member of the bank's board.

To make matters worse, Bill reminded me that I not only needed to borrow some money, I needed to do so in the form of a personal loan. Unlike loans I had made to finance my races for state office, the repayment of this one could not be guaranteed by friends. Under federal law, this one had to be on my signature alone. James E. Clyburn would be betting the ranch on this one. I gulped and picked up the phone.

Fortunately it was not exactly a "cold call." I had served on bank boards for several years—Citizens and Southern and C&S/Sovran, in particular—and had made some good contacts and friendships along the way. Now I was wondering how those contacts and friendships might hold up in this situation. It wasn't long before I had my answer. The friendships turned out to be in good condition, and the first call led to my negotiating a one hundred thousand dollar personal loan.

I was simultaneously gratified and terrified. As I signed my name to that loan agreement, my hand was trembling, and I could only imagine the consequences if the ad didn't reach its mark and, worse still, if I lost the election. If I had been motivated before, I was downright afire with incentive now.

The loan responded to Bill's number two issue. I had made my financial commitment to the campaign and had driven myself to the point of deep financial distress. The unaddressed issue remained question number one. What was the "values piece"? What was going to be the theme of this miraculous TV buy that was going to reach into the living rooms of white voters in the Sixth Congressional District and convince them to vote for this black guy? What great wisdom was going to empower me to reach across racial chasms that had divided South Carolina for generations? And more important, would it be good enough for me to be able to repay my one hundred thousand dollar personal loan?

For once Bill DeLoach didn't have a quick answer. The "theme," he said, would come from a speech before a live audience. I agreed there was certain spontaneity to this approach. Good themes rarely come out of brainstorming sessions held in campaign offices by a weary candidate and staff members inspired by little more than stale sandwiches and flat sodas. Good ideas come from the passion of public appearances and human contacts.

Searching for a Theme

Bill and I had chosen for an early testing of my candidacy an invitation I had received from the Reverend Anthony Dicks to deliver the Men's Day address at the Friendship Baptist Church on House Street in Columbia. It was a small, all-black congregation, but Bill thought I might somehow impart a racially ecumenical message in that set-ting. What Bill did not know, however, was that I rarely make direct political refer-ences when I speak at those kinds of events, and I did not do so in this instance.

I chose to close my remarks with a story I had used frequently about an incident that occurred with my dad and me when I was a preteenager. It took place on a day when he and I were leaving my grandfather John Dizzley's home in Lee County. Driv-ing out to the main road we came upon a tree limb lying across the road in front of us.

As my dad swerved to avoid the limb, I said rather casually, "Somebody ought to move that thing."

Dad slammed on the brakes so hard that he literally threw me into the dash-board of the car. "Well?" he said to me.

"Well, what?" I answered, a little confused and distraught.

"Well," he said, "aren't you somebody? Get out of the car and move the limb."

I proceeded to get out of the car and do as Dad told me, tugging, pushing and pulling until I had gotten the limb out of the roadway. I got back into the car, and we continued our trip to Sumter. Not a single word was spoken between us the rest of the way home. Strategic silence was often Dad's way of putting an exclamation point to one of his impromptu lessons. Obviously the strategy worked on me. I not only remembered the lesson, I was using it in speeches forty years later.

The Men's Day audience at Friendship Baptist seemed to like the story too. And, as it turned out, so did Bill DeLoach. "That's the theme," he decided, apparently see-ing in it a family story, a father-and-son story with a theme of self-reliance. At a time when political attack ads were becoming popular and effective, it had a wholesome quality to it. I, on the other hand, wasn't so sure.

As I often did, I deferred to Bill's judgment. We called Bill Carrick, a politi-cal consultant from Aiken who had become successful and well-known on the West Coast. I had known Bill from my earliest days of political activity, and he had helped me get elected as the first African American president of the South Carolina Young Democrats. He and Bill DeLoach had gotten to know one another while working to-gether on Dick Riley's successful gubernatorial campaign. Bill Carrick had never lost touch with his South Carolina roots, and he, I decided, could bring his high level of professionalism to the ad, along with his keen sense of South Carolina politics and culture. In other words he would spend my hundred thousand dollars well.

And he did. The campaign flew Bill Carrick to South Carolina to make an ad out of the tree-limb story, and everybody, including me, loved it. When I saw the finished product, I saw how wrong I had been with my early reservation about the theme. I thought it was not only a terrific piece of campaign material, it also removed a lingering concern I had harbored since we began discussing this particularly project.

The tree-limb ad had no racial message whatsoever. If anything, it showed that basic human values reach across whatever artificial lines we may erect to separate people from each other. That was basically the message I had been trying to convey from the beginning of the campaign. Race wasn't the issue; human values were. Dad had been teaching that lesson all along and—as usual—he was right.

The campaign had left the Clyburn family physically exhausted and emotionally drained, which is something we always try to keep from the voters we greet on Election Day. That's the day we dress up in our finest, flash smiles to voters standing in line, wave to reporters, and show to our friends that we have indeed survived all the trials and tribulations of a long ordeal.

Inside we're worried about the turnout; we're wracking our brains to make certain there was nothing we overlooked; and we're praying that there's no big surprise awaiting us that will disrupt our hopes and expectations.

Those are only some of the worrisome things that occupy a candidate and a candidate's family. I had certainly known my share of Election Day disappointments, and I had learned well the regimen of showing the stiff upper lip and fighting back the real emotions.

There was no reason to feel negative about this day though, and I was spending time going over logistical things and paying homage to family rituals. As was our habit, Emily and I arose around 5:30 and had breakfast in our customary Election Day silence. We departed in the early morning sunlight of a pretty August day at around 6:45, and I drove the two minutes it took for us to get from our home on Juniper Street to Greenview Park, the polling place for the city's well-known Greenview precinct. Voting had always been a family affair with the Clyburns, and we were joined by two of our daughters—Jennifer and Angela. Much had changed since the last election. Jennifer had gotten married just a few days earlier, and Angela had enrolled in college. Our first-born, Mignon, would be casting her vote in Charleston, where she had been born and where she vowed she would make her home.

In the car the four of us observed a continuation of our tomblike silence. But in my case it was more than a ritual silence. I was beginning to feel some pressure, which had begun a day earlier with a call from the Associated Press asking when and where I would be voting. There was some elevated interest in the race, and there were some potentially troublesome moments ahead.

Diane Feldman, my superstar Washington pollster, had called three weeks earlier with a good-news/bad-news report. The good news was that her interpretation of the data from her tracking polls had led her to conclude that there was a good chance I could win the primary on the first ballot. South Carolina law required a candidate to win 50 percent plus one vote in a multicandidate primary race in order to qualify for a first ballot victory.

The bad news, as Bill DeLoach related to me, was that, as the frontrunner, if I did not win on the first ballot, whoever came in second would rise to my level almost instantly, and the runoff could be a real dogfight. Bill did not need to remind me of that consequence. I had finished among the top vote getters in my first primary race for the State House from Charleston County and had lost in the general election, and I had finished first in the 1978 primary for secretary of state and had lost in the runoff. Those memories clouded my thoughts as we proceeded to the polling place. When we arrived at the Greenview precinct, however, my mood changed almost immediately. It was a pretty day. The turnout looked good, and the scene of Jennifer, Angela, and Emily working the crowd with great vigor and good humor sent my spirits rising. Greenview had been something of a bellwether precinct for black politics for years. There were about two thousand registered voters—most of them African American—and it was a place where political activism was bred and encouraged. Turnouts were usually high, and political candidates could often judge their chances by what seemed to be the mood of Greenview voters.

I was moved by what I saw that morning at Greenview, and by the time I dropped Emily and the daughters by our home and drove to campaign headquarters in downtown Columbia, I was ready to head out into the district to observe the usual Election Day ritual of visiting precincts. I don't know how many voters get swayed by the appearance of a candidate at a polling place, but I knew that there were certain precincts I wanted to visit just to let them see my face and know how much I appreciated what they were doing. I could also get some insight into how things were going.

In informing me that I had a chance to win the election on the first ballot, Diane Feldman had said her polling information indicated that I should spend the last ten days of the campaign in six counties—Marion, Florence, Sumter, Richland, Orangeburg, and Williamsburg. These were not only the most populous of the sixteen counties in the sprawling district; they were also the places where my opponents were running the hardest. I disagreed with Diane slightly, suggesting that I should spend some time in Charleston. She reminded me that I was paying her the big bucks to advise me on such matters, and that I should follow her recommendations. I did.

On Election Day I headed back into the same areas, visiting precincts in Florence, Sumter, and Richland Counties, some of them for strategic purposes and some for sentimental reasons. Awaiting me, I hoped, would be some indications that things were going well, that I could relax, and that there were no bad breakdowns along the way.

At our first destination, Florence, we set out for the Mount Zion AME Church precinct. It was a place where all manner of interesting crosscurrents seemed to be in play, particularly as they involved Frank Gilbert, the state senator who was my chief rival. Anybody who knows anything about black politics knows that two of the most important elements at the local level are family and church. At the Mount Zion AME Church precinct, those factors were coming together in a complicated and somewhat overlapping way.

With my Pee Dee area campaign chair Ruth Smith (right) and her daughter, Carole (left), during a 1994 campaign event in Florence.

Frank Gilbert had recently joined Mount Zion AME Church. The pastor there was an active and vocal supporter of Frank's candidacy. Ruth Smith, my Pee Dee area campaign coordinator was a lifelong AME and longtime member of Mount Zion. To complicate the AME scene even further, Ruth Smith's brother, Mingo Singleton, was the presiding elder of that AME district, and he was a vocal supporter of my candidacy.

Meanwhile I was getting much support from Frank Gilbert's former church, Trinity Baptist. The pastor, the Reverend W. P. Diggs, had backed me in my earlier races for secretary of state and his daughter, Mary Lynn, had worked on my campaign staff. He had spoken on my behalf during the congressional race. Also Charlene Lowery was a very active member of Trinity. All this made for some interesting forces at work in the election, and I was anxious to see things firsthand at the Mount Zion precinct on Election Day.

When I arrived, Ruth Smith was there to greet me, and she helped me work the lines. She also went to great lengths to introduce me to every precinct worker, and I appreciated the friendly and cordial manner with which they greeted me. But there wasn't the rush of support I detected at Greenview. I came away a little uncertain about how I was going to do in this precinct where Frank Gilbert and I were going toe-to-toe, or should I say, pulpit-to-pulpit?

After visiting two more precincts I made my way to Sumter along U.S. Highway 76, stopping at precincts in Timmonsville, Lynchburg, and Mayesville—the birthplace of civil rights and education champion Mary McLeod Bethune. These were not large polling places where elections were going to be won or lost. But they were places of memories from my growing up in Sumter, and on this day when my whole life might be changing, I wanted to revisit my childhood for a few moments.

Connections

As I neared Sumter, I had all the warm and familiar feelings of coming home on what might be the most important political day in my life. I also knew, however, that my opponent, Ken Mosley from Orangeburg, had targeted Sumter as a place of special concentration for his campaign. The last thing I wanted to happen was to have Ken Mosley do well in my own hometown.

I entered Sumter from the east. My plan was to visit polling places in South Sumter, as well as the Clyburn Beauty Shop in the western part of town. But my eyes caught a sign—"Vote Here Today"—in front of a church on East Calhoun Street, and I pulled over to the curb for a moment. I remembered attending a funeral at that church as a child, and the eulogy had been delivered by Reverend J. Herbert Nelson. I often attended services at Orangeburg's St. Luke Presbyterian, whose pastor was the Reverend Nelson when I was in college. J. Herbert, who had also served as president of the NAACP and was a man I much admired, had helped broaden my religious views beyond those of the fundamentalist Church of God. For some reason I always associated him with this particular church.

Upon entering the church, I noticed machines for Democrats on one side of the room, and Republicans on the other. The Republican machines were idle, but there were two precinct workers tending the machines and I waved to them as I made my way to the Democratic side of the room, where a few people were voting. It only took me a few minutes to greet and shake hands with the voters, one of whom was a former classmate. As I was preparing to leave, one of the Republicans came over, shook my hand, and asked if he could have a word with me.

He turned out to be a Republican activist named John Hoar, a local attorney who—to my surprise—had an abiding interest in black political leaders in the state. He told me of his particular interest in the last black man to represent South Carolina in the U.S. Congress, George Washington Murray, whom he described with some obvious pride as "a Republican with Sumter connections." I told him I shared his interest in Congressman Murray, who had spent fifteen years in Sumter as a schoolteacher and who served in Congress from 1893 to 1897. It is interesting, I was thinking, that a white Republican from Sumter in 1992 would have this kind of interest in a black congressman who had served a century earlier. I was running late on my campaign trail, however, and I glanced at my watch and eased toward the door.

His next comment stopped me in my tracks. He made me aware that he had conducted research into Congressman Murray and that research had produced an interesting possibility. "Did you know, Mr. Clyburn," he asked, "that you may have a family connection with Congressman Murray?"

As it turned out, I did know of that possibility, and acknowledged as much. "Yes," I said, simply, "I'm aware of that." He seemed pleased with my answer, as if my response confirmed his own research.

But my information, which I did not tell him at the time, hardly came from research. It came from that tortuous process of pursuing black genealogy, not in the archives of documented family records, but from memories handed down from generation to generation.

That's how I came to know of the possible family relation I had with George Washington Murray. And it had come only a few weeks earlier through an encounter with my second cousin Johnny Lloyd, whose grandfather and my grandmother were brother and sister. Johnny and his brother, Marion, were active in local politics in Lee County, and Johnny had invited me to speak at the small St. Matthews United Methodist Church in Kershaw County. The St. Matthews Church was located near where the family roots of Governor John C. West and my father virtually came together. West was born and raised on a Black River Road farm in the Charlotte Thompson community, and his voting precinct was at the St. Matthews United Methodist Church. My father's mother, Phoebe Lloyd, was born in the Spring Hill community, only a few miles down the road from Charlotte Thompson.

I knew that the area was rich with the Lloyd family, and that St. Matthews was one of two churches, the other being Emmanuel United Methodist, that had been home to the Lloyds. As my brothers and I grew up, Dad made certain we visited the various members of the Lloyd family, particularly his uncles Richard, Willie, and Enoch.

I took some time to chat with Johnny prior to the speech, intending to discuss the pending program and maybe get caught up on some personal news. I wasn't prepared for the topic he chose. He opened our conversation by asking me if I was aware of the historic significance of the upcoming congressional election. I nodded, and launched into a conversation about George Washington Murray, his role in the founding of South Carolina State College, and his service as the last black congressman from the state.

"No, no," Johnny said, waving his hand and shutting off my academic mutterings. "Did you realize that Murray was family?"

My eyes must have widened, and for a moment I hesitated. Then I asked him what proof there was. I knew, as did he, that the Lloyd family history was clouded with the kind of mysteries and contradictions that my dad used to cover with the simple qualification "or so they told me." Johnny referred me to his mother, my Uncle Willie's wife. A few days later, I called her. Like my dad, she spoke with some reticence and great caution. She confirmed the Murray connection up to a point. She said to me with determination and conviction, "Back then, some things happened without the benefit of marriage."

I knew exactly what she meant, and always felt my father knew. I realized that she would not be revealing this kind of deep Lloyd family secret unless she was confident of its reliability and that she wanted it to be passed along through the family's word-of-mouth channels of history. It also seemed to explain why my questions at a previous Lloyd-Joy family reunion had been answered by Ms. Mary Montgomery who suggested that I stop by her house and she would answer my questions. I have come to regret that I never did.

Of course I wasn't going to tell that story to my new white Republican friend from Sumter, and maybe I didn't need too. I simply told him I would be interested in seeing his research on the subject and would appreciate his passing it along to me. He did send me some interesting information that has been helpful in further clouding the issue. At any rate he seemed pleased at my interest and attention, and the conversation ended with him saying that as a Republican, he realized that the next congressman from the Sixth District would be a black Democrat. Like Congressman Murray, he said, he was confident that it would be "someone with Sumter connections."

With that I continued my Sumter tour, and I tried to get my mind back on the business at hand. It seemed interesting that on a day when my political future was at stake I had spent a few moments rambling through my family history. Now it was time to get back to work. I was freshly motivated. I was not just seeking to win an election to Congress; I was setting out to make family history or continue a legacy.

I visited several precincts in South Sumter and then paid a visit to the Clyburn Beauty Shop. There, I was told a nice campaign anecdote from Ida Davis Smith, who had worked at the Clyburn Beauty Shop since the 1950s. It seemed my opponent Ken Mosley had stopped by there one day to seek their support. Ida told me that she was only too delighted to suggest to Mr. Moseley that he take a look at the name out in front of the building. "That might help you understand where our votes and support are going," she said she told him. I grinned broadly at the story, and I left the beauty shop with my spirits rising even more sharply. I renewed my silent hope that the property where the beauty shop had been in business for more than forty years would one day pass to Mom's granddaughter Dia, the daughter of my brother Charles.

My Second Wind

The visit to Sumter was upbeat, but I was getting weary. On the way back to Columbia, I planned to stop by the Eastover precinct in Lower Richland and I was feeling my energy ebb. I made a quick stop at the Eastover precinct, and by the time I got to the Prince Hall Masonic Lodge on Gervais Street in Columbia, my adrenalin was flowing again, and I had gotten a second wind. The Masonic hall was the polling place for Ward 9, and, like Greenview it was a place of make-or-break importance for black political candidates. I knew it was where Herbert Fielding and John Roy Harper had made a big push, so I was prepared for a mixed reception. As it turned out, my anxiety was misplaced. I got nothing but positive feelings in the cavernous Prince Hall Masonic building, where I had spent so many important times during my twenty years in Columbia and the travels one makes on the road to becoming a thirty-third degree Mason. With each stop, my confidence was growing. I was finding this Election Day to be far different from those in previous years. What was happening? Were things going this well or was I becoming delusional?

I dropped by my campaign headquarters a few blocks up Gervais Street and decided to head home for a nap. But my energy level was still high, so I decided to make a stop at the Fairwold Precinct. It was not a large precinct, but it was special to me for several reasons.

The polling place was located in the old Fairwold Middle School, recently renamed W. G. Sanders Middle School, where all three of our daughters had attended and where Emily had been its first librarian. It was also a precinct where Ira and

Thernel Scott lived and worked the polls regularly. They were not only important to me politically, they were good friends who had helped me in some of my earlier political and public ventures. I also knew that if I did not visit the Fairwold precinct, they would never forgive me. And I would not have blamed them.

Thernel Scott was a transit bus driver for the South Carolina Electric and Gas Company, and as such, he saw and interacted with more people in a day than I did in a week. He was my "ear-to-the-ground," and after a long day of campaigning I would often stop by their home to wind down, get caught up on Thernel's "political intelligence," and have a short visit with my favorite Uncle Jack, as in Daniels.

Ira was part of IBM's early initiatives in the area of diversity, and through that corporate setting she proved invaluable to me in the aftermath of an early political setback. It went back to the days after my statewide loss in the race for secretary of state in 1978. I wound up with a considerable campaign debt, and decided on a one-night program to try to retire as much of the debt as possible. These were the days of the *Dean Martin Celebrity Roast* program, a television show in which various celebrities were the object of mostly good humored comic abuse. It was a big hit on television, and I decided to try the format as a local enterprise, using political friends as the "roasters." I called it a "Roast and Toast" program, and I was the first object of the comic scorn of my friends.

I guess a lot of people enjoyed heaping their wrathful humor on me because the first roast proved to be a financial success. We not only raised enough money to retire the debt, we had enough left over to form the Palmetto Issues Conference (PIC), a nonprofit forum for political discourse and a vehicle for continuing the "Roast and Toast" programs. John West agreed to be the second "roastee." After that the enterprise became something of a regular part of the political scene each year. We even roasted Strom Thurmond one year, and when we roasted Bob Royall, Carroll Campbell did the toast. In that kind of respectable, bipartisan setting, Ira Scott was able to bring IBM on board as a corporate mainstay. It became an invaluable part of our PIC initiatives and accorded a lot of ongoing credibility to the "Roast and Toast" programs.

Another outgrowth of PIC was the First Palmetto Issues Classic golf tournament in 1979. We later renamed this annual event the Rudolph Canzater Memorial Classic after a dear friend who had helped to organize this college-scholarship fund raiser and died at age forty-nine of an aortic aneurism.

I could tell Ira and Thernel had been expecting me at the Fairwold precinct, and their caustic comments let me know that I would have paid a heavy price in the way of friendly rebukes if I had not done so. Few people were voting, and I attributed it to the time of day. With my energy on the wane again, I greeted the few voters, then bade Ira and Thernel farewell and headed home for a nap.

Election Night

As I drifted into my short but deep nap, thoughts of previous election nights stayed with me, nights when I had lost. Would tonight be different? Who knows? But as I awoke from my nap around 5:45, I knew I would have my answer in a few hours.

A lasting legacy of the PIC Classic, mulligan money raised through the renamed Rudolph Canzater Memorial Classic is donated to youth golf programs such as this First Tee group in Columbia, South Carolina.

After a quick shower, I decided to discard the blue-gray suit I had worn during the day and chose one that was a deeper blue. It was one that always made me feel good, and it usually drew favorable comments. It should have; it was the most expensive suit I had ever bought. It had thin maroon lines that went well with the made-for-television maroon tie I would be wearing that night.

Emily and I dressed for the evening in the same tomblike silence with which we had begun the day. We left home around 6:30 and headed for the (Clarion) Town House Hotel, which for years had been a political landmark in South Carolina's capital city. My garnet and blue campaign signs, in the school colors of our alma mater, S.C. State, were scattered along our route from home to the Town House. The good showing of signs reflected something I had discovered during the campaign. Experienced campaign workers learn the travel routes of their candidates and make sure that those routes were well covered with signs. Although I had often chastised them for the practice, I was pleased with it on this particular night. As I tried to get control of myself, it was good to feel the welcoming warmth of my yard signs along what had all the appearance of a victory route.

Bill DeLoach met us at the hotel door, and we observed another of the Election Day rituals. The candidate, his family, and close friends would await the results in the privacy of an upstairs suite of rooms. The remainder of the friends, supporters, bystanders, politically curious, and ever-inquiring members of the news media would await the outcome in a downstairs ballroom, which was well equipped with snacks and plenty of liquid refreshments of both the hard and soft variety.

Bill quickly whisked Emily and me to our upstairs holding area. The place was already crowded with friends and campaign workers, and I felt obligated to work the room with my smiley face firmly planted in place. Bill noted the tension growing as I lapsed into yet another campaign exercise, and he ushered Emily and me into an adjoining room, where we had some quiet, privacy, and peace. There was a two-cushion sofa in the room, and since no one seemed to want to sit next to the candidate, I took off my jacket and stretched out as much as I could. I couldn't get comfortable, though, so I wound up pulling my feet up onto the sofa and curling into what looked like the fetal position. Wouldn't that have made a great page one picture? "Candidate Clyburn Awaits Election Results in Fetal Position." I quickly assumed a more conventional posture on the sofa and straightened my tie.

It was seven o'clock, and there was something of a hush in the room as we all realized that polls were closing and that whatever was going to happen that day had already happened. It was just a matter of counting the votes and announcing the people's verdict. I took a deep breath and felt my stomach churning. I was nervous as hell.

The phone rang, breaking the silence, and Bill answered it. I watched anxiously and saw a small smile come to his face. He thanked the caller and turned to me to provide the contents of the call. It came from a beautician friend of his who had worked the polls in Holly Hill, an old farming town in the lower part of Orangeburg County. She wanted Bill to know that a steady stream of elderly white women had voted on the Democratic side in that particular precinct, something of a rarity in democratic primaries in majority-black Holly Hill. Almost all of them, she told Bill, had said they wanted to vote for "the man with the tree limb." I almost let out a whoop. This was only one telephone call from one precinct, but the message could not have been better. What a way to start election night!

The next call continued the good news. It was from Mattie Rabb Williams, Ike Williams's former wife. She had spent the day working the polls at Ward Nine, where I had visited only a few hours earlier. I braced myself for the results, remembering that this was a place where Herbert Fielding and John Roy Harper were expected to do well. Mattie had stayed until the votes had been tabulated. She gave Bill the results, and he passed them along to me: Clyburn 168, Fielding 13, Harper 22, Gilbert 9, Mosley 34. I felt my knees weaken. Suddenly the idea of winning this thing became a reality in my mind.

A few minutes later the results came from the other two polling places I had visited in Columbia. I had carried Greenview with 78 percent and Fairwold with 79 percent, and I was being projected to carry the entire Richland County with 68 percent. Sixty-eight percent of the vote in a five-man race! It was surpassing my cautious hopes and expectations.

Bill started working the phones, looking for reports from outposts that would be slower to report their results. He was trying to reach people such as Ruth Smith and Charlene Lowery in Florence, Milton Troy and Frank Hart in Marion, and all those neighborhoods in my hometown of Sumter.

And then, before many of the local results were reported to us, the word came that the Associated Press had declared me the winner. I took another deep breath and tried to contain myself and hold in my emotions. Twenty-two years were not too long a lapse of time for me to get over the 1970 election in Charleston, when I had been declared a winner, only to learn a few hours later that things had been reversed.

But Bill DeLoach was having none of that restraint. He began shouting, "It worked! It worked! It's in the bag"—referring to the television commercial about the tree limb that seemed to have worked so well in that Holly Hill precinct. For me being declared the winner was only the first part of the story, however. Now the question was whether there would be a runoff.

As more results were reported to us from around the district, news became increasingly good. I would not get the results from each of the precincts in the sixteen-county district for several more days, but in a matter of a few more minutes, the television stations were projecting that I was going to win with more than 50 percent. That's when it hit me. I was going to be the Democratic nominee for Congress from the Sixth District of South Carolina. I had broken my three-race election losing streak. Jim Clyburn might well be going to Washington in January as the South Carolina congressman from the Sixth District. It felt good.

It was time to think back to defining moments and people who had made it happen; Diane Feldman and her projections three weeks earlier that I could win on the first ballot; Bill DeLoach and the idea he sold to me about the thirty-second commercial; the one hundred thousand dollar loan in which I had gambled my own economic security on winning the race.

There was Robin Tallon, whose gracious withdrawal had made me the favorite to win; the plant owner in Andrews who had so generously urged me to support the needs of his workers over his own; the white Republican in Sumter who expressed confidence that the next Sixth District representative would be a black congressman "with Sumter connections" like George Washington Murray a century earlier.

Even though the general election lay five months away, I allowed myself at that moment to feel like the winner. I jumped to my feet and began thanking and accepting congratulations from those who had by now crowded the three-room suite. Then, I put on the jacket to my expensive dark-blue suit, straightened my maroon tie again, and headed downstairs with Emily to join what would surely be the biggest, most joyful celebration of my political life.

I wasn't disappointed. Hundreds of friends and supporters were crowded into the ballroom, and it did not take long for me to realize that they had been visiting the refreshment stations with great frequency. There was a lot of noise and bright television lights, which made it seem as if we were on some sort of enlarged stage. And through it all, I spotted my good and faithful friend Kay Patterson. His personal check for one thousand dollars had been one of the first acts of good faith for me in the campaign, and he had supported my candidacy over that of two of his Senate colleagues, Herbert Fielding and Frank Gilbert. Before I began moving through the crowd, I spoke to Kay and told him what his presence in my campaign had meant to me. Then I moved into the rest of that vast ballroom, discovering friends who represented so many aspects of my life.

There were those who had been part of my "Young Democrats" days two decades earlier. Neither they nor I were very young Democrats anymore. There were people from my high school days at Lincoln in Sumter and Mather in Camden. There were many from that extraordinary group of men and women who had been classmates and schoolmates at South Carolina State, people who had been there "when the water blew" and had helped to launch a revolution at that institution.

There were more recent friends from my nearly eighteen years as Human Affairs commissioner; people who worked so hard to establish what we liked to call the "firm, but fair" administration by which we broke through the barriers of criticism and cynicism over whether the human rights of minorities could be evenly adjudicated.

It was a rare and heady moment. I was in a room of hundreds of people who were not just my friends and political supporters. They were the men and women who had made me what I was at that moment.

In the midst of it all, I spotted Thelma Baker, my secretary at the Human Affairs Commission, and she came over to me with her young grandson. Without hesitation, I picked him up and hoisted him into my arms. The flash bulbs went off, and that picture—of Justin and a broadly beaming Jim Clyburn—told the story on the front page of the *State* newspaper the next morning better than any words could have conveyed.

After a while, I was ushered to the podium. I made a few remarks with Kay Patterson, family members, and a few friends at my side. In front of the podium behind which we stood was a tree limb. Bill had thought of everything. Try as I might, I have no recollection of what I said. I was in a trance. Chalk it up to the exhilaration of the moment, the weariness that was creeping into my body, or the fact that I had nothing on my mind except gratitude and appreciation to that great throng of friends.

The next day, the *State* quoted me as saying, "I'm very flattered by this showing of confidence. I believe this will do a whole lot to make young people of this state recognize that if you work hard, if you're fair and honest with people, the rewards will be great." And I should have added, "Three strikes and you're out is a baseball rule."

The newspaper showed that with all but a few precincts reporting, I carried more than 55 percent of the vote in the district, winning every one of the counties except Charleston, where Herbert was winning his home county by 286 votes. In Orangeburg it looked as though I had won over Ken Mosley in his home county by one vote, but in none of the other counties was the race very close.

In his coverage of the election, the *State*'s political reporter, Lee Bandy, wrote, "Clyburn left his opponents . . . in the dust. It was a major feat. Most analysts had predicted a runoff in the crowded 6th District race."

All those fine words and numbers greeted me in the next morning's newspapers. But on that election night, as the crowds began to thin, Emily and I could feel only the exhaustion of what had been almost a twenty-four-hour work day. We returned home in the wee hours, and once the exhilaration of the evening began to dissipate, we made our way wearily to bed.

I found it hard to get to sleep. I was worried that the doorbell might ring, as it had earlier in my political life, to tell me that it was all a mistake.

The doorbell, thank goodness, never rang.

23 *General Election, 1992*

It would have been perfectly normal for the general election of 1992, coming ten weeks after the energetic and emotional Democratic primary, to seem anticlimactic. As it turned out, it was.

I learned what I needed to know about my opponent early in the campaign. As I was driving into Florence one day along Evans Street, I noticed the car in front of me had a decal of the official flag of the Confederacy on its bumper. Few people recognize the "real" Confederate flag, which has a circle of stars on a blue field in the upper left corner, and three bars, one white, and two red, hence the nickname for the flag, "Stars and Bars." This flag is far less recognizable to the general public than the "Navy Jack" that flew atop the State House.

Anyone whose bumper bears the decal of the official flag of the Confederacy, I figured, is a full-time southerner who probably takes the state's history and all things southern seriously and personally. As we approached the intersection the traffic light turned red, and we pulled alongside the car with the Confederate flag decal. I looked over, and much to my surprise, the driver was John Chase, my Republican opponent in the general election. At that moment, I knew that whatever race baiting he would employ in the campaign against me ran much deeper than a tactic to get white votes in the general election.

The election campaign turned out to run pretty much along those lines. Mr. Chase rarely brought up an issue that did not have a direct racial angle, or one that was only slightly disguised. Unlike the primary race, in which my four opponents and I shared some basic values, this contest was run against an opponent with whom I rarely even made philosophical or political contact. His positions were a throwback to the days when race dictated the issues, and he was apparently satisfied to make that distinction his campaign platform. He believed, I guessed, there was a sufficiently large reservoir of ill will over race that he could wave his Confederate flag, mutter a few code words, raise a few wedge issues, and drive me into a defensive position.

I decided not to take the bait. My margin of victory had been a comfortable one in the primary, and I was satisfied that, while I would not carry a majority of the white vote, I would do well enough with white voters to feel politically secure and confident. It was my plan to win enough white votes to go to Washington legitimately representing more of the district than the 58 percent with whom I shared a racial identity. I stuck with my game plan.

One of the early opportunities to engage in combat was Mr. Chase's decision to attack me on the food-stamp issue. Food stamps always seem to offer a field day for those who wished to belittle black and low-income people and, in this case, a black candidate. Somehow, despite evidence to the contrary, the stereotype lingers that only black people used food stamps, and Mr. "Confederate Flag" just couldn't resist the temptation. He aired a television ad attacking a proposal I had made for issuing Electronic Benefits Transfer (EBT) cards, rather than the traditional paper coupons, for food-stamp recipients to use at the checkout counter. Mr. Chase's ad showed a distorted picture of me superimposed over an American Express card and claimed that I wanted to give every food-stamp user a credit card. It was so over-the-top and racially mean-spirited that several television stations refused to air it. Of course some did.

My proposal had nothing to do with providing "credit" for food-stamp users. It simply offered an easier, less costly, and more efficient way for qualified recipients to use whatever food-stamp value would have been issued to them anyhow, and it was a damn sight easier for supermarket checkout personnel to use, as is now the case. As far as potential fraud and cheating were concerned, it provided a much cleaner way to assure the integrity and accountability of the Food Stamp program itself. Of course, in the world of sound-bite racial politics, all that reasoning got swept up in the emotion of abusing black people.

Blaming the Poor People

I actually did have an ax to grind along those lines. In the initial debate over the establishment of food stamps years earlier, one of the opponents of the program, a Mr. Smith of Virginia, had insisted that coupons be used so that recipients would be "shamed" at the checkout counter. Somehow that exercise in humiliation, I guess, was supposed to enrich the experience of those customers who did not use food stamps. I never understood what motivated people to enjoy the idea of degrading other people, but Mr. Smith must have thought it would be great fun. I have always found the whole idea of punishing people for being poor to be one of the uglier aspects of American society, and this particular version stuck in my craw for years. I vowed if I ever had the chance to confront it, I would. This election campaign gave me just such an opportunity.

My opponent, I was happy to point out, didn't even have the support of his own Republican governor on this issue. The EBT device, which he was likening to an American Express card, actually had considerable support among many governors, Democratic and Republican. Included in that number was South Carolina's GOP governor, Carroll A. Campbell, with whom I had developed a good working relationship and for whom I had a high degree of respect. He and I had actually discussed the EBT, and when Mr. Chase decided to attack me on the issue, Governor Campbell and I had a few good chuckles.

The food stamps proposal wasn't Mr. Chase's only racial blind spot. When I laid out significant proposals as early as the Democratic primary campaign to deal with the widespread rural poverty in the Sixth District, Mr. Chase decided that rural poverty also equated to black people, and he performed his knee-jerk response against it.

Another candidate in the Republican primary at the time, Delores DeCosta, a black female, joined him initially in opposition but later recanted, offering a set of proposals similar to my own.

That left Mr. Chase waving his Confederate flag alone, apparently not aware of the fact that my proposals for rural economic development had a rich background in Republican Party politics. It went back as far as the 1968 urban riots in the wake of the assassination of Dr. Martin Luther King. George Romney, a Mormon of great social conscience, was governor of Michigan at the time, and he walked the riot-torn streets of Detroit and talked with the victims of the violence and destruction, most of them African American. Among other things, he asked about their backgrounds, why they had come to Detroit, and where their original homes had been. To his surprise, a large number of the transplanted Detroiters had come from Williamsburg County, South Carolina.

Governor Romney was planning a run for president at the time and was positioning himself as a Republican with a social agenda. He decided that one approach to the urban riots was to determine the root causes that had prompted so many people to migrate northward to cities such as Detroit. What was it in their hometowns in the South that had caused them to leave?

To amplify that interest, Governor Romney made a high-profile visit to Williamsburg County, accompanied by South Carolina's Senator Strom Thurmond, a fellow Republican. Their visit caught a lot of national attention and highlighted conditions in the rural South, which had for decades been causing southern people by the tens of thousands—white and black—to abandon their homes in search of better opportunities elsewhere in the nation. One of the people much impressed by Governor Romney's visit and his subsequent plan to improve the lot of rural southerners was a young guy named Jim Clyburn, who was serving as director of the Neighborhood Youth Corps in Charleston County and was already seeing firsthand the living conditions that were causing so much hardship among the people of our area. As it turned out, Romney's campaign for the presidency imploded over his comment that he was "brainwashed" in forming his views on the Vietnam War, and we never got to know the full impact of that visit or his thinking about what was needed to address the economic needs of our state and nation at the time.

The GOP Influence

But Romney's visit left an enduring impact on me, and I was deeply impressed by the insight and political courage of this high-profile Republican from a big industrial state in the Midwest. I internalized and incubated those thoughts, holding them for the time when I might be able to bring them to political light as part of my own agenda.

I was also paying attention to the views of Jack Kemp, the much-heralded professional football player from the old American Football League who came to Congress in 1971. Kemp was a deeply committed Republican of the conservative variety, but like Romney, he had great sensitivity to the social and economic conditions around him. His football days in the AFL made him a natural advocate of racial fairness and he was a strong supporter of Affirmative Action. His representation of a poor industrial area of his home district in Buffalo, New York, sensitized him to the kinds of economic troubles facing "Rust Belt" cities throughout the East and Midwest. It was from Jack Kemp that I learned the concept of Enterprise Zones, a major program that he popularized during his years of service. Kemp was a fiscal conservative of the first order, but his support of a wide range of antipoverty programs earned him high regard among leaders of both parties at the time.

It was from those two Republicans that I began forming strong opinions about measures to combat the rampant economic distress of the Sixth District in South Carolina, and their influence led directly to my advocacy of Enterprise Zones legislation during my campaign and my first term in Congress. The Republican roots of my plans for upgrading the economic condition of the district made the positions of my Republican opponent in the congressional race absolutely farcical.

There was one other stereotype that Mr. Chase decided to employ during the campaign. A black Democrat, he decided, must automatically be antibusiness, and he launched a big effort to describe me as such. What he had missed apparently was the fact that two of the state's largest banks, Citizens and Southern and C&S/Sovran—predecessors to today's Bank of America—apparently considered me sufficiently pro-business to invite me to join their statewide boards of directors. He apparently also missed the fact that I was a businessman myself. I was co-owner and copublisher, along with my daughter Mignon, of the *Coastal Times*, a lowcountry weekly newspaper headquartered in Charleston. Mr. Chase was apparently too tangled up in things such as the Confederate flag and food stamps to see me for who I really was and debate me on the legitimate issues of the campaign.

Issues aside, I was becoming increasingly aware that a congressional district is not a single, organic entity. It is many counties, cities, towns, neighborhoods, country roads, schools, shopping centers, churches, and farming communities. One strategy, particularly for the spread-out Sixth District, did not fit all locations, and I worked hard to have a local special identity wherever possible.

The local connection proved more important than I had originally calculated. For one thing, a lot of the people in the district seemed to want their candidate to live in the Pee Dee region itself, and I became sensitive to that fact, particularly as it applied to my hometown of Sumter. While I referred often to my growing up in Sumter, I also knew some people did not consider Sumter to be in the Pee Dee. To counter that consideration, I spent time discussing my early days of accompanying my dad to church conferences and revival meetings in Pee Dee towns such as Darlington, Hartsville, Lamar, and Timmonsville. It helped that I could talk about my relationship with the Church of God sanctuaries at the corner of Lee and Pine Streets in Darlington, on Sixth Street in Hartsville, and on Brockington Street in Timmonsville. It also helped that a lot of Pee Dee people had attended Morris College in Sumter, and I made certain they knew that it was the alma mater of both my parents. For all the energy and anxiety I was expending in sparring with my opponent over issues, I was appreciating how important it was for people to consider that their congressman was "home folks."

Family, Friends, and Church Politics

The campaign, for the most part, was going well. My long and strong relationships with beauty-shop and barber-shop operators were paying off throughout the entire district. In Orangeburg I still had plenty of good friends from S.C State and Claflin, and my connections with the Church of God on Treadwell Street and St. Luke Presbyterian were being translated into political support there. The Churches of God identities were helping me in Bamberg, Colleton, Dorchester, Richland, and my birthplace of Sumter. The AME bishop and churches were doing their thing, and the organizations I had put together for the primary were still functioning well in the heavily black counties of Marion, Williamsburg, and Clarendon.

Only Florence seemed uncertain. It had the largest white population, and it was where I heard most often the parochial suspicion that I was not from the Pee Dee. In addition to being Mr. Chase's home, it was the home of Senator Frank Gilbert, who had finished second in the Democratic primary. I tried to assess how important Florence might be in the overall Sixth District, so I took some time to review the history of voting patterns and turnout in the three previous elections. Nothing in that review caused me to feel any alarm about the upcoming contest—even if I did poorly among all the voters in Florence County, black and white—which I did not think would happen.

Relax Clyburn, I thought. I had worked hard, and our organization was functioning well throughout the district. We're going to win this thing. Enjoy it. And we did. On Election Day there was none of the edgy silence and anxiety of the primary day. I went through the routine of visiting precincts across the district, a different set from those I had targeted during the primary. This time I was not looking for news or inside information. I was taking my victory lap, and the mood was celebratory. I was using the time to thank the staff, thank the workers, and thank the voters. They knew they were seeing their new congressman, and I wanted to look the role.

As I had during the primary, I took some time to think back about the campaign and to fix in my mind the people who had kept me focused, helped to shape the victory, and made this extraordinary moment possible.

Keeping Focused

One of those people was Marjorie Amos Frazier, who had called me one day during my first year in the governor's office. Her call was much like the one I got from Judge Richard Fields.

The events that led up to that call started in my hometown of Sumter, where I had gone to do an early morning convocation at Morris College. I had spent the evening before visiting with my dad, who was still having difficulty coming to grips with something he never could have imagined, outliving two wives. I spent the night at a motel near the Morris campus.

The next morning I had breakfast in the motel's restaurant with the lady who was the college adviser for the group that was sponsoring the event. After breakfast, I escorted her to her car and returned to my room.

My car was parked directly in front of my room. When I exited my room about ten minutes later, someone called out to me from the second level directly above me. I looked up and it was a gentleman I often saw in Charleston. I knew him only by his last name, Rice. I waved to him, and we chatted for a moment.

I did not think any more about the chance meeting until about two weeks later when Phil Grose laid a copy of a newspaper in front of me. The headline blasted an ominous statement and question: "Women Were the Downfall of Adam Clayton Powell. Is the Governor's Aide James Clyburn Headed in the Same Direction?"

Phil informed me that copies of the publication had been placed on the desks of every member of the General Assembly. The picture that accompanied the article showed me seemingly coming out of a motel room. I suddenly recalled that chance encounter in Sumter. I knew that the gentleman who greeted me was a muckraker who occasionally contributed to that publication, but I had given that fact no thought that morning. I was giving it a lot of thought now.

Later that day, as I sat at my desk pondering the issue, my phone rang, and it was Marjorie Amos Frazier. Someone in Charleston had brought the article to her attention, and she asked whether or not I had seen it. I told her that I had and started trying to explain the circumstances. Marjorie cut me off in the middle of a sentence. She told me that the circumstances behind the article did not matter. "Get in your car," she admonished, "point it towards Charleston, and when you get here go straight home."

The trip from Columbia to Charleston is about a two-hour drive, and maybe that's all it took. But it felt like an eternity.

When I arrived at home there was a copy of that newspaper on the dining-room table. I sat down and started pretending to read it again. After a while Emily sat at the table and I started trying to explain. She listened, and just as things seemed to get pretty tense she offered that there was food in the refrigerator if I wanted something to eat.

I had done enough stage performances to recognize and appreciate a good cue when I heard one. I immediately got up from the table and rushed to the refrigerator. This was long before microwave ovens, and it took a while for me to prepare whatever I ate that evening. Under the circumstances, I am sure I took even longer than I needed to. When I sat back down to eat, Emily changed the subject. I felt relieved and also perplexed, but I was not about to revisit the issue if I could avoid it.

Later that evening, after Emily had retired to bed and my stalling was even obvious to me, I went up to bed. I laid there for a while, very much awake and feeling certain that Emily was awake as well. She broke the silence with laughter. This really threw me into a quandary, but hearing her laugh was a great relief. When I asked about the laughter she asked whether or not I had taken a good look at the picture that accompanied the article. When I replied that I thought I had, she told me to take another look. She was still laughing.

I jumped out of bed, rushed down the stairs, and picked up the newspaper. While I was standing there gazing at it trying to determine the source of her amusement, Emily appeared on the landing at the top of the stairs and asked, "When was the last time you wore those horn-rimmed glasses?" I had bought those glasses because I thought they made me look more mature, but Emily hated them, and when I was about to go to Columbia to start my tenure on the governor's staff she had insisted that I get new wire frames, which she selected. As if to underscore her disdain for those horn-rimmed glasses, she held on to them and put them in her pocketbook as we left the optometrist's office.

I never saw or thought about them again. Emily had put them in one of her dresser drawers, so I could not have been wearing them that night in Sumter. I found out later that the picture had been cropped from one that had been taken of me and three other people sometime earlier in the Staley Building at South Carolina State College, and had been superimposed on another photograph to make it fit the circumstances that Mr. Rice wished to convey.

I also found out later that Marjorie Amos Frazier had called Emily before phoning me. I am sure they talked about much more during that call, but neither one of them has ever told me anything about their conversation. I do know that, when Emily read the article and saw the picture, she went to the drawer where she had put those glasses, and they were still there. And there she was, standing at the top of that staircase holding them in her hand. The relief I felt was indescribable, and when I finally drifted off to sleep, I slept well.

I do not know this for sure, but I have gleaned from conversations I had with Marjorie about the incident that she most likely thought that the picture was current and that the article accurately portrayed a true set of circumstances, and under the circumstances, she concluded, I needed some mature guidance or things could come crashing down.

Marjorie knew that I was now operating in an arena that I knew little about, and whether I knew it or not, I was going to need the help of people like her. She was still helping me as Emily and I stood next to her hospital bed the week before she died. The three minutes I was allotted to bring remarks at her funeral were not near enough to share all that Marjorie Amos Frazier and that call meant to me. I can only hope my comments did justice to our relationship.

Facing the Future

But this time, as I drove out and about through the district, I began to look ahead. I began to take mental snapshots of the countryside, and I began to ponder what kind of congressman I would actually be.

Would I find ways to help the people so much in need across the vast stretches of rural poverty in the district?

Would I have the energy to listen and learn as I stepped into a brand new job at a relatively advanced stage of my career?

Would I maintain the confidence of those white voters at that Holly Hill precinct and the Florence Rotary Club?

Would I find ways to serve both races fairly and effectively so that I would be known not as the black congressman but simply the congressman?

The final margin of victory was predictable, about 65 to 35 percent, a margin that has stood up for most of my reelections in the years that have followed. We had a good celebration to observe the victory that night in Columbia, not the uproarious and spontaneous party of ten weeks earlier after the primary victory, but a triumphant observance befitting the kind of inner satisfaction we were all feeling.

I got to bed a little earlier that night, but I had a few moments before I drifted off to create some imaginary visits in my mind. I conjured up visions of Mom and Dad joining me on that election night and I was listening for what they might have said to me.

"Remember?" Mom would probably be saying. "Remember when I told you that things were going to change? Remember when I said that if you stayed in school and studied hard, you would be able to realize your dreams? You've done it, Son, and I'm very proud."

And Dad, trying to suppress a smile and retain his gruff exterior, would shake my hand firmly, look me steadily in the eye and say, "Well, Partner?" Dad seldom called me "Son" or "James." He often called me "Partner."

I would wait for him to continue, and he would say, "Well, Partner, you've got a big job ahead of you. Get a good night's rest so you can start fresh first thing in the morning."

As always, I did just that.

PART NINE

Mr. Clyburn Goes to Washington

My security detail was seated behind me. . . . I suddenly felt a presence in front of me. I looked up, and the flight attendant, who looked to be a thirty-something African American, was staring at me. She quickly retreated to the cockpit, returning shortly to inform my detail that the captain needed to see him. He returned with a rather amused look on his face. When I inquired, he told me that the flight attendant had reported to the pilot that I was in violation of the airline's policy because prisoners were not allowed to sit on the exit rows. My business suit, tie, and briefcase notwithstanding, that flight attendant's only experiences with black passengers boarding airplanes with armed escorts were with prisoners.

24 | *Arriving in Congress*

Nineteen-ninety three was quite a year for America. Bill Clinton was inaugurated as the forty-second president, and Democrats held the majority in both houses of Congress. Michael Jordan scored his twenty thousandth point for the Chicago Bulls. The Dallas Cowboys won the Super Bowl. Shaquille O'Neal was a rookie with the Orlando Magic.

Jim Clyburn was a rookie too, starting his first year as congressman from the Sixth District of South Carolina. Unlike Shaq, however, I was fifty-two years old, an age when a lot of people are considering retirement instead of starting up a new career. One veteran reporter in Washington seemed to delight in suggesting that I would not have much time to build the kind of seniority needed to get much done in the House of Representatives. I felt like telling him that I was *fifty*-two, not *eighty*-two.

Others enjoyed pointing out that it had taken federal legislation to force the State of South Carolina to create a congressional district in which a majority of the population was African American. Creating such a district, they contended, represented an extraordinary piece of special legislation.

What was extraordinary, I usually responded, was the fact that in a state where 28 percent of the population was black, the congressional delegation was 100 percent white and had been that way for ninety-five years. What was extraordinary was the fact that for nearly a century, through the exercise of unconstitutional gerrymandering, South Carolina had somehow managed to ignore the principle of one-man-one-vote and create six finely sculpted districts that were all at least 58 percent white. What was extraordinary was that the State of South Carolina had not—on its own—seen the obvious unfairness of all this and had chosen not to do anything about it on its own.

But as I had learned on that memorable afternoon in my mother's beauty salon when her childhood friend tried to diminish the dreams of an ambitious black youngster, I was not going to let anyone rain on this parade. I knew I had to make up for a lot of lost time if I was going to be a successful fifty-two-year-old rookie in Congress. I decided that a first step in that direction would be to run for the presidency of the freshman class.

When I disclosed that ambition to Lee Bandy, a veteran Washington journalist who was the political reporter for the *State* newspaper in Columbia, he literally laughed out loud. Lee was quick to inform me—with some delight—that there were several candidates for the presidency, at least one of whom was from California, which boasted sixteen new members. Another probable candidate was Eva Clayton, an African American female who represented the First Congressional District in eastern North Carolina. Eva had gained immediate seniority in the class by filling the unexpired term of Walter B. Jones Sr., who had died in office, and she became the first woman ever to win election to Congress from North Carolina.

Forming Friendships and Alliances

These were formidable obstacles. There were 110 freshmen in that class, the largest since 1949, and I was not certain how this fifty-two-year-old rookie from South Carolina would fare in such competition. Then I got a call from longtime friend John Winburn, a lobbyist who knew his way around Capitol Hill and a South Carolinian with an impressive history of Democratic Party activities.

John Winburn had been a tremendous help to me in my primary and general election victories. I trusted him and respected his insight. He told me that running for president of the freshman class, regardless of the outcome, would be a good way for me to make myself known. He also thought I might be able to pull it off.

John had served on the staff of Congressman Ken Holland of the Fifth District of South Carolina. When Ken chose not to run for reelection in 1982, John decided to go for it himself. In a five-man race in the Democratic primary, John finished a strong second but lost in the runoff to John Spratt, who went on to give many years of distinguished service from the Fifth District.

I first got to know John Winburn during that race. He was an acquaintance of Bill DeLoach, who was helping John and asked me to get involved in the campaign. I had lost my first race for secretary of state only four years earlier, and I knew several of the candidates in the Fifth District race. I was reluctant to help out at that stage.

John Winburn's showing in the first primary was impressive. As an underdog to the better-known Spratt, he had attracted almost twenty thousand votes, and it looked as if he had an outside chance in the runoff. I agreed to help out in two counties where I had family members and friends, Sumter and Lee. John Spratt won the race by almost 55 to 45 percent, but John Winburn was grateful to me because the only two counties he carried were Sumter and Lee.

When I declared my candidacy for the Sixth District seat, he offered to help, and hosted a function for me in Washington. After I won, he was an invaluable friend and opened a lot of important doors for me. The most important of those doors was with then–Speaker of the House, Tom Foley of Washington State, and Majority Leader Dick Gephardt of Missouri. Bill DeLoach had suggested it, but it took Winburn and his business partner, Ed Jenkins, a former congressman himself, to pull it off. We were told that the meeting with Foley and Gephardt would last only ten minutes, which suited me fine. I just wanted the face time, and John and Ed wanted the fodder to feed that remarkable Washington rumor mill, which only insiders like them can operate.

The meeting turned out to last twice as long as expected. Foley and Gephardt seemed particularly impressed that I had gotten more than 55 percent of the vote in a

Bill DeLoach and Speaker of the House Thomas Foley with Emily and me at a 1993 event honoring me in Columbia, South Carolina.

five-candidate primary. It was not only a rarity in such a multicandidate race; it also surprised a lot of the Washington crowd, who didn't think I had a chance to win at all.

Over the course of our conversation, I was able to mention my plans to run for freshman class president. Although there was no official endorsement, there were a sufficient number of staff people in the room for word of my planned candidacy to be broadly circulated. Thanks to Winburn and Jenkins, the rumors eventually included a suggestion-by-association that Foley and Gephardt had even blessed the candidacy. In the days before blogs, tweets, and Facebook, the Washington rumor machine was all that was needed in the way of offhand journalism in the nation's capital. I was getting a lot of exposure from this alternative network of unofficial information.

For all the support I was gaining from these carefully orchestrated communications, however, I believed that Eva Clayton still had the inside track, and I had a lot of respect for her. I had known Eva before coming to Congress. We both served on the board of the Southern Regional Council in Atlanta. I also realized that Eva was not the only African American freshman from North Carolina that year. Mel Watt of Charlotte, an attorney who had been involved in Harvey Gantt's political campaigns, was representing North Carolina's Twelfth District and could be expected to support his fellow Tar Heel State candidate. It wasn't lost on me either that 1993 had been declared the "Year of the Woman" by the United Nations, and in those days of ascending political progressivism in America, the freshman class in the U.S. House of Representatives would have great motivation to select a woman—particularly an

African American woman—as their leader. All these things were on my mind as Bill DeLoach and I conferred.

Finding an Accommodation

Bill and I decided it was time to look for a compromise, so I sought out a potential intermediary between Eva Clayton and me. It was Carrie Meek of Miami, an African American member of the freshman class who had won a decisive victory to represent the Twelfth District in South Florida.

Carrie had also served with Eva and me on the Southern Regional Council board, and she and I had several mutual friends and professional acquaintances. I also knew that she could be persuasive. She was so popular in South Florida that she had only token opposition in the general election. While a lot of us were at home campaigning for election, she was up in Washington campaigning for status in the upcoming Congress. It paid off. Carrie achieved the unusual distinction of becoming a freshman member of the House Appropriations Committee.

I was comfortable talking with Carrie with some frankness, and I was confident that she could probably sell a compromise to the rest of the freshman caucus. She had heard the rumors that I had hit it off well with Speaker Foley and Majority Leader Gephardt. I offered my suggested resolution of the contest between Eva Clayton and me. We would both be president. Eva would serve the first year of the session (1993) and I would serve in the second year (1994). She would be president during the UN's "Year of the Woman." We would both be winners.

And that's how it played out. Eva's name and my name were placed in nomination and we were the only nominees. Once nominations were closed, Carrie made the motion that we be declared copresidents along the lines we had discussed. After some brief comments, the motion was seconded and carried. Eva Clayton and Jim Clyburn were both winners. This marvelously eclectic 110-member freshman class of the One Hundred Third Congress, whose roster contained districts from coast to coast and whose membership was energized by fresh new faces of leadership from the African American and Hispanic populations, would be headed by a couple of black Carolinians. I knew there was something I really liked about compromises.

Getting Down to Business

Because of the historic nature of my election, Bill DeLoach felt that we needed to have a ceremonial swearing-in program in Columbia to allow those hardworking volunteers and well-wishers who would not be able to go to Washington an opportunity to savor the moment. The ceremony was a deeply moving and briskly instructive moment in my new life. It took place in the State House in Columbia and was attended by members of the state's leadership corps with whom I had long-standing working relationships, mostly of a positive nature. Our Republican governor, Carroll Campbell, was there. All but one member of the South Carolina congressional delegation were there. Senators Fritz Hollings and Strom Thurmond, Democratic congressmen Butler Derrick and John Spratt and Republicans Bob Inglis and Floyd Spence attended. Only Arthur Ravenel, the Republican from Charleston, was missing. It was a

My ceremonial swearing-in at the South Carolina State House with the state's 1993 congressional delegation: Rep. Bob Inglis (Fourth District), Rep. Floyd Spence (Second District), Senator Ernest Hollings, myself, Rep. Butler Derrick (Third District), Senator Strom Thurmond, Rep. John Spratt (Fifth District). First District representative Arthur Ravenel did not attend. Clyburn Papers, South Carolina State University.

Former governor and U.S. ambassador to Saudi Arabia John West congratulating me at my ceremonial swearing-in as the first African American to represent South Carolina in Congress in nearly a century. Clyburn Papers, South Carolina State University.

good send-off for me, and I appreciated the show of goodwill and bipartisanship to get my congressional career under way.

There were, however, other things on my mind that day, sobering thoughts about why I was really there and what I would be trying to accomplish in my new job. I thought back to my experiences at the Commission for Farm Workers, and I thought of those frontline political years on Governor West's staff. Still fresh in my mind was the battle for human equality I had fought during my almost eighteen years as Human Affairs Commissioner. All that was becoming an aggregate definition of mission and a compelling sense of urgency for me. On that day I was in the process of putting aside the joys of victory and honor at winning the seat, and taking on the realities of work and responsibility I had been chosen to address.

All that came home quickly to me when I was approached by an elderly white man who wished me well and then took me aside for a brief piece of advice. "Now when you get up there," he said in a friendly way, "be sure and get a seat on the Armed Services Committee." That one moment of conversation with a constituent brought it all home to me quickly and personally. My job was being defined for me by a man who had such a significant stake in my performance that he was steering me toward a House committee where I could be of most service to him. That short comment carried a lot of symbolic weight with me that day and in the days thereafter.

It turned out not to be particularly good advice, however. Of the six South Carolina congressmen at the time, three were already serving on the Armed Services Committee: Spratt, Spence, and Ravenel. From the days when Mendel Rivers of Charleston served as chairman of the Armed Services Committee and steered many military installations to our state, South Carolina's association with the committee was well known. I didn't think my addition as a fourth South Carolina member would be all that beneficial to the state or to me as a freshman congressman.

There was other guidance available to me on committee selection as well. All during the election campaign, as I made trips from one end of the Sixth District to the other, I was frequently reminded of the importance of agriculture. The Pee Dee region of the state had traditionally anchored the Sixth District, and the bulk of that region's economy turned on farming. The vast plains of the area had once been the home of tobacco farming, and that business was dying. Lee County was once the largest cotton-producing county in the state. Many people advised me that a good congressman representing the Pee Dee would need to be on the Agriculture Committee.

A Political Hero and Model

I went to Washington with a distinct model of congressional service in mind, that of one of my political heroes, William Jennings Bryan Dorn. For a quarter of a century Bryan was the congressman from the Third District. I know of no one who more effectively combined service to his nation and service to his state. Even though his home was in Greenwood County and he served a district far removed from my lowcountry home, he became known to me, and many others, as "South Carolina's Congressman" because of his influence in Washington and his generosity of spirit and willingness to help people, wherever they might reside.

I got to know him when, as the youthful director of the Neighborhood Youth Corps in Charleston, I took a group of youngsters to Washington to acquaint them with our nation's capital and how the business of government is conducted. Unfortunately my experience with our congressional delegation to that point had been largely that of closed doors. But while we were touring the Capitol, Senator Fritz Hollings met with the students, and Bryan Dorn, the congressman from Greenwood, was the only

House member who opened his doors to us. There wasn't a vote anywhere in that group for him because not one of us lived in his district. His kindness stuck in the impressionable minds of my Youth Corps members, and he had a lifelong friend in me.

There weren't many black voters in South Carolina's Third District, but that didn't keep Bryan from having an influence in racially progressive matters in our state. He and his family supported my campaign to become the first black president of the South Carolina Young Democrats. He also joined hands with me in my efforts to get Governor West to back the hanging of a portrait of Mary McLeod Bethune in the State House. Bryan admired Mrs. Bethune as a civil rights pioneer and prominent educator. Bryan's intervention brought much-needed influence to the effort and helped us lower yet another racial barrier in tradition-bound South Carolina.

We later joined forces again in lowering that barrier a little further. We worked together to have the portrait of Dr. Benjamin E. Mays hung in the House Chamber of the State House. Dr. Mays was born on a farm near Epworth in Greenwood County, attended high school at S.C. State College, and went on to earn a Ph.D. from the University of Chicago and serve as president of Morehouse College in Atlanta, where he became the early mentor of a young idealistic student by the name of Martin Luther King Jr.

Bryan Dorn's efforts to honor Dr. Mays were joined later by his good friend Senator John Drummond of Greenwood, who helped us to save Dr. Mays's boyhood home from destruction and have it physically preserved and moved.

Bryan's committees in Washington were Public Works (Transportation and Infrastructure) and Veterans' Affairs. His association with the latter committee was a particularly powerful and productive one for our state. In my case it also proved to be fortunate because it made my decision to remain on Governor West's staff, after a year of commuting, economically feasible. Bryan had used his influence within the Veterans Administration to help Emily return to her old job as a librarian at the VA hospital in Columbia, a job that made our move to Columbia infinitely more practical. Emily was also encouraging me to seek a seat on the Veterans' Affairs Committee. Her affinity for this committee was deep and personal.

Her only brother, Arthur England, had died while on active duty in the army, and her uncle, her mother's brother, Joseph Henry Washington, was serving on the USS *Arizona* on that fateful day, December 7, 1941, when Pearl Harbor was attacked. Emily was always concerned that, although Uncle Joe survived and had appeared on the *This Is Your Life* television program in connection with his involvement with the bombing of Pearl Harbor, he would never talk with anybody about his experiences in the navy. He would say only that they were humiliating and painful.

Congress later named the VA hospital in Columbia the William Jennings Bryan Dorn Medical Center. But in my mind, the institution had already had that name for years. Bryan left Congress to run for governor, and I wanted to follow in Bryan Dorn's footsteps in Washington, so I decided his two committees—Public Works and Veterans' Affairs—would be my best choices. I reached that decision not just out of my admiration for him, but also with the belief that those committees could be most beneficial to the Sixth District. In fact, at the time of my election, the Sixth District was ranked sixteenth of the 435 districts in the number of constituents receiving veterans' benefits.

While I realized that the fate of tobacco farmers was in peril, I also knew that the economy of the entire district was declining across a broader spectrum of activities. We were already experiencing a significant drop in textiles and textile-related industries, including the growing of its basic raw material—cotton. Whatever economic future there would be for the people of the Sixth District—I believed—lay in the travel and tourism industry. I therefore set out to gain membership on the Public Works Committee, where much potential support for tourism-related projects lay.

Learning the Hard Way

As it turned out, however, I made a tactical error, probably a "dumb freshman mistake." Instead of placing Public Works and Veterans' Affairs on my list of choices, I went through what I considered to be only an obligatory request for membership on "exclusive committees:" Appropriations and Ways and Means. I knew my chances of being chosen for those committees were almost zero. On the night the House Steering and Policy Committee met to make committee assignments, I realized how serious the mistake was.

I placed a call to Butler Derrick, who had replaced Bryan Dorn as Third District congressman and had risen rapidly through the ranks in the House. Butler was in his eleventh term and was a chief deputy whip in the House and a member of the Steering and Policy Committee. Butler was a fine political operator and a good friend. We had come to know each other when I was in the governor's office and he was a member of the South Carolina House of Representatives from Edgefield County. He and I shared great admiration for Bryan Dorn, and I didn't hesitate to invoke that relationship when things got tense in our conversation.

My call to Butler Derrick was only a few minutes before the committee met. I could tell Butler was a little bit miffed because I was putting him in something of a tough position. As it turned out, he was able to deliver. He called me later that evening to inform me that I had been placed on the Public Works Committee. He even apologized for not getting me placed any higher than seventh in seniority among the new members. I was deeply relieved that I was on the committee in any capacity, and I was much impressed and grateful that Butler Derrick was able to produce under such difficult conditions. I was learning the ways of Washington through trial and error, and my experiences in the freshman-class elections and the workings of the Steering and Policy Committee were providing two good early lessons.

Another good lesson awaited me when the Public Works Committee met for organization and subcommittee assignments. Being seventh in freshmen seniority turned out to be my lucky number. I was one slot ahead of Corrine Brown, an African American classmate who represented the Third District in Florida. Both of us wanted a seat on the Aviation subcommittee. During the bidding process, we were seated in order of seniority and I noticed that she was getting pretty nervous. I could even hear her mumbling a little prayer that a slot on the subcommittee would still be available when the bidding got to her.

I asked Corrine why getting on that subcommittee was so important to her. She professed that her chances of reelection might well rest on her being able to serve on that subcommittee. As it turned out there was only one place left on the Aviation subcommittee when it came my turn to choose, and in a slightly dramatic fashion, I passed and let Corrine take the last position on that subcommittee.

She was grateful, and I only half jokingly told her that I would let her know at some undetermined point in the future what my price would be. She has maintained to this day that she has never stopped paying for that gesture. And I have to concede that there may be some modicum of truth to that. In all my leadership races, she has been one of the first people I have approached for help and support, reminding her every time of her "debt" to me. To her great credit, she has never failed to "pay" for that 1993 gesture.

Building Some Friendships

The other great by-product from that exchange with Corrine Brown was the development of a relationship with Jim Oberstar, the veteran congressman who represented the Eighth District in northern Minnesota. Jim, an acknowledged expert on matters of aviation and aviation safety, noticed my gesture to Corrine and commented to me on how magnanimous he thought it was.

Jim was beginning his tenth term at the time, and his friendship became an important one to me. While his voting record was probably a bit to the left of mine, he often mentioned my gesture to Corrine Brown over the years, and I believe it may have had a lot to do with his placing me on the House-Senate Conference Committee a few years later during the reauthorization of the federal highway bill, TEA-21, in 1996. In 2007 Jim became chairman of the House Committee on Transportation and Infrastructure, a committee of untold potential benefit to the well-being and economic success of South Carolina.

As I listen to the puffed-up and distorted claims of the political obstructionists who have fought to keep financial aid out of South Carolina in recent years, I think of Jim Oberstar and the enormous good that came to the state from my friendship with him.

In a matter of months, I was learning the ways of Washington in the sense of the political gives-and-takes in matters of my own personal career. Give-and-take, as I was learning, was not unlike much of what I had done elsewhere for most of my life. I was comfortable with it, and I was beginning to develop some confidence. I was also learning names and faces, building friendships, and developing alliances that could only enhance my ability to serve the people of the Sixth District.

To do my job, to bring attention to the needs of an economically troubled state such as ours, would require many friendships and working alliances with the 435 members of the Congress, particularly the 110 members of the freshman class. It was the beginning of a career in which I built a political infrastructure in the U.S. Congress one personality at a time. For a small-town rookie from Sumter, South Carolina, it was the only way I knew how to do things. As it turned out, it became the style and basis of my political career in Washington.

25 | *Playing Hardball Clinton Style*

For all the promise of the Clinton presidency and the One Hundred Third Congress, things got off to a rocky start. The president's first choice for attorney general, Zoë Baird, was discovered to have undocumented immigrants in her employ, causing her name to be withdrawn from consideration. And the president's early attention to the fate of gays in the military set off an early firestorm of national controversy at a time when he should have been enjoying some undiluted momentum from his election win.

There was a perception that the president had fumbled the opening kickoff, and in the Congress there was some uncertainty and hesitation. Democrats had solid majorities in both houses, but even those majorities seemed to create their own peril. There is no political monster more dangerous than overconfidence, and that monster began showing its fearful head early.

It was decided, for example, that these Democratic majorities were sufficient to exclude Republicans from a role in developing and passing the 1993–94 budget, making compromises or concessions across party lines unnecessary.

The strategy, while mathematically sound, was politically hazardous for two reasons. First, it placed great pressure on the Democratic leadership in each house to deliver the needed votes. Second, it played right into the hands of Newt Gingrich and other Republican leaders spoiling for a big-time fight in the 1994 elections. It gave the GOP a clear and open invitation to oppose whatever they chose to oppose and in whatever fashion they chose to employ.

It didn't help Bill Clinton's Washington strategies either that he was an "outsider." That role, which played so well at ballot-box time in November, was useless when it came to lining up votes for congressional support of White House initiatives. Just ask Jimmy Carter. The states of Georgia and Arkansas are not very good power bases from which to organize large-scale political campaigns within the halls of Congress. That meant that Bill Clinton had to cobble together his majorities on an issue-by-issue basis, even among his fellow Democrats. He was good at it; he was one of the most effective arm twisters I'd ever met. But it was a grueling and politically expensive exercise for him.

This fact was evident in one of my first exposures to political hardball in the Congress. The president's budget resolution, which is basically the spending plan for the coming fiscal year, had passed. It was adopted by the House in mid-March on an entirely partisan vote, 243-183, and about a week later it cleared the Senate, 54-45.

But the budget-resolution vote was only preliminary to the real battle, which came in May when the budget document itself was submitted for approval.

In the meantime the president had suffered a major defeat with the downfall of a modest economic-stimulus package. About half the size of a similar program instituted by the Reagan administration in 1981, Clinton's plan called for about $16.5 billion, including $4.3 billion in extended unemployment benefits.

Republicans, along with some moderate Democrats, ganged up on the president to gut the stimulus program, and only the extension of unemployment benefits survived. It was a painful defeat, and the public approval ratings for his economic plan fell by about a third in the intervening three months.

The Price of Success

That was the condition of things when the Clinton budget arrived on Capitol Hill in May of 1993. By then it had become the product of a wounded president, and the next few months represented my introduction to the fine art of political deal making. I began to notice that a lot of games were being played. The closer we got to the vote the more intense the games got. People were making all kinds of requests and demands. And some of them did not seem to make a whole lot of sense to me. In fact I saw very little redeeming value in most of them.

All the "requesters" and "demanders" seemed to be getting a hearing with the president, however, and I've never been bashful about trying to acquire a fair share of largesse for the people of the Sixth District in South Carolina. Critics have attacked me often and viciously in later years for my willingness to find special ways to bring money, programs, and other resources into the state and into the district, often in the form of legislative "earmarks." Such criticism always baffled me, and I've never understood why I should be expected to apologize for helping the people of my district, or feel defensive about improving the economic conditions of the state. If you've never seen the face of poverty stalk a neighborhood or watched disease attack entire communities, then I guess you can be ideological about preserving the purity of some "market-driven" economic system. Never made much sense to me.

I guess you could call my dealings with President Clinton as my first foray into finding special ways to help poor communities in South Carolina and the rest of the nation. My price for supporting the Clinton budget of 1993, I decided, would be the establishment of Empowerment Zones to provide means of boosting economic opportunities in disadvantaged communities. It was a concept I had promoted in my campaign. It was also a concept that was in the 1992 National Democratic Party platform. But platforms, whether at state level or national level, seem to lose their traction once conventions and elections have passed. As I began my lobbying effort to have Empowerment Zones included in the 1993 Clinton budget, I realized I had to start virtually from scratch. My early contacts with various members of the freshman class as well as with a few veterans generated little interest or enthusiasm. My next thought was to visit Representative Charles Rangel, the iconic Harlem congressman who represented New York's Fifteenth District and whose name had been so long identified with efforts to lift the economic status of poor Americans.

What I heard from Charlie was the position of a Ways and Means Committee member and the interests of an urban congressman. My orientation was that of a member of the Transportation and Infrastructure Committee and the representative of mostly rural communities in need of infrastructure development and jobs. Charlie kept talking about the need for tax credits, and I kept talking about the need for cash infusion and investments. In short I didn't get very far with the congressman from Harlem.

The Gang of Five

That's when I decided the effort needed a little more political muscle. So I went to four members of the freshman class who were notably fearless when it came to political risk taking.

Cynthia McKinney was the outspoken and aggressive representative from Georgia's Eleventh District. I had come to know her father, Billy McKinney, during our days as civil rights activists. Whenever I saw him, he would always say, "I'm counting on you to take care of my daughter." Nobody needed to take care of Cynthia. She was a powerful intellect and political battler, who some years later introduced articles of impeachment against President George W. Bush, Vice President Dick Cheney, and Secretary of State Condoleezza Rice. I had formed a good political friendship with Cynthia, and she was an ideal cohort in the instigation of some "hardball."

Other fellow freshmen I recruited to the team were also high-energy colleagues. Bennie Thompson represented the Second District in Mississippi. Bennie was no stranger to advocacy either. Later he distinguished himself for his energetic advancement of relief for Gulf Coast victims of Hurricanes Katrina and Rita in 2005, and with a little bit of luck and some help from his friend from South Carolina, he became chairman of the Homeland Security Committee.

Congressmen Earl Hilliard and Bennie Thompson joining me at my annual Rudolph Canzater Memorial Classic golf tournament in 1999.

Earl Hilliard was from Alabama's Seventh District, which included Birmingham. He took a nonsanctioned trip to Libya in 1997 on a fact-finding mission, and that trip—plus his pro-Arab positions—were believed to have led to his defeat in 2002. But he was—and still is—my friend.

Sanford Bishop represented the Second District in Georgia. He was the most conservative of the five of us and later gained some notoriety by becoming one of four members of the Congressional Black Caucus to vote for the 2002 resolution authorizing the Iraqi War. He was a "blue dog Democrat," meaning that years later he was among the toughest votes for me as House majority whip to swing behind a White House proposal. He did, however, publicly support the election of Barack Obama as president, and he made a good colleague in our political challenge to President Clinton's 1993–94 budget.

On a very personal note, it should be stated that none of my three male "Gang of Five" colleagues was a member of my social fraternity, Omega Psi Phi. A sign of my growing political maturity was the fact that I could join forces with two members of Kappa Alpha Psi—Sanford Bishop and Bennie Thompson—and one member of Alpha Phi Alpha, Earl Hilliard. Here was true diversity at work.

While we were all African Americans serving our first year in Congress, our districts ranged from the urban to the rural and from the upper- and middle-income to the deeply impoverished. The message we were sending was that there was not a "one-size-fits-all" solution to the needs of America's long-neglected, disadvantaged communities. It was a message coming from states of the Old Confederacy on a fundamental issue that applied throughout the entire nation. All of us were genuinely southern and proudly black. It was clear to us that Charlie Rangel needed to uphold some representations he had made to President Clinton, and we decided to make it very difficult for the Harlem congressman to do so.

It wasn't long before Charlie Rangel was coming around to our way of thinking, and with him on board, the president began to pay attention and eventually saw his way clear to include funding in his budget for the establishment of Empowerment Zones and Enterprise Communities in both the Commerce and Agriculture Departments.

More skirmishes over the budget remained. The most memorable was over an onerous part of the president's decision to impose a tax broadly based on many energy sources. It was to be measured by the British Thermal Unit (BTU), a term most of us hadn't heard since college physics classes. And it certainly had little political appeal to any of us or our constituencies. It led to a commonly heard refrain among Democrats on the Hill even today: "Beware of getting BTUed."

Its genesis grew out of a meeting of the Democratic Caucus that was held in the hall of the House and attended by President Clinton. Many members were leery of any tax, and this one was very tough for a lot of them. They made it clear that they wanted the president to succeed, but they did not want to take a tough vote for something with which the Senate might not agree. The president doubled down in his pitch and assured us that if we voted for it he would fight to keep it when the bill got to the Senate.

Things did not turn out that way. The House vote on the budget on the floor was 219-213, with 38 Democrats voting against it and no Republicans voting for it. I often joke that after that bill left the House on its way to the Senate, that BTU tax fell out of the bill somewhere in or near Statuary Hall. In the Senate, the BTU tax was replaced by a 4.3 cent per gallon tax on gasoline, and with that, things headed for a showdown. The feeling among House members was that they had been screwed, or as it has come to be known, "BTUed."

The Senate passed the budget bill only on a tie-breaking vote by Vice President Gore. Since the houses adopted different versions of the bill, there remained the conference committee reconciliation of the differences and the battles subsequent to that action. The final vote in the House for the conference committee version was 218-216, still with no Republicans voting for it, and Gore's tie-breaking vote was again necessary to rescue the budget in the Senate.

I thought back to that "Gang of Five" proud southerners—McKinney, Thompson, Hilliard, Bishop and Clyburn—who had held out for Empowerment Zones funding, and I quietly numbered us as being among the "swing votes" who made passage of the 1993–94 budget possible. Of course a lot of people could claim to be "swing votes" in that turbulent budget year.

Charlie Rangel was less quiet about his role in the fight to fund Empowerment Zones. An online biography had this account: "He [Rangel] played a significant role in the creation of the 1995 Upper Manhattan Empowerment Zone Development and the national Empowerment Zone Act, which helped change the economic face of Harlem and other inner city areas." I have no doubt that his interest and support was necessary for the president to accept our recommendations. I also have no doubt that without the coalition of Georgia, Alabama, Mississippi, and South Carolina freshmen, the Empowerment Zones would not have been in that budget.

Empowering People in Need

My first "hardball" experience was a positive one. I had learned another lesson on how things were done on Capitol Hill. In addition I had made some important friends—Cynthia McKinney, Bennie Thompson, Earl Hilliard, and Sanford Bishop. And maybe I had even caught the attention of the iconic congressman from Harlem, Charles Rangel. I found out in later years that indeed I had, but it would be some time before that attention turned into respect, the kind of respect that the crusty old southern owner of the Charleston Fun Bowl Eugene Skinner had admonished me about. Mainly for me, however, the outcome of the 1993 budget fight was measured in the payout to South Carolinians. Of the thirty HUD-administered urban programs across the nation, the Sumter-Columbia Empowerment Zone was one of the earliest designations. Of the thirty rural programs administered by the Department of Agriculture, three were in South Carolina—the Williamsburg/Lake City Enterprise Community, the Charleston/North Charleston Enterprise Community, and the Allendale Alive Enterprise Community.

I'm aware that Harlem was also the recipient of a major project, and certain areas of the states of Alabama, Mississippi, and Georgia managed to receive priority attention. Good things often get done in unorthodox ways, and we were learning the ropes under the pressure of real-world conditions. We were finding ways to combat that historic tragedy of disadvantaged Americans.

As I have said on many occasions in the past, people to whom special things have been done to deprive them of their full status and opportunities as Americans, need special things to be done *for* them in order to eliminate or remedy the current effects of those injustices. The Empowerment Zone legislation was just such a special act of human recovery, and helped lay the foundation for the 10-20-30 formula that I was able to get into the American Recovery and Reinvestment Act, which is beginning to get some bipartisan traction in the Congress for inclusion in other legislation as well.

26 | *My First Bill*

The education of the neophyte congressman from South Carolina was well under way in the 1993–94 session when I set out to introduce my first bill in the House of Representatives. By then I had learned that introducing a piece of legislation was one thing, getting it passed was another.

Having been blessed by the experiences of getting the Empowerment Zone authorization and my campaign to gain the copresidency of the freshman class, I had come to learn that nothing gets done single-handedly in the Congress. I also recognized that leverage is an important political tool, particularly when it's leverage with the White House. A final crucial element, I had learned, was the influence of the standing committee on which a member sits.

All those factors came into play as my first legislative proposal hit the House desk early in 1994. It was a matter of deep personal importance to me, and—as it turned out—a matter of deep political complexity in South Carolina, and Washington as well.

It all began years earlier with my curiosity as to why the federal building on Laurel Street between Assembly and Main Streets in Columbia was named just that, the "Federal Building." In a state where practically everything—office buildings, football stadiums, highways, bridges, public parks, and even interchanges on interstate highways—seemed to bear the names of notable South Carolinians, this building had stood for decades untitled with anything other than its generic designation.

At our first congressional staff meeting, I asked Bill DeLoach, who was now serving as my chief of staff, to look into why the building had no name. Then I told him my purpose for the inquiry. I wished to have the building named for Matthew J. Perry Jr., the man who had served with so much distinction as a federal court judge and whose work as civil rights champion had so powerfully reshaped the federal community in which we exist.

Matthew Perry was also powerfully ingrained in my own being as hero, mentor, friend, great model of human achievement, and fraternity brother. If there was one person who had changed the face of South Carolina and had enhanced my own opportunities for personal and professional growth, it was Matthew Perry. Having him as the subject of my first bill in the Congress was not only a matter of great symbolism, it was a down payment on the great debt owed to him by me and all the other people of the state.

Shaking hands with Judge Matthew J. Perry Jr. before addressing the judge's first naturalization ceremony. Clyburn Papers, South Carolina State University.

Shortly after the 1993 session of Congress had convened, I was given the opportunity to speak on behalf of legislation naming the Thurgood Marshall Federal Judicial Center in Washington. It was my first speech on the floor of the House, and I spent a few minutes discussing Justice Marshall's impact on the desegregation of public schools in South Carolina and elsewhere in the nation. I said, "He was a man who took us on a journey of courage for many years."

As I spoke those words, I realized that I was also describing Matthew Perry, and I envisioned the day when I could apply that same kind of thinking and rhetoric to his great life and career and the journey of courage that he had brought to my own state.

Bill DeLoach came back with the report that there seemed to be no particular reason the federal building in Columbia was unnamed, and he thought the way should be clear to have the building named for Matthew Perry. He cautioned me, however, to make certain before I went far with my plan that Matthew Perry himself was comfortable with it. It would be, in the minds of many, the first federal building in South Carolina to be named for an African American, and that in and of itself could cause a stir. I knew, however, that the Veterans Administration hospital in Charleston had been named for a young African American Medal of Honor winner who graduated from Burke High School and was fatally wounded in Vietnam in a heroic act that saved the lives of his fellow soldiers.

The Project Becomes Larger

Matthew had a reputation for being overly modest, a reputation with which I also have some acquaintance. But I also knew that neither one of us was as modest as our reputations might indicate. We just worked a little harder than others in high-profile public positions at keeping our egos in check. At any rate I called Matthew to tell him what I had in mind. When I conveyed my plan to have the federal building named after him, he was gracious and expressed his appreciation. Then—true to form—he privately passed along some information of which I was not aware.

He told me that the United States Justice Department had authorized a new courthouse for Columbia. After a polite pause, he let me know, in his own courtly way, that he would be more interested in having the new courthouse bear his name, rather than the office building at the corner of Laurel and Assembly Streets. That revelation, I realized, escalated the project by many magnitudes. But it also made the final outcome much more appropriate. What could be more meaningful than having an edifice of the federal court, where Matthew Perry had won so many landmark decisions on behalf of black Americans, bear his name as a permanent testament to his role in our history?

I smiled, and for an instant I recalled the early moments when I had first seen this man and then finally met him. I remembered Mom taking me as a teenager to the courthouse in Sumter to show me the kind of man "you can be when you grow up." I remembered Matthew Perry choosing me as the lead witness to provide testimony on behalf of S.C. State and Claflin students who were arrested for a civil rights demonstration in Orangeburg in 1960.

Now, more than three decades later, it was my turn to be advising Matthew Perry. I told him that I would eagerly and enthusiastically look into the possibility of having the proposed new courthouse named in his honor. But once the effort became public—as I knew it would rather quickly—I needed his commitment that he would be supportive when asked to comment. The worst thing that could happen, I thought, would be for him to express any reticence, or even modesty, at the prospect of the courthouse being named after him. At that point, Matthew Perry assured me that he would not say or do anything to undercut the effort.

With that understanding, I went to work on what had suddenly become a tougher—and far more important—project than I had earlier anticipated. It had also become a lot closer to my heart.

Bill DeLoach set about to conduct some initial research and found—just as Matthew had said—that a new courthouse had been authorized for Columbia but had not been funded. That meant that I would not only have to fight to have the building named in Matthew Perry's honor, I would also have to fight to get the building funded and constructed. This was getting real complicated.

Things didn't get any easier when a public uproar arose nationally over the cost of new or under-construction federal courthouses at Foley Square in Lower Manhattan, New York City, and on the Boston, Massachusetts waterfront. The New York building, with its twenty-seven-story tower and 900,000 square feet of working space, was estimated at $412 million, and the Boston courthouse, with 765,000 square feet, was $167 million. By twenty-first-century standards, these costs may not seem all that high. By 1994 standards, however, they were considered by many to be lavish and outrageous. I had nothing so spectacular in mind for Columbia. But the controversy over the New York and Boston courthouses was reaching scandal-like proportions and it had gotten the attention of President Clinton. The president had made some public statements to the effect that he would oppose the construction of any new federal courthouses. So, as is often the case, timing meant everything, and the timing for initiating a new federal courthouse project didn't seem good.

It was about then that it occurred to me that I owed my friend and fellow congressman Butler Derrick even more gratitude than I had originally believed. The Public Works Committee was exactly where I could be most effective in advancing the cause of the Matthew Perry Courthouse. This committee is where the authorization process for such buildings begins. I was also about to realize the benefit of doing a good deed for a colleague. When I passed and allowed Congresswoman Corrine Brown to have that seat on the Aviation subcommittee, I landed a third subcommittee —Buildings and Grounds. All naming bills start in that subcommittee.

My first thought was to buy some time in order for things to cool down over the cost of courthouses and to use that time as a member of the Building and Grounds subcommittee to learn as much as possible about the process. Several projects involving the naming of public buildings were coming before us, and I started asking questions. One of the questions I asked each time was whether the person after whom the building was to be named was living or deceased. Some were, and some weren't. After a few such inquiries, I began getting cold stares from my colleagues. But I never offered an explanation.

Taking on Strom Thurmond

Within a matter of days an even more serious complication arose. It was brought to my attention that Senator Strom Thurmond, after whom the existing fifteen-story federal office building and adjacent courthouse in Columbia had been named, was referring to the proposed new building as the "Strom Thurmond Annex." In his mind, I suppose, that meant that he had already decided on the name. In reality, however, the new courthouse would actually be located on a city block completely separate from the existing courthouse and at least a block away. Hardly an annex, I thought.

The possibility of a clash with Thurmond was changing the whole scale of things. What had started out as the fairly simple matter of naming a building after a prominent South Carolinian was taking on new dimensions and challenges. I was expecting a fight over funding the new courthouse, but now I was entering the dangerous territory of a disagreement with Strom Thurmond over something of a delicate personal nature.

It was regrettable that it had come to that. By our count, there were twenty-seven entities in the state that bore Strom Thurmond's name. But deep inside me, I relished the opportunity of going to battle for Matthew Perry after he had gone to battle so many times for me and so many others. There was, in fact, something entirely fitting about Thurmond and Perry being at opposite ends of this issue. They had been there many times before, and I found a certain kind of historic justice about the battle being fought one more time.

Even before the Thurmond issue arose I had already begun gathering the support of the five other members of the South Carolina congressional delegation. For a while things proceeded smoothly. Once a hearing on the bill was scheduled, I notified the South Carolina delegation of the date. Each member agreed either to give testimony personally or to write a letter to the subcommittee in support.

Then strange things began to happen. As the time for the hearing drew near, defections began. All the South Carolina Republicans abandoned me, some saying that their hearts were with me but their heads were being bludgeoned by the senior senator. John Spratt and Butler Derrick stayed with me, but Butler was wavering. He and Thurmond were from the same hometown of Edgefield, and I understood how personal and prickly politics in close-knit small towns could be.

The bill cleared the subcommittee without opposition, and some of the members came to realize why I had been asking the questions about naming buildings for living people. I did not want to get tripped up on a technicality, and my "due diligence" on the issue paid off. The question was not even raised, at least not yet.

My feeling of victory, however, was short-lived. Once the Matthew Perry Courthouse bill received the full committee's recommendation for the Suspension Calendar, the mild skirmish became all-out war, and I began to feel the full force of a peeved Strom Thurmond. Without my knowledge, he had contacted the White House—the same White House that was occupied by my fellow Democrat Bill Clinton—and he had obtained what is known as an "Administrative Objection" on the bill, a courtesy extended to the president on issues where important policy was involved. Important policy? Did the people of Peoria, Illinois, really care about the name of a courthouse in Columbia, South Carolina? This was not an "Administrative Objection." This was a slap across the face of James E. Clyburn, freshman congressman from South Carolina, and it was being applied by my good friend the Democratic president.

An Unexpected Intervention

The letter from the White House was signed by Sheila Foster Anthony, sister of Vince Foster and wife of Beryl Anthony Jr., a congressman from Arkansas. Though Sheila Anthony's name was affixed at the bottom of the letter, I took it as a missive directly from the president himself. The reason for the objection, the letter explained, was that the "book on Matthew Perry's life was not yet closed." As if the "book" on Senator Thurmond's life was? I was furious.

I had been blindsided by a letter from "my" president, who was siding with Strom Thurmond against me. How could Bill Clinton, whose support from black Americans was so powerful, betray me and oppose an honor for a great American such as Matthew Perry? To cool my anger, I counted to ten very slowly. And as Mark Twain once said, if counting to ten isn't enough, then count to twenty. I counted much higher than that.

Once I calmed down, I began to rethink the lessons I had learned about "hardball" experience on Capitol Hill. I began to remember how the element of "leverage" came into play in Washington, and how I had parlayed a vote for the Bill Clinton 1993 budget into a commitment from him to include funding for the Empowerment Zones in that budget. Would the same technique work for the Matthew Perry Courthouse? I began looking for a vehicle.

It so happened that about that time the president was launching his campaign to organize support for another major piece of legislation: the Violent Crime Control and Law Enforcement Act of 1994. It had originally been written by Senator Joe Biden of Delaware, and it was the largest crime bill in the history of the nation, $9.7 billion for prisons and $6.1 billion for prevention programs. The bill also provided for two hundred thousand new police officers, and it attracted a lot of public sentiment and support.

As was customary with his administration, Bill Clinton was struggling to put together the votes. On another battlefront at the time, things were not going well with his mammoth health-care bill, and he very much needed a legislative victory. He needed it so much, in fact, that he was once again resorting to one-on-one phone calls to Senate and House members.

I waited for my call from Bill Clinton and prepared for the conversation. When it came one afternoon and I was asked to "hold the line for the president," I had my thoughts well composed. "Can you help me on this one?" came the request a few moments later, and I responded, "I'm not so sure, Mr. President." "Why is that?" he asked with only a slight rise of surprise in his voice.

"Well, Mr. President . . ." I began, and I quickly told him about what I considered to be the ill-advised letter from Sheila Foster Anthony. He didn't seem aware of what I was talking about and quickly attributed it to "a misunderstanding." I then launched into a discussion about Matthew Perry and what he had meant in my life. I even went back as far as my first contact with him in the Sumter County courthouse. By the time I had gotten halfway through my comments on Judge Perry, I could tell, even on the telephone, that the president was figuratively throwing up his hands and conceding. He said he would "look into" the matter, and I took that to mean he would withdraw his administrative objection to the bill. With that, I committed my support to the Violent Crime Control and Law Enforcement Act, which passed a few weeks later, giving the president an important congressional victory. Bill Clinton proved good to his word about removing his objection to my bill, and I thought to myself that I was becoming a pretty good horse trader.

Things Get Personal

Getting the president to withdraw his objection was one thing; dealing with Senator Thurmond was quite another. While my position on naming the courthouse for Matthew Perry was getting some attention and support from major newspapers, Thurmond's pride was formidable, and it was going to take something more than a few prickly editorials to dissuade him from his desire to have yet another public structure named in his honor.

I was also beginning to realize that for all the political disagreements I may have had with the senator over the years, they had usually been at long-range, like soldiers lobbing artillery shells at each other. This, on the other hand, was a direct conflict, like hand-to-hand combat, and it was a little daunting.

During this time, as fate would have it, I got a phone call from John Napier asking to see me about an issue in which he had an interest. John was a Republican from Bennettsville who had preceded me as congressman from the Sixth District, serving one term (1981–83) before losing in his bid for reelection to Democrat Robin Tallon. Despite our political differences, John and I got along well. We had come to know each other during my 1978 and 1986 campaigns for secretary of state. His law partner and later circuit judge Edward Cottingham was a big supporter of mine.

As he stood up to leave our meeting, John made the familiar parting comment, "Let me know if there's anything I can ever do for you." Well in this particular case, there was, and I said so. John hesitated and then took his seat again. Our conversation took a new direction.

I knew that John Napier was a Strom Thurmond protégé and had served on his Washington staff in the mid-1970s. I also knew that John's politics were fairly moderate on social issues, and that he held Matthew Perry in high esteem.

We chatted for a while about Judge Perry, and I told him of my efforts to honor the judge by naming the new courthouse in Columbia in his honor. John nodded, smiled, and said it would be the appropriate thing to do. I did not know how much he knew of the brewing controversy between Thurmond and me over the naming of the building. We were just having a friendly chat about the plan.

I then decided to make certain that John was aware of the senator's opposition, and I proceeded to fill him in on what had transpired up to that point. He seemed a little surprised, but I was still not certain what he knew about the issue or whether he knew how hard I intended to fight.

What I was fairly certain about, however, was that John did not know about some historical information I had just acquired and what I was prepared to do with it. Thanks to some good staff work I had learned that the naming of the existing Strom Thurmond Building and U.S. Courthouse on Assembly Street in Columbia, which had opened in 1979, had never gotten congressional approval. It was not by oversight either. I pointed out to John that on at least two occasions, the legislation had failed in the Congress, probably by objections in the House of Representatives. While Thurmond had become an icon in the U.S. Senate, his fan base in the House wasn't all that strong. The building had been named after Thurmond by administrative fiat and could be overridden by congressional action.

It was hardball time. If the senator persisted in his opposition to the naming of the courthouse after Matthew Perry, I told John, I was prepared to use the legislative history I had acquired to seek statutory authority to rename the existing Strom Thurmond Building and U.S. Courthouse. While I fully realized that passage of such legislation was unlikely, I also realized that it might have enough traction to clear the House and become a matter of some political embarrassment to the senator. Things could get downright testy.

John expressed disbelief that I would go to such lengths, and I assured him that I was not only prepared to do so, but that I was planning to do so in a matter of days. At that point John repeated his offer to be of some assistance. This time the offer was more clearly focused. I again accepted his offer, and provided more specific details.

I suggested that because of his long-standing friendship with the senator, John might try to intercede and seek a peaceful settlement that would clear the way for the naming of the new building for Judge Perry. I made it clear that I had no interest in a public fight, but it was Thursday, and I told John my bill was coming up on the Suspension Calendar on the following Monday. Being a former congressman, John knew congressional procedures, and he realized he would have to work fast to head off the escalated debate which lay only four days ahead.

An Artful Negotiation

And he did. John called me that evening only minutes before I was scheduled to deliver a banquet speech in Charleston, with news of his conversation with the senator's staff. In a grand act of statesmanship and diplomacy, he had worked it out so that the senator would drop his opposition.

The only condition would be my agreeing to make it clear in my floor remarks that the new courthouse was to be distinctly separate from the existing Strom Thurmond Building. That was an easy concession on my part; in fact it was no concession at all. That had been my position all along.

And so it came to pass. My first bill in Congress was adopted in both houses with scarcely a murmur. A little over two years later, an article in the May 12, 1996, issue of the *State* newspaper reported that the courthouse project had cleared its second major congressional hurdle with the approval of $3.5 million for the design of the 200,000 square foot building. The funding went along with $4 million which had been authorized to purchase the 3.7 acre block in the middle of downtown Columbia.

The article, by Charles Pope, reported, "It wasn't easy to win approval to attach his [Perry's] name to the courthouse. When Clyburn pushed the idea in 1994, Thurmond objected, arguing that it was an annex to the existing building and therefore should be named after him. Thurmond lost the battle, but the Perry courthouse soon became imperiled by a brief scandal about the cost of federal courthouses. . . . So far, however, the Perry courthouse has survived and Clyburn said . . . he has gotten assurances from the White House that the project will be fully funded."

It was good to read such an accurate report of the events, which had taken place two years earlier, and to know that the public could share my own feelings of joy in the approval and support being accorded the historic recognition of Matthew Perry as a great American.

For the record the eventual cost was estimated at a little less than $60 million, a far cry from the $412 million that had been appropriated to build the federal courthouse in Lower Manhattan and had set off such alarms with President Clinton.

It gave me more than a little delight on February 26, 2004—eleven years after I had spoken of Thurgood Marshall's "journey of courage"—to rise again on the floor of the U.S. House of Representatives and talk of Matthew Perry's own journey: "The dedication of a United States courthouse in his honor in the shadow of his birthplace that was once cloaked in the scourge of segregation signals a new era in South Carolina brought about in large measure by the dogged determination of Matthew Perry and his unbending faith that justice will prevail. His vision and veracity led him to

Speaking at the dedication of the Matthew J. Perry U.S. Courthouse in April 2004 with Judge Perry and his wife, Hallie, looking on.

challenge the Jim Crow laws of his time, and he succeeded in providing faith and hope to an entire generation of South Carolinians."

There they stand today—the Strom Thurmond Federal Building and U.S. Courthouse at 1935 Assembly Street and about a block away—separate and distinct—the Matthew J. Perry U.S. Courthouse at 901 Richland Street. Like testaments to two eras of the state's history, they are arrayed side by side as monuments to the changing and evolving nature of the law and the notion of justice. And when the lights go down every night, they probably eye each other warily, making certain that neither encroaches on the territory or jurisdiction of the other.

27 : *Building Friendships*

Back in the 1960s, weekend evenings at Fun Bowl in Charleston were often followed by a stop at Brooks Restaurant. Its proprietor, Albert Brooks, and I became good friends and were inducted into the Omega Psi Phi Fraternity together. Omega's motto is "Friendship is essential to the soul," and Albert's favorite saying was, "Friendship is as Friendship does." I took both that motto and Albert's adage to heart and put both to full use in my leadership pursuits.

CBC Chair

During our second term Bennie Thompson the Kappa, Earl Hilliard the Alpha, and I cemented our friendship during early morning walks from Capitol Hill to the Lincoln Memorial. On one of those mornings, during our third term, Bennie suggested that I consider running for chair of the Congressional Black Caucus (CBC). Maxine Waters was CBC chair at the time and had recently appointed me to chair the CBC's Annual Legislative Conference for the second consecutive year. I was getting pretty high marks in that capacity and was developing significant political and personal relationships inside and outside the Beltway. I told Bennie I was doubtful that the CBC would tolerate a chairman from the Deep South.

Several walks later Bennie broached the subject again. He told me he had checked into my regional concern, and it did not seem to be a problem. He said that, if I ran, he doubted I would have any opposition. This made the prospect rather inviting. I subsequently discussed it with family, friends, and several other members. It appeared Bennie was right. So I decided to run.

When the elections were called, Bennie nominated me, and the vote was unanimous. I was overwhelmed and unsure how best to express appreciation for the faith and confidence the members had placed in me. So when I stood up to address them, I did as I often do in such situations. I relied on one of my dad's stories.

One day when my dad overheard me boasting about something, he told me the story of a minister who had been called to a church that had great difficulty keeping a pastor. Dad said that after a year the minister was still there and felt compelled to ask one of the parishioners why he had been so successful. "I have been here for a year," the pastor said to the parishioner, "and everybody knows that before I came here y'all couldn't keep a pastor. Please tell me why have I been so successful when so many others before me failed?"

*Sitting across from President Bill Clinton, at the first White House meeting of the Congressional
Black Caucus after I became the group's chair in 1999. William J. Clinton Presidential Library.*

According to Dad, the parishioner looked at the pastor and said, "well preacher,
you see the members of this church, we really don't want a pastor and you are the
closest thing to nothing we've ever had." So I said to my fellow caucus members that I
was hopeful that such was not the case in that instance. I promised them that I would
work hard to make them proud of having put their faith and confidence in me.

Appropriations Committee

Meanwhile I was also seeking a seat on the Appropriations Committee. I knew how
difficult it was to get on that committee, so I sought John Spratt's guidance. John
asked whether or not I had the support of Democratic leader Dick Gephardt. I replied that I had not spoken with Dick yet and asked for John's advice as to how best
to approach him. He told me that the leader usually puts up a slate, and whoever is
on that slate usually wins. So I should try to get on the leader's slate.

When I subsequently asked Dick Gephardt for his support for one of the six
Democratic seats that were open, he said he had commitments to four people and was
still thinking about the other two. I requested that, if he could not support me, would
he consider leaving at least one of the other two seats open. He did not say yes, but
he did not say no. So I informed John Spratt that I was going to take my chances.

John asked how I planned to pull it off. I told him that my first move was
to have him nominate me. I knew how highly regarded John was by everybody in
our House Democratic Caucus, and I felt I had developed friendships with enough
members of the Steering and Policy Committee to be successful, if Gephardt left an
opening.

Gephardt left the opening, and Spratt nominated me. What a speech he gave. As he spoke, I watched the members' expressions. His speech closed the deal. I became one of the six new Democrats on the committee.

Then came some luck. Although there were twenty-seven Democratic seats on the committee, there was only enough money for twenty-two staff assistants. Consequently only one of the six new people would be able to get an appropriations staffer. That would be determined by seniority, and the order of seniority would be determined by lot. The six names were placed in a hat, and my name was the first one drawn.

The political gods were smiling on me in a big way. After only six years in Congress, I was chair of the Congressional Black Caucus and a member of an exclusive committee. The big question at that point was would I have the time to do justice to both positions.

A Friendly Gesture

Several weeks later, a Republican member of the Appropriations Committee, Michael Forbes of New York, decided to switch parties, and negotiated a deal with Democratic leader Dick Gephardt, to stay on the committee. The plan Gephardt presented to our caucus to keep Mr. Forbes on the committee seemed very problematic to me, but I did not say anything in the meeting. When I got back to my office, however, I called Gephardt and told him that I felt his plan was fraught with problems.

Dick sound a little irritated when he asked if I had a better idea. I told him that if he were to respond favorably to a memorandum I would send him, he could have my seat. He asked me to send the memo and I did. In the memo I laid out the priorities I was pursuing on behalf of my constituents and their representatives, and requested assurances that he would make them a part of any leadership requests that I knew he would be making.

Gephardt responded with a meeting that was attended by whip David Bonior, ranking member Dave Obey, an Office of Management and Budget staffer Sylvia Matthews Burwell, and the chair and vice chair of the Democratic Caucus. We went down my wish list, and various people around the table pledged assistance. With that, and a guarantee that I would maintain my seniority, I took leave from the committee.

Quite a few members questioned my sanity. Emily privately chastised me. Senator Fritz Hollings publicly expressed dismay. But I was comfortable with my decision because it allowed me to maximize the time I needed to spend on CBC activities while practicing my fraternity's motto and Albert Brook's adage. Charlie Rangel wanted to know what I really wanted. I told him to stay tuned.

Vice Chair

When my two-year CBC chairmanship came to an end, I decided to seek the vice chairmanship of the House Democratic Caucus. Al Wynn of Maryland had sought the position previously, and I had been a part of the whip operation of his unsuccessful bid. When I sounded him out to see if he was planning to run again, he assured me that he wasn't and would be happy to support me if I ran. One day, during my period of contemplation, I was approached by Congressman Ed Towns of New York seeking my support for Gregory Meeks to be vice chair. I told him that I was contemplating running for the position myself and was hopeful that I would have his support.

After that conversation, I knew that it would not take long for the word to get out so I got with Bennie Thompson, and we launched the campaign. Then word came that Zoe Lofgren of California was getting into the race. That set up a race between two African American males, one from New York, the other from South Carolina, and a white female from California; a race that also pitted me against representatives from two big states with large Democratic delegations.

The odds looked daunting. But, not only had I cultivated relationships with members, I had pretty good relationships with many staffers as well. I was also receiving high fives and well wishes from cafeteria employees, Capitol policemen, subway operators, and the workers who cleaned the hallways and offices and polished the furniture. I felt good about my chances.

I sent the customary letter to every member of the House Democratic Caucus. The centerpiece of the letter was a little political adage often used by South Carolina politicians: "The best way to tell what a person will do is to look at what he has done." I wrote that "caucus leaders should be willing to put the caucus's interests above their own." I reminded the members that I had demonstrated my willingness to do that when I stepped off of the Appropriations Committee to allow our caucus to resolve a serious issue in an orderly fashion.

But I felt the need to do something further to distinguish me from my opponents. So on my letter to the New York and California members—and other members in their regions—I wrote a message that, if circumstances were to develop that the first ballot were not definitive and I was in a runoff against a member other than the one from their region, please consider making me your second choice. The impact was beyond my wildest expectations. Many members mentioned that note to me.

On the day of the election, I could tell by the expressions on the faces of my colleagues that my efforts had taken hold. Just before the meeting started, Bill Lipinski who had not had much to say to me since I leapfrogged him and nine other senior Democrats to land on the TEA-21 Conference Committee, walked up to me and said, "You've got my vote." I was taken aback but very pleased.

All three of us were nominated, and when the votes were tallied, I was two votes shy of the required 50 percent plus one, and Gregory Meeks was in second place. Realizing that my "make-me-your-second-choice" campaign had been well received, he withdrew and asked that I be elected by acclamation. I was.

House Democratic Caucus Chair

I served as vice chair for the next three years and once again seemed to be in the right place at the right time. A resignation from the Senate took place in New Jersey setting up a governor's appointment and Bob Menendez, who was serving as caucus chair, was chosen to fill the seat. So when Menendez got appointed to the Senate, I was unanimously elected chair—after another outstanding nominating speech by John Spratt. When he concluded, there were more than a few tearful eyes in the room. Kendrick

Meek, who had succeeded his mother in the Congress, still talks about John's remarks. I served as chair of the House Democratic Caucus for the final year of the One Hundred Ninth Congress.

I went into the 2004 elections feeling rather confident that it was the year we were going to get out of the wilderness. I sincerely felt that the public's reaction to the results of the 2000 elections and the subsequent Supreme Court decision in *Bush v. Gore* were all that was needed to make our tenth year in the wilderness our last. But in the final four or five weeks of the 2004 campaign I started getting some unsettling reports and experiencing some cruel and unusual treatment from faith voters.

The treatment was especially severe in Ohio and Michigan. In Columbus, Ohio, an expected group of fifty or sixty black ministers turned out to be only five or six. None of my repeated phone calls to the pastor of the Church of God in that area, whose wife was my mother's godchild, were returned. In Cincinnati an AME father and son team hosted a group, and they did not hold back. It was brutal.

On one trip to Michigan, Congressman John Dingle and I were greeted at a church by a group passing out leaflets that were patently false. On another occasion, a meeting with a group of African American ministers that had been pulled together by Congresswoman Carolyn Kilpatrick at the Detroit airport was about as unpleasant an experience as I have ever had. I started feeling that we were going to be in the wilderness for at least two more years, and we were.

Keeping Faith

Reflecting on why we failed in 2004, I kept thinking about a radio interview I heard two or three days after the election. The lady being interviewed admitted that the Democratic Party's policies seemed more in tune with her social needs, but that was secondary to her religious considerations when it came to voting. She expressed that the Republican Party seemed to better reflect her religious values. That lady's comments haunted me. Consequently I sat down and sent Minority Leader Nancy Pelosi a memorandum, which read in part:

> All of us have read the headlines trumpeting that Republicans won the election because their stances on moral issues were more in tune with ordinary Americans than the Democrats.
>
> As the son of a minister and an ardent believer in the Judeo-Christian ethic into which I was born and by which I was raised; when contemplating certain issues, I sometimes ask myself, how would Solomon advise or what would Jesus do?
>
> I often reflect upon Dr. Martin Luther King Jr.'s reminder that, "Life's most persistent and urgent question is: What are you doing for others?"

How do Democrats speak in a language that engages persons of faith?

We cannot have a conversation about faith and politics without involving the faith community, and especially the Black clergy. In recent years the African-American community has been an integral and arguably the most consistently reliable component of the Democratic Party. The Black Church is still the corner-stone of that community. It is how slavery was endured for 244 years, Jim Crow tolerated for another 100 years, and many past and current protests are sustained.

Democrats need to reengage African-American clergy in substantive ways. We need to be more community based as we address the long-term economic, social, and moral health of not just African-Americans but all Americans.

Democrats must reach into those various communities and forge new and stronger relationships. We must also be willing to introduce ourselves to African-Americans of faith who have little identity and no experience with the Civil Rights Movements of the 50's and 60's. We must start meaningful conversations with them and make certain that these conversations cross cultural, ethnic, and economic plains.

Framing our moral vision in terms of our policy

In his "Letter from the Birmingham City Jail," Dr. Martin Luther King skillfully reveals how social justice is a moral issue that links human souls together. He writes, "We are caught in an inescapable network of mutuality, tied in a single garment of destiny. What affects one directly affects all indirectly." Dr. King enabled us to understand that it is the duty of persons of faith and the charge of persons in politics to stand for justice and morality. We as Democrats must remind the American people of our moral vision and, I hope, our soulful commitment.

It is imperative that Democrats learn to talk the talk going forward as well as we have walked the walk in the past. It does not matter very much what religious persuasion one professes or denomination one embraces. There is a huge difference in conveying deep moral convictions and attending formal services every Saturday or Sunday. In our efforts to reach the faithful, Democrats should not lose sight of that distinction. By speaking in terms of morality and fundamental values we can bridge the gap between us and those voters who claim religious beliefs as their primary motivation in deciding for whom to vote.

Pelosi's Response

About two weeks later Nancy Pelosi approached me with a proposition. She said that she was going to appoint a Faith Working Group and wanted me to head it. I responded that I felt one of the ministers in our caucus might be better suited for that assignment, but Nancy said she had detected a certain faith component in my speeches and writings and felt I should do it. Of course this was rather flattering. On reflecting I realized clearly that Nancy understood some of the dangers such a position could encounter if someone too closely identified with one religion or denomination headed the effort.

How would one navigate discussions of faith issues among Christians, Jews, Muslims, and Buddhists, all of which are represented in our House Democratic Caucus? Where do you draw the line between Catholics and Protestants, not to mention the quagmire that could await you within the various Protestant denominations that are so prominent within our caucus: Baptists, Methodists, Presbyterians, and Pentecostals? How would nonbelievers fit into these discussions? And we did have a few of those in our caucus.

I told Nancy I would have to think about it. But I didn't just think about it, I discussed it with my pastor, the Reverend Joe Darby, of Morris Brown AME Church in Charleston. When I asked what he thought I should do, Reverend Darby responded that he thought I should reread the book of James.

Now the book of James has always been one of my favorite books of the Bible. Not just because of my name, although that does not hurt, but because it's such a short book. You can read it in one sitting and really feel proud of yourself. But it had been sometime since I had read it.

So I sat down to reread the book of James. When I got to the second chapter, I clearly saw what my pastor wanted me to ponder. But I was still not fully satisfied. I felt the need to dig a little deeper. So I had a second talk with Joe Darby. We discussed the history of this epistle and what led James to write it.

We reviewed the great debate that was taking place among the believers as to how to further the work that they had been recruited to do and had committed themselves to continue. As those who have studied this issue know, James wrote his epistle around 44 A.D., at a time when Jesus' followers were having a debate as to what was required of them. Some argued that all that was required was to just express their faith, testify if you please. James disagreed. He wrote that "if your brother or sister comes to you hungry or naked, it is not enough to tell them to go in faith, you feed them and you clothe them, because faith without works is dead."

That conversation with Reverend Darby and my subsequent reflections were transformational. I was ready for my next conversation with Nancy and to take on a new challenge of rebuilding my party's relationships with faith voters. And I do believe that the results of the 2006 national elections are testimonials to the success of the Faith Working Group.

Majority Whip

As we were going out for the 2006 elections I felt change in the air. The pundits were saying we had a tremendous opportunity to win back control of the House, so before we left for the final stretch, I announced to the CBC that if we came back in the majority, I planned to run for House majority whip. I told them that I would not establish the traditional whip operation that was usually employed for such campaigns but wanted the entire CBC to function in that capacity.

In the final days of the campaign—which Democrats won—Mel Watt, who was chair of the CBC, dispatched G. K. Butterfield to join me on the campaign trail to make sure I made the calls and did the follow through that was necessary for such efforts to be successful. Those calls were educational. The vast majority of them were pleasant and productive, and some were humorous. I often laugh with Congressman Jim McDermott about our conversation. Jim gave an emphatic "yes" when I asked for his vote but expressed some reticence about putting a whip in a black man's hand.

Rahm Emanuel was chair of the Democratic Congressional Campaign Committee (DCCC), and justifiably expected to be rewarded for a successful effort. But in addition to my work with faith leaders, I had logged a lot of miles, and had raised a lot more money than I had been assessed. Did I not have a right to expect to be rewarded as well? The problem was that both of us saw our reward as being House majority whip.

In the meantime a third member started making waves. Diane DeGette of Colorado announced that she planned to run for whip and had the support of John Lewis. Of course we put that to rest rather quickly. Then we got word that John Tanner of Tennessee, a leader of the "blue dogs," was making phone calls for Rahm. I called CBC blue dog member, Sanford Bishop. He immediately went to work to "nip that in the bud." As things heated up, I received a call from one of my "K Street" supporters, who reported that he was at a luncheon on the Hill, where the speaker, one of my colleagues, had just questioned my worthiness even to run for whip. Her take was that whatever Rahm wanted, Rahm should get. I immediately confronted her. Although she denied it, she was on notice that my relationships were multiracial and multifaceted, and that my intentions were real.

Then came various news stories, which were surely planted by Rahm and/or his supporters; subtly playing the race card, though by no means openly. Their slant was that I was not a traditional candidate for whip. As a black southerner, I did not have the ability to raise money. One reporter confronted me with the question, "Don't you have a reputation of not paying your dues." When I asked where she had gotten such information, she said, "a little bird told me." I told her she should feed her bird better seeds. The fact of the matter was and is that I always overpaid my dues.

Finally I met with Leader Pelosi and made it clear that I was going for bust in the whip race and the CBC was solidly in my corner. The next day I got a call from Rahm. He said he had decided against running for whip, but that I should understand that if he did run, he would win. I told him I understood that, and appreciated his magnanimous gesture. I was elected unanimously.

Assistant Democratic Leader

Four years later—in November 2010—House Democrats lost the majority, and speculations started flying all over the place as to what Nancy Pelosi was going to do. Steny Hoyer started positioning himself to run for minority leader if Nancy were to step down, and I started positioning myself to run for minority whip if Steny were to step up. But all those activities came to a halt when Nancy decided to stay put.

I told Steny that, despite rumors to the contrary, I was not going to challenge him for whip for several reasons. The main one being the one thing you learn as whip; how to count. Steny proffered the popular notion that all of us should step back a notch. Nancy back to leader, him back to whip, and me back to chair of the House Democratic Caucus. That also seemed to be Nancy's position. But I did not like that idea for two reasons: John Larson and Xavier Becerra. John would be pushed back to vice chair, and Xavier would be pushed from the table.

*Two former House majority whips, Bill Gray (left) and Roy Blunt (right) in a ceremonial
"passing of the whip" to me on the day I became majority whip, January 2007.*

I had done some research and I knew that our rules allowed for the establishment
of various leadership positions and one of them was assistant Democratic leader. I felt
that a better resolution would be to establish that position in our caucus. Some sentiments were expressed to make the position assistant to the leader and appointed by
the leader, which had been previously done. We in the CBC thought that the position
should be titled "assistant leader" as our rules allow, and be elected. Nancy Pelosi
expressed her support for the position being elected and staffed. That settled it, and I
was unanimously elected assistant Democratic leader, and have since been reelected.

Keeping It Real

In spite of these milestones and heady accomplishments, I do not allow myself to lose
sight of the realities of who I am, what I am, and where I am. I was reminded of those
circumstances rather dramatically shortly after I was sworn in as House majority whip.
I was flying to Myrtle Beach to address the annual meeting of a group of educators to
whom I had committed long before the November elections that made my elevation
to the whip position possible.

I was accompanied by a member of the security detail that is assigned to the
whips and leaders of both parties and the Speaker of the House. As is customary we
boarded the plane a few minutes before the other passengers, and the security detail
stopped at the cockpit to present his paperwork and credentials to the pilot. I spoke
to the flight attendant and made my way back to 8-D, an exit-row aisle seat. I stored

my topcoat and briefcase in the overhead bin and sat down to glance over my notes for the speech I was about to deliver. My security detail was seated behind me in 9-D.

I suddenly felt a presence in front of me. I looked up, and the flight attendant, who looked to be a thirty-something African American, was staring at me. She quickly retreated to the cockpit, returning shortly to inform my detail that the captain needed to see him. He returned with a rather amused look on his face. When I inquired, he told me that the flight attendant had reported to the pilot that I was in violation of the airline's policy because prisoners were not allowed to sit on the exit rows.

My business suit, tie and briefcase notwithstanding, that flight attendant's only experiences with black passengers boarding airplanes with armed escorts were with prisoners. That blessed experience serves to keep it real for me.

PART
TEN

Treading
and Toiling

*. . . Emily and I set a goal of raising $1 million . . . to
establish the James E. and Emily E. Clyburn Endowment
for Archives and History at South Carolina State University.
I announced our intentions in a speech at an annual meeting
of the Washington, D.C. alumni chapter. When I mentioned
the million dollar figure, I could see on the faces of those
assembled that they thought I had spent too much time at the
bar during the reception.. . . . No matter how tortuous I have
found many of my experiences to be, I have never questioned
their efficacies or failed to find a blessing in all of them—with
the possible exception of my efforts on behalf of S.C. State.
Every time I think of my experiences with almost every aspect
of the institution, I understand why I keep "Duty as Seen by
[Abraham] Lincoln" hanging on a wall of my office.*

28 *Wandering in the Wilderness*

The 1994 elections resulted in the Republicans gaining control of the House for the first time in forty years. It seemed that none of us Democrats saw it coming, but we should have. The arrogance of being in power for forty years shone brightly among the leaders of our caucus. Some committee and subcommittee chairmen were literally unapproachable. John Dingle and Joe Moakley were notable exceptions. Almost everybody was talking with significant disdain about the high-and-mightiness of most other chairmen.

I experienced some of that with the chairman of the Judiciary Committee. Having spent almost eighteen years directing a quasijudicial state agency, I thought I could make a significant contribution as a member of the Judiciary Committee. But, when I approached the chair requesting his support for one of the vacancies on his committee, he asked whether I was a lawyer. When I told him that I was not, he slowly cast his eyes up toward the tally board. I had been warned that his response would be something akin to what it was, and I was prepared with what I thought would be an appropriate retort. I told the gentleman that although I was not a lawyer, as head of a quasijudicial agency for eighteen years, I had hired and supervised a few of them and had even fired one. He looked at me rather disdainfully but did not respond.

Several months later I ran into that gentleman in Taiwan when the schedule of a congressional delegation that I was heading crossed paths with one that he was heading. We merged the two groups for a meeting with local officials, and seniority dictated that he preside at that meeting. He could not have been more gracious when he introduced me. He was one of the casualties of November 1994.

Going into the minority after just one term was a tremendous blow to my plans. I wanted to make a significant impact on the communities of which I had been such an integral part for all of my life. I wanted to put pipes in ditches that were dug to catch water draining from roads that were scraped when they should have been paved. I wanted to build bridges to reconnect communities that had been busted up to get commuters back and forth from their homes in suburbia to their downtown office buildings. I wanted to put water systems in those rural communities where the people should not drink, cook with, or bathe in the only water that was available. In short I wanted to improve the quality of life of people I had grown up with, gone to school with, and worshipped with—the voters who had seen fit to send me to represent them in Washington.

Losing fifty-four seats meant that Democrats were going to be something they had not been in more than a generation: the loyal opposition. I understood that. I also understood what that meant for me. The loyal opposition's role is to oppose. I had not campaigned to be the loyal opposition, but for that matter neither had I campaigned to enjoy the fruits of being in the majority.

I had campaigned to bring hope and change to the communities of the Sixth Congressional District of South Carolina. People who voted for me knew little and cared even less about inside-the-Beltway shenanigans. They were looking for me to fulfill the promises I had made to put "service above self and principles above politics." I had given them every reason to believe that I could, and they had every right to believe that I would. I had enjoyed reasonable success serving in state government during the administration of four governors, two Democrats and two Republicans. So working with Republicans was not foreign to me.

But that was South Carolina; this was Washington. Could I have as much success in Washington as I had bridging the political divide in South Carolina? How could I fulfill expectations as a member of the loyal opposition and maintain sufficient relationships with the new majority to serve my constituents effectively? While contemplating the real dilemma I was facing, I thought about one of the blessed experiences I often reflected on while serving as Human Affairs commissioner.

During my first year in the governor's office, I commuted home to Charleston every weekend. One Friday, as I was preparing to leave the office for that drive back home, I received a phone call from Tom Netting, the television reporter who brought me the devastating news on election night in 1970 that I had lost rather than won a seat in the South Carolina House of Representatives. He wanted my reaction to a controversy in Charleston that some people thought would have an adverse impact on the black community and requested an on-camera interview when I got to Charleston.

When I arrived at 16 Darlington Avenue around 3:30 that afternoon, the reporter was there with his tripod already set up on my front lawn. I stepped out of the car, stood before his camera, and started raising hell. When I finished the interview, I was feeling really good and could hardly wait to see how I looked and sounded on the news reports that evening. When I saw the telecast that evening I was pleased with my performance and went to bed feeling quite proud of myself.

Early the next morning I received a phone call from attorney Richard Fields, whose law office was a regular meeting place for various political gatherings. Over the years, Richard had become a great friend and a reliable mentor in whom I often confided. He asked if I could stop by his office after church the next day, around 1:30 P.M. I assured him that I could, and I did.

Richard and I had always held our little meetings in his law library, but this time he invited me into his private office and directed me to have a seat in the chair in front of his desk. Richard told me that he had seen my Friday evening comments on television and wanted to share something with me. He related an experience he had earlier

With my mentor Judge Richard Fields (left), 2011. Photograph courtesy of the Medical University of South Carolina.

in his career representing a client who had fatally shot a person. Richard said the client paid him a five thousand dollar retainer.

When the case was set for trial, Richard retained an investigator to help him prepare a defense. After the investigator found that there were four or five witnesses who were prepared to testify against his client, Richard said, they decided the best course of action would be to "cop a plea." Because of a few extenuating circumstances, the solicitor agreed to allow his client to plead guilty to a lesser charge that allowed for a five-year jail sentence plus a period of probation. Richard's client rejected it. He demanded his day in court and reminded Richard that he had been paid five thousand dollars for his services.

Richard said the facts were so overwhelming against his client that not much of a defense could be mounted. So he put on a real show, challenging the prosecutor and voicing frequent objections to the point of drawing contempt warnings from the judge. Richard told me the jury stayed out about twenty minutes before returning a guilty verdict, and the judge handed down a sentence of twenty-five years. As Richard prepared to leave the courtroom looking a little dejected, his client tapped him on the shoulder and said, "Don't feel bad lawyer. That judge may have given me twenty-five years, but you damn sure gave him hell."

Richard told me he thought I could have a good future in politics, but I needed to make a decision. He said, "You need to decide whether you are going to use your talents to improve opportunities for the black community or spend your time and energy giving white folks hell."

During my four years in the governor's office and almost eighteen as Human Affairs commissioner, I often found myself reflecting on that little session with Richard Fields. As I contemplated my newfound position in the minority, I thought about that session again. I decided that in my role as the loyal opposition I would maintain civility and develop relationships. I would work as hard as I could across party lines and not be afraid to meet an opponent more than half way.

Even when you're in the majority, it is not unusual for your proposals to end up as committee bills or in the chairman's mark. And when you are in the minority, it is as if none of your ideas make any sense unless a comma is added, a word changed, or someone in the majority has their name on it.

Emily had always insisted that I use billboards in my campaigns. I had learned from my research and experiences that a billboard message should not be more than nine words, preferably seven. Consequently, in 1992 I had bought 100 percent billboard coverage with an eight-word message: "*JIM CLYBURN*: Principles above Politics, Service above Self." It was clear to me that it was time to put my 1992 precept into practice.

29   *Principles above Politics*

During our twelve years in the wilderness there were many noteworthy achievements that I feel were real national game changers. And all of them received significant bipartisan support.

Protecting Protectors

Several members of the Flight Attendants Association, one of whom was a constituent, started visiting with me during my first year in Congress to discuss two of their priorities: whistle-blower protection for airline employees and a ban on smoking on airliners. I had no problem with either of these issues, but I had taken to heart a lesson taught to me by a long-serving white state senator from Orangeburg, Marshall Williams. He was very southern and very conservative but rather progressive by South Carolina standards.

During my tenure in the governor's office, Senator Williams periodically dropped into my office to chat and offer political advice. During one of those visits, he informed me that he had some concerns about my having recently commented on an issue that was quite controversial. He reminded me of an earlier controversy I had commented on. He told me that he generally agreed with me but felt I was taking on too much. He summarized his visit with some advice I took to heart. "Remember my friend," he said to me, "you can't ride every horse in the circus." So I said to the flight attendants that I would be pleased to champion their whistle-blower protection issue, but although I agreed with their smoking ban, I did not feel comfortable taking on that issue at that time. Consequently, on March 28, 1996, during the One Hundred Fourth Congress, I introduced HR 3187, the Aviation Safety Protection Act of 1996.

Ironically, on May 11, 1996, ValuJet flight 592 crashed into the Everglades outside of Miami, Florida. The investigation raised questions about canisters on board that may have been impermissible and whether or not they contributed to the cause of the crash. It was also implied that some airline employees were aware of the situation but did not say anything out of fear for their jobs.

The Subcommittee on Aviation held a hearing on my bill on July 10, 1996. I had 73 cosponsors. In spite of strong bipartisan support, it became clear to me that my bill would not see the light of day. So we set out to find a Republican who might step up on the issue and were successful. On March 4, 1997, in the One Hundred Fifth

Congress, Representative Sherwood Boehlert of New York, a member of the Subcommittee on Aviation, introduced HR 915, the Aviation Safety Protection Act of 1997. I and 127 other members signed on as cosponsors of the bill. Protecting those who are trying to protect us should be a no-brainer. But, as often happens, bottom-line profits trumped common sense and public safety, and every now and then we pay a heavy price. Such was the case with the ValuJet crash. Yet the airlines continued their opposition to the bill and nothing happened.

Two years later, on March 3, 1999, Congressman Boehlert introduced HR 953, the Aviation Safety Protection Act of 1999. It had 101 cosponsors. Congressman Boehlert and I worked to successfully get the bill incorporated in the Aviation Reauthorization Bill, and on April 5, 2000, the Wendell H. Ford Aviation Act became Public Law 106-181.

We became heroes to the airline flight attendants and pilots. They held a big rally in room 2167 of the Rayburn House Office Building and passed out T-shirts with the outline of a big whistle on them and the words "Our Hero." But I was declared persona non grata by the Airline Owners Association and was no longer invited to their events.

I received the ultimate vindication, however, when shortly after the 2001 shoe bomber incident at Logan International Airport in Boston, I received a letter from the flight attendants, informing me that the attendant whose actions probably averted a disaster said that she felt embolden by our law.

Honoring Our Heritage

I became aware that a bill to establish several new Heritage Corridors was expected to move through Congress. I knew that the last time such a bill was considered, efforts to include South Carolina failed. I also knew that the previous attempt was for a corridor roughly along the route of the old Hamburg railroad that the *Best Friend* rolled on. A replica of this historic train is in the South Carolina State Museum.

This issue had the kind of historic ambience I have always liked. It also had the potential to be sufficiently bipartisan for me to reach across the aisle and get something done for several challenged communities in some of the rural parts of my state and district. Although another route for the corridor might have had a broader impact on the Sixth District, I decided to stick with the previously designated route. If approved, the corridor would benefit the state and allow me to burnish my bipartisanships. It would also allow me to keep a commitment I made to Ruth Gulledge— mother of Mike Gulledge of Abbeville County, a former member of the South Carolina legislature. She was big on historic preservation and had supported me when I ran for secretary of state. And of course the corridor would run through small portions of the Sixth District and end in Charleston.

The partisan divide in Washington was getting wider and wider, and I knew that my name on the bill would doom it for defeat. So I approached Republican congressman Lindsey Graham and explained to him what I wanted to do and why. I asked him to put his name on my bill. He demurred, protesting that it would be unfair. But I assured him that I really did not care about getting credit. After some cajoling he agreed to put his name on the bill, and it became Public Law 104-333. The South Carolina National Heritage Corridor has been in existence since November 1996.

Needless to say, I was happy with the result. And although Governor David Beasley touted it as a Republican-created economic engine for the state, I knew better, and so did he.

Saving Affirmative Action

The combined twenty-one years I spent in the governor's office and at the Human Affairs Commission made me very sensitive to diversity issues. So I had more than a passing interest in the plethora of court challenges to affirmative action programs. Ever since the United States Supreme Court decision in *Crosan v. City of Richmond,* a ruling that those of us in the equal employment opportunity arena had warned could be problematic, legal challenges to various affirmative action programs were being successful. That is, until *Aderand II,* when the Supreme Court supplied a roadmap for what it suggested would be constitutionally permissible. It was pretty much what many of us had been saying for years, and it came just in the nick of time.

In 1998, as Congress was considering reauthorization of the Transportation Act, one of the big issues was whether or not the affirmative action section could survive. The betting was that it would not. Also being debated was the amount and type of funding Congress would approve. President Bill Clinton and Speaker of the House Newt Gingrich decided to limit the bill to approximately $170 billion and not allow any earmarks.

Congressman Bud Shuster, a Republican from Pennsylvania, was chair of the Transportation and Infrastructure Committee, of which I was a member at the time. The ranking member was Democrat Jim Oberstar of Minnesota. Chairman Shuster was a big proponent of earmarks, as I am, and Jim Oberstar was a big supporter of affirmative action programs, as I was then—and still am. Bud wanted to defeat the bill, but he did not have enough votes on his side of the aisle to do so. He wanted a big highway project in his district and needed an earmark to do it. I saw this as an opportunity to save the affirmative action program. I developed a plan and presented it to the Congressional Black Caucus. At that time the CBC had thirty-six voting members, and they authorized me to use their votes to negotiate a possible deal with Shuster.

Before approaching Shuster I met with members of the newly formed blue dog coalition, the more conservative members of the Democratic Caucus, and gave them a quick tutorial in what affirmative action was and what it was not. I also shared with them my plan to ask Shuster to protect the affirmative action program in the transportation bill by inserting the Aderand "roadmap" into the legislation.

It was not an easy sell, but Congressman Charlie Stenholm and the blue dogs agreed not to oppose my plan. Besides they also wanted earmarks. I then approached Shuster. He told me that if I could deliver thirty Black Caucus votes against the rule, we had a deal. The record shows that thirty-four of the thirty-six voting CBC members voted against the rule, and Gingrich's bill was defeated.

Subsequently, following urgings from my staff and transportation officials in my state, I lobbied Jim Oberstar to get on the Conference Committee. Jim Oberstar passed over nine more senior Democrats, and placed me on the Conference. It was the only way for a black person to be at the table, and he agreed that a black presence in the room would lessen the chances of the affirmative action provision being stripped out.

I got to every meeting long before they started, and stayed until after the last member left the room. Thanks to the intestinal fortitude of Jim Oberstar and my strong bladder, the Transportation Equity Act for the Twenty-first Century (TEA-21) kept the affirmative action set-aside program, and it has stayed in all transportation reauthorization bills ever since.

Helping HBCUs

Although I am often given the credit, the fact of the matter is, the genesis of the historically black colleges and universities (HBCU) preservation and restoration of historic buildings and sites program does not rest with me. As far as I can determine it was started by Democrats Bob Clement of Tennessee and my classmate Alcee Hastings of Florida as a special deal to restore Jubilee Hall at Fisk University. When Alcee, a Fisk graduate, sought my support for funding the program the second year in a row, I decided that what was good for Fisk was probably good for a few other HBCUs with which I was familiar. I developed a plan.

I approached my friends Bennie Thompson of Mississippi and Earl Hilliard of Alabama with my plan to put up an amendment to add some money for historic buildings on HBCU campuses in our districts. It worked, but it also attracted the attention of a few other CBC members. This presented a real problem for future efforts.

I decided that the best way to move forward was to request that the National Park Service conduct a survey of all HBCUs in the country to identify historic buildings and sites on their campuses and determine the cost of preserving and restoring them. I discovered that if a member of Congress were to request the study, it might take years, but if an official caucus were to make the request, it would receive priority consideration. This was a no-brainer for me.

I approached Maxine Waters, who was chair of the Congressional Black Caucus at the time, and she presented the plan to the full caucus, which voted unanimously to request the survey. Some HBCUs were suspicious of the effort, and many did not have the personnel or the resources to supply all the information that was requested. We invited the schools to the Park Service Headquarters in Washington, to answer their questions and allay their fears and suspicions. There were quite a few hiccups along the way, but the survey was eventually concluded. It revealed that there were 712 historic buildings and sites on the campuses of HBCUs, and according to the General Accounting Office, the restoration of all of them would cost $755 million. That presented a big problem. The rules and procedures of the National Park Service also presented problems. Under the Park Service's criteria as to what buildings got funded, it was possible that those of us who worked to secure the funds could very well have our schools left out. Also many of these schools were having real difficulty raising the required dollar-for-dollar match. That meant a $4 million project required the school to raise $2 million.

With Claflin University president Henry Tisdale and Congressman Dick Gephardt, on the day I brought the House minority leader to visit Claflin's Ministers' Hall, a building restored using funding secured through the enactment of the HBCU historic preservation bill.

For many of these schools, that was a hill too steep to climb. After some consultations and contemplations, I decided that the match needed to be reduced, and all members with HBCUs in their districts needed to be accommodated. But none of this was possible without some bipartisanship.

I had developed a cordial relationship with Republican James John Duncan of Tennessee, who had sponsored a community breakfast in my honor during a visit I made to Knoxville College, an HBCU located in his district. Duncan and I discovered that we shared birth dates, July twenty-first. That little factoid accorded us an added commonality. So I approached him with what I wanted to do. He agreed, but as one can imagine, he became the lead sponsor of the bill.

The bill we got passed authorized $10 million a year for ten years and lowered the match requirement to 70/30. I have not surveyed every HBCU campus to determine the full impact of this program, but in South Carolina, buildings have been renovated and restored on the campuses of Allen, Claflin, and South Carolina State Universities and Voorhees College.

Hatch's Help

Probably the most popular singular undertaking of my congressional career has been my effort to preserve and protect the Gullah/Geechee culture. It probably would have failed were it not for the timely intervention of Republican senator Orrin Hatch of Utah.

The sights, sounds, and tastes of Gullah/Geechee, a unique blend of African and European cultures found along the coasts of North and South Carolina, Georgia, and northern Florida, have been intriguing to me since the first time I visited Charleston as a young lad. Marrying a native of Moncks Corner, spending our first ten years together in Charleston, and running a migrant and seasonal farm worker program throughout the lowcountry reinforced the intrigue. And I thought I had really arrived when soon after I joined Governor West's staff, the South Carolina Educational Television network asked me to narrate a film they were doing to highlight Charleston's basket weavers, one of the keeper groups of the Gullah/Geechee culture.

They make their baskets from sweetgrass, which is becoming scarcer every day. In fact much of the Gullah culture is slowly slipping away although many small enclaves of the culture remain. Many conservationists and preservationists believe that the Gullah/Geechee traditions and art are worth saving.

In these communities, you can still find houses trimmed in indigo—to ward off evil spirits. You can hear talk of life before the "cumyas," as recent arrivals to the area are called, and the problems they visit upon the "benyas," those whose domicile can be traced back to early plantation life in the region. You can enjoy traditional spirituals such as "Kumbaya" (come by here) sung in unfamiliar dialect to a unique beat called "common meter." You can watch nimble hands weave gorgeous sweetgrass baskets with skills handed down through generations. You can also enjoy the aroma and tastes of "hoppin' John," sweet-potato pie, or benne wafers, all Gullah specialties that have become parts of our modern culture.

These communities, called Gullah in North and South Carolina and Geechee in Georgia and Florida, were developed by former slaves who began their freedom in isolated and remote villages, where they nurtured and sustained their way of life for generations. I decided that this was a cause worth embracing, and I secured an earmark to have the National Park Service conduct a three-year-study of the Gullah/Geechee coast.

This study focused a good deal of attention on the region, and shortly after the study got underway, the Gullah/Geechee region was named one of the eleven most endangered sites by the National Trust for Historic Preservation. The study found that these unique slices of history and traditions were endangered. I responded to the study by introducing the Gullah/Geechee Cultural Heritage Act, to implement the Park Service's recommendations. The legislation received overwhelming support in both the House and Senate, but time ran out before we could reconcile differences.

I reintroduced the bill in 2005 with some significant changes to address the overwhelming grassroots response, much of it decrying my omission of Gullah communities in North Carolina and Geechee communities in Florida. So my later legislation corrected this oversight by establishing the corridor along the lines laid out in the study. The bill authorized one million dollars for ten years and established a Gullah/Geechee Culture Heritage Corridor Commission to help federal, state, and local authorities manage the corridor and its assets. The new bill was cosponsored by Representatives Henry Brown (R-SC), Joe Wilson (R-SC), Mike McIntyre (D-NC),

Speaker Nancy Pelosi conducting a ceremonial swearing-in for me and my family
after I became House majority whip. We used a Gullah Bible for the ceremony.

Jack Kingston (R-GA), Ander Crenshaw (R-FL), Corrine Brown (D-FL), and John
Mica (R-FL).

In spite of this strong support, the bill was being subjected to the same dilatory
tactics as my previous legislation. But as fate would have it, just a few days before
we were to go out for the 2006 election-year break, Connie Myers, an Orangeburg
County native, hosted a reception in my honor. John Haddow, a golfing buddy and
former staffer for Orrin Hatch, was in attendance. Suddenly a light came on.

A couple of years earlier, to keep a promise I had made to Haddow, Emily and I
attended Senator Hatch's annual Utah Charities event in Park City, Utah. During the
banquet Senator Hatch recognized our presence, and as we were leaving, he assured
me that he considered my attendance an act of friendship and stood ready to return
the gesture if ever I needed him to do so.

I told Haddow about my dilemma and shared with him the contents of the bill
and my reasons for seeking its passage. I really poured it on pretty heavy; even claiming that the creditability of my reelection campaign, if not my reelection itself, could
turn on my getting the bill passed. I reminded him of the senator's promise and told
him who I understood was holding up my sorely needed legislation.

Connie lived near Capitol Hill, and in the middle of her reception a vote was
called, so I rushed back to the Capitol for the vote. I returned to the reception about
thirty minutes later, and Haddow was still there. He told me that he had already gotten in touch with Senator Hatch and that I should call him the next morning around
11:00 A.M.

The next morning Senator Hatch called me around 10:00 A.M. He told me he wanted to be helpful and needed to know a little more about this "goolah" bill.

After correcting his mispronunciation of "Gullah," I told him a little bit of Gullah/Geechee history and shared with him how I thought he could help. About three hours later, I got a call telling me that the bill had been "hotwired." It passed around 5:00 P.M. that day.

Building key relationships at the 2012 RBC Heritage Pro-Am with (l-r) Jim Albaugh, CEO of Boeing Commercial Airplanes; professional golfer Ernie Els; Senator Lindsey Graham (R-SC); and Senator Johnny Isakson (R-GA).

While I was rather pleased with the impact I was having at the national level, I was just as focused on issues that were important to my constituents and the citizens of South Carolina.

Lake Marion Regional Water Agency

Two weeks after I was elected, Bill DeLoach pulled together a group of state agency heads, many of whom I had worked with for almost two decades. For the most part these were folks who had been supportive of my candidacy, and some had helped me develop the platform on which I campaigned. Bill thought it would be good for me to hear from them as to how I could best go about keeping the many promises I had made in the heat of campaigning.

Much to my surprise, Bill had kept copious notes and had compiled a list which he shared with the group in advance of the meeting. There was substantial agreement among them that if I were going to keep my promises, I would have to find a cure for the infrastructure problems that were prevalent throughout the district, most especially along the I-95 corridor.

Following that meeting, I met with Robert "Bob" Royall, who was heading Governor Carroll Campbell's Commerce Department. Bob had supported my political efforts over the years, and was an "honoree" at one of the "Roasts and Toasts" that I hosted for several years. He had retired as president of C&S National Bank of South Carolina, on whose board I had served as a member of the audit committee and chair of the Communities Reinvestment Act (CRA) Committee.

Bob had his staff put together a powerful and persuasive presentation that was a real eye-opener for me. Their presentation was a real blessing and reinforced the recommendations of the ad hoc committee of agency heads I had met with earlier. Everything kept coming back to one thing: potable water.

The meeting with Bob Royall and his staff convinced me that a regional water system near Santee made a lot of sense. They also made it clear that I was going to need significant cooperation from local elected officials and community leaders along the I-95 corridor.

The price tag for a water-treatment plant on Lake Marion had been placed at $150 million, which made it all the more necessary to go regional in order to make the case for that amount of funding.

I began by hosting a meeting at Camp Daniels with all the possible stakeholders I could identify throughout Orangeburg, Sumter, Clarendon, Calhoun, Dorchester, and Colleton Counties. The attendance was great, but the idea did not have unanimous support. My work was cut out for me.

There were a few doubters and some who were just plain ornery. I was not too sure whether or not it was because of continued animosity over the creation of the majority minority district or the opposition to infrastructure investments in several rural communities. I had become aware of this opposition while working in the governor's office, when I came across a memorandum that had been sent to the state's leadership by economic development specialists who had been hired to help recruit industry to the state. That memorandum listed ten counties—all but one of which was on the I-95 corridor—that should be avoided when courting prospects. All these counties had majority black populations. The theory was that black people were more prone than white people to join unions, and the lack of organized labor was one of their recruiting tools. No matter the reason, I was determined to get my project authorized and funded.

Getting elected president of the freshman class for the second session of the One Hundred Third Congress brought me to the attention of quite a few people who probably would not have noticed me otherwise; two of them were Norm Mineta and Jim Oberstar, the number one and number two ranking Democrats on what was then the Public Works Committee. Both were very helpful to my efforts, and those relationships paid off handsomely.

There were many hits and misses and quite a few ups and downs, but the Lake Marion Regional Water Agency became a reality.

The Honda Accord

Honda decided to erect a facility that would manufacture four-wheel all-terrain vehicles in South Carolina. The Florence/Pee Dee area was in contention for the facility, and "the powers that be" made an all-out effort to get selected. But when Honda selected the Pee Dee area for the plant, a problem developed regarding where to locate the facility.

The "powers that be" decided that the best location for the facility was in an area that included a piece of property owned by a family named Tucker. There was a house on the property that Mr. Tucker claimed was of significant historical value, and he was demanding compensation far beyond the price that was considered reasonable.

The negotiations were not going well, and Robert Williams, the hard charging president of Pee Dee Electric Cooperative, got intricately involved. Robert Williams, a friend I held in very high regard, was not particularly diplomatic—especially when he felt he was being screwed. And that is exactly what Mr. Tucker was doing to him and everybody else. One of the things I learned from my friend Teaky at the Charleston bowling alley was "when you have your hand in a lion's mouth you have to ease it out." Unfortunately Robert Williams was not as blessed as I was to have known and benefited from Teaky's wisdom.

It became clear that Mr. Tucker was not going to sell, at least not to Robert Williams and his group. Consequently "the powers that be" started looking for another piece of property.

One of the people on the Honda team was a young African American, Wendell Buggs, whose father and uncle were schoolmates of mine at S.C. State. I had also met some of the Honda officials from Japan, and as it would be said in Gullah vernacular, our spirits mixed well. During one of our meetings, Wendell told me that the Japanese officials were not going to let the failure to secure the Tucker property torpedo the project. They were committed to South Carolina and to building the plant in the Sixth Congressional District. This was music to my ears, and I began to work a little bit harder to help get it done.

Sometime later, I received a call from Wendell telling me that a suitable piece of property had been found near Latta in Dillon County, and they were going to move rather swiftly to close the deal. Wendell was shocked when I expressed grave disappointment. I reminded him of their promise to locate the plant in the Sixth Congressional District. He told me that he was under the impression that Latta was in the Sixth District, but I assured him that Latta was not. Then I asked Wendell what was so objectionable about the Timmonsville site, and he said he was unaware of a Timmonsville site. Well I had learned that Florence County owned a piece of property adjacent to Interstate 95 just outside Timmonsville. The citizens of Timmonsville had been promised that the site was for industrial development, and if an industry were to locate on that property, there was $10 million in highway construction funds available to construct appropriate access to I-95.

Mitchell Kirby, the county councilman from that area, had taken me to the site and had told me about the promise. I told Wendell where it was, and he promised to look into it and get back to me.

When Wendell got back to me, he said that the site was perfect and that he was at a loss as to why they had not been shown it before. Well I understood why, and if Wendell had seen that previously discussed memorandum, he would have also. As one might imagine, "the powers that be," including my good friend and brother Bob Royall, were not very happy with me. But the Honda plant now sits on that site, and there is a diamond-shaped interchange called Honda Way that allows access to I-95. Everybody finally got on one accord without having to purchase one.

Sumter/Columbia Empowerment Zone

Two of the four places I have called home at one time or another are Sumter, my birthplace, and Columbia, where I currently reside. I had worked hard to get the Empowerment Zone/Enterprise Communities legislation authorized and funded, and I felt I deserved to have one in my district. We had received two enterprise communities, Charleston/North Charleston and Williamsburg/Lake City, but I wanted one of the big ones, an Empowerment Zone. Columbia had applied for one in the first round, and Mayor Bob Coble felt that they had a good application but lost out to politics. I agreed.

I did some back channeling and asked Mayor Bob Coble to apply again. He was not inclined to do so, but when I told him that, if the new application were made regional, I thought it would be successful, he expressed some interest and asked which jurisdictions I had in mind for the region.

My staff and I went back and forth as to who would be a good partner for Columbia in such a situation. Orangeburg was their recommendation. I told them I thought Sumter might be better. They told me Sumter would be good, but argued that Orangeburg was better. I listened politely and respectfully retorted that everything they said was meritorious but one important element was missing that favored Sumter. Sumter is my birthplace. They understood.

So the Sumter-Columbia Empowerment Zone was conceptualized, and I called Mayor Steve Creech of Sumter. His city administrator was not all that enamored with the idea, but we worked through that as well. Mayor Coble agreed to the new arrangement, and the application was submitted. After a few meetings with then HUD Secretary Andrew Cuomo, who is now governor of New York, and his senior adviser, Alvin Brown, who is now the mayor of Jacksonville, Florida, the Sumter/Columbia Empowerment Zone was approved and funded.

It meant an authorization of $10 million a year for ten years. What a way to repay the people of Sumter, a city that always meant so much to me and the entire Clyburn family.

Hometown Honor

One day, while I was attending a meeting in the Sumter Opera House, Mayor Joe McElveen, who had succeeded Steve Creech, asked me to stop by his office next door. I did, and he showed me some plans they had for an intermodal transportation facility. He thought it was something that Sumter really needed, and I had had enough interaction with the board members of their Regional Transportation Authority to agree.

They had developed alternative plans for the facility, one of which called for a new building. Another plan was to renovate an old warehouse, a stately building shrouded in history. I told Mayor McElveen that I would be glad to help and could get real excited if they made the renovation of the old warehouse their preferred location. He told me that it was in fact their first choice.

I had two reasons for wanting to locate the facility in that old building. One was pretty noble, my love for historic restoration and preservation. The other was a little less noble, and might even be considered petty by some.

The building is located just a couple of blocks from the old Greyhound bus station from which I was often chased while selling those bags of boiled peanuts. A few of us young, budding entrepreneurs felt people getting off the bus after a long ride from "up North" might be prone to buy a bag of salted boiled peanuts that they probably had not tasted since their last visit home. Those peanuts could also be good snacks for those who were about to board the bus for the trip up North. Not everybody could afford to ride the Atlantic Coastline's "chicken-bone special."

We were often chased away by bus station employees, one of whom was a deaf mute. I still remember the day he kicked me while chasing me off the premises. I kept thinking about that not-so-blessed experience as Mayor McElveen was sharing his vision with me. I thought, wouldn't it be great to be the catalyst for this new intermodal facility that would be receiving Greyhound bus passengers that I was not allowed to serve as a kid.

The mayor told me that they needed $6 million in federal funds to do the project. It was a much bigger need than I had anticipated, but I promised to do my best. I went to work and was very pleased to be able to announce at a subsequent Sumter Chamber of Commerce retreat that we had successfully secured the funds to get the project done.

Five years later, hundreds of Sumterites and folks from surrounding areas attended the dedication of the new intermodal facility, which the board of the Regional Transportation Authority had named the James E. Clyburn Intermodal Transportation Center.

Although many family members attended, I kept thinking about the two I felt sure were smiling from above. It was an unbelievable experience and a real hometown honor.

IAAM

During a visit to my Washington office, Charleston's mayor, Joe Riley, shared with me his vision of establishing an African American Museum in Charleston, and wanted me to chair a steering committee that he planned to appoint to launch the effort. I thought I could give productive service to the effort, so after a discussion with Emily, I agreed to do so.

It took no longer than our first meeting for me to get a flavor for what I was going to encounter. The mayor had put together a good steering committee of some pretty strong-willed people, one of whom was Edward Ball, author of the book *Slaves in the Family*. This book about his privileged white family's shared blood with slaves and former slaves had gotten pretty good press. I had not read the book, but Emily and her sister Mattie had, and we had discussed it.

At our first meeting of the steering committee, Mr. Ball insisted that the museum be a slave museum. I strongly disagreed, and so did others on the steering committee. When Mr. Ball did not get his way, he took his case to the media, and I responded in kind. I have not seen him since our second or third meeting.

Media reports of Mr. Ball's assertions caused significant reactions from many locals, as I knew it would. Charlestonians were almost unanimous in their opinions that the museum should not be a slave museum but an African American museum. Things got rather uncomfortable in some quarters of the local community, which led to a few touchy situations and discussions in our meetings. But we worked our way through all of them.

A lot of time was spent trying to figure out what would be the best name for the museum. I favored "International African American Museum" and am very pleased that name carried the day. I love the acronym, IAAM.

In spite of some pretty testy meetings, I really enjoyed serving on the steering committee and was pleased to successfully direct some congressional funding towards the effort. But I found it necessary to resign from the committee because of a peculiar circumstance. One evening as I reviewed material for the committee meeting to receive recommendations from a subcommittee that had been working on selecting the design group for the project, I noticed a collage that contained images of me and my eldest daughter, Mignon.

Mignon happened to drop by our home that evening, and I asked if she had any idea what that was about. She said that it was done by my nephew, her cousin Derrick, who is the son of my brother Charles from a relationship prior to his marriage to Emily's cousin Gwendolyn. Derrick lived in New Mexico, and his firm had partnered with the Ohio firm that the subcommittee unanimously decided upon to design the museum.

I agonized all weekend and during the drive down to Charleston decided I should resign from the committee. Before the meeting I took Mayor Riley aside and informed him of the dilemma. He felt it was not a real dilemma if fully disclosed. He quipped that this was another indication of how good the Clyburn DNA must be. I told him that I was flattered by his gene pool assessment but the project's detractors and Jim Clyburn haters would have a field day accusing me of familial favoritism. I felt that it would be in everybody's best interest for me to resign from the steering committee. I later shared the problem with members of the board. The feeling among them was the same as Mayor Riley's, so I continued to preside over the meeting.

Derrick and his firm made an excellent presentation, and I could understand why the subcommittee had settled on them after initially voting to recommend a group on which hometown hero Harvey Gantt was a partner. But at the end of the meeting, I informed them that this would be my last meeting as chair of the steering committee. On finding out why, Derrick suggested that maybe he should leave the project. I told him that my involvement was to get the project launched, which had been accomplished, and I had more than enough other things to do and meetings to attend. For me it was a labor of love, but for him it could be the consummate career builder and professional achievement. I hope to live long enough to see the IAMM in Charleston, and the National African American museum in Washington, D.C., completed.

Briggs-De Laine-Pearson Connector

Not all my efforts were as pleasant and productive as those mentioned above. And not all South Carolina elected officials have been a pleasure to work with. Long before our public battles over stimulus funding and health-care reform, Governor Mark Sanford and I were locking horns over issues that were extremely important to significant numbers of my constituents. Such was the case with the Briggs-De Laine-Pearson Connector.

The project was originally called the Clarendon/Calhoun Causeway. Later State Senator John Matthews—with encouragement from my staff—proposed renaming it the James E. Clyburn Connector, and the legislature approved a bill to do so. My detractors, many of them using derisive statements, implied that my real interest in this connector was to erect a monument to myself. These accusations were distracting and destructive; so I asked John Matthews to rename the connector in honor of Harry and Eliza Briggs, the Reverend J. A. De Laine, and Levi Pearson in recognition of their civil rights activism that led to the *Brown v. Board of Education* decision. He did, but that did not stop the opponents.

The connector became one of the most controversial issues of my congressional career, and it still lingers. It should never have been controversial, and it wasn't my idea although I became its most visible champion. I was introduced to the idea during a meeting with elected officials along the I-95 corridor.

David Summers, who was chair of the Calhoun County Council, stated that there was something that he thought would really improve the quality of life in Calhoun County and that area. When Lake Marion was first created, he said, residents were promised that a bridge would be built to reconnect areas that were divided by the new lake. He spoke about the depressed value of land in the area, which made it difficult for them to address the social and economic needs of their citizens.

He also told me about studies that had been conducted supporting the economic benefits that such a bridge would have on Sumter, Lee, Orangeburg, and Calhoun counties. He closed his comments with a rather emotional recapitulation of how his father died in a car wreck trying to get home from Sumter, having had to travel the circuitous route that was necessary because the bridge had not been built as promised. I told him that I was not aware of the history he shared or the studies he referenced, but I would certainly look into them and get back to him.

Our research revealed that the legislature had approved such a bridge but no funding had ever been appropriated for it. The vote for the bridge was bipartisan and nearly unanimous. Two of the legislators who had voted for the bridge were still alive, and after seeing news reports of my decision to look at the issue, both of them called me. They told me that the real reason the bridge wasn't built was because the communities that would have benefited the most did not have sufficient political clout. I knew what they meant. The vast majority of the people who lived in the area of the proposed connector were black.

After reviewing the studies, all of which supported the efficacy of building such a bridge, I decided to pursue it. I had no idea what viciousness such an undertaking would unleash. People with friends in high places went after me with a vengeance. The e-mails were nasty, the phone calls threatening, and environmental groups were at best disingenuous.

A meeting with several environmental groups produced two action items. First, they were to share with me the findings of their economic-development consultant who they claimed had already begun developing some plans to address the economically depressed communities around Lake Marion. It has been more than fifteen years, and I am still waiting to receive those findings as promised. Second, I assured them that I would request a detailed environmental impact study (EIS), and I committed to them that I would not pursue funding for the connector if the EIS concluded that it would be harmful to the environment or a threat to wildlife in the area. They refused, however, to commit to dropping their opposition if the EIS concluded the connector would not be harmful to the environment.

The results of the EIS were as I had hoped. The 9.6 mile project connecting State Highway 120, running through Sumter and Clarendon counties, and State Highway 33, running through Orangeburg and Calhoun counties, including a 2.8 mile bridge, would not harm the area's environment or threaten its wildlife. But my friends in the environmental community refused to accept the results and continued their opposition, making all kinds of specious claims and legal threats, which they have followed up on.

The EIS also validated the conclusions of two earlier economic and social-impact studies. Although reasonable environmentalists would applaud these findings, anybody who followed the controversy closely knew that reasonableness was not a virtue of the opponents of the connector. They threw honesty and good faith to the wind.

The websites of many of the connector's opponents were replete with racially charged rhetoric, character assassinations, and simplistic arguments. Consider this posting by a member of the board of the South Carolina Wildlife Federation: "I have the distinct pleasure of passing by Rep. Clyburn's office on Gervais Street every day. And nearly every day there are cars out front with the Clyburn bumper sticker. Most of the time, I see Cadillacs. This morning there was a . . . Porsche Boxster. . . . It really gets to me that these people that are supposed to be 'giving' their time for the betterment of the state are spending their $'s in such ways. I would be a lot happier if I knew Clyburn's personal vehicle was a big Crown Vic. Do you suppose that they will use Clyburn's bridge as a straight track for Porches?" Could this apparent attempt to stereotype lifestyle choices be yet another cover-up for the oft-stated belief that infrastructure improvements in predominantly African American communities are wasteful government expenditures?

Whatever it was, it certainly was not isolated. The South Carolina Coastal Conservation League had argued just as fervently against my efforts to provide safe drinking water to two black communities in rural Berkeley County to replace fecal- and mineral-contaminated wells. The league claimed it would make the area attractive to developers and create "sprawl."

I was told that in a public meeting one of the representatives of the Coastal Conservation League blatantly stated that "those people have been drinking that water for 200 years and they seem to be doing okay." This same group, whose stated mission is to protect the coastal environment, offered to drop its lawsuit against a project they were opposing in a majority white area of the lowcountry in exchange for help against the connector project.

The connector's opponents seized on a part of the report that said 3.29 acres of wetlands would be impacted by the project; yet none of these wetlands was in any way connected to Lake Marion. Some in fact were man-made and helped to create the catch-22 in which so many communities I represent find themselves.

The man-made wetlands are ditches that were dug to drain roads in black communities, rather than paving them, as was done in white communities. Now that these communities have a congressperson who is committed to seeking equity and fair play for them, the environmentalists have decided to use against these communities the things they were forced to endure.

They also resorted to some bare-knuckled partisan politics and recruited the governor and four of his fellow Republican congressmen to their cause. At their behest the governor requested a cost-benefit analysis of the project.

Now I have no problem with an objective, nonpartisan study, as the EIS was. But this analysis the governor requested was selective and unprecedented. It was a classic case of disparate treatment. Reading and listening to some of the expressions from opponents of my efforts, I get a greater appreciation of the Good Book's admonition that "where there is no vision the people perish." These detractors could not see, or did not wish to see, the connections between poor health, inadequate education, and unemployment in these communities and the government-imposed isolation they suffer.

Why was all the water we tested in the area of the proposed bridge deemed unfit for human consumption?

Why were the poverty levels in the census tracts of the connector's footprints often five times the state's average?

Why was the I-95 corridor called the buckle of the stroke belt in South Carolina?

Why were the incidences of diabetes and numbers of deaths from prostate cancer among black males among the highest in the nation?

It was very clear to me that our state and its people were suffering from a lack of visionary leadership. When I envisioned the fifty-mile corridor this connector would create between Sumter and Orangeburg, I could see the hundreds of residents who live there and the thousands who would visit and recreate there, receiving the benefits of safe drinking water and better accessibility to jobs, educational opportunities, and health facilities. I could see biking and hiking trails. I could see the economic impact of conference and retreat centers, hunting and fishing lodges, assisted living communities, and vacation sites.

This experience was a real eye-opener for me. So many whom I had thought were truly interested in protecting the environment were really more interested in launching a cause célèbre or making headlines.

Nobody is any more interested in clean air, safe drinking water, and a pristine environment than I am, but I often find myself asking the question found in the title of a book written by one of the South's more enlightened elected officials, Governor Terry Sanford of North Carolina: *But What about the People?*

What I found most disconcerting was Governor Mark Sanford's actions in all this. He called me one night to "give [me] a heads up" about a letter he had just written to the secretary of transportation, requesting a cost-benefit analysis of the bridge project. He told me that he had no problems with the project but was responding to some of his neighbors. He said that he felt that my "perch" (the term he used) on the Transportation and Infrastructure Committee pretty much ensured that I would be able to move forward with the project.

I told the governor that I thought the project was meritorious and would be pleased to share the findings of the EIS study with him. He told me that he would not be in his office for a while because he was on his way to fulfill the training requirements of his recent enlistment in the Reserves.

In fact, he said that he was driving himself and at the time was somewhere between Atlanta and Chattanooga. He then gratuitously asked me about Mignon. I found that strange, because we served together in Washington for six years, and he had never mentioned Mignon to me before. I told him that she was doing well but was a little bit anxious about her upcoming reelection to the Public Service Commission.

At that moment it became clear why he had asked about Mignon. I was shocked when he said he thought that the public service commissioners were his appointees. I assured him that they were not, and he seemed disappointed to learn that some leverage he thought he had did not exist.

When I hung up the phone I shared the conversation with Emily. Her immediate reaction was that I would be a fool to believe his line that his letter was an innocent gesture. It was not very long before I found out Emily was right.

A few months later the governor's neighbors and a few of my environmentalist "friends" filed a lawsuit against the bridge. Because the highway department had conducted the environmental impact study, they were the main object of the lawsuit. So I called the governor to discuss the matter. I could not believe it when Mark Sanford said to me that he had no recollection of our prior conversation on the subject.

But this was just the beginning of my many differences with Governor Sanford.

South Carolina State University

The Morrill Act established institutions of higher education that would offer instruction in agriculture, mechanic arts, and military science. It was signed into law by President Abraham Lincoln on July 2, 1862, six months before the effective date of the Emancipation Proclamation. Consequently it is easy to understand why it became necessary for Congress to enact the Second Morrill Act in 1890 to create higher educational opportunities for former slaves and their descendants in the former Confederate states.

S.C. State was established by the Second Morrill Act and immediately became shrouded in controversy. Despite their being called land-grant schools, these institutions were not granted any land—as Congress had done for the schools created under the 1862 Morrill Act. The appropriated funds could be used for only instruction and facilities. The states had to provide the land, and South Carolina refused to do so. Consequently the Methodist Church, which had established Claflin University on land it owned in Orangeburg, donated some of that land to establish a public institution of higher education for "colored" students.

S.C. State was, and still is, South Carolina's only predominantly black four-year public institution of higher education. Many influential people and elected officials in the state still refuse to sufficiently support S.C. State, and they are getting help from some very unlikely sources.

Many of the school's troubles over the last ten years have lain largely at the doorsteps of former governor Mark Sanford, and a few current and former elected officials and board members. Their antics precipitated a warning from the Southern Association of Colleges and Universities for micromanaging and egregious interference in the day-to-day operations of the university, the kind of activity that would not be tolerated at any other institution in the state.

In the beginning, I was somewhat amused when S.C. State became the subject of a campaign of obvious half-truths and manufactured controversies by a few malcontents and media sensationalists. But it was not long before I realized that there was nothing amusing about what was taking place. When I ran for Congress, I promised to stay focused on the future but not to lose sight of the past. In my opinion that meant doing everything I could to help right past wrongs, and the lack of funding and offerings at S.C. State was and still is among those past wrongs.

A U.S. District Court found in 1972 that southern states, including South Carolina, were not taking substantial steps to desegregate public higher education institutions. The same court found five years later that state plans to address this inequity were ineffective, and under Governor Richard Riley's leadership, South Carolina sought to implement a plan that would meet the court's approval. Governor Riley appointed me to a blue ribbon committee that he tasked with developing a response to the court's ruling, and he named W. W. "Hootie" Johnson to chair the committee. Service on that committee was a real blessed experience, and I developed a great deal of respect for "Hootie." Our efforts led to South Carolina's becoming compliant, and I learned some lifelong lessons.

The centerpiece of our court-approved plan was the assigning of a unique mission to each state-supported higher education institution. S.C. State's unique mission was a doctorate in education (Ed.D.). Supposedly anybody wanting to get a doctorate in education from a South Carolina state-supported institution would have to get it from South Carolina State College (now University). The thinking was this mission would help to diversify the S.C. State student body. It worked but not for long.

Several years later the Higher Education Commission allowed an out-of-state institution, Nova University, to offer a similar degree. So in 1998, when Congress was increasing the number of university transportation centers under the "Transportation Equity Act for the Twenty-first Century" (TEA-21), I saw an opportunity to restore a unique mission to S.C. State.

It took some effort, but I managed to get one of the Transportation Centers included in TEA-21 placed at S.C. State. The reaction was immediate and vociferous. And just as it was back in the 1890s, some very influential people—in very high places—felt that S.C. State was not deserving of such a significant designation and financial support from the federal government.

Unfortunately the school's detractors undertook a campaign of manufactured controversies to discredit the school, its administration, and the Transportation Center project. A couple of my detractors, who are also enablers for those who want to see S.C. State shuttered, began feeding half-truths and untruths to a Charleston's *Post and Courier* reporter, who began writing sensational stories, most of which were figments of her imagination. She claimed that nearly $50 million federal dollars were missing from the funding for the Transportation Center.

In the middle of my 2010 campaign for reelection, I sat down with the paper's editorial board and asked, as I had done in telephone interviews with the reporter, why they were so persistent in writing such obvious untruths. I am still waiting for a substantive answer. The money for funding the construction of the Transportation Center was a cost-reimbursement grant, which means that you do not receive the money until you incur the cost and your requests for reimbursement have been vetted by the funding agency.

So how is it plausible to assert that S.C. State authorities were inept for not drawing down the money that was appropriated to erect the building and at the same time be guilty of misspending the millions of dollars that were never drawn down in the first place? Creating a catch-22 is a regular tactic of those whose objective is to maintain the status quo or manufacture controversy. I don't know a whole lot about accounting systems, and I would never make excuses for inefficiency or incompetence. But even if and when they do exist, neither rises to misappropriation of funds.

The Presidential Debate

During the run-up to the 2008 presidential election, S.C. State experienced one of its proudest moments, and I was pleased to be the impetus for it.

When the Democratic National Committee was trying to decide which states would be allowed into the preprimary window, it was generally accepted that one of them would be a southern state with a high African American population.

A contest broke out among Alabama, Mississippi, and South Carolina. South Carolina's Democratic Party chair, Joe Erwin, requested my help in his efforts to make the case for South Carolina. I was pleased to help, and South Carolina got the nod, for the first in the South primary. We also got three presidential debates, and I had a hand in them as well.

One debate was at the Citadel, which is located in the Sixth District. The last one before the January twenty-sixth primary election was at Myrtle Beach. It was sponsored by the Congressional Black Caucus Institute, which was established during my chairmanship of the caucus. Neither of these two debates was particularly newsworthy except for a retort directed toward Senator Hillary Clinton by Senator Barack Obama, and my Bill needs to "chill" comment made to John Roberts on a news show a few hours before the Myrtle Beach debate.

The first debate, however, was held at S.C. State on April 26, 2007, and it was particularly noteworthy and newsworthy.

When I agreed to help Chairman Erwin secure a preprimary slot for South Carolina, I hinted that S.C. State would be a good venue for one of the debates. Shortly after it was announced that South Carolina would be one of the preprimary states, Chairman Erwin told me that he was in discussions with S.C. State president Andrew Hugine about the school's hosting a debate.

Chairman Erwin was excited about the possibility and used his experiences and contacts to make it happen. I was ecstatic. I saw this as a real public relations coup for S.C. State, one that would be worth millions of dollars in publicity for the school, and I mistakenly thought that every S.C. State graduate would be as pleased as I was. But I should have known better, considering that a few of my detractors are S.C. State graduates. I was absolutely shocked at some of their reactions, especially when one of the presidential front runners was African American. And even more shocking were the quarters from which much of it emanated.

I first saw the envy on display at the press conference we held on the campus to announce that S.C. State would host a debate. Chairman Erwin and President Hugine made the announcement. I attended, but did not speak. It was clear, however, that some board members felt they should have spoken.

I saw further evidence of that attitude on the night of the debate. When I walked out onto the stage with the candidates, I saw Governor Mark Sanford being escorted toward the seats that had been reserved for him and S.C. State's board chairman. I recognized them in my comments, but when I left the stage and took my seat, which was a row behind them in the audience, one of my classmates seated directly behind me leaned over and said that when I walked out onto the stage the governor looked as though he would much rather had seen a black snake.

The morning after the debate I headed to Clemson, where I was to deliver a lecture. I received a call telling me that S.C. State was reporting it had already received several thousand hits on its website. I was absolutely beside myself. To me this was going to allow the school to turn the corner, but when it comes to S.C. State, nothing is apparent.

The impact of this favorable publicity was evident the following September, when the school had a much higher rate of applicant acceptances than was usually the case, and it was ill-prepared for the several hundred more students than usual who showed up. This to me was a positive. But for those who were hell-bent on discrediting the institution, this was grounds to fire President Hugine. And that is what they did.

Later when the board's chairman ran for reelection to the board, he was challenged by Patricia Brown Lott, with whom I shared the campuses of both S.C. State and C. A. Brown. It was no secret that I, and most of the alumni, preferred her in this contest. Although she was elected to the board some two years later, she failed on her first attempt. The chairman was not very graceful in victory. He celebrated his four-vote victory by declaring, "The whip got whipped." I maintain, however, that the real loser in this instance was my beloved S.C. State University.

The S.C. State Endowment

In addition to establishing a unique mission for S.C. State, Governor Riley's blue ribbon committee also promised to help enhance S.C. State's endowment, which was negligible and by most standards still is. That promise was not kept.

I had always been bothered by this, and I spoke about it often at various alumni functions. I would often ask alumni groups to establish endowments at the school in their alumni chapters' names rather than making annual contributions to various funds and causes. My pleas seemed to always fall on deaf ears. It occurred to me that maybe I was once again espousing a precept when maybe I needed to set an example.

So in 2005 Emily and I set a goal of raising $1 million over the next several years to establish the James E. and Emily E. Clyburn Endowment for Archives and History at S.C. State University. I announced our intentions in a speech at an annual meeting of the Washington, D.C., alumni chapter. When I mentioned the million dollar figure, I could see on the faces of those assembled that they thought I had spent too much time at the bar during the reception.

I am pleased that to date, Emily and I have raised nearly $2 million in private sector dollars for the endowment and need-based scholarships. In addition our scholarship fund (The James E. Clyburn Research and Scholarship Foundation) underwrote, to the tune of $65,000, the first two years of the traveling exhibition of the Smithsonian Museums' *From Africa to Gullah II, Word, Shout, Song: Lorenzo Dow Turner Connecting Communities through Language.* Our only condition was that the first stop for the exhibition had to be on the campus of S.C. State. Turner's first experiences with the Gullah language took place during a summer he spent on the campus of S.C. State College in 1938. The second stop was at Avery Institute in Charleston.

No matter how tortuous I have found many of my experiences to be, I have never questioned their efficacies or failed to find a blessing in all of them—with the possible exception of my efforts on behalf of S.C. State.

Every time I think of my experiences with almost every aspect of the institution, I understand why I keep "Duty as Seen by [Abraham] Lincoln" hanging on a wall of my office.

Celebrating the Honda Accord with a Honda official and Governor David Beasley.

PART ELEVEN

The Age of Obama

When it came my time to speak I made it clear what my primary concerns were. I was very concerned about a stimulus package that failed to give due consideration to those communities that were traditionally overlooked during such governmental action. . . . I started out by saying that up to that point in my life, Harry Truman was my favorite president. But I assured the president-elect that he could do something about changing that. I said that my fondness for Truman was grounded in his "Fair Deal" policies as opposed to Roosevelt's "New Deal," which seems to be preferred by most Democrats. I went on to explain that many of the policies of the New Deal were unfair to people of color and a raw deal for many of the communities I represented.

3-V Day: Victory, Validation, Vindication

On that historic January 20, 2009—the day Barack Obama was inaugurated as our forty-fourth president—America was in a celebratory mood. And for good reason.

Obama's victory on November 4, 2008, had not only crashed through yet another racial barrier, it had offered great hope for millions of Americans, most of whom felt good about themselves and had high hopes for their futures.

I felt pretty good myself. I told a reporter from my hometown newspaper, *The Item,* "This is the greatest day, I think, in the history of the country." It was the same newspaper I used to read growing up, and it was the paper I searched for articles for the daily report to my parents about an important event that took place that day. This would have been a good one.

I told the reporter, Mary Dolan, "It is almost incredible the feelings I have been having all week." Down deep, two words kept rushing into my mind: validation and vindication. I saw Barack Obama's victory as a validation of Dr. Martin Luther King's "I Have a Dream" speech.

The word "vindication" kept coming to mind as well. Vindication of those who adhered to the dream; vindication for the sacrifices made by my parents and other parents of their generation and the generations that preceded them; vindication for the struggles that took place on all the Amelia Streets of our nation by young men and women who risked their lives and well-being for the cause of human and civil rights; vindication for all those Americans who fought for the right to vote and put their lives and well-being on the line.

I also felt personally vindicated. I felt vindicated for counseling my children to believe in themselves and this nation's promise. I felt vindicated for having maintained the faith of my father and the tenacity of my mother. I felt vindicated for having told all those students I had taught that they could grow up to be anything they wanted to be if they stayed in school, studied hard and stayed out of trouble.

There were many times when I wondered if maybe I were being a little too optimistic and idealistic. Suddenly I realized I had been telling them the truth after all, that the shackles of limited expectations had been removed from the lives of black Americans. Obama's historic victory validated King's dream, and vindicated those who had held fast to that dream. November 4, 2008, was truly 3-V Day.

On that cold January day, I stepped out from the canopy at the West Front of the Capitol building and into the bright sunlight that flushed the inaugural platform, having been appointed by Speaker Nancy Pelosi to lead the congressional delegation into the history books. I took my seat not more than fifteen feet from where Barack Obama would take the oath of office and passed the time chatting with retired Supreme Court justice Sandra Day O'Connor. Mrs. O'Connor had made history herself as the first woman ever appointed to the United States Supreme Court.

I looked out over the throngs of Americans who were gathered on the mall to observe the confluence of civil rights fulfillment and political triumph. I wondered what kind of speech we would be hearing in just a few minutes, and I thought back to some of those memorable speeches of the past—the stirring, almost poetic words of John F. Kennedy, the resolute words of Franklin Roosevelt, and the challenges of Harry Truman. I thought back to the spiritual defiance of Martin Luther King, who had spoken so powerfully four decades earlier at the other end of the mall, the very spot where millions of his adherents now celebrated.

The speech we heard that day was none of those, and perhaps it should not have been. Like FDR, Obama was trying to lead us out of an economic misery that was driving millions of people into desperation. But this was not a stem-winding oration, as Roosevelt delivered in 1932. The new president spoke to his twenty-first-century audience in a conversational, reassuring tone in words of friendship and familiarity. "The challenges facing us," he said, "are serious and they are many. They will not be easily met or in a short span of time. But know this, America. They will be met."

As his words rang out, and as the bursts of applause interrupted him with an almost churchlike cadence, I felt a part of it all, and I felt a part of America as I had never felt before. I was sixty-eight years old, but I felt young, as if a stage of my life had just begun. I thought about my dad and when he observed his sixty-eighth birthday. It was 1965, the year of the passage of the Voting Rights Act, which made possible my service in Congress and the election of Barack Obama as president. My dad, the carpenter and preacher, had helped to build the foundation of the inaugural platform on which I was sitting and the context of the speech Barack Obama was delivering. Few people on that platform could know the depths of the feeling I was experiencing at that moment.

That feeling had actually been building during the days prior to the inauguration. On the Monday before Obama took office, the Congressional Black Caucus celebrated the life of Dr. King at the historic Metropolitan AME Church, where Frederick Douglass and many African American pioneers had worshipped. I was one of the speakers and used the occasion to recall my first meeting with Dr. King.

That meeting occurred during a weekend in October 1960, a few months after the first lunch-counter sit-ins by four North Carolina A&T students in Greensboro, North Carolina, and the March fifteenth mass arrests in Orangeburg, South Carolina. The Student Nonviolent Coordinating Committee (SNCC) had been launched earlier that year, and some of the students involved were feeling some disenchantment with the whole idea of nonviolence. A call went out for a second meeting of SNCC. Several students from S.C. State and Claflin University responded to the call. I was among them.

Leading the congressional procession at the 2009 inauguration of President Obama. Joyce Hamlett, first person of color to serve as assistant to the sergeant of arms, is carrying the mace.

The SNCC meeting was held in Atlanta on the campus of Morehouse College. And there was significant discord. This was a tenuous moment in the movement, and a fragmented student engagement could very well have a devastating impact on the overall effort.

It was decided that we needed to meet with Dr. King himself, and a "short meeting" was arranged. The "short meeting" lasted until 4:00 A.M. Dr. King was engaging, avuncular, and amazing. I walked out of that room a changed man. And I have never been the same again.

What lay ahead for us were more demonstrations in the streets, imprisonments in the jails, and convictions in the courtrooms of Orangeburg, Rock Hill, and Columbia—and the eventual overturning of those convictions by the U.S. Supreme Court. That "short meeting" not only changed my life, it changed history.

The manifestation of that historic adjustment was evident in no small measure in the election of Barack Obama to the highest office in the land. It was hard to imagine any person who had not recognized the historical significance of Obama's election. Even those who resented the thought could not deny the profundity of that moment.

The theme of the Congressional Black Caucus's celebration on the Monday before Obama's inauguration was the validation of Dr. King's dream. The high spot of the day was the keynote address by Bishop Desmond Tutu, the South African Nobel Peace Prize winner. He likened Obama's election to that of Nelson Mandela, the first democratically elected president of South Africa, who had spent twenty-seven years of his life in prison protesting the apartheid regime that ruled that nation. Bishop Tutu recalled after Mandela's election a friend telling his wife, "Darling, please don't wake me. I like this dream."

The day before Obama's inauguration, Bishop Tutu had similar feelings. He said, "Is this for real? Is tomorrow for real? Oh, no, no, no. It can't be true. A black man! President of the United States! In the White House!" Bishop Tutu spoke what was on the minds and in the hearts of many of us. We were watching in blissful disbelief the joy of human reconciliation taking place right before our eyes.

The comparisons were many, but the most frequent was the linking of Obama's election with Dr. Martin Luther King. That's as it should be. Without Dr. King there would have been no Voting Rights Act of 1965. Without Dr. King there would have been no Congressman Jim Clyburn. Without Dr. King there would have been no President Barack Obama. It was that simple.

And yet it seemed that in all the euphoria of January 20, 2009, we may have lost sight of the true nature of Dr. King's mission. As we rushed to embrace the words of the Lincoln Memorial speech that America thought it knew so well, the speech that came to be known as the "I Have a Dream" speech, we may have unintentionally distorted things. We may have chosen to remember Dr. King more as a dreamer and less as a fighter.

That was another of the important revelations that came to mind in those powerful moments leading up to Obama's inaugural.

As part of our family's observance of the inauguration, three generations of Clyburns—my wife, Emily, and me; our three daughters: Mignon, Jennifer, and Angela, and our son-in-law, Walter, and grandchildren, Walter and Sydney, had gathered the day before Obama took office to watch a video of the Dr. King's entire Lincoln Memorial speech. My brother Charles and his wife, Gwendolyn, and their children and grandchildren joined us.

The whole idea was for us not simply to revel in the historic significance of the moment, but to continue the process of learning and understanding what was going on around us. My daughter Jennifer, a public-school teacher, decided to forego a possible bonus for not missing a teaching day. The grandchildren and their parents felt that being a part of the inauguration of the forty-fourth president of the United States, the first African American president, was worth giving up a chance of receiving a certificate for perfect attendance.

I had agreed to a request by the Cable News Network (CNN) to film us watching the speech. Afterward, the CNN reporter who was sitting with us asked for our reactions. He started by asking my grandson, who was thirteen at the time and sitting to my immediate left, whether or not he had ever heard the speech before.

I nearly died when he was a wee bit hesitant in responding. I was greatly relieved when he said that he had heard and read part of it before, the part about the dream. And when asked what they thought of the speech, he and his cousins all responded by focusing on various parts of the speech that were King's well-thought-out written text for that occasion, particularly the part about not responding to violence with violence.

When the conversation turned to the occasion for which we there, the children shared some of their experiences in school concerning many of their white classmates' reactions to Senator Obama's campaign and election, most of which were negative. Maybe I should have realized, from what those youngsters were telling us about what they were hearing from their classmates, that reactions to a President Obama were not going to be all positive, either politically or socially, any more so than the reactions many had to the United States Supreme Court after it issued its *Brown* decision. Then my first born, Mignon, who holds a banking and finance degree from a university that would not even accept me for admission when I graduated from high school four decades earlier, offered a quiet and thoughtful response. She did not dwell on the well-known portions of the speech either. Instead she called attention to the portions of Dr. King's text in which he said that he "refused to believe that there were insufficient funds in the great vaults of opportunity in this nation."

For the TV news reporter it may have been an unexpected answer, but not for me.

Although she was less than eighteen months old at the time of Dr. King's Lincoln Memorial speech, Mignon and I shared the belief that it contained portions more important than the "I Have a Dream" passages. It seemed to me, in fact, that Dr. King's originally intended theme might have been something other than the idealism of "I Have a Dream," an addition to his prepared speech that he included at the public urging of Mahalia Jackson. It seemed to me that he was exhorting the thousands of Americans who had come to Washington for the rally to think in terms beyond idealism and to examine some realities, primarily the realities of limited economic opportunities that history had imposed on black Americans. What a relief it was for me to see and hear the other two generations of Clyburns viewing the speech much the same way as Dr. King had intended.

I believe Dr. King intended for the speech to urge black Americans to grasp the larger views of civil rights—not just political rights and legal rights—but human rights and economic rights as well. He used the practical language of finance in those early passages of the speech, describing the Declaration of Independence as a "promissory note" and contending that America had defaulted on that note to its black citizens. It was in that context that Dr. King went on to explore the consequences and remedies for that failed transaction: "America has given the Negro people a bad check, a check which has come back marked 'insufficient funds.' But we refuse to believe that the bank of justice is bankrupt. We refuse to believe that there are insufficient funds in the great vaults of opportunity of this nation."

I have held onto the belief over the years that a lot of Dr. King's stirring conclusions may have been extemporaneous, but that he may have preferred that the address be remembered as his "Vaults of Opportunity" speech.

Opportunities for achievement in civil rights appear like comets that flash across the sky, only to disappear in the darkness of political reaction and retrenchment. It is not a linear progression; it is a sporadic phenomenon that allows for hurried exploitation of the moment. Dr. King knew this when he scolded the white ministers who urged him to slow down his march for racial equality.

That's what made Mignon's comment to the CNN reporter so pertinent. Dr. King's rhetoric drove us to high idealistic planes, but his feet were always firmly planted. Mignon said to the reporter that it occurred to her last November, with the election of Barack Obama, that we may have finally discovered the combination to the vaults of opportunity. And now that it is open, how will we put its contents to good use?

My daughter, who now serves as a member of the Federal Communications Commission, may have been overly optimistic or premature in her assessment of where we stand. There is no question that Dr. King's deeply held beliefs about expectations and opportunity still lay unfulfilled as we inaugurated our first black president.

But euphoria can be an intoxicant for some, and there were among us those who began to mistake wishful thinking for reality. They began to fantasize about a world where race no longer divided the population politically, socially, and economically. The election of a black president, it seemed to them, was sufficient to wipe out generations and centuries of ill will and mistrust between the races.

About a week after the inauguration, the respected Public Radio commentator Daniel Schorr talked about the coining of the term "postracial." He said it's what Obama signaled in his South Carolina victory speech when he talked about a former Strom Thurmond supporter who was now knocking on doors for the Obama campaign. Schorr went on to mention "the *Economist*'s reference to a "postracial triumph," and the *New Yorker*'s description of a "postracial generation." He concluded that it may be "a little too early to speak of a generation of colorblind voters, but maybe color blurred." John West probably would have liked that distinction.

For my part I had begun to worry about such overstatements as early as the Democratic convention in August. I told a reporter for the *Chicago Tribune*, Dawn Turner Trice, that Obama's election could serve as a huge step toward moving beyond deep racial divisions. But it was only a step. "Race got locked in with our country's founding," she quoted me as saying. "Even after the 13th, 14th, and 15th Amendments, members of Congress allowed separate but equal to be the law of the land until 1954 and the *Brown v. Board of Education* Supreme Court decision that ended legal segregation in schools." I was remembering the exhilaration of my classmates and me when we heard about that decision while walking home from school May 17, 1954.

That exhilaration was everywhere in Denver during the Democratic convention, particularly among younger delegates. It reached a fervent pitch in Chicago's Grant Park on election night. The people of my age group were more somber and more emotional about it. We remembered a lot of things the younger generation had not known and would never know. Their zeal in itself was uplifting to those of us who had trudged the streets of protest to make this happen.

In all the euphoria, there was much attention paid to the fact that Obama's acceptance speech in Denver came exactly forty-five years after Dr. Martin Luther King's "I Have a Dream" address to tens of thousands at the Lincoln Memorial in Washington on August 28, 1963. Lee Tant of the *Orangeburg Times and Democrat* asked me for my opinion of Obama's acceptance speech at the convention. I said at the time that I would give him an "A" for rousing the base of the party, addressing the world, and laying out the differences between himself and Senator John McCain.

I believed that Obama deserved more of a "B" in highlighting the historical signifi-cance of his acceptance speech being given on the forty-fifth anniversary of Dr. King's famous speech.

Lost in the moment was the fact that Dr. King had delivered his Lincoln Memo-rial speech only 134 days after he had issued his "Letter from a Birmingham Jail." Among the many themes of that epistle was the admonition to white ministers who had been critical of what they felt was the too-rapid pace of Dr. King's demonstra-tions. They felt he was rushing things. He responded in the letter to the ministers by writing: "For years now, I have heard the word 'Wait!' It rings in the ears of every Negro with piercing familiarity. This 'Wait' has almost always meant 'Never.'"

Three and a half months later—on that historic August twenty-eighth—those thoughts were clearly on Dr. King's mind when he spoke at the Lincoln Memorial. "We have come to this hallowed spot," he told the Washington assemblage "to re-mind America of the fierce urgency of now. This is no time to engage in the luxury of cooling off or to take the tranquilizing drug of gradualism. Now is the time to rise from the dark and desolate valleys of segregation to the sunlit path of racial justice. Now is the time to open the doors of opportunity to all God's children. Now is the time to lift our nation from the quick sands of racial injustice to the solid rock of brotherhood. It would be fatal to overlook the urgency of the moment."

I told Lee Tant after the acceptance speech at the Democratic convention that I would have loved Obama to say what Dr. King was really talking about that day. The substance of Dr. King's speech was really about the fierce urgency of now. It wasn't about a dream. For all the warm feelings people may have gotten from his inspiring exhortations about racial harmony, Dr. King was imploring us with a sense of fierce urgency to make good use of our time to accomplish those things that needed to be done.

If there was a linkup between Dr. King and Mr. Obama in the president's first in-augural address, it came in this passage: "The success of our economy," he said, "has always depended not just on the size of our gross domestic product, but on the reach of our prosperity, on the ability to extend opportunity to every willing heart—not out of charity, but because it is the surest route to our common good."

It may not have registered as such with most of that exuberant throng at the in-auguration, but Mr. Obama was letting us know that he understood things, that he "got it." He saw full participation in the nation's economic mobilization, not only as the only means of achieving Dr. King's dream of economic rights for all people, but also as the means of achieving the nation's full economic potential.

That's what was at the heart of much of Obama's remarkable early agenda: mas-sive economic rescue legislation to protect jobs, stabilize governmental services, and launch a comprehensive reform of health care. He attempted to make all citizens se-cure and capable of achieving their own individual potentials. I think Dr. King would have approved. I just wish Mr. Obama had drawn those connections more urgently himself. It would have led us more clearly to the work agenda Dr. King left for us.

Two weeks before Obama's inauguration, I had my own occasion to offer some observations about the historical perspective of the moment. I was speaking to a group of about 450 at an annual breakfast at the University of South Carolina commemorating Dr. King. I chose another of his speeches to discuss. I reminded them of the words spoken during his speech on April 3, 1968: "I just want to do God's will. And he's allowed me to go up to the mountaintop. And I've looked over. And I've seen the Promised Land. I may not get there with you. But I want you to know tonight that we, as a people, will get to the Promised Land."

The next day Dr. King was shot dead at a Memphis motel. I guess I am something of a fatalist, and I wonder about things. I wonder about our own quest for the Promised Land, and I think of the forty years described in the Bible that elapsed between Moses's message to the Israelites about a Promised Land and their actual arrival there. It was forty years between Dr. King's death and the election of Barack Obama as president.

Unlike those proclaiming the end of racial politics, I do not believe we have reached a Promised Land. But I do not know if these things are mere coincidences either. As I told the group at USC that morning, "I do believe that Obama's election was ordained."

At times of political madness, there is some solace in words and beliefs from a higher, more stable source.

With my daughters at the April 2000 march to demand the Confederate Battle Flag be taken off the state capitol and out of the House and Senate Chambers.

32 : *Barack and Me*

I first met Barack Hussein Obama in Boston, Massachusetts, at the 2004 Democratic National Convention. I first heard of him when he ran in the 2000 Democratic primary for the First Congressional District in Illinois against the incumbent Bobby L. Rush. Bobby and I were sworn into Congress together in 1993, and while I did not get involved in the 2000 race, my sentiments were with Bobby Rush, who was not only my classmate and a son of the South, but had seconded my nomination to be president of the freshman class for the Second Session of the One Hundred Third Congress. Bobby had developed quite a political reach across the poverty-wracked First District in South Chicago, and his politics were the politics of those of us who had moved to political activism as the next tool for social change.

Barack Obama was the director of the nonprofit Project Vote and had become known as a good fund-raiser with connections in the upper levels of Michigan Avenue. He had been described in a January 16, 1996, *Village Voice* article as part of a "new breed of foundation-hatched black communitarian voices . . . a smooth Harvard lawyer with impeccable do-good credentials." In the Gullah parlance I had come to know and respect in South Carolina, Rush was a "benya," and Obama was a "cumya." He lost to Bobby nearly two-to-one.

But much like me after my heart-breaking loss to a "benya" in 1970, Barack Obama did not let a little thing like a defeat stymie his ambitions. By the time he and I met, he was the Democratic nominee for the U.S. Senate from Illinois and was widely considered to be an up-and-comer in Democratic Party circles.

Our first meeting was by chance as we were preparing for our speeches at the 2004 Democratic Convention. It was Obama's first convention address, and it was my second. But he was the keynoter, and I was one of scores of three- or four-minute evening fillers whose remarks few—if anyone—would remember.

It goes without saying that Barack's keynote address was historic and memorable, and it launched his pursuit of the presidency of the United States. I have since heard him deliver other memorable speeches, including his March 18, 2008, Philadelphia speech on race, his powerful 2009 inaugural address, and his soul-stirring address following the 2011 shootings at Tucson, Arizona.

After his 2004 election to the United States Senate, Obama came to several of the weekly meetings of the Congressional Black Caucus, and we often sat next to each other and exchanged small talk. We would not have a substantive discussion of his presidential aspirations until one day as we were gearing up for the 2006 election cycle. We sat down for a one-on-one over sandwiches and sodas in the little hideaway on the first floor of the Capitol, which I occupied at the time as chair of the House Democratic Caucus.

He told me what he had in mind, and this time we didn't waste a lot of time on small talk. There had been black presidential candidates before, and we had duly given them "favorite son" or "favorite daughter" status before joining in the affirmation of support for a white candidate. In my own case I had supported nontraditional candidates as diverse as Shirley Chisholm and Frank Church, and I had even said some nice things about George Romney at one time and was the only nonwhite member on the official flight to Richard Nixon's funeral.

The prospect of a competitive black candidate for the presidency, however—for all its historic implications—could be fraught with incalculable complications. Every black Democrat in America would be subjected to constant scrutiny as to whether our loyalties lay with race or party. It was too early in the process for me to do anything more than anticipate those complications as Obama and I had our brief meeting. I was mostly listening. I wondered about his loss to Bobby Rush and about the description of Obama as a "smooth Harvard lawyer . . . with impeccable do-gooder credentials," and I began to manufacture the image of him attending a barbecue fundraiser in Kingstree and working the crowd at my "World Famous Fish Fry," an event that began as a thank you to my statewide supporters and grassroots Democratic Party activists and has grown into a critical political event for state and national candidates.

Then I realized that Barack Obama was not running for president of Williamsburg County or South Carolina. There were places in America where a "smooth Harvard lawyer" would be just fine. America had been through two disastrous terms with a Republican president who had plunged us into unconscionable wars in the Middle East and had devastated the economy with lopsided economic policies that favored the wealthy.

I felt that America needed a good Democratic president, first and foremost, black or white. It would be my job to help determine who would be best qualified for that job. As our conversation continued, I began to realize that the person best qualified for that job might well be a black man.

I knew that should South Carolina be successful in its pursuit of the "first in the South primary," I could very well find myself between the proverbial "rock and a hard place." But, being the political pragmatist that I consider myself to be, and as the knowledgeable politician that I thought I was, I told myself that Democratic Party voters in Iowa, New Hampshire, and Nevada would render my chances of being in such a predicament highly unlikely.

Aside from being the most successful black politician America has ever known, Barack Obama, I found, was my kind of guy. He would make a good Omega. But there is nothing automatic about the friendship between the black president from Chicago and this black congressman from South Carolina. We both have had to work

At the first 2007 Democratic Presidential Debate (fifth from left), held at South Carolina State University, with presidential hopefuls Mike Gravel, Barack Obama, Chris Dodd, John Edwards, Dennis Kucinich, Joe Biden, Bill Richardson, and Hillary Clinton. Photograph by Clevis Harrison.

at it, and we have succeeded most of the time. When we didn't agree, it sometimes became newsworthy.

There was the occasion when Shirley Sherrod was fired from an Agriculture Department position based on a badly distorted videotape that seemed to show her admitting to discrimination against white farmers, when the opposite was actually true. Her firing amounted to a political drive-by shooting, and I—and many of my colleagues—erupted. *New York Times* columnist Maureen Dowd was only too happy to observe the conflict and record the exchange.

"I don't think a single black person was consulted before Shirley Sherrod was fired," she quoted me as saying. "The President's getting hurt real bad; he needs some black people around him. Some people over there are not sensitive at all about race. They really feel that the extent to which he allows himself to talk about race would tend to pigeonhole him or cost him support when a lot of people saw the election as a way to get the issue behind us. I don't think people elected him to disengage on race. Just the opposite."

The president and I quickly became reengaged after that column appeared in the *Times* on July 26, several days after Shirley Sherrod's firing. I was invited to the White House for a one-on-one conversation with the president. We discussed the incident in some detail, as well as how we might avoid such public clashes in the future. I had been harboring some sentiment about what I considered the president's rightward leanings anyhow, and I told him that I felt compelled to continue speaking openly and candidly to the press. Without being the least bit argumentative, he let me know that such would be fine with him. "Just one request, though," he said, "speak with me first."

Launching the Recovery

Soon after returning from his postelection vacation in his home state of Hawaii, President-elect Barack Obama hosted the bicameral, bipartisan leadership of the Congress at a Capitol Hill meeting to discuss ways and means to jump-start an economic recovery.

Until the final ninety days of the 2008 presidential campaign, arguably the most discussed issue during the campaign was what the candidates would do to reform our health-care system. And it was generally felt that health-care reform was probably going to be President Obama's signature effort, and of course it was. But it was not his priority. There are those who now argue that it was a mistake for him to take it on before tackling jobs and the economy. But that is only true for those who feel that an administration can't do more than one thing at a time.

The fact of the matter is that the economy was of paramount importance to the president-elect and us Democrats and had been ever since that fateful September 2008 visit to Capitol Hill by President Bush's secretary of the treasury, Henry Paulson. I was in the room for that late afternoon and evening meeting, and partisan politics was the last thing on any of our minds when we left. As a consequence of the information revealed in that meeting—that we could be just days away from an economic collapse—and subsequent reactions from members of the Republican Conference and Democratic Caucus, both presidential candidates suspended their campaigns and rushed back to Washington to huddle with their advisers and respective congressional leaders.

At this first meeting with legislative leaders, President-elect Obama did not talk about health care. The meeting was all about what would be the best prescription for an ailing economy that was hemorrhaging more than 700,000 jobs per month. The president made a valiant pitch for a legislative package that could be supported by both bodies and both parties. Of course he did not get the bipartisan support he sought, and I never thought he would.

Getting bipartisan cooperation was not what was uppermost on my mind, and when it came my time to speak during the round-robin format that is usually used at these meetings, I made it clear what my primary concerns were. I was very concerned about a stimulus package that failed to give due consideration to those communities that were traditionally overlooked during such governmental action. I made my argument in a way that seemed to cause a little discomfort to a few at the table, although everybody agreed that our country was at a point where it had not been since the early 1930s.

I started out by saying that up to that point in my life, Harry Truman was my favorite president. But I assured the president-elect that he could do something about changing that. I said that my fondness for Truman was grounded in his "Fair Deal" policies as opposed to Roosevelt's "New Deal," which seems to be preferred by most Democrats. I went on to explain that many of the policies of the New Deal were unfair to people of color and a raw deal for many of the communities I represented.

After a lot of contentious debate, the House approved a $990 billion bill, which unfortunately, for all intents and purposes, was dead on arrival in the Senate. It had nearly all the things I thought needed to be in a recovery package, but I had some grave concerns about equity for rural and minority communities. And that concern was well-placed.

Funding for Broadband deployment is a good example. When the bill left the House it contained $5 billion for Broadband deployment, $2.5 billion to be administered by the Department of Commerce and $2.5 billion to be administered by the Department of Agriculture. When the bill got back from the Senate it had $7 billion for Broadband, and, as I had feared, all of it to be administered by the Department of Commerce.

I was very vocal in my opposition to the Senate's version. I told Speaker Pelosi that I did not trust the Department of Commerce to be sufficiently vigilant in getting adequate resources for Broadband deployment into rural communities. I felt that the agency responsible for the development of rural communities, the United States Department of Agriculture, should administer the Broadband money in rural areas. Speaker Pelosi understood but was having great difficulty getting folks at the White House to cooperate. We were going back and forth in real time, utilizing the so-called ping-pong procedure. At a crucial point in the negotiations, the Speaker put me on the phone with the president.

I explained my concerns to the president. He seemed to understand, but it was clear to me that he was much more interested in getting the bill done than he was in dealing with my issue. I did not relent. In the final analysis, the Department of Agriculture got the $2.5 billion back, leaving $4.5 billion for the Department of Commerce.

I was championing two other causes that I thought were very important to my district and scores of rural committees all across the country: rural energy savings and gubernatorial discretions.

Three or four governors had begun making noises about not wanting any of the stimulus money to come to their states. One of them was the governor of South Carolina, Mark Sanford.

I was determined to do whatever I could to get those monies into those states and into the communities where they were sorely needed. I was very public in my opposition to Governor Sanford's position, and I started getting phone calls and e-mails from elected officials in South Carolina and other states where governors were threatening to refuse the money. The Speaker of the Mississippi House of Representatives invited me to come and meet with the Mississippi House Democratic Caucus. It was a productive and informative meeting.

After that meeting in Mississippi, and meetings with several legislators and regional governmental officials in South Carolina, I approached David Obey, chair of the Appropriations Committee, with my wish to include language in the American Recovery and Reinvestment Act (ARRA) that would allow state legislatures to receive and control recovery funds in instances where governors were being recalcitrant. David was very progovernor, and our discussion was not pleasant. But thanks to Nancy Pelosi, I was able to get language included that satisfied my concerns.

Many in the Democratic Caucus and some in the media began referring to the governors' work-around wording as the Clyburn Amendment. I suspect it was that moniker, as much if not more than his political convictions that led Governor Sanford to double down in his opposition to receiving the funds. He sued the legislature to keep the money out. But thanks to the South Carolina Supreme Court, we prevailed.

But the achievement of which I was most proud was getting language inserted into the Rural Development section of ARRA directing funds to the neediest rural communities. I called it the 10-20-30 Amendment. The concept being that at least 10 percent of the Rural Development funds would be invested in those communities where 20 percent or more of the populations have been stuck beneath the poverty level for the last thirty years.

I don't know what impact that formula has had throughout the country, but in South Carolina's Sixth Congressional District the impact was great. We saw water systems developed in communities that had been trying to get safe drinking water for more than half a century. Communities such as Branchville in Orangeburg County, Britton's Neck in Marion County (where 51 miles of water lines were laid), and Williamsburg County (where 132 miles of water lines were funded).

I subsequently explored with President Obama and the Office of Management and Budget the possibility of utilizing the 10-20-30 formula, or some similar method of appropriating funds, throughout the budget to enhance the fortunes of persistently impoverished communities. There seems to be significant bipartisan support for the concept, but we haven't gotten there yet. I remain hopeful.

33   *Reforming Health Care*

I have spent a lot of time trying to figure out how we got caught so flat-footed during the August 2009 recess. We—and the health-care debate—were dealt a severe setback. We left Washington for the summer break rather upbeat. The three relevant House committees, Ways and Means, Commerce, and Education and Labor, had produced a good product, and we headed home to extol its virtues at town-hall meetings. The Senate committee on Health, Education, Labor and Pensions (HELP) had already produced a bill, and many of us felt that, when we returned after Labor Day, we would quickly pass a House version and head to a conference with the Senate.

I have always prepared for the possibility of problems at town-hall meetings. Consequently I always hold them in well-lit, well-patrolled areas that would discourage too much chicanery from taking place.

One of my meetings was at the Drew Wellness Center in Columbia, and I had a second meeting at the International Longshoreman's Hall in Charleston. Both these sites are located on well-traveled thoroughfares, and functions held at both of them are usually well attended by diverse audiences. But I did not take anything for granted. I dispersed a significant number of staff members throughout the audiences. Sure enough, some people came to the town-hall meetings intending to be disruptive. But we were able to contain them and did have what I considered to be productive meetings.

My meetings were sharp contrasts to what I was seeing on television across the country. Dick Armey's Tea Party was proving to be well-funded and thoroughly coached, if not highly trained, in disruptive techniques and tactics. August 2009 was a disastrous month for us.

When we returned to Washington after Labor Day, the general feeling was that health-care reform was dead. In fact, many of the pretty astute members of the House Democratic Caucus publicly pronounced it so. But at our first caucus meeting I was pleasantly surprised to see that many members had really been emboldened by the experience. Of course there were various ideas as to how to move forward. Some people felt that we should break the bill up and pass it in small pieces. Some felt that we should just do something really small, declare a victory, and revisit the issue at some later time. There was also serious debate taking place in the White House. But Speaker Pelosi never relented. She wanted to move forward comprehensively. She wanted to go big, and so did I.

Healthy Reflections

I opened my local newspaper on Saturday morning, January 9, 2010, and was greeted by a blaring headline that read, "Clyburn Quiet while Other Black Lawmakers Criticize Obama." The headline was rather jolting but hardly inaccurate. I had been rather muted in my responses to the many inquiries and questions that were coming my way as President Obama seemed to be backing farther and farther away from some of the promises made during the campaign, and the hopes and expectations of many from the more progressive wing of our party.

While the Barack Obama presidential campaign was an important interlude in our nation's pursuit of a more perfect union for folks in my generation; for many others, working in that campaign was the fad of the moment, the hip thing to do. For me President Obama's campaign was about life or death, if not life and death.

The health-care issue was very important to House Democrats and very personal with me. Watching your mother celebrate her fifty-fifth birthday while dying from multiple myeloma is something you never quite get over. Spending every dime she had saved for that house she was never going to build leaves an emotional scar that is very hard to heal.

Couple that with growing up with two brothers, dreaming about the day when I would be a father developing the kind of partnership with my son that I had with my father. That too, was not to be. The good Lord blessed me with three lovely daughters. So it is not hard for one to imagine what emotions I felt when my first grandchild was a boy.

But Walter A Clyburn Reed arrived two months before he was expected, weighing in at less than four pounds. He had three operations before he was ten pounds and spent his first ninety days in the intensive-care unit. I watched my wife sit by that child's bedside every one of those ninety days. I watched my daughter Jennifer and son-in-law Walter as they wandered helplessly up and down the corridors of the hospital. And I remembered their euphoria when they made the final payment on the copayment required by their insurance policy.

During the debate, I often reflected on the night I stepped out of a political event to receive the frantic call from my daughters telling me that they were taking their mother to the emergency room. Emily had been complaining for some time, so I was quite concerned. It was the next morning before I could get a flight home, but that phone call left me in no mood for the kind of discussions that usually take place at political dinners such as the one I was attending honoring Elijah Cummings, who had just been elected chair of the Congressional Black Caucus.

So I excused myself and drove home. In my gut, I felt that something bad was wrong. Later that night I was informed by my daughters that, although the emergency-room tests did not find anything wrong, they had insisted that Emily be admitted, and she was.

When I landed in Columbia the next morning I went directly to the hospital, arriving just ahead of the doctor. He told us that whatever the problem was, it seemed to have dissipated. He attempted to conclude our discussion by asking Emily how she was feeling. Emily replied that something was wrong. He seemed taken aback but decided that they would chemically induce a condition that simulated a stress test. They did so the next day, and she failed the test. Subsequently they injected a dye that clearly revealed four blockages and the possibility of a fifth. Two days later, Emily underwent five-vessel bypass heart surgery.

Throughout the health-care debate I often found myself wondering: What would have happened if our children had not resisted the initial ER attempt to send Emily home and if Emily were not so well insured—or had not spoken up when her doctor expressed doubts that anything was seriously wrong? Would "A.C." be enjoying his sophomore year in college and showing no ill effects from those first critical months if his parents did not have health insurance? I also thought about having to spend my mother's entire savings trying to keep her comfortable.

These blessed experiences made health-care reform rather personal to me.

Healthy Complaints

A few days before that headline appeared in my local newspaper, we had a Democratic leadership meeting in Washington and held a "press avail" afterwards. The first questioner raised the complaint that President Obama was not keeping his campaign promise to have the health-care reform debate fully transparent. In fact he had promised that the public would be allowed to look in on the conferences and listen to the discussions and debate via C-SPAN.

The second question had to do with an unidentified member of the Democratic Caucus, who was complaining that too much was being done in private gatherings and that it would show a total lack of democracy to produce a bill without a full House and Senate conference. All this signaled real difficulties going forward.

It was also revealed during that earlier leadership meeting that Speaker Pelosi and Majority Leader Steny Hoyer would be going to the White House later that evening to discuss the final push to reconcile those differences. And, as had been the case in several recent instances, it was my first knowledge of such a meeting. But I had long since gotten used to the fact that, whenever it was possible for me to be excluded from a White House meeting, the president's chief of staff would make certain I was. I had gotten over being bothered by such slights. Besides I have always had an aversion to meetings for the sake of meeting, and in all too many instances that is what these things were all about.

When I got back to my office after the press avail, my chief of staff raised the issue of the White House meeting. I told him that I had just been made aware of the meeting but had not been invited to participate. The media were doing extensive reporting on the meeting, and I started getting inquiries from members of the Tri-Caucus (the CBC, Hispanic, and Asian Pacific Americans) complaining about my lack of participation in these meetings. Later I received an e-mail stating that there would be another Democratic leadership meeting at ten o'clock the next morning, Wednesday, January sixth.

I got to the office before nine o'clock the next morning and placed a call to my health-care staffer, Barvetta Singletary, who had taken over the duties that had been the purview of A. J. Jones, who had gone off to greener pastures. A. J. had a well-deserved sterling reputation on health-policy issues, and many people wondered whether or not I would be able to replace him. Few people knew that my chief of staff, Yebbie Watkins, had anticipated that A. J. would soon receive an offer he should not refuse, so he and A. J. had begun preparing Barvetta to step in if A. J. were to leave.

Barvetta had not only stepped in, but she had also stepped up, in a big way, much to almost everybody's surprise, except maybe Yebbie's and mine. She had gained the confidence and respect of most of the other Capitol Hill staffers. So I knew that although I had not been invited to the previous evening meeting at the White House, Barvetta would have been briefed about the meeting along with all other House and Senate staffers.

When she returned my call, it was just as I had thought. She was in a meeting with other staffers getting updated on the White House meeting. When we finally got together, it was only fifteen minutes before the Democratic leadership meeting was to begin. Consequently I ran a few minutes late for the meeting because I was determined to have sufficient knowledge before going into that room to vigorously support, or fiercely oppose, whatever seemed to be the direction we would be taking.

On my way to the meeting I received an e-mail from one of my staffers indicating that Speaker Pelosi had called the office wanting to know whether or not I was going to attend. I surmised that some staff-to-staff discussions had taken place between her staff and mine, and she was aware that I and the minority caucuses were not pleased with being left out of these White House health-care discussions.

When I walked into the Speaker's conference room I took my usual seat, the second chair to the right of the Speaker. I listened intently and did not have much to say. It was clear to me from what was being said that affordability for low- to moderate-income people was not getting the kind of attention that I felt it needed to get at those meetings. It also seemed to me that the national exchange was on the chopping block in favor of a state-by-state approach. As insulting as backing away from the national exchange was to me, I still refrained from saying anything. I spoke at the meeting only when complaints were raised about an issue that had become known as the "Cornhusker Compromise," Senator Ben Nelson's amendment that granted Nebraska 100 percent federal support to cover additional expenses that might be incurred by Medicaid recipients.

The issue had engendered significant opposition, and South Carolina senator Lindsey Graham had called for a lawsuit. In response the attorney general of South Carolina had moved to pull together fourteen or fifteen other state attorneys general to move in that direction.

I spoke up in favor of equity for the other forty-nine states. This evoked a slight discussion as to whether or not I meant equality for all the states. I insisted on using the word "equity," because I have always been sensitive to the argument that many poorer states, including South Carolina, got much greater returns from the federal government for certain social programs, such as Medicaid, than we pay in. So I have always insisted that whenever this kind of argument gets underway, I focus on equity rather than equality. That has always been my position on civil rights and affirmative-action issues as well.

I had made it clear at a recent media roundtable in my district office right after the Senate passed its bill that, rather than get all exercised over what Senator Nelson had gotten for Nebraska, I would be pushing to get a similar deal for South Carolina and other states similarly affected. Two days after I made that statement, Governor Mark Sanford released a letter that he said he had sent to me requesting my assistance in getting a better deal for South Carolina. Of course I had not received his letter, but as was usually the case with Governor Sanford, regardless of the effort, he always seemed to be several days late and millions of dollars short.

Healthy Differences

The meeting lasted for about two hours, and Speaker Pelosi announced that there would be another bicameral leadership meeting at the White House at 2:20 P.M. When our meeting adjourned the Speaker invited some of us into her office for a meeting after the meeting. It turned out that it was to decide who would take the lead on what discussions during the 2:20 P.M. White House meeting. She made it clear that this time I was being invited to attend.

Of course I had no intentions of attending the White House meeting, so as the discussions developed and various assignments were being made I remained quiet. The Speaker seemed a little uncomfortable with my demeanor and lack of participation, so after a while she assigned me a role for the meeting.

At that time I informed her that I did not plan to attend. She and the others in the room were taken aback by my announcement. I explained that I was scheduled to participate in a retirement ceremony at the Pentagon at two o'clock and would be leaving immediately from there to catch a plane home to participate in the funeral services of the mother of one of my district employees.

It was clear to me that the Speaker was not pleased, although she expressed sympathy for the bereavement of my staffer. When the meeting ended, I attempted to make a quick exit and was approached by one of the meeting participants who expressed regret that I would not be attending. During his comments he underscored the discomfort he and others had with my not being invited to attend the meeting the night before. Most members of the Democratic Caucus know that I pretty much practice listening at least twice as much as I do talking, but would never fail to speak up and defend our party's principles.

Everybody also knew that I was not all that impressed by high sounding phrases like "bending the cost curve" and never hesitated to say so. My interests were whether or not we paid sufficient attention to affordability and accessibility. How much funding could we provide to community health centers and prevention programs? Everybody knew that I would be relentless and vocal in my support for both, and that did not sit too well with some in the Obama administration.

We were standing just outside the Speaker's office. She could see us, and no doubt detected what the conversation was all about. In fact there was a lot of chatter about the images TV cameras had captured of the Speaker and majority leader arriving at the White House for the meeting the night before, and there was a lot of speculation as to why I had not been in attendance. She asked me back into her office and made it clear that the others needed to allow the two of us to go one-on-one. It was obvious she felt there was more to my not attending the meeting than that which I had expressed earlier.

The fact of the matter is that I had committed to speak at a retirement ceremony at the Pentagon for the nephew of a very supportive constituent and college school-mate, K. D. Lowery, and the funeral service was for the mother of my casework supervisor, Carole Smith. So I told the Speaker that this was in fact the case. But I also told her that it was clear to me that I was not particularly welcomed at these White House meetings, and that I always got the feeling the president's people, and maybe the president himself, would rather that I not be there.

She knew as well as I did that Rahm Emanuel would rather that I not be in any White House meeting. Everybody in our caucus was aware of the tension between Rahm and me, and of course she understood as well as I did as to why that was. The Speaker then shared with me some of the conversations she had with various people during the August break. She wanted to make it clear, without having to say so directly, that she understood my feelings and why I had them. Our one-on-one lasted for about fifteen minutes before I excused myself to get over to the Pentagon.

The next morning, I went to Florence for the home-going services for Ruth Elizabeth Singleton Smith, who had been critical to my 1992 successes. The services were being held at Mount Zion AME Church, which had figured so prominently in the 1992 Democratic primary that started me on my way to Congress. Ruth had been one of my staunchest supporters in the 1992 campaign.

It was rather interesting that Ruth would be laid to rest in the middle of the health-care debate. She had been a polio victim in her childhood, and the illness had left her with a decided limp. Ruth had a tremendous sense of humor, and after spotting Florence City Councilman Billy Williams in the sanctuary as I rose to speak, I decided to share an anecdote about an experience Billy and I had with Ruth during a critical moment in that 1992 primary race.

In a pep talk to our volunteers one evening, Ruth urged them not to let the rumor mill stem their enthusiasm and then wowed them by vowing that "Jim Clyburn is going to Washington even if I have to carry him there on my back." The mourners appreciated the irony of that vow when I shared it, just as much as Billy and I had on the day that Ruth made it.

Emily attended the services with me, and afterward we headed to St. George for a meeting with the directors of the Regional Councils of Government along the I-95 corridor. These folks are responsible for much of the community and economic development efforts in those counties. They had accommodated my obligation to participate in Ruth's services by moving our scheduled 10:00 A.M. meeting to 2:30 P.M.

When feeling pressure, I have a habit of making myself really busy, sometimes burying myself in work, especially when the sources of the pressure are beyond my control. So I had instructed the staff to fill my schedule with as many appointments as time and circumstances would permit. But my mind was on health care. I was wondering what might have occurred in that meeting the day before the one I had strategically failed to attend. After the St. George meeting, we headed back to Columbia.

I left Columbia early the next morning and headed to Charleston to do a 10:00 A.M. TV interview. After that interview, I held a 10:30 meeting with Mayor Joe Riley of Charleston and Jim Newsome, head of the South Carolina Ports Authority to discuss funding for the port and local infrastructure projects. The mayor wanted help for a cruise-ship passenger terminal and the flooding problems in the Fishburne Street area, and Jim Newsome wanted support for deepening the harbors in Charleston and Georgetown. I was hoping that I would not seem too detached because, to a great extent, I was just going through the motions. My mind was on health care.

I left that meeting around 11:15 to attend an 11:30 A.M. meeting with David Rivers and his fellow board members of the Charleston Department of Public Works. This meeting was also about infrastructure funding, this time to repair and expand the deteriorating wastewater tunnels that lie one hundred feet beneath the streets of Charleston.

Although the price tags on the projects we were discussing were almost unimaginable, discussing them gave me a brief break from thinking about things over which I had no control. And I was enjoying being among old friends, a real respite from the back biting and throat cutting that was going on up in Washington.

After a great discussion and a lowcountry lunch, I left that meeting and rushed over to the Medical University of South Carolina for a meeting with President Ray Greenberg to discuss additional funding for the Ernest F. Hollings Cancer Center and to receive an update on the plans for the research center the MUSC board of trustees had recently voted to name in my honor.

The extended Clyburn family at the dedication of the James E. Clyburn Research Center at the Medical University of South Carolina in 2011. Photograph courtesy of the Medical University of South Carolina.

During all of these meetings my Blackberry was vibrating pretty constantly. Lunch had been punctured by a call from the *Wall Street Journal,* and in the middle of the meeting with Dr. Greenberg, a staffer interrupted to inform me that I needed to make myself available for a conference call with President Obama and the rest of the House leadership in about fifteen minutes. I kind of deducted from all of this that I was being brought back into the health-care discussions, and I decided that I was not going to be as quiet going forward as I had been in the past.

The Blair House Summit

In my not-so-humble opinion, the turning point in the health-care debate came in February 2010 at the Blair House Summit with the bipartisan leadership of both Houses. When I was called on to speak, I decided to keep it simple. I expressed my strong feelings that we should not lose sight of the necessity to incentivize prevention programs and increase the number of federally qualified community health-care centers; both of which could dramatically drive down the cost of health care. I shared with them what I had heard during a visit I had the day before with Dillon County officials who wanted my help to secure funds to double the size of their emergency room.

They said that about 40 percent of the folks coming into their ER were seeking primary-care services, and not all of them were without health insurance. Some of them were using the ER because they didn't have health insurance, but many others were coming there because they could not afford their deductibles and copayments. I wholeheartedly endorsed substantially increasing the number of federally qualified community health centers, regardless of whatever else might or might not be in the legislation.

I had not focused on it at the time, but I was scheduled to attend a meeting of the Association of Community Health Centers later that evening. When I arrived, the reception I received was awesome. Most of them had caught my comments at the Blair House meeting via C-SPAN, and the attendees rewarded me with a standing ovation and thunderous applause. And media reports the next day gave the president's Blair House performance very high marks.

Getting off the Sixty-Vote Treadmill

Although the Blair House Summit may have changed the narrative and raised the level of the debate, I believe that the road to passage of the Affordable Care Act began in Massachusetts, and I don't mean Romney's health-care plan.

I had been saying for months—and was being chastised for it by my friends at MoveOn.org and in other liberal quarters—that the magic number to pass the health-care bill should be fifty plus one, not sixty. I was well aware that the budget resolution called for the reconciliation process to be used for health care and education, and I was convinced that the pursuit of sixty votes was ruining the chances of both.

Losing the Kennedy seat in Massachusetts was embarrassing to us Democrats and looked to many to be a tragedy for the health-care debate. But it allowed us to get off of the sixty-vote treadmill, and in my opinion that was not a bad thing. This is not

President Obama visiting the House Democratic Caucus to sell the Affordable Care Act, November 2009: Assistant to the Speaker Chris Van Hollen, Majority Whip Jim Clyburn, Speaker of the House Nancy Pelosi, President Obama, Majority Leader Steny Hoyer, Democratic Caucus Chair John Larson, and Democratic Caucus Vice Chair Xavier Becerra.

sour grapes; I certainly wanted Democrats to hold that seat, and I am convinced that we lost it because of the reason we were losing so many other races. Developing issues from focus groups, conducting campaigns on poll-tested platforms, and listening only to media consultants while ignoring the tried-and-true methods of how Democrats win elections, was and is problematic for me. Not putting boots on the ground with the feet of local GOTV (get out the vote) experts in them is a recipe for defeat.

The weekend before that election I was doing Martin Luther King Jr. events up in Michigan. Because I was hearing so much disheartening news from Massachusetts, I decided to call my cousin Willie Mae Clyburn Allen, who at the time was serving in the Massachusetts House of Delegates. Although her brother Bill, who serves in the South Carolina legislature, and I are pretty close these days, and our families often vacation together, when we were growing up Willie Mae was my favorite cousin in their household, and she occasionally spent weekends with us in Sumter. Willie Mae was actively involved with and highly respected by veteran groups and held a high-level position with the Prince Hall Masonry Eastern Stars. I wanted to get a feel from her as to what was going on in Massachusetts. Why were the prospects of holding the seat so bleak? After all, that was the seat of Senator Edward Kennedy. Surely it would not go to a Republican.

What she told me was familiar and continues to plague our prospects and efforts today. She told me that just a few minutes before I called, she learned—for the first time—that a GOTV rally was to be held in her legislative district at 5:00 P.M. the next afternoon. The campaign seemed to be ignoring the GOTV ground game.

The Republican win in Massachusetts gave the GOP the forty-one votes they needed to conduct an effective filibuster without any help from Democrats. And it made us Democrats come face-to-face with a new reality. We held marathon sessions at the White House, and the meetings were about as intense as they were long. Getting the House and Senate on the same page was not easy, but I thought the president was doing a pretty good job of getting us to where we needed to be. But even after the White House meetings had gotten us to a good place, there were still some loose ends that needed to be wrapped up.

The debate was becoming more and more contentious, and the push for a full House and Senate conference to hash out differences in the House- and Senate-passed plans was becoming less and less likely. I was one of those who felt that a full-fledged conference was not necessarily the best way to go. On the other hand, it was clear that there was a strong feeling among some from the more moderate wing of our Democratic Caucus, that a full conference was the only way to go. So we continued to have bicameral meetings.

It just seemed that the closer we got to agreeing on a bill the more reticent one of the senators would get. Of course it is not at all unusual for the House to get jerked around by the Senate.

One night during one of those contentious meetings, I got into an exchange with one of the senators, who was pushing to pass the bill outside the reconciliation process. Such would require sixty votes and would leave education exposed to a similar fate. I felt strongly that this tactic would put both health-care reform and education at jeopardy.

I argued with the gentleman that doing so would be once again walking away from those in our caucus who saw both health care and education as being important to our base. I reminded him of the debate we had earlier, which resulted in leaving funding for the black farmers settlement out of the American Recovery and Reinvestment Act.

The senator retorted by telling me how long he and his brother had been involved in the black farmers' issue. His comments and demeanor seemed condescending to me, and I took grave exception. Raising my voice a few more decibels than usual and digging a bit deeper into my diaphragm for lower octaves than were necessary, I reminded the gentleman of how long I had been black.

An uneasy quiet enveloped the room, which I punctured with a piercing argument for proceeding under the reconciliation process. I also dug in on getting significant increases for preventive-health programs and additional community health centers. Thanks to persistence on the Senate side by Senator Bernie Sanders and a favorable ruling from the Senate parliamentarian, we proceeded under the reconciliation process and got both education and health care reforms.

34 | *Reducing the Deficit*

A telephone call from Nancy Pelosi is not unusual. But when I answered her April 11, 2011, call, her salutation was very formal and businesslike. I knew right away that this was not an ordinary call. Unless she is asking for money, Nancy seldom goes directly to the point, but this time she did.

When Nancy said that she was appointing me to the so-called Biden Group, I was glad we were not in a face-to-face meeting. It was all that I could do to contain my glee, and I couldn't wait for the call to end so I could share the news.

I immediately called my chief of staff, Yebbie Watkins, and my personal and political confidant, Bennie Thompson, with the news. Later I called Emily, my most severe outside-the-Beltway critic. But I was cautious with all of them. I told them that there was a good possibility I would be appointed to the much-talked-about group to study and make recommendations to Congress as to how to confront the country's debt and deficits. I felt that this was too good to be true, that something could still go terribly wrong.

In his 2011 State of the Union Address, President Barack Obama called on Congress to create a sixteen-member committee of four Democrats and four Republicans from the Senate, and four Democrats and four Republicans from the House. Their job would be to fashion a plan to address our nation's debt and deficits. The president named Vice President Joe Biden to chair the committee.

Immediately after the president's speech that night, I started receiving e-mails and texts from colleagues, staffers, and former staffers suggesting that I make a push for a seat on the proposed committee. Although I did not think about it during the speech, these messages started me to giving it some thought.

Republicans, being much less diverse and a little more "clubbie" than us Democrats, criticized the size of the proposed committee as being too large to be effective. Subsequently Senate Republican leader Mitch McConnell announced that he was going to appoint only one senator, Republican whip John Kyl. Speaker of the House John Boehner followed suit and announced that he would appoint only one congressman, House Republican leader Eric Cantor.

I thought that I could probably land one of the four House Democratic seats, but if Democratic leaders Reid and Pelosi followed the Republicans lead and appointed only one from each body, there was absolutely no chance that I would be

*With Congressmen Bennie Thompson and Cedric Richmond on the first day
of the One Hundred Thirteenth Congress, January 3, 2013*

the one House member. It would go to Chris Van Hollen, the ranking member on the House Budget Committee.

Although I had not made many public comments about our deficits and debt and not said a whole lot about the debt-ceiling debate that was raging, I had internalized some lessons from my blessed experiences. I had been taught from childhood to live within my means and keep my credit clean. Those teachings had profound impacts on me. Throughout my adult life I have never had a problem waiting until I could afford a purchase before making one. Consequently there has never been a day in my life when I have fretted over being able to pay a bill that is due.

I took this lesson to Congress, much to the chagrin of the Christian Coalition. In their heyday, the Christian Coalition was the premier political organization of evangelical Christians and faith voters, highly respected in some quarters and greatly feared in others. Every election cycle they published their little voter guides, scoring five or six issues they claimed were important to people of faith and distributed them in churches two or three Sundays before an election. Most Democrats seemed to fear those little palm cards, but I was never fazed by them and was never shy about expressing the low esteem I held for the group.

My state Democratic Party chairman once cautioned me to tone down my criticism of the Christian Coalition because it might hurt my future in politics. I listened to him respectfully, but I could not wait for the next opportunity to level criticism against that crowd. I always treated the Christian Coalition as what I thought they were—an arm of the Republican Party.

There was a significant incident rather early in my congressional career that supported my opinion about the Christian Coalition. During the budget debate in 1995, I was casting votes for things I thought would be important planks in the platform upon which I planned to build and sustain a political career and establish a record that would make future political pursuits easier for young black South Carolinians. Some of those issues had been touted by Republicans and were a part of Newt Gingrich's Contract with America. To the dismay of some of my Democratic colleagues, I voted against "unfunded mandates," and to the displeasure of others, I voted for the Balanced Budget Amendment (BBA). Both were issues conservatives felt were exclusively theirs and many liberals disdained. My votes in favor of these two most important issues put the Christian Coalition in a quandary as to what to do about their opposition to my reelection when they published their voter guides for the 1996 elections.

The BBA was central to their cause, and it was important for them to put their check mark under the "against" column in the box next to my name. During the budget debate, several amendments to the BBA legislation were offered, one of which was to require a two-thirds vote in order to raise taxes. I voted against that amendment. So the Christian Coalition cured their dilemma by doing a special voter guide for my race. They used that vote rather than my BBA vote, in order to achieve the result they wanted. Throughout that campaign, I had a lot of fun calling attention to that obvious act of disingenuousness. It helped to underscore that they were pushing the Republican Party's agenda and were not good practitioners of the religious principles their name would imply.

But I wanted to be on that committee for another, much more personal, reason. Right-wing bloggers and talking heads had taken great joy in denigrating my efforts to stay at the leadership table in the House of Representatives after Democrats lost the majority in the 2010 elections, which resulted in the compromise through which I was named assistant Democratic leader. Rush Limbaugh had been gleeful in his proposal that an appropriate leadership job for me would be "driving Ms. Nancy," his satirical takeoff on actor Morgan Freeman's character in the movie *Driving Miss Daisy*. The *Black Commentator*, a right-wing instrument for pseudo-black conservatives, castigated my efforts, as they almost always did in response to any position taken by a member of the Congressional Black Caucus.

Some of my close friends were also skeptical of the new leadership arrangement. On May 10, 2011, a *Washington Post* reporter quoted my Democratic colleague and congressional classmate Alcee Hastings of Florida as saying that my role as assistant Democratic leader was "a work in progress." That reporter also quoted Democrat Emanuel Cleaver of Missouri, who was chair of the Congressional Black Caucus, as saying that his initial reaction to my new leadership position was "anger. However, it has turned out to be something we can all feel good about. . . . They're utilizing his talents."

Three days later, on May 13, 2011, David Rogers, an astute and experienced Capitol Hill observer writing for *Politico,* quoted me as saying, "These cuts have to be fair. The sacrifice has to be shared." Mr. Rogers also quoted me as saying during that interview that in search for common ground, I made it a practice to "fish in many ponds."

Of course, I am not a fisherman and, looking for me at the 11:00 A.M. hour on Sunday mornings, one could have as much a chance of finding me fishing golf balls out of a pond or lake as in a church pew. Nobody was as happy as I was when so many Protestant churches, mine included, added early morning worship services, something Catholics have always done. Being able to spend two hours in a church pew on Sunday mornings before spending four hours on a golf course is my idea of what heaven on earth is all about.

I learned in church pews that we are expected to protect the least among us. On golf courses I learned that everybody is expected to play by the same set of rules, regardless of what positions they hold or what their social status might be.

Like most politicians, I believe that sometimes it is better to be lucky than good, and I got lucky. The Senate Democratic leader, Senator Harry Reid, announced that he was not going to follow the Republicans lead and would be appointing two to the committee. He appointed Senator Max Baucus, chair of the Senate Budget Committee, and Senator Dan Inouye, chair of the Senate Appropriations Committee. Nancy Pelosi announced that she would probably appoint two members as well. This provided an opening that Pelosi herself had laid the foundation for much earlier. In proposing my new leadership arrangement, she had structured an appropriations role as a significant part of my assistant Democratic leader portfolio, and she had reinforced that role at every possible opportunity inside our caucus and to the media.

When my appointment to the Biden Committee was made public, it generated the expected reactions from the usual suspects among Capitol Hill staffers and in various elements of the media, the same ones who had proclaimed that I did not fit the traditional mold of a party's whip.

Finding common ground is what I have tried to be about throughout my public service career. In doing so, I try to be respectful and expect to be respected. I don't make it a practice of laughing at things that I do not find to be funny or scratching where I don't itch. And as I often say, and said at the time of my appointment to the Biden Group, if the distance between my opponent and me is five steps, I don't mind taking three of them.

The Biden Group

At our first meeting, Vice President Biden concluded his opening remarks by saying, "Nothing is agreed too, until everything is agreed too." He repeated that mantra often during every meeting. If I heard him say it once, I must have heard him say it a hundred times. It's a refrain that still rings in my ears.

Also at that first meeting, Jack Lew, director of the Office of Management and Budget, and Treasury Secretary Timothy Geitner presented a detailed overview of the gravity of our financial situation and the importance of raising the debt ceiling. We were provided handouts comparing President Barack Obama's budget proposal, the Ryan/Republican budget, the Bowles-Simpson Commission proposal, and the Domenici-Rivlin committee proposal. There were things in all of them that would cause difficulties for me.

During discussions of the comparisons, Cantor defended the Ryan/Republican budget, which—among many things I found unacceptable—proposed to block grant Supplemental Nutrition Assistance Programs (SNAP) and Medicaid. That is, they wanted to fold all the funding into one big block and leave it up to the states to decide how the funds got allocated. After one discussion, he summarized his presentation by saying, "as far as safety-net programs, we take a block grant approach."

When Cantor made that comment, I asked him whether or not there were other options to block granting he was willing to discuss. I said to him, as respectfully and as firmly as I knew how, that because of the histories of his state (Virginia) and mine (South Carolina), I was never going to agree to the block granting of SNAP programs or Medicaid.

Other members of the committee drew lines in the sand regarding their priorities. Republicans made it clear that they were not willing to put any revenue on the table, and Democrats made it clear that without additional revenue there could be no agreements on entitlement cuts. Republicans insisted that defense should not be touched and Democrats declared that Medicare was off-limits. Trying to figure out how to proceed, Vice President Biden summed up our dilemma this way: "What we know is the House won't pass something with revenue, a Constitutional Amendment won't pass the Senate, and the President will not sign anything without revenue."

I also had problems with raising the age for Medicare eligibility and Social Security benefits. I thought, and still think, that it is unfair to set retirement for mine workers and others working in hazardous conditions at the same age as for people working in air-conditioned offices.

Around our second or third meeting I began to feel a little uncomfortable with some things that were being reported by the media. I was honoring our pledge not to discuss our deliberations publicly, but it was pretty clear to me that not everybody was abiding by that agreement. I was also reading and hearing comments from some of my Democratic Caucus colleagues indicating that many of them were feeling a little uncomfortable with some of our efforts. I started feeling the need to give myself some cover, so I formed a little kitchen cabinet, much as I had with my senior whips during my tenure as majority whip. I met with them regularly before and after Biden Group meetings.

The Biden Group went through the federal budget function by function. In meeting after meeting Democrats continued to identify areas where cuts might be amenable, and in every instance Republicans refused to engage in a conversation about raising revenue. The vice president kept trying and conciliating to the point that I really felt he was being much too deferential.

On June 2, 2011, President Obama invited the entire Democratic Caucus to the White House. It became clear from various members' comments that there was a lot of anxiety among them about the Biden Group's deliberations. And it was not helpful to the anxiety I was feeling when the president's comments and references in that meeting seemed to indicate that he was not aware that I was a member of the Biden Group. When I was finally recognized in that meeting, I made it clear that preserving

Medicare and protecting Medicaid were my top priorities. I also said that Democrats needed to stand firm for fair and equitable revenue raisers.

I argued that we would lose the message war if we didn't approach our work in a way that the public perceived was fair and equitable. I maintained that we had two recent models to guide us in our messaging: The Clinton tax increase, which spurred 22 million new jobs, and the Bush tax cuts that got us historically high debts and unprecedented deep deficits. I made it clear that I believed that some had already sacrificed enough. When I finished my comments, it was clear to the president and everybody else that I was certainly in the room and not as a potted plant. When we returned to our committee meetings, we fought over budget caps and firewalls between defense and nondefense, with Democrats wanting firewalls and the Republicans not wanting them. We discussed what to do about the sustainable growth rate, the so-called doctors' fix. We discussed whether or not there should be a change in the way we calculate the consumer price index (CPI).

We argued over whether or not war savings, the Overseas Contingency Operations account (OCO), should be a part of our considerations. The Republicans maintained that counting them was gimmickry, even though Congressman Paul Ryan of Wisconsin had used them in putting together the Republicans budget, and the Congressional Budget Office scores them as real savings. We also debated preserving the payroll tax cut. For the most part, our differences fell along party lines. Although at one point Senator Max Baucus of Montana threw fellow House Democrats a curve ball on Medicaid and during one discussion threatened to walk away from the table over the issue of farm subsidies.

We were trying to achieve a $1.2 trillion down payment on $4 trillion in deficit reduction. Democrats felt that a $1.2 trillion deal had to have $300–400 billion in revenue to accompany the $800–900 billion in cuts we had identified as palatable. Republicans were saying it had to be all cuts. For Democrats that was a nonstarter.

We held nine meetings, averaging about ninety minutes each. Around the eighth meeting Vice President Biden announced that time was running out. He started talking about ways to make a graceful exit and kicking everything up a level. For the vice president and senators, that meant up to the president. For us members of the House, that meant Speaker John Boehner.

A Not So Grand Bargain

Just before our tenth and last scheduled meeting, Eric Cantor announced that he was withdrawing from the talks. His announcement was quickly followed by Senator Jon Kyl's announcement that he was also withdrawing. Later that same day, it was reported that President Obama and Speaker Boehner had been meeting privately. I guess they knew we would not be able to reach an agreement.

For several days their discussions dominated Capitol Hill news. Although it seemed as if they had reached some sort of general agreement, it did not seem to be one that most Democrats were all that excited about, and as it turned out, it was not one that Speaker Boehner was able to sell to the Republican conference.

On August 2, 2011, President Obama signed into law the Budget Control Act (BCA) of 2011. Among other things it created the Congressional Joint Select Committee on Deficit Reduction to propose further reductions that will amount to at least $1.5 trillion in budgetary savings over ten years.

The Super Committee

When the "grand bargain" eluded President Obama and Speaker Boehner, attention turned to the Congressional Joint Select Committee on Deficit Reduction. It was almost immediately nicknamed the "Super Committee." It was going to be a committee of twelve, three Democrats and three Republicans from the House and three Democrats and three Republicans from the Senate. Speculation was running wild as to who would be on the committee.

Senate Majority Leader Harry Reid appointed Democratic senators John Kerry, Max Baucus, and Patty Murray. The Senate minority leader appointed Republican senators Jon Kyl, Rob Portman, and Pat Toomey. Speaker Boehner appointed Republican representatives Jeb Hensarling, Dave Camp, and Fred Upton, and minority leader Nancy Pelosi appointed Democratic representatives Chris Van Hollen, Xavier Becerra, and me.

I was in Tunica, Mississippi, attending the Annual Meeting of the Congressional Black Caucus Institute when I received Leader Pelosi's call. This time she was not so direct. She told me that she would like to have my input as to who I thought her three should be. Of course we were talking about only two because Chris Van Holland was a lock to be on the committee.

We discussed the value of having diversity on the committee and maintaining Democratic Party values. After we seemed to have reached consensus on which member might be the second appointment, she sort of set me back on my heels when she asked, "if not you, who would you suggest my third appointment should be?"

I stood firmly for making sure that the diversity of Democratic Caucus and commitments to our constituents be honored. I offered the names of several members who I thought would remain true to both missions. After a little back and forth, our conversation ended with me feeling relatively sure that Xavier Becerra would be one of the two. I kind of felt that I might be the other, but I did not know for sure until it was announced.

My appointment to the Super Committee pretty much zipped the lips of my critics. I did not expect nor did I want approval from the Rush Limbaughs of the world or the editorial boards of publications such as the *Black Commentator*. But I knew that this appointment and my subsequent service on the committee would give substance to my political efforts and solidify my political standing.

Shortly after my appointment was announced, I wrote an opinion piece for the *Washington Post*. It was printed on September 5, 2011, the day before our first meeting, and was subsequently reprinted in several South Carolina newspapers. I wrote in part:

> I am entering the Committee's negotiations with a clear vision, an open mind and willingness to find common ground. I have always said if the distance between

me and my opponent are five steps, I don't mind taking three. Real deficit reduction, however, must have three components—jobs, cuts and revenue.

Jobs: During the August recess I held a town hall meeting. . . . People didn't want to hear about cuts or revenue; they wanted to hear about jobs. We cannot put the economy back on track until we put people back to work. Job creation will generate tax revenue and reduce the need for government assistance.

Cuts: Targeting waste, fraud and abuse; eliminating unnecessary and duplicative spending; and ending military adventurism need not be accompanied by slashing essential services like education, and shredding our safety nets: Social Security, Medicare and Medicaid. . . . The GAO has recently identified 34 areas where federal agencies or offices offer overlapping and duplicative programs. Streamlining could save billions.

Revenue: While I think our current tax code is unfair and in need of massive overhaul, the Super Committee does not have the time or resources to sufficiently reform the tax code. But we do have time to reduce inequities, close loopholes and eliminate outdated and unnecessary tax subsidies. . . . We need to work together to address these urgent priorities. . . .

We, as a Super Committee, cannot let our differences cause too much disagreement. Debt and deficit reduction should be wrapped into a strong cord of job creation, budget cuts, and revenue raisers. Pursuing them separately will weaken our efforts and could doom our mission.

The cochairs of the Super Committee were Senator Patty Murray of Washington and Congressman Jeb Hensarling of Texas. In preparation for our first meeting, both sides caucused separately. Patty Murray hosted our first meeting over lunch. Each one of us took turns sharing a little bit about ourselves and how we viewed our mission. As we proceeded, I detected a developing theme with which I was not particularly comfortable.

Several expressed how difficult this effort was going to be. When it came time for me to share how my experiences had shaped my views of our mission, I stated: "To me, this is not hard. Let me tell you what's hard." I continued, "Hard is challenging centuries of values and mores in the segregated South. Sitting in southern jails wondering when or whether you are going to get out; facing law enforcement officers who are more interested in defending practices than administering justice; and being able to tell from the looks in their eyes that they were looking for any excuse to do you physical harm. That's what's hard."

At the first meeting of the full committee, we had a similar get-to-know-each-other session. Senator Rob Portman and I had served on an ethics panel together sitting in judgment of one of our colleagues who had been accused of violating the rules of the House. It is always hard for a member to sit in judgment of a colleague, and in this instance, the colleague being accused was—and still remains—a very close friend of mine.

Rob chaired the panel and was aware of that friendship and how difficult that task was for me. He shared with the group a little bit about that not-so-blessed experience, which was concluded with a unanimous decision. He told the committee that he remembered how excruciatingly painful that task was for me and that he knew from the totality of that experience that I could, and would, make tough decisions.

We kicked off our public meetings with a hearing on September 13, 2011. Our only witness was Douglas W. Elmendorf, director of the Congressional Budget Office (CBO). While we were in that hearing, a news report was released that the nation's poverty rate had increased to 15.1 percent. So I mentioned this when it became my turn to ask questions of the witness. I questioned Mr. Elmendorf on the impact of unemployment on the amount of revenue going into the federal coffers. Of course it is pretty elementary that the higher the unemployment the lower the revenue. But I was trying to lay a foundation for later discussions, and I was highly pleased with his responses to my questions.

Our second public hearing was on September 22, 2011. It was on "Revenue Options and Reforming the Tax Code." Thomas A. Barthold, chief of staff of the Joint Committee on Taxation, was our lone witness. We held a third public hearing on October 26, 2011, the day after the CBO released a study titled "Trends in the Distribution of Household Income between 1979 and 2007," and Dr. Elmendorf returned as our lone witness.

This time my questions to Dr. Elmendorf focused on the findings of that study, which covered twenty-eight years, a full generation. It found that the lower twentieth percentile of households experienced an increase in income of only 18 percent, while the eighty-first to ninety-ninth percentiles had a 65 percent increase in household income. The top percentile had enjoyed an increase in their household income of 275 percent while the middle 60 percent had averaged approximately a 40 percent increase in their household income.

I asked for his suggestions as to what Congress should do about these findings, and was just as pleased with his answers this time as I was with his earlier testimony.

I was in favor of a big bargain. I had picked up the mantle of Nancy Pelosi's "3Bs" approach: "Big, Bold, and Balanced." I also desperately wanted to avoid the sequestration. In all my public statements, I made it very clear that I wanted the $4 trillion deal that the president and Speaker had failed to achieve.

But I and the other Democrats made it crystal clear that we were not going to make the mistakes of the Biden Group, putting cuts on the table without Republicans laying out some revenue raisers.

Our meetings were cordial if not very productive. And I thought all Democrats were of one accord, until we walked into a meeting one day, and Becerra asked whether or not I was aware of Senator Baucus's plan. I was not. He then told me that Baucus was about to present a plan that was being referred to in the media as the Democrats' plan. But Baucus had not shared that plan with the Democrats, at least not all the Democrats, and when he presented it, I listened in silence. Baucus's proposal was big, and it was bold, but it was not balanced. In that instance, to me, two out of three was bad.

When I got a chance to speak I made it clear that this was not the Democrats' plan, and I did not think it was democratic. I reminded everybody of the position I took in my Washington Post op-ed piece: any plan that I supported would need to have a balance of cuts, revenue, and jobs. Becerra spoke in support of my positions, and not long after that meeting I began seeing and reading reports in the media that the two of us, Becerra and I, were standing in the way of a deal.

Now I can understand, and will sometimes excuse, leaks by members or their staffs. But misrepresentations and total fabrications are not the stuff from which productive relationships are built. What profit or satisfaction anyone gets out of such leaks I have never been able to understand. But they are pretty much the norm in Washington, D.C.

Another big and bold, but imbalanced plan was put forward by Senator Pat Toomey. It was being touted as the "Republican Plan." But the media were reporting that it was the only plan on the table and that Democrats had not presented a plan. Toomey's plan was based on so-called dynamic scoring. That is to say, if this were to happen and that were to occur, and if the wealthy among us were given some additional tax cuts, then the dynamism that flows from it all will create growth. Then, at some point in the great by and by, a few good things would start trickling down to the masses. Most Democrats and a lot of independents considered such a plan to be suspicious—if not voodoo—economics, not to mention how such would be scored by the CBO.

I was sufficiently incensed over some of the media reactions to Toomey's plan that I accepted an invitation to appear with him on Fox News. I was also concerned over reports that Democrats did not have a plan. We always had a plan, and I had one of my own that had been thoroughly vetted by my kitchen cabinet and several others in the Democratic Caucus.

I had even consulted with those in my caucus who felt that it might not be all that bad—and might even be good—for the Super Committee to fail. These people were reasoning that because entitlements were protected, a failure might allow what they felt were much-needed cuts to defense and might let the Bush tax cuts expire. Of course, although I agreed with them on the Bush tax cuts, I was fighting to avoid cuts in both defense and entitlements.

After all the made-up stories began to surface, I decided that as soon as the opportunity presented itself, I was going to push my plan. I got that opportunity a few days later in a meeting of the Democrats on the committee. I told them that I had spent several days putting together what might not be a big number, but I believe it was a big deal.

My plan was a $1.2 trillion down payment that contained some structural changes in Social Security and Medicare but did not involve raising the Medicare eligibility or Social Security retirement ages. I reminded them that there were fiscal issues and political issues to deal with, but that I had taken into account what I was hearing in meetings of the twelve-member group, our Democrats-only meetings, as well as what I was hearing from constituents.

After my presentation, a few of the members seemed surprised, and Becerra voiced some reservations about my having put modifications to the consumer price index on the table. Of course I had informed him before the meeting that I was going to do so, and he had informed me of his lack of enthusiasm for my proposal. Senator Kerry questioned me rather closely but concluded that my proposal was instructive and my willingness to address Social Security and Medicare was very constructive.

Despite all the talk about a big deal, some discussions about a small deal, and a few hints about a medium deal, in the end there was no deal. Those sitting at the table got close to each other's views once or twice, but we were never close to a deal. Throughout the process, I often said to members and the media that, if it were left up to the twelve people in the room, I thought an agreement could be reached. But that was never the case.

There was always that thirteenth person who never attended a single meeting but whose presence was always in the room. Tax cutter Grover Norquist, founder of Americans for Tax Reform, made it clear that even the closing of a loophole was considered by him and his funders to be a tax increase, and those signed pledges not to raise taxes that he had collected from Republican politicians over a period of nearly twenty years were considered to be a blood oath. Mr. Norquist seemed to strike fear into the hearts and minds of all Republicans. Consequently he and his supporters were able to enjoy success while the committee and the rest of the country endured failure.

PART TWELVE

Blessed by the Past

Today the small thinkers like to belittle public service and make it sound like some sort of social evil. . . . They have railed against government and used that argument to justify their campaigns to cut taxes for the greedy, deny services to the needy, and reduce government across a broad range of activities. In the world of Lewis Powell, whenever there is conflict between government and business, business should always win. In my world, there should always be a search for proper balance between business and labor; policy and practice; efficiency and effectiveness; government and the governed.

35   *Genuinely Southern*

"Dum spiro spero" (While I breathe, I hope) is South Carolina's motto. I learned it as a child, taught it as a public school teacher, and recite it at almost all of my graduation speeches, regardless of grade level. I have been stimulated and incentivized by that motto and many other maxims that have echoed in my ears over the years. My mother's axiom "I believe I could live in Hell for three months if I felt I was going to get out," my dad's admonition "The world would much rather see a sermon than to hear one," Professor Howell's sociology lesson "We are but the sum total of our experiences," and from my in-laws, that old Gullah/Geechee gnome "What goes around comes around." If there is a synergy generated by these aphorisms, my story is the epitome of the result.

My past has been shaped by God's good graces, several strokes of good luck, a caring and nurturing family, and a plethora of loyal and supportive friends.

Emily's Jolt

Good luck in my personal choices was underscored a few months after I moved from Charleston back to Columbia in 1971. I was invited back to Charleston to address a housing and community-development conference at the Francis Marion Hotel. Emily took the trip with me. I was so hypersensitive about the speech that I didn't trust myself to write it on my own. So I appealed to Phil Grose, the governor's chief speech writer, for some professional help. Phil was also my supervisor in the governor's office, and became my chief collaborator on this book project.

It was my first attempt at delivering a speech that I had not written myself. So when Phil handed me his treatment of the thoughts I had shared with him, I read and reread it several times, pushing and pulling here and there so that the flow would better accommodate Phil's and my cultural differences. I was satisfied with the finished product and thought I delivered it rather well. At the conclusion of my remarks the applause was thunderous, and the audience of four-hundred-plus rose to their feet. As best as I can remember, it was the first time I had ever received a standing ovation.

We were returning to Columbia immediately after the speech, and I could hardly wait to get in the car and hear Emily's assessment. When we got onto I-26 for the one-hundred-plus-mile drive to Columbia, I waited for her to say something about the speech. Instead, she opened a book and started reading.

As we approached Aviation Avenue, about ten miles from downtown Charleston, I could not take the deafening silence any longer, so I asked Emily what she thought about the speech. Without looking up she sort of whispered, "I just wonder when you are going to stop talking about South Carolina's problems and start doing something about them."

Her response was about as sobering as the "brag gently, weep softly" note she left on my mirror the morning after that tumultuous primary victory party. It created a deafening silence that lasted the rest of the way home.

I was still reeling from Emily's jolt the next morning. I started asking myself some questions: Was my speechmaking doing anything to change things for those students I stood before for three years at C. A. Brown? How would a well-received speech change conditions for those migrants and seasonal farm workers I abandoned when I moved into that little office on the first floor of the State House? What impact would that standing ovation have on my children and the millions of other children who looked like them? Was I more interested in garnering headlines than making headway? What would Edna Lukens and Rowena Tobias think? I was very uncomfortable with the conclusions I drew from that little exercise in self-analysis.

The Blessings of Children

To date I have been blessed with three daughters, two sons-in-law, two granddaughters, and one grandson. As I go about my duties and responsibilities to the people of South Carolina's Sixth Congressional District, I often think about the dreams and aspirations Emily and I had for our children and ourselves, our experiences and challenges of watching them grow up and mature, and the challenges they now face as adults and parents themselves.

But I think about those experiences and Emily's subtle and sobering lessons in more personal ways as well. As I was concluding this project, Mignon, our eldest, had just been appointed acting chair of the Federal Communications Commission (FCC), becoming the first woman to head the agency. She was appointed to the FCC by President Barack Obama in 2009 after serving almost twelve years as a member, two years as chair, of the South Carolina Public Service Commission (PSC). Prior to being elected to the PSC, she spent ten years publishing the *Coastal Times,* a black-oriented weekly newspaper that she and I co-owned.

Jennifer, our yelling baby, as the second child is often called in the Gullah/Geechee culture, was serving as a teacher at Dent Middle School, completing her twentieth year in the South Carolina public-school system, nineteen as a teacher. I occasionally share with audiences the discussion I had with Jennifer when she was selecting a major at the University of South Carolina. When she told me that she had decided to major in political science, I expressed my disapproval with a stern lecture about the difference between political science and the practice of politics. It all fell on deaf ears. She graduated from the University of South Carolina with a bachelor's degree in political science.

During her senior year she learned that college seniors could earn a few extra bucks as substitute teachers and signed up. She fell in love with the art. A few weeks before graduation, she told me that she had decided to go to graduate school and wanted to know whether I would assist. I reminded her of our earlier conversation and told her that I had footed the bill for four years, and if she wanted to get a graduate degree, she would have to do so on her own dime. "By the way," I asked, "in what field do you plan to get a master's degree?" She replied that she wanted to get it in teaching. I was stunned but pleased, and whipped out my credit card to assist.

The one year that Jennifer did not teach was spent at the State Department of Education. She had volunteered in Inez Tenenbaum's campaign for state superintendent of education, and when Inez won, she offered Jennifer a position in her administration. Several months later, during one of the family breakfasts that we regularly have when I am at home, I noticed that Jennifer seemed a little out of sorts. I asked if everything was all right, and she said yes, but I knew better.

Fearing that there might be a domestic problem I did not pursue the inquiry then, but I called her the next day. When I repeated my question she sort of blurted out that she hated her job. She declared that she was going to finish out the year in the state office and was going back into the classroom, and she did. I was just as proud of this decision as I was pleased with her earlier decision to enter the teaching profession. During my work on this book, she and her husband, Walter A. Reed, a native of Mississippi, were raising two children, Walter A Clyburn Reed and Sydney Alexis Reed.

During this effort, our youngest daughter, Angela, was working in the development office at Benedict College, from which she graduated in 1998. She and her husband, Cecil, a native of Lynchburg, South Carolina, are parents of my third grandchild: Layla Joann Clyburn Hannibal, who was born on December 3, 2011, the fourteenth birthday of her cousin Sydney.

An incident with Angela at the beginning of her junior year at Keenan High School in Columbia has haunted me for years. In the weeks that followed the Conway controversy, all three girls were having some very unpleasant experiences with their peers. One day I received a call from one of Angela's teachers informing me that she was afraid the taunting Angela was receiving from her classmates because of my Conway decision was so intense that it might cause some permanent psychological damage. She thought it might be helpful if I would come to the school and explain my Conway decision to Angela's classmates. I was happy to do so, and I did so.

A few years ago, during one of our weekend family breakfasts, the Conway controversy came up and I mentioned my visit to Angela's classroom. Angela looked at me rather puzzled and asked what I was talking about. Even after some prodding, Angela professed no memory of my having that discussion with her and her classmates. That was shocking, and I am still haunted by it.

Reflections

Over the years, I have often drawn from my blessed experiences with my children when I've wanted to make a point or drive home a message. My most favorite is one I often use during my arguments in defense of government efforts to eliminate the current effects of past discrimination.

*With Emily and our daughters—Angela, Mignon, and Jennifer—at our
fiftieth wedding anniversary celebration in 2011.*

To buttress my contention that such efforts are not preferential treatment, I often use the distinct differences in my daughters' personalities, differences that are obvious and prominent in spite of their growing up in the same household and having the same parents. Often, when declaring them as having the same mother and father, I would say, similarly to what my dad often said when speaking of his parentage, "at least as far as I know." That line seemed to always help with the atmospherics in the room, especially when broaching such a controversial subject as Affirmative Action.

I would talk about Mignon's independence, which was constantly on display during our ten years in business together. Whenever we had significant differences she would listen quietly, and when I laid down my father-knows-best final directive, she would never talk back. But when the newspaper came out the next week, she would have done exactly what she said she was going to do.

I would contrast that to Jennifer's regular search for her dad's support, in spite of being married with two children. In these speeches, I would say that whenever Jennifer called asking my advice, I would often tell her, "Go ask your husband; I gave you away."

And then there is Angela, highly opinionated and argumentative. But I always appreciated and admired her big heart. Angela has always pursued the last word, even when feeling the need to mumble inaudibly. My punch line for her with audiences was to use a dramatic pause in referring to her as "my free spirit."

I would say to audiences that because of my daughters' differences, I treated them differently. It did not mean that I loved one any more than I loved the others. It simply meant that their needs are different, and I treat them according to their needs. In fact, I would often say that affirmative action does not foster the same or equal treatment, but fair and equitable treatment. I would say that in order to treat people fairly, you sometimes have to treat them differently. The ultimate in fairness, I often concluded, is to treat people and communities according to their needs.

Emily and the girls, and even my two sons-in-law, often protest my using them as guinea pigs and examples. I do believe, however, that they appreciate being of assistance to me in those pertinent moments of discourse, however uncomfortable it may sometimes make them feel.

In June 2011 I watched our children plan the celebration of Emily's and my fiftieth wedding anniversary, which because of Mignon's schedule they held two weeks after the actual date of June twenty-fourth. I found myself reflecting on their past and contemplating their futures. I recalled the day Mignon was to take that crosstown trip to start her freshman year at the University of South Carolina. I sat down with her to have that father-to-daughter conversation that for weeks Emily had been urging me to have. As is sometimes the case with me, why do today what can easily be put off until tomorrow? But on that day, I had run out of tomorrows.

So I called Mignon to the kitchen table—much as my mother had done with me some years earlier when she admonished me not to pay any attention to that beauty-shop customer's suggestion that I should tamp down my aspirations to be a part of South Carolina's political structure.

My talk with Mignon was a rather clumsy sendoff, and I stumbled through some advice about leaving the family unit that had been her protection for seventeen years. I closed with a warning that she would face some challenges that could prove vexing during her campus experiences.

I explained to her that being my daughter could very well generate some favorable experiences for her and some unfavorable treatment as well. I told her that she should not get overly concerned about either, because over time they would pretty well even out. But I concluded our little talk by telling her that she was bound to face some challenges solely because of her gender and skin color, and that those scenarios would probably never even out. Those were the circumstances, I told her, that she would have to work to overcome.

Mignon did not say much during our little chat and said nothing when it ended. And I did not ask her to comment or respond. Three months later she called to ask if I could drive her home for the Thanksgiving holidays.

I picked her up the next afternoon, and as we drove down Bull Street, a car passed us sporting a bumper sticker touting "George Rogers for Heisman." Mignon asked me whether or not I noticed the bumper sticker, and I told her that I had. She asked whether or not I thought that driver would put a "Clyburn for Secretary of State" bumper sticker on his car. I responded that chances were great that he would not.

When I asked the import of her query, she responded by recalling our "kitchen table" conversation. She said she was not so sure what I meant until she attended USC's recent homecoming game. She told me that the black homecoming queen had been loudly booed when she was introduced at halftime, and she noticed that the loudest boos came from the section of the stands that cheered the loudest when George Rogers—the South Carolina running back who won the Heisman in 1980— was introduced at the beginning of the game. She told me that it occurred to her at that moment that one of the challenges we faced is that many white people did not have a problem being entertained by black people but did not want to be represented by them.

Several months later, I mentioned that incident during remarks I made to a Leadership Columbia class. At the conclusion of my comments, Columbia City Councilman Luther Battiste told me that he and his wife, Judy, were in attendance at that game, and when the "boos" rang out, she cried. Since the election of Barack Obama as the forty-fourth president of the United States, I have often thought about that incident.

Echoes and Whispers

The writing of this book has accorded me opportunities to reflect on the outstanding people and blessed experiences I have enjoyed and endured throughout my life, people and experiences that have helped me come to regard myself as "proudly black and genuinely southern."

The big people who have had the greatest influence on me are not necessarily famous people. This project has accorded me the opportunity to reflect on two of the biggest people I ever knew—Almeta Dizzley and Enos Lloyd Clyburn, who cast their eyes above the hopelessness of Jim Crow South Carolina.

I thought about my mom telling me not to listen to the small thoughts of her friend that day in the beauty parlor discouraging me about my ambitions to become a political leader in the state; or to suck it up and weather the silent treatment from my high school superintendent, which I was sure to escape if I could hold fast for three months.

I thought about my dad telling his small-minded parishioner to never again utter the phrase "I've been down so long, getting up don't cross my mind."

I thought of my former students, who believed my encouragement that they could be whatever they wanted in life, even though I harbored great doubts.

I am the sum total of my life experiences and—looking back—those blessed experiences were, as the last line of the second verse of "Blessed Assurance" says, "Echoes of mercy, whispers of love."

36 *Proudly Black*

Many of us felt that the struggles for human decency and dignity ended with passage of the 1964 Civil Rights Act, the 1965 Voting Rights Act, the 1968 Fair Housing Act, major health-care legislation for the poor and the elderly, and the many court orders and legislative fiats that affirmed that the U.S. Constitution did indeed apply to all people. This was how I felt entering the governor's office back in 1971. Even so, I knew my job would be no walk in the park.

It's one thing to be viewed as the symbol of racial peace and progress in South Carolina as the first black executive on a governor's staff. It's another thing to establish economic and social stability for a professional wife and two (soon to be three) young daughters. The "Charleston shuffle" we were forced to perform, moving up and down Interstate 26 with great frequency, was pretty stressful. But stress or no stress, the Charleston shuffle was a necessary dance to perform, because there were still forces out there determined to undo the progress that had been made. It was expected that there would be efforts to push back against the social and political gains we had begun to realize. And many of us who were beneficiaries of those gains expected even more.

Back in 1971 many of those expectations came to rest in that little office I proudly occupied in the governor's suite. They made my life interesting. Trying to reconcile the various elements of black political activists in the state, the vast majority of whom were Democrats, into some semblance of solidarity was an awesome challenge. It was common among establishment types in those days to think of black people as some sort of monolithic political entity that saw all things alike. Nothing could have been further from the truth. Factions among black people were diverse and scattered across the state in many sizes, shapes, and forms. But in 1971 there was one thing black South Carolinians had in common: they expected a great deal from John West, who they had supported by the tens of thousands.

Broadening the Issue

The year 1971 was a particularly edgy one. The civil rights furor had begun to die down, but the antiwar and antidraft activities were even more ferocious. In March of 1971 a bomb exploded in the U.S. Capitol, and in late April five hundred thousand people marched in Washington to protest American involvement in Vietnam. In June of that year, the *New York Times* began publishing the "Pentagon Papers," a secret military history of the nation's presence in Vietnam. In August race-oriented riots broke out in Camden, New Jersey, devastating the Philadelphia suburb and signaling yet another urban center in distress.

I remembered having grave concerns about the extent of the violence. While most Americans took precautions to protect their families during these times of trouble, there were other reactions to the unrest that went a lot farther than personal safety. President Nixon, who had successfully exploited this unrest with his "southern strategy" during the 1968 presidential campaign, began exercising the kind of bunker mentality that eventually led to his resignation from office. Others were looking long-term at measures that could reshape the entire political landscape in America.

They were taking aim at what they perceived to be much more than troublesome public eruptions against unpopular public policies, practices, and statutes. They sensed that the entire system was under assault from alien forces within and without American leadership itself. Unlike the Joseph McCarthy uprising of two decades earlier—which had something of a carnival atmosphere to it—this one was quiet, almost clandestine.

The Big People

Matthew J. Perry Jr. passed away on July 29, 2011. He was a few days short of his ninetieth birthday, a day on which I had arranged for him to celebrate at a meeting with President Obama. As it turned out, Judge Perry had another important meeting that took priority over meeting our country's first black president.

Matt didn't miss many meetings. He never really retired from his duties as judge or from his role as a South Carolinian whose presence brought dignity and status to any event. Three weeks earlier, Matt had honored Emily and me with his presence at our fiftieth wedding anniversary celebration. It was typical that he was still giving of himself even as he reached the end of his days.

His passing prompted an outpouring of praise from many who knew him as a friend and valued leader. I was among those who eulogized him on August 4, 2011, and with forewarning, took much more than my allotted three minutes.

Matthew Perry was a big man. He thought big thoughts, dreamed big dreams, and created big ideas. He dared to take on a world of discrimination and prejudice, and in doing so he shattered many barriers. He helped to create a whole new world of unity and opportunity that more faithfully reflected the words upon which our nation's Constitution was based. Matthew Perry helped define what "We, the People" really meant: big people who thought big thoughts and did big things.

As I thought about his life and others around him, I began to realize that there was a palpable separation between big people and small people. And it was a politically defining one. The big people who strode the earth looked beyond the simple and the immediate. They saw beyond the horizons and the sunrises. John F. Kennedy challenged us to reach the moon, and Martin Luther King Jr. took us to the mountaintop. Both men saw a human dimension to all we do. In recent times though, we have seen the politically small people scrambling for attention and rising in public prominence.

They adopt many names and references. Some of them hide behind the country's predominate religion by calling themselves names such as "Christian Coalition." Others seize on a patriotic moment in American history by calling themselves the "Tea Party." But for the most part, there has not been much that's religious or patriotic about all of this. Their impact has been remarkably negative and profoundly destructive.

Their "issues," if you can call them that, seem to have an exclusionary element to them, building chain-link fences across the southern border of the country to keep out Hispanics, wondering aloud if America's first black president is a Muslim, and insisting on seeing his birth certificate and college transcript. Their influence on debates over complicated issues such as health-care reform, deficit reduction, and raising the debt ceiling of the federal government was invariably ill-informed, simplistic, and damaging to the overall settlement of the issues. They are small-time political grandstanders, by whatever name they choose to give themselves, and they have played a toxic role in the conduct of business in our democratic system.

Some people thought these small-minded reactions were spontaneous and even somewhat natural. I didn't. For years I would often say to my staffs and friends that "somebody had a meeting."

What seemed to some to be a spontaneous uprising from economically desperate people was strategic and calculating in opposing whatever initiatives President Obama put forward. They opposed policies that would generate jobs; they opposed programs that would stabilize the nation's economy; they even took up positions against the nation's worldwide credit standing. In many instances their targets were racial and economic minorities, and they were not too bashful about making it known.

If there had just been a spontaneous uprising of unhappy working people, the shallowness of the thinking might have been understandable. But, to the dismay of many of us who believed that extremists were an influential element within the conservative forces, such did not prove to be the case. The grimly inhuman insistence that the needy and vulnerable people of America should bear the burden of programmatic cuts to satisfy deficit reduction requirements proved to be something of a mainstream tenet of American conservatism.

Narrow Vision

In the midst of the promotion of this malignancy and narrow thinking among some business leaders, I received a deeply disturbing letter from the U.S. Chamber of Commerce only days after I was appointed to the Super Committee. The letter, presumably speaking on behalf of a major segment of American business, demanded that the committee address "entitlement programs." No mention was made of a role for American business in finding new sources of revenue to stabilize the economy or generate jobs. There was only the same old tired insistence on more tax cuts for a sector already bloated with favors from generous political friends. The Chamber of Commerce letter came not only as a reflection of the utter indifference of business leadership toward the plight of the poor, it sounded a disturbing note of self-defeating nonchalance about the overall condition of the nation's economy. A much different perspective from the businessman in Andrews, South Carolina, who advised me that his interests and those of his employees, who live in my district, might sometimes collide, but as their representative, I should not forget them. He could see the world beyond his bottom line. What happened to that big-picture vision?

I am among those who attribute many current business leaders' positions to a document generated some four decades earlier which had come to be known as the "Powell Manifesto," a private memo from the then corporate attorney Lewis Powell urging a greater role in political activities for the business community. Powell, who was soon to be appointed to the U.S. Supreme Court by President Nixon, advocated a more active role in the nation's political affairs by the business community.

Lewis Powell, an astute corporate attorney, conveyed his dire feelings in a memorandum to his good friend Eugene B. Sydnor of the U.S. Chamber of Commerce. Powell, who became a crucial swing vote during his days on the Supreme Court, wrote, "No thoughtful person can question that the American economic system is under broad attack."

For its day Powell's recitation of the bad guys was something of a departure from the social critics who generally saw the enemies of the system as creatures such as draft dodgers, marijuana users, long-haired hippies, and Afro-wearing, dashiki-clad black activists. Powell envisioned enemies who were cosmic and often unseen on the surface. He worried about "socialists, communists, Marxists, intellectuals and leftists." They could be your next door neighbor or your son's college professor. He saw government regulation and government intrusion as further sources of antibusiness activity.

Powell believed business had been soft and passive during the turmoil of the 1960s and 1970s. He urged the creation of centers where research could lead to the development of pro-business positions and political advocacy. He planted the seeds of ideological institutions that later blossomed into aggressive think tanks. In time, organizations such as the Cato Institute, the Heritage Foundation, and the Manhattan Institute grew out of Powell's ideas and became entities that applied themselves "vigorously to the preservation of the system."

There are no means by which the influence of the "Powell Manifesto" could be measured. There is no doubt, however, that this private memorandum came to the attention of policy makers of many political persuasions and that it provided a blueprint for much of America's conservative movement of the last quarter of the twentieth century. The ease with which terms such as "socialists" and "leftist" found their way into conservative doctrine of today, and the ready acceptance of antigovernment positions as a simple justification for business-centered activities, can readily be traced to the Powell memo of decades ago.

Ronald Reagan became an early champion of this New Right with his suggestion that there was something inherently bad about government. His personal oratorical and political skills brought popularity to such notions as limited taxation, reduced business regulation, and fierce antiunion sentiments. He found dangers on college campuses and in TV and newspaper editorial rooms. He quoted an article contending that Yale University was "graduating scores of young men who despise the American political and economic system." He urged American business to become vigilant in monitoring such hazardous places. He advocated the development of counter systems to the suspicious institutions, espoused greed as good, and created the "Welfare Queen."

By the second decade of the twenty-first century, there was in place an apparent orthodoxy of tax cuts, program reductions, and service cutbacks that virtually defied challenge in many political circles. Even so, it came as a shock to me as we undertook the difficult task of finding ways to reduce annual program expenditures to learn that the political separation between what I considered mainstream conservatism and political extremism had become a very narrow one, if it existed at all.

Battles Revisited

I began to realize that a lot of the battles of earlier political generations are being refought, only this time on different turf and under more dangerous conditions. The steps we had taken one by one and year by year—school desegregation, voting rights, equal employment opportunities, public accommodations, medical assistance for the poor, medical care for the elderly, nutritional supplement for the young, health insurance for all, and many, many more—are under a full-scale attack, not just from extremists but from mainstream political opposition, which have become unified in common cause against the poor, the elderly, and the infirm. Those things about which I tried to educate my students and from which I have tried to insulate my children, seem to be cascading back to the future.

Unlike previous times, however, the arguments are made in obscure, abstract, statistical terms. There are no discussions of things such as a War on Poverty or a Great Society. Human beings and human aspirations and human consequences are left out of these equations. We talk about deficit reductions, debt ceilings, and even "balanced budgets." And in all that hushed debate over the fate of millions of Americans, a scarce few voices are raised to take up the cause of those losing their benefits, losing their hopes, and losing their access to longer and better lives for their families, their children, and their grandchildren. "Entitlement programs" are being debated, not human beings and human outcomes.

The pundits are spending a lot of time fretting about "liberals" and "conservatives," blue states and red states, partisan polarization and approval ratings. Securing our borders and the global economy. There is an air of detachment, and issues seem to come out of a textbook or primer that provides its own set of definitions and applications. The closest the "inside-the-Beltway" guys ever got to the realities of the people of my district was when they spoke, sometimes with raised eyebrows and a little disdain in their voices, about "entitlement programs."

To most of the Sixth District of South Carolina, this discussion is not about "liberals" or "conservatives." To the people who have lost jobs, these are not "entitlement programs." Whenever I hear that term my blood pressure rises. Along the streets of the small towns and across the countryside of the South Carolina lowcountry, these are survival programs. These are opportunity programs. These are programs of hope and dignity for thousands of people whose lives have been damaged by economic conditions beyond their control.

To the less fortunate, these are programs of income supplement, nutritional support, and life-saving medical assistance, which they receive from Social Security, Medicare, and Medicaid. These programs have been the lifeblood of America for generations, and they were created by big people—big people with names such as Roosevelt, Truman, Kennedy, and Johnson—who believed that Americans deserved better than lives of fear and deprivation. Big people with big ideas believe that children deserve hope for the future and the elderly deserve some degree of security in their advancing years. There is no bigger idea than the concept of human hope and human dignity.

So as I thought about people such as Matthew Perry and Septima Clark, Martin Luther King Jr. and Whitney Young, Theodore Roosevelt and Harry Truman, and many other giant spirits who once graced our planet and had made us proud to be Americans, I wondered about the small timers who impeded their way and the smallness of the issues that seemed to be at stake. I realized that even in my younger days, the areas of contention seemed almost trivial.

How could it be that we drew battle lines over whether my college friends and I could sit down for a cup of coffee at a lunch counter in downtown Orangeburg, South Carolina? How could we have gone to war over whether black folks could sit in any vacant seats they chose on buses and trains? How could we have created an entire civil rights campaign over whether people who could occupy the same foxholes in Korea and Vietnam could sit in the same waiting room in a bus station?

Big and Small

I began to realize that much of the political differences and the partisan strife in our nation may not lie between the Left and the Right, the blue states and the red states, the conservatives and the liberals, the Republicans and the Democrats. It's between the big thinkers, the big people, the big dreamers who gaze beyond horizons, and the small people who worry about things like who can buy cups of coffee and where, and whether the president of the United States would show his birth certificate and college transcript, and how quickly we can build chain-link fences between college campuses and across the country's southern border. It's between people who see the complexity and the broad implications of the decisions we make and those who would trivialize the entire process and would have you believe that governing is just a series of multiple-choice questions.

Looking back, I see that in many ways the battles we are fighting and the battles my parents undertook are not all that different. In my congressional service the foes haven't worn sheets and used the "N" word so much, but in many ways our opponents are quite similar to those who fought against Social Security in the 1930s, integration of the armed forces in the 1940s, desegregation of public schools in the 1950s, the civil rights acts of the 1960s, and equal employment opportunity in the 1970s. Unlike the earlier debates, however, today's discussions have an overlay of terminology and media-related distinctions that sometimes obscure the real issues and their motives.

These same small thinkers choose to overlook the trillions of dollars squandered on the monstrously foolish wars in the Middle East, the waste fraud and abuse by providers of medical care, and the additional trillions of dollars of revenue lost in the high-end tax cuts. For the record, the costs of the Iraqi and Afghanistan wars, plus other new defense expenses, came to almost $1.5 trillion during the Bush era (2002–9). Add to that the lost revenues of $1.8 trillion coming from the "Bush tax cuts" for upper-income folks, and there are almost $3.2 trillion dollars in new costs generated by these two "conservative" initiatives alone. Compared to that, new net costs of the "entitlement programs" and the health-care reform programs of the 2010 legislation amount to $152 billion. All told, the cost of Bush-era new programs was $5.07 trillion. By comparison the Obama initiatives, even projected through 2017, amount to $1.44 trillion. So who is the spendthrift? You go figure.

In Washington billions of dollars and trillions of dollars are almost unreal to many of us, and we toss these numbers around like abstractions. As that great statesman Everett Dirksen, who I greatly admired, once famously said, "A hundred billion here and a hundred billion there, and pretty soon we're talking real money."

The Real Big Money

We are talking big money, even in Washington terms. But the real big money comes at the other end of the delivery chain, at the place where corporate and governmental decisions have their ultimate impact. As the debate over health-care reform came down to its final weeks and days, I reminded people of Dr. King's statement a half-century earlier: "Of all the forms of inequality, injustice in health care is the most shocking and inhumane."

I told my colleagues in the Congress of a constituent from Florence who had just been informed by her insurance carrier that because of her eight-year-old daughter's cancer treatments, her family had reached its lifetime benefits limit. "What could be more inhumane," I asked the Congress, "than telling that mother that the life-saving treatments for her daughter must end?"

I look back on all of this with some puzzlement. It's not really about demonizing insurance companies or assailing opponents with spicy rhetoric. That's the business of the consultants and the spin doctors who get paid richly to create the political wedges and make the daily headlines and generate the political heat to fill up the twenty-four-hour news channels. It should be no big revelation that insurance companies cancel policies of needy customers who can't keep up their premiums. It happens all the time and is part of their regular operation. After all, they're in business to make money, not solve social problems. They're not shy about telling you that either and they do so with some regularity.

So whose responsibility is the family who lost coverage because their eight-year-old daughter's cancer treatments have used up all of their benefits for all their lifetimes? Whose responsibility is it to help the middle-aged woman who called into a radio program to tell me of how she had paid premiums all her life on a health-care policy only to be dropped when she contracted cancer? I'll tell you whose responsibility it is. It's mine. I'm the one who is supposed to solve human problems—social problems, economic problems, political problems, and, yes, health-care problems. Sometimes I can. Sometimes I can't. But I'm elected to try to help those people in the

Sixth Congressional District of South Carolina who are among the neediest of any congressional district in the nation and I proudly give it my best shot.

I travel my district on weekends. I hold briefings for the news media. I hold forums to solicit the viewpoints of local leaders. I visit churches, beauty and barber shops, and country stores where people gather on weekends to exchange views and discuss events of the day. And when I ask how things are going, I do a lot of listening.

When I return to Washington I enter a different world. Given my seniority and leadership position in the House of Representatives, I am often accorded a role of influence. I occasionally play golf with the president, I am invited on the Sunday morning talk shows, and I'm often asked to spar with the talking heads on the weekly political shows. We discuss things such as the budget and spending limitations, deficit reductions and debt ceilings. We talk politics, about who is winning or losing, like a football or baseball game.

I'm never asked about the family in Williamsburg County who lost their home and had to "double up" with a neighbor. I'm never asked about the roofer who hasn't had work in five months because of the housing slowdown and has no health insurance for his infant son. I'm never asked about the jobless people in Allendale County, where there has been a steady nearly 20 percent unemployment rate for months.

The Human Disconnect

There is a sense of disconnect in it all. An entire political philosophy has evolved. Not only does it oppose efforts to assist America's most needy, its backers brag about it. Candidates line up to run for president in one party promising grandly to repeal the Affordable Care Act, an act they derisively call "Obamacare"—this from people who flaunt such terms as "family values" and "religious principles." There seems to be a new focus on efforts to promote family suffering and to practice moral indifference.

For my part the Affordable Care Act is a giant step toward the goals of several generations of leaders who thought big thoughts and cared about people. I proudly call it the twenty-first century Civil Rights Act, and I believe that big people such as Roy Wilkins, Whitney Young, and Martin Luther King Jr. would approve—as would Mary McLeod Bethune, Septima Clark, and Rosa Parks.

In my home state, however, the small thinkers are in control. In their particular brand of political eccentricity they practice a kind of "talking in tongues." They speak of the nation's capital—Washington, D.C.—as if it were the headquarters of some alien power. They reject hundreds of millions of dollars in educational support and medical assistance, very often with no explanation other than the fact that the money "came from Washington."

Whatever happened to "Yes, We Can"? Have we ceded the field of battle to political bullies who disrupted our town-hall meetings and broke our concentration? Did we become so wrapped up in the abstractions of the billions and trillions that we lost sight of the tens, twenties, and thirties? Did we lose sight of the fact that until Americans go back to work, until we use whatever public and private resources are available to stimulate job creation, the nation's economy will continue to be flat and many proud Americans will continue to lose hope?

Did we forget that racial and prejudicial thinking still makes up a shamefully large portion of our nation's political thought, and unless we continue to fight it at every turn, it becomes a part of our accepted way of life? Did we lose the energy to fight off the small thinkers who find insidious ways to divert our attention and impede our efforts? Or did we just get old and tired?

History Lessons

Our current situation is not new. There was another time when the cause of racial and human justice seemed stuck in inertia. In the years immediately following the 1954 Supreme Court decision in *Brown v. Board of Education,* nothing much happened in the Deep South. Many Americans, who had struggled and risked their lives and careers to promote educational opportunity, saw their work seemingly going for naught. Civil rights organizations were undergoing pressure and outright threats from most of the South's white leadership and many of our black and progressive white leaders were becoming reluctant to continue the fight.

Then, seemingly out of nowhere, came renewed energy and new initiatives. On the campuses of colleges and universities came the clear message that the fight was not over; it would just be fought in a different setting. In Greensboro, North Carolina, students from North Carolina A&T sat down at a lunch counter to begin a new era of standing up to indignities and atrocities. They were soon joined by students at South Carolina State and Claflin Colleges in Orangeburg, Benedict and Allen in Columbia, Friendship Junior College in Rock Hill, Voorhees in Denmark, Morris College in Sumter, and other colleges and schools throughout the South, who sat down at lunch counters and ordered coffee and doughnuts. And when they were denied service and arrested because of the color of their skin, a whole new dimension of public expression took form and became a powerful force for change and political power. From that pool of assertive and aggressive young men and women, came new leaders who took their places at the tables of change in America and who turned public service and political activity into vehicles of new opportunity for millions of previously disadvantaged citizens.

Today the small thinkers like to belittle public service and make it sound like some sort of social evil. They have railed against government and used that argument to justify their campaigns to cut taxes for the greedy, deny services to the needy, and reduce government across a broad range of activities. In the world of Lewis Powell, whenever there is conflict between government and business, business should always win. In my world, there should always be a search for proper balance between business and labor, policy and practice, efficiency and effectiveness, government and the governed.

The outlook of the "Powell Manifesto" must be revisited. The notion of government as somehow impeding economic growth and social progress is phony. It is a piece of propaganda that damages the very premise of representative government. Americans should rejoice that there is a vehicle for change, that there is a resource to accommodate human progress, and that there is a platform upon which the premise of equal justice can be exercised. Americans should not be told that their nation's capital is an evil place, that their political system is unworthy, and that their government is something to be demeaned and trivialized.

In 2012, as prospective candidates traveled the country campaigning for the presidential nomination of their party, one of them—a swaggering Texan—came into my district and spoke to a group of wealthy doctors. If elected, he promised, he would do all in his power to repeal "Obamacare." The doctors cheered and gave him a lot of money. If this hero of the wealthy had bothered to travel one mile in any direction of the hospital complex where he spoke, he would have found communities where more than half the residents were uninsured and where their only hope for health-care coverage came about because Obama cared. He would have found within the same zip code, families who could no longer afford life-supporting prescription drugs and were developing dangerous medical conditions as a result.

As he bragged about his intentions to deny these needy people access to health care and family security, he might have also noted that he was visiting a section of South Carolina with one of the country's highest incidences of deaths from heart attack, stroke, and prostate cancer; not to mention the mile-high rates of renal failure and amputations because of diabetes. He might have learned that one of the causes for these unflattering statistics was the lack of access to regular health and preventive medical care. That part of the story didn't make the Sunday morning talk shows. It probably wasn't in the lunchtime discussions of the doctors that day in the large medical complex where he spoke, or the conversations at the local country clubs that weekend.

But it was a topic of many anguished discussions at rural churches the following Sunday. It was the topic of discussions at barber shops, and grocery stores, and service stations where people congregate to discuss their needs, hopes and troubles. And it is always a part of their conversations with this congressman, who proudly represents their interests in our nation's capital.

It needs to be a topic of conversations in many other locations. It needs to get the attention of state political leaders who shrug nonchalantly at the idea that they have any responsibility for helping the desperately poor. It belongs in the pulpits of wealthy churches that ship great amounts of money overseas for world missions but do not recognize the need for missions of mercy in their own communities.

Most prominently, it belongs on the campuses of colleges and universities all over the nation and not just among those that bear the designation "historically black" either. It needs to be discussed in classrooms, in sorority and fraternity meetings, at technical and community colleges, and various other places where students talk about what they're going to do with their futures.

Colleges and universities should not be places where students just learn how to make as much money as they can as fast as they can. They should be places where people learn what their roles in society can be, and how they can help to advance the cause of human progress and human compassion and what it really means to be proud Americans.

History lessons can be real blessings, but only if we have learned them.

Epilogue

To my children
Mignon; Jennifer and Walt; Angela and Cecil;
their children Walter, Sydney, and Layla; and
all others who may be similarly impacted:

It recently occurred to me that I was younger than Sydney when I walked out of Sumter's Emanuel United Methodist Church back in 1953 to join the fight for social justice and equality, and I was Walter's age when I joined the student movement that was launched in 1960. Today much of that past seems to have become part of our futures. It is clear to me that over the next several years, we will find ourselves fighting battles to retain the dignity and maintain the rights that your parents and grandparents fought to gain decades ago.

It is my fervent hope that you will rise to the occasion and meet those challenges. I hope our colleges and universities will once again become places where students are taught to confront challenges and overcome obstacles. Whatever may be your chosen endeavors—public service, professional pursuits, or business leadership—please reject the notion that government is nothing more than a necessary evil.

Government is not an evil thing. It is the fervor that keeps us focused and the glue that keeps the many as one as we pursue "a more perfect union." I hope you will learn that serving the public is not to be disparaged and that caring for your fellow man is not some sort of "socialist" or "leftist" endeavor.

As many of my generation did, you should become a cadre of idealists who believe there is something noble about the democracy that serves the American people. As Americans and South Carolinians, I hope you are as proudly black and genuinely southern as your parents and grandparents were.

You should welcome all visitors and new arrivals to our state and region with open arms, and please reject the notion that there is something wrong with protecting the feeble and caring for the needy. There is great joy to be found in helping to further the dreams and aspirations of those who need to be educated and nurtured.

Those who have spent their productive years helping to create the smiling faces and beautiful places that I have grown to love and believe you will also—if you haven't already—should feel appreciated. All of God's children should feel hopeful, and all our seniors deserve to feel safe and secure in their golden years.

Those of you who are contemplating professional pursuits should not consider big medical facilities and office buildings you may occupy as places where wealthy practitioners espouse the cause of their own professions with little or no regard for those who are less fortunate and whose cause they have vowed to serve.

Those of you who may seek to pursue public service should make regular visits to the communities you wish to serve and talk with people about their needs and concerns. Study the realities and possible consequences of the vital programs that are all too often discussed and dismissed with much disdain in certain quarters. Listen to their pleas for safe schools, roads, and drinking water; for clean air, sanitary conditions, and other basic needs most of us take for granted.

Those of you who start businesses will do well to get to know those you wish to be patrons as well as those you may seek to hire. Try to bring hope to their dreams of a better and brighter future for themselves and their children. Your generations—and what is left of mine—should make sure that all Americans understand that, as it has been for centuries, education is the single most important ingredient in the lives of young people and should never be sacrificed on the altar of austerity or their ability to pay.

Finally, regardless of what profession or vocation you may choose to pursue, find something to do for which you are not paid. You are expected and are obligated to earn your pay. But you will find that you will be appreciated for the things you do beyond your obligations. And believe me, those are the things that will accord you the greatest satisfaction and fulfillment.

Our struggle today continues to be one where those with the big ideas are battling against the small thinkers who would lead the nation down the narrow roads of selfish indulgence and self-destruction.

Just as my generation did, you must reject the politics of chain-link fences and replace them with the inclusionary dreams that Martin Luther King Jr. so eloquently extolled.

You must reject spiteful suspicions such as those aimed at our nation's first black president. Rejoice in the notion that our nation has achieved yet another level of human maturity. Please reject the dashing of hopes, the trampling of dreams, and the limiting of expectations.

America is running short of big people who are willing to tackle big issues, pursue big ideas, and make big commitments to the human condition. Martin Luther King Jr. and Septima Clark, Lyndon Baines Johnson and Everett Dirksen, Mary McLeod Bethune and Esau Jenkins, and countless others have left us great legacies. They must be replaced with professional careerists whose personal commitments are genuine, and handshakes are ironclad contracts. Those who seek your assistance should never be shrugged off by nonchalance and indifference.

You must help replace today's big thinkers with visionary leaders who see our country as a land of opportunity for all Americans and as a beacon of hope for peoples around the world who yearn to be free.

You must help replace them with men and women who believe that public service is a noble calling that provides opportunities for blessed experiences. You must ignore protestations to the contrary and reject the naysayers and prophets of gloom and doom.

The promise of America is as valid as it ever was; the American dream is still worthy of pursuit; and the creation of a "more perfect union" must always be our goal.

That, after all, is the real entitlement and responsibility of every American, isn't it?

The Clyburns who attended the awarding of Reverend E. L. Clyburn's posthumous degree from Morris College in 2003.

INDEX

Page references given in *italics* indicate illustrations or material contained in their captions.